Kingdom Overthrown

Kingdom Overthrown

Ireland and the Battle for Europe, 1688–1691

Gerard Fitzgibbon

NEW ISLAND

KINGDOM OVERTHROWN

First published in 2015 by
New Island Books
16 Priory Hall Office Park
Stillorgan
County Dublin
Republic of Ireland.

www.newisland.ie

PRINT ISBN: 978-1-84840-475-5
EPUB ISBN: 978-1-84840-476-2
MOBI ISBN: 978-1-84840-477-9

British Library Cataloguing Data.
A CIP catalogue record for this book is available from the British Library.

Typeset by JVR Creative India
Cover design by Mariel Deegan
Printed by ScandBook AB, Sweden

10 9 8 7 6 5 4 3 2 1

Contents

For Mum and Dad,

and Martha

Introduction

I was born in England to Irish parents. When I was a boy my father gave me an old storybook of Greek legends, which told me of the feats of Perseus, Hercules, Odysseus and Jason. The idea that bizarre and marvellous things might live in the past was what first kindled my love of history. When I went to secondary school in Ilford, I learned about the industrial revolution and the Great War and Britain's firm, proud strides into the twentieth century. Then, in 1998, my family moved to Ireland. Sitting in a new school and opening a new textbook, I found a strange story staring back at me. History, I was now told, actually began with Parnell, the Home Rule movement, and Ireland's final fight for independence. England was no longer a proud old dame, but a tyrant. I read and listened, but it took a while to fully understand. Every nation teaches its children the story of how it won. It follows, therefore, that defeats and humiliations are tucked away. Most Irish men and women of my generation can speak comfortably about Michael Collins and Eamon de Valera. Ask them about Richard Talbot or James II, however, and many will shrug. This is not criticism; it is simply what we were all taught.

In the six years that I spent working as a journalist at an Irish regional newspaper, I always sought the human within every story. The world is built on numbers and stone, but people built it. When I look at a four-hundred-year-old wall, I think of the man who laid the bricks. When I read about Ulysses Grant or Simon Bolivar or Edward IV, I picture them as men, tapping their fingers and struggling with the weight of a cause. It helps to remember that history always begins as dirt, blood and water. Only time and teaching turn it into ink. In Ireland, this ancient and beautiful old rock, history is all around us. It is up to us whether or not we choose to see it.

This book is a narrative account of what we now call the Williamite War in Ireland. It is told as a story, not a succession of inevitable events and conclusions. The war and the constitutional crisis that spawned it was a violent, dramatic, and visceral time, and much of it spun on luck. The conflict meant something different to everyone it swallowed: to James Stuart, it was a fight to regain his kingdoms. For William of Orange and Louis XIV of France, it was a new frontier in a great European brawl. To the gentry and noblemen who took commissions and raised regiments, it was a battle for Ireland's land, and the wealth and prestige that flowed from it. For the common folk of Ireland, Protestant and Catholic alike, it was a war for the right of their king to secure their religion. The tale of passion, tragedy and heroism that these men and women shared does not deserve to be told in black, white or grey.

This book exists because I, like so many of my generation, was vaguely aware that this war took place but had little sense of its breathtaking scale, cost and consequences. In school we are not taught that it was the only continental war ever fought in Ireland, or that in the Battle of Aughrim it witnessed the bloodiest single day in Irish history. We walk through the streets of Pennywell in Limerick, but never think of the titanic hand-to-hand struggle that took place under our feet. We stand on the old walls of Derry and look out at the proud city that has grown around them, but we cannot see the wretched forest of tents and corpses that once clogged the horizon. The story of this war has been reduced to anecdotes and folded away. I believe it is time to bring it back to life.

It is necessary to clarify a few things before this story begins. All dates in this book are taken from the old Julian calendar, which was still in use in England and Ireland at the time, not the modern Gregorian calendar, which exists today. There is roughly an eleven-day lag between the two, but I have kept to the old style simply because these were the dates used by every diarist, printer and clerk. Distances and measurements are likewise given in the old imperial format of miles, yards and inches. There is also some prickly housekeeping to be addressed. Whether the great citadel of Ulster is named Londonderry or Derry can split opinion like a pickaxe. I have sought to tread water by referring to the county by the former name, and the city by the latter. I accept that this is a crude compromise that may offend someone, or everyone, but that is the risk I must take.

My generation has known more of peace than war. We are one of the few in human history able to say that. The Troubles of Northern Ireland, though not yet confined to memory, are slowly being left behind. There is distance enough now, perhaps, to read about the men who fought and died at Athlone and the Boyne without choking on the prejudices of the past. Little good comes from being bound by history, but it should not be ignored either. This book was not written to massage a particular point of view, or to challenge facts that already exist. Nor is it a biography of James II, William III, Richard Talbot or any other man. I have not sought to explore rumour, innuendo, sexuality or gossip. It is a book about people, mighty and poor alike, standing in muddy battlefields or draughty palaces, each finding themselves sucked into a great and furious moment. It is a human history.

Gerard Fitzgibbon
Summer, 2015

Acknowledgements

This book would not exist were it not for the help, direct and otherwise, of so many people. Firstly, I would like to thank the team at New Island Books for bringing my idea to life, particularly Eoin Purcell for taking the project on and Dan Bolger for seeing it through. I owe much to my editor, Emma Dunne, for helping turn a squishy first draft into something more. Emma's patience, insight and extraordinary eye for detail have been invaluable, and I am truly grateful that she was part of this journey.

I also wish to thank the teachers, lecturers and storytellers who kept me hooked on history throughout my life. There is the late Mr Farrar, history teacher at Ilford County High School, who once got us to re-enact the assassination of Archduke Franz Ferdinand in class, and encouraged us to use items from our pencil cases as improvised explosives. Then there is Professor Roger Sarty of Wilfried Laurier University in Waterloo, Ontario, who delivered the most memorable lecture I ever attended: a three-hour, grippingly detailed account of combined arms warfare in the Second World War, delivered without a single page of notes for reference. Closer to home, I wish to thank Dr Ruan O'Donnell of the University of Limerick for his frank and honest advice, and Dr Padraig Lenihan, formerly of UL and now of NUI Galway, who is one of the finest scholars of seventeenth-century-Ireland and provided me with valuable advice back when this book was just an idea.

I also wish to thank two men I have never met, but without whom I doubt this book would exist: the late J. G. Simms, whose work on Jacobite Ireland in the sixties and seventies is the keystone of every journal and book on the subject that followed; and Roger Crowley, author of *Empires of the Sea*, the finest narrative history book ever written and the one work that I will forever try and fail to emulate. I also wish to thank my old editor at the *Limerick Leader*, Alan English, who taught me the valuable lesson that sometimes a writer just needs to get out of the way.

I must thank my family for all their love, support and encouragement. My parents, Helen and Pat, my sisters Joanne, Julie and Jenny and my little niece Emma have done more for me than I will ever be able to repay. Finally, I owe the greatest debt to Martha, who lay awake with me every night, reading every page. Her praise was always honest, her criticism gentle, and her love undisguised. She is the reason this book is more than just a forgotten dream.

Part One

Legacy

'This blessed plot, this earth, this realm, this England'.

William Shakespeare, *Richard II*, Act II, scene i.

1

Pieces of Paper

The fortress sat on the cliff like a crown of stone. Its walls seemed to rise up out of the earth like vines, tangling their way around the high keep that guarded the passage into south-east England. To the sailors and merchants who spent their days haggling and cursing in the port below, the sight of the great castle of Dover looming over them was nothing strange. But on the morning of 25 May 1660, a young prince standing on the deck of a great flagship offshore could barely take his eyes off it. Charles Stuart, the exiled heir to the throne, was a knot of excitement and nerves. He was tall and slender and bore the long bulbous nose of all royal inbreeding. With his dense dark hair, brown eyes and faintly sallow skin, he had more than just a little of his Medici grandmother in him. Charles was just a few days shy of his thirtieth birthday, but he had already known a lifetime's worth of danger and ruin. Now, at last, his tide was sweeping in. Dressed in lavish silk finery finished with a cape of blue, crimson and gold, Charles climbed down into a small dinghy with his younger brothers, James and Henry, and was slowly rowed towards the shore. As the heaving crowd that had been gathering along the beach since dawn drew closer into view, the air suddenly cracked as the cannons of Dover castle fired a thunderous salute. The fortress was welcoming its new master.

When Charles finally reached the shore, he was swallowed in a wave of noise and adulation. Hardened soldiers fell at his feet and kissed his hands. An 'infinite' crowd of 'horsemen, citizens and noblemen of all sorts' thronged the streets of Dover, as if they had all refused to trust the pamphlets and proclamations and reckoned that the only way to believe that the king had finally returned would be to see him with their own eyes.[1] Charles eventually climbed into a waiting carriage and was whisked away towards Canterbury. As he stared out into a sea of faces, he saw hope and relief in the eyes looking back at him. But there were wounds as well, hidden beneath the smiles and trumpets and civic gifts. The three kingdoms of England, Ireland and Scotland, which Charles had come to claim as his birthright now that Oliver Cromwell's commonwealth had finally fallen to pieces, had been shredded by civil wars. Today at least, as he climbed ashore at Dover, Charles Stuart felt a fair wind at his back. But in these dark and changeable times few were brave enough to guess what weather lay ahead.

*

The letters started arriving immediately. At first, the correspondence piling up on the desks of the royal secretaries of Whitehall Palace was fairly standard – sailors looking for back pay, for example, or merchant seamen seeking protection from pirates. But very soon the petitions for favour, mercy and fortune began to flood through the door. In just the first weeks after Charles had arrived in London on 29 May 1660, his thirtieth birthday, the young man who had at last inherited his father's throne received hundreds of letters from old allies seeking favour, peasants pleading for work and others who had fought for the Stuarts in the civil war and had lost everything because of it. The road back had been a long and tortuous path for Charles and his kingdoms, and it ended where it had all began: in Westminster, the beating heart of the realm.[2]

In April 1661, almost a year after his return at Dover, King Charles II was formally crowned in Westminster Abbey in a ceremony rich with pageantry, hymns and ancient oaths. The magnificent cathedral was crammed with dignitaries dressed in velvet and cloth-of-gold, while outside in the streets bonfires were lit, rivers of wine were poured and 10,000 people jostled for a glimpse of the king on whom so much now depended. The last of the formalities was over. Charles II now wore a crown that had been vacant since 1649 when his father, Charles I, was convicted of treason by parliament, marched on to a scaffold in Whitehall and beheaded. The new king had been groomed since childhood to one day ascend to the throne, and though the path he was forced to walk had been soiled by filth and gore, the young Charles trusted his footing. He had come to understand that the fate of the crown, and the course of history itself, was ultimately balanced on simple pieces of paper. Charles and his people had learned, and would learn again, that letters, charters and warrants could create and destroy so much.[3]

*

It started with the Plantagenets, the medieval line of kings that conquered Wales, snatched Ireland, fought wars with France out of ancient habit and ultimately tore itself to pieces in the Wars of the Roses. Magna Carta, the most famous document in English history, hatched an awkward bargain between the

Plantagenets and their often-restless noblemen. It sought to restrict the king's previously unchecked and God-given power through laws, in return for which the lords and barons of the realm would continue to collect taxes, raise armies and finance the crown's cripplingly expensive wars. The king, in turn, was expected to sit and hear his subjects' grievances in a convention that evolved into a parliament. Over time, the rulers and the ruled came to see one another as a murky burden. Hardly a single king reigned without tasting some flavour of revolt. When the crown's reckoning finally arrived, it would not be clean or quiet.

In January 1642 Charles I, who had once gone eleven years without calling parliament and was labelled a tyrant by his enemies, barged into the House of Commons with 400 soldiers and demanded the arrest of several of its members for high treason. The commons refused to hand them over, and a bonfire of hate and suspicion that had been piling up across all three of the Stuart kingdoms finally ignited. Scotland had already risen in rebellion, as the Presbyterians of the north struck out to defend their faith against the controls of the crown's established Protestant Church. In Ireland, some of the last maverick Catholic Gaels of Ulster had sparked an uprising against English settlers, which had since spilled out across the island in a spiral of atrocities. And now, at last, the rival supporters of the crown and parliament in England cracked open their armouries and began to march against each other. The next nine years would be a haunting era of cruelty and barbarism, as tens of thousands of people died from starvation, disease and battle across the British Isles. The war between Charles and the forces of parliament, led by Oliver Cromwell, was a brutal and lingering struggle. It ended with the historic execution of Charles in January 1649, which followed the passing of a law barely a few hours earlier ensuring that the throne would remain vacant after his death.

The warrant for Charles's execution – which infamously charged him as a 'tyrant, a traitor, a murderer, and a public enemy' – and the fifty-nine men who signed it, including Cromwell himself, would never be forgotten.

The crown became a ghostly relic. The executed king's eldest son and heir, the teenage prince Charles, was forced into exile. In 1651, aged just twenty-one, Charles returned to England and led a doomed invasion to retake the crown from the north. After his army was routed on the battlefield, Charles was smuggled to safety in disguise and barely made it out of England alive. For the next decade he was a king without a country, keeping a small court on the continent and surviving on the patronage of benefactors like his cousin, the young King Louis XIV of France. But his thoughts were trapped in England, and Charles never stopped waiting for the day when fate's hand would turn. His patience was eventually rewarded. After the execution of Charles I in 1649, Cromwell had invaded Ireland, dissolved parliament and ruled the three kingdoms as a military dictator under the title of lord protector. After his death in 1658, the realm began to slide once more into darkness. Cromwell's son Richard briefly succeeded him as lord protector, but he had none of his father's brutal authority and could not prevent power from slipping through his hands. The army withdrew their support for his regime, and rival blocs within the old parliament began to eye each other suspiciously. Another civil war gathered on the horizon like a tempest. Then, in December 1659, General George Monck, one of Cromwell's old deputies and the commander of the army in Scotland, decided to step forward and seize the moment. He had seen the rape and pillage and murder of the civil war with his own eyes; he knew the history of the Wars of the Roses 200 years earlier, when rival branches of the Plantagenet tree tore England to shreds. Monck and his allies were terrified at the thought of another power vacuum. He gathered his men, marched south and on 3 February 1660 he arrived in London at the head of almost 6,000 troops. Monck seized control of the capital and cleared the way for Charles Stuart, the lost prince, to return at last.

Another historic piece of paper arrived from across the sea. Charles had been in secret correspondence with Monck for some time, and on 4 April he wrote an open letter to the people of his father's kingdoms swearing his 'desire and longing' to finally end the darkness of the civil war and return the realm to peace. Charles's famous 'Declaration of Breda' promised to pardon a great many people of a great many things – all except the regicides, the men who had signed his father's death warrant. Charles would later have them hunted down one by one: some escaped to Europe or the Americas; others were already dead. The rest were captured and tried, and several suffered the traitor's death of being hung, drawn and quartered. Cromwell's rotting corpse was dug up and beheaded, and the lord protector's skull was stuck on a spear outside Westminster Hall, where the trial of Charles I had taken place. The Declaration of Breda offered Monck, his soldiers and his supporters two key promises: that Charles would not interfere with 'their lives, liberties or estates' and that he would settle their unpaid wages. It was all they needed to hear. With the army now on his side, Charles was invited home. On 1 May 1660 the House of Commons met in London and proclaimed Charles as their king, and within a month he had climbed ashore at Dover, where the first person to greet him was General Monck, the relieved architect of a bloodless restoration.

*

As the spring of 1660 melted into summer, and the kingdoms were caught in a carnival of joy and relief, it would have seemed to many that one of the most terrible chapters in English, Irish and Scottish history was finally over. But trouble was only hiding in the shadows, biding its time. The Declaration of Breda was heavy on promises but light on detail, and soon Charles would have to come up with answers to many of the murky questions he inherited from Cromwell. One of the most volatile problems was land and deciding who now owned it all. Nowhere would this prove more dangerous than in Ireland, the great thorn in England's side.

2

Predatory Incursion

Only one Englishman has ever been Bishop of Rome: a monk from Hertfordshire named Nicholas Breakspear, who was elected as Pope Adrian IV in 1154. Adrian was an administrator, and he liked a challenge. As a cardinal, he had been sent as papal legate into the wilds of Scandinavia, and as pope he remained determined to stretch out the church's arms. Staring at a map of Europe, Adrian glanced towards his homeland and then, across a narrow slither of sea, at Ireland, one of the Vatican's old headaches. Hard on the edge of the continent, Ireland was home to a Celtic brand of Christianity whose practices and habits did not sit well with Rome. Many priests did not practice chastity – the Archdeacon of Clogher, for example, claimed to have fathered eight children. To a distant eye, the Irish were seen as 'wallowing in vice', without a true church to guide them. It was foggy propaganda, but it was useful. In 1155 Adrian signed a papal bull which granted ownership of Ireland to Henry II, King of England and Duke of Normandy and Aquitaine. With a sharp knowledge of canon law, Adrian decided that Ireland was his prize to give because of an obscure 800-year-old document

– revealed centuries later to be a forgery – in which Emperor Constantine apparently handed control of the western half of his empire, including all of the islands of Europe, to Rome. Hoping to inspire Henry II to become one of Christ's champions, Adrian urged him to 'enter into the island of Ireland in order to subject the people to the laws, and extirpate the vices that have there taken root'. Adrian also wished, conveniently, to levy an annual tax on the island of one penny per household, payable directly to the Vatican.[1]

Henry II, the first king of the Plantagenet dynasty, hailed from Anjou in the north-west of France, and he had grown up with a very French idea of kingship. He liked tough armies, thick walls and obedient vassals. He was energetic, broad-shouldered and had a devilish temper. But he also had a shrewd eye for opportunity, and when he finally decided to take up Rome's invitation to claim Ireland in October 1171 – long after Pope Adrian himself had died – he did so because it suited the times. Henry was still privately terrified of God's judgement after the scandalous murder of his best-friend-turned-bitter-enemy Thomas à Becket, the archbishop who was hacked to pieces in Canterbury Cathedral the previous year by four knights who thought they were doing the king a favour. Taking up a papal crusade was generally good for the soul, but there were other benefits. Invading Ireland would allow Henry to take care of another problem: in 1169 he had sponsored a band of Norman barons to travel to Ireland and forcibly restore the deposed king of Leinster, who had travelled to France and pleaded for Henry's help. By 1171 these barons, led by the likes of the Earl of Pembroke, the famous 'Strongbow', had spread out across Ireland and become very powerful, very quickly. Celtic storytellers would long rue the 'predatory incursion' of these barons and mercenaries, who fought pitched battles, burned homes and churches, seized livestock and turned much of the island into 'a trembling sod'. Lawlessness and murder was one thing, but Henry's real concern was the risk that these barons would grow rich in Ireland, raise their own armies and come back to challenge him. Like all the Plantagenets who would follow him, Henry saw a potential enemy in every ally. He decided that it was time to put the barons back in their place.[2]

In October 1171 Henry landed in the southern Irish port of Waterford with a fleet of 400 ships and 4,000 men, including hundreds of thickly armed knights and 'earls and barons of great worth'. The 'rich and bold' King of England arrived with an overwhelming show of colour and strength. As he marched to Cashel, Lismore and Dublin, Ireland's native chieftains and the rowdy Norman barons had no choice but to come and pay homage to the great king, who now carried the self-appointed title of 'lord of Ireland'. Henry began shuffling the country around to his liking, confiscating and re-granting estates under new terms, and generally flexing his muscle. Everywhere he went, he brought a copy of Adrian's bull with him, swinging it like a hammer. Henry spent six months in Ireland before he was called away to deal with a rebellion in France led by his eldest son. But by then, the visit had served its purpose. The new Pope Alexander III praised Henry's short and swift work in subduing a 'barbarous nation'. Ireland had been wrenched into Rome's sphere of control, and the Vatican was pleased. What had been a brief and mildly distracting voyage for one of the most powerful rulers in Europe had in fact opened up a bloody new chapter in history. The English had arrived in Ireland. One way or another, they would never leave.[3]

*

Ireland became the crown's most lethal frontier, a wild west where law could never be counted on and danger hid in every crevice. It opened the gate for the demise of the tyrant

Richard II, who was usurped by his cousin Henry while he was away putting down a rebellion across the Irish Sea in 1399. The lesson was clear: Ireland was trouble. Royal authority in the island rolled back and forth like a spring tide. As the feuding heirs of the Plantagenet dynasty fought each other to a standstill in the Wars of the Roses, Ireland slipped from their control. The descendants of the first Norman settlers had once controlled two-thirds of the island, but by the fifteenth century their footprint could only be found in and around Dublin, in the exposed plains of Leinster and Munster and in a handful of large ports such as Limerick, Cork and Drogheda. In the wild and rugged lands of Ulster and Connaught, royal power barely existed in the fiefdoms of Gaelic warlords. In those places where English influence remained strongest, however, the old Norman families flowered into a minor aristocracy prim with culture, refinement and status. They took surnames like Butler and FitzGerald; they built stunning homes, such as the great castle of Kilkenny; they practised music and fashion and commerce and passed titles and estates on to their heirs. These earls of Ormonde and Desmond and Clanricarde became known as the 'Old English', and in the golden days of their influence they were the crown's right hand in Ireland. Then Martin Luther nailed his theses to a church door in Saxony in 1517, and the quiet thud of his hammer rippled over every blade of grass in Europe. The greatest continental crisis since the Black Death – the Reformation – would creep into the three kingdoms, cloaked beneath a row over a king's thirst for a new wife. Ireland was about to be tugged into a stark and violent future.

Henry VIII, the second king of the House of Tudor, was a force of nature. He had inherited his father's deep distrust of anything he could not control, and when the Vatican refused his petitions to have his marriage to Queen Catherine of Aragon annulled, Henry broke with Rome and established himself as supreme head of the church in England in 1534. He set aside Catherine, married his mistress Anne Boleyn and systematically began to scrub out all traces of church power and wealth in his lands. Henry tore down religious monuments, cracked open tombs, confiscated the lands of the monastic orders and rinsed the spiritual footprint of Rome from his realm. Ireland did not escape this fate. In 1537 Irish friaries and churches were subjected to the same assaults that had been carried out with such brutal efficiency in England. 'Scarcely had there ever come so great a persecution,' Celtic storytellers lamented. Henry did not stop. In 1541 the loyal Irish parliament passed an act that turned the island into a full kingdom of its own, with a crown that it immediately granted to Henry and his heirs. Henry was a scholar of history and canon law and knew that the legal foundation of English rule in Ireland could be traced right back to the wishes of the Vatican, sealed within the words of Adrian IV's papal bull. Rome could – and did – try to give Ireland away to other Catholic rulers, such as the Habsburgs of Spain, once Henry had been excommunicated. But with a sword and a pen, Henry had tightened his grip on Ireland.[4]

The Old English nobles in Dublin, Kilkenny and Limerick watched with horror. They continued to plead loyalty to the crown, but almost all of them refused to abandon Rome and join Henry's new church, which they saw as a heresy of 'pride, vain-glory, avarice and lust'. Henry was rarely patient or forgiving, and neither was his daughter Elizabeth, who ultimately succeeded her half-brother Edward and half-sister Mary to the throne in 1558. She would finish, with brutal vigour, that which her father had begun.[5]

*

The template was drawn with blood and earth, one inch at a time. Queen Mary, Henry VIII's eldest daughter, began in 1557 when she sponsored the first major expeditions by English settlers into the interior of Leinster. In 1583, when a second uprising in less than twenty years by the Earl of Desmond and his supporters was crushed, Queen Elizabeth took her sister's canvas and stretched it to unimaginable proportions. The lands of the Desmond rebels in Munster were confiscated by a bill of attainder, and tens of thousands of acres were handed to new English Protestant settlers. It was social engineering on an unseen scale. Elizabeth did not need to weigh the merits: for most of her long reign she felt besieged by enemies real and imagined and carved her father's church into a shield. The Church of England was given total legal supremacy in her lands, and the crown began to violently suppress dissenting faiths, which Elizabeth came to see as the creeds of her enemies. The fact that Madrid and the Vatican had sent military aid to the Desmond rebels only tightened her belief that Catholics, with their ultimate loyalty to Rome, could never be trusted and would have to be rooted out, one generation at a time. By 1598 there were 12,000 English settlers scattered across 500,000 acres of former Desmond lands in Munster. Each of them spoke English instead of Gaelic, each of them obeyed English law and all of them were members of Elizabeth's Protestant church, paying taxes directly to the English exchequer. Irish Catholics, whether they had Norman or Gaelic blood, watched anxiously. Elizabeth had shown her hand and was prepared to snatch the wealth and estates that gave Ireland's Catholic nobles their lingering power. In 1590, when a Gaelic clan leader in Monaghan was hanged for resisting a plan for an English settlement on his lands, the fuse was lit. The earls of Tyrone and Tyrconnell, the most famous and powerful Gaelic lords in Ulster, understood that they were next. Before they might be left with nothing to defend, they chose to attack. Gaelic Ireland went to war.

The Nine Years War between the crown and forces led by the earls of Tyrone and Tyrconnell dragged Ireland into catastrophe.

At first, the royal forces were pummelled to the brink of defeat. Led by Hugh O'Neill, the Earl of Tyrone, the rebels rooted the crown's soldiers out of Ulster and charged south. In 1598 Elizabeth's great plantation of Munster was swept aside as English settlers were driven from the land, seeking refuge in walled towns or fleeing back across the Irish Sea. Madrid, which never missed an opportunity to harass and undermine Elizabeth, offered its support to the rebels. Clinging to Ireland by her fingernails, Elizabeth fought back. She sanctioned a massive build-up of soldiers, weapons and war materiel, and by 1599 there were 17,000 English and Welsh troops in Ireland. They were put to devastating use. Under the command of Charles Blount, Baron Mountjoy, the royal forces burned, starved and pillaged Ireland into submission. The uprising was finally quenched in 1601 when the armies of Ulster and a small Spanish relief force were scattered near the port of Kinsale in Cork. The Nine Years War had claimed the lives of some 130,000 people, most of them destitute Gaelic peasants who died from starvation and disease. Tudor power now penetrated deep into every corner of Ireland, a kingdom that was now little more than a ragged shell.

*

Elizabeth died in 1603. She was unmarried, and it was claimed that she had never once taken a man to her bed. The crown now passed to her distant cousin James Stuart, the king of Scotland, whose ascension formally unified the three kingdoms under one ruler for the first time. One of James's first tasks was to clear away the wreckage of the Nine Years War, which was formally concluded with the Treaty of Mellifont, signed in an old abbey near Drogheda in 1603. The treaty spared the lives of the Gaelic earls who had led the uprising but forced them to abandon the ancient feudal powers that had made them princes in their own lands. It was a humbling, embarrassing slight that effectively reduced Hugh O'Neill and his kinsmen to large landowners. The shroud of suspicion that had ignited the war never truly lifted. In 1607, as O'Neill was preparing to travel to England for an audience with James, he caught a whiff of a rumour that he was to be arrested on his arrival and implicated in a Spanish plot against the king. Along with Rory O'Donnell, the new Earl of Tyrconnell, O'Neill realised that his life was at risk. In a swift and utterly unexpected move, the two earls quickly gathered together their families and a small retinue of servants and decided to flee to Spain, hoping to petition King Philip III to support their ailing cause. On 4 September 1607 the most powerful old warlords in Gaelic Ulster sailed out from Lough Swilly on a doomed crusade. 'The winds had not wafted from Ireland, in modern times, a party of one ship who have been more illustrious or noble,' Gaelic storytellers lamented.[6]

Time was creeping on, and the earls were about to be left behind. Philip III was bankrupt and could not risk an expensive war with England for the sake of sheltering a few rebellious Irishmen. He refused to allow the earls to enter Spain or reside in his territories in Flanders. O'Neill and O'Donnell were shuffled around the palaces of Europe like a hot potato before finally settling in Rome. Ignored and forced to live on a tiny allowance from the pope, the earls and their campaign to liberate their island were drowned in the concert of European politics. Idle and heartbroken, the last princes of Gaelic Ulster slowly succumbed to poverty and fever by the Tiber.

The flight of the earls was an astonishing gift for King James. In 1608, with the vast northern estates of Tyrone and Tyrconnell now up for grabs, parliament passed a law of attainder condemning O'Neill and O'Donnell as rebels and stripped them of their lands and wealth. The estates were then hewn into chunks of between 1,000 and 2,000 acres and offered to new waves of English and Scottish Protestant settlers. Mary and Elizabeth's template was rolled out once more. Over the next thirty-five years, roughly 100,000 new settlers took up the crown's invitation to settle in Ulster, completely remaking the ancient den of Irish Gaelic power. The crown sought to pave over all traces of Gaelic heritage in the north, and even took steps to prohibit the new settlers from employing Catholics on their land. Chronic labour shortages, however, forced this 'New English' class of Protestant landlords into a bitter working arrangement with Gaelic-speaking natives who despised them. The tension would fester and pass from one generation to the next like an heirloom. Ulster became a deep pot of paranoia and hate, ready to boil.

In just over a hundred years, the old notion of English power in Ireland that had lingered since the days of Henry II's first campaign had been transformed. Crown law now extended into every province, and through defeat and misadventure the old roots of Gaelic power in Munster and Ulster had been scorched. The earls of Tyrone and Tyrconnell had disappeared into the sea like jetsam. At the turn of the seventeenth century, Ireland was bound tighter than ever to her master in London. Dublin, Kilkenny, Cork, Galway and Limerick became cities of English language, teaching, commerce and dress. The visible differences between native and settler began to blur; only the quiet, inherited hatred of old remained. Religion, rather than language or bloodlines, was the new wedge driven deep into the heart of the kingdom. As the wars of reformation and counter-reformation ripped across Europe, faith became a vicious instrument. In Ulster, more than anywhere else in Ireland, Catholic and Protestant waited nervously for a violent reckoning. The wait would not be long.

3

Avalanche

The Protestant prisoners were marched for six miles in the piercing cold of November. Guns and swords poked at their backs, and most had their hands bound. They had spent more than a week in captivity and were all starving and terrified. On and on they marched, until finally the prisoners reached a thick stone bridge tilting over the River Bann in Portadown. One by one they were forced onto the bridge, stripped naked and driven into the river at gunpoint. Wails and screams were choked in the current, as the river dragged one prisoner after another to a wet grave. Rebels waiting on the bank shot anyone who swam to the shore and kicked their corpses back into the river. In a hard winter of 1641, Ulster's great volcano of hate finally erupted. As its violence began to trickle down into the rest of the kingdom, it started an avalanche that would doom Ireland to decades of war and fire.

In February 1641 a small group of Gaelic Irish landowners had hatched a plot to seize Dublin, drive the hated English settlers out of Ulster and finish what their old brethren had started in the Nine Years War. The madness of the times, they felt, had created a perfect opportunity. Charles I's tyrannical streak was drawing him towards an almost inevitable conflict with Westminster. In Scotland, Presbyterians fighting to protect their church from royal control had risen in rebellion, scattered the king's army at Newburn and went on to menacingly occupy the north of England. Charles's authority was disintegrating, one crumb at a time. The Gaelic Irish plotters, led by Rory O'Moore and Phelim O'Neill, decided that this was their moment.

Ireland under the Stuarts was no place for the decadent lifestyles of the remaining Gaelic nobles. The earls of Tyrone and Tyrconnell had fled, and those left behind suffered under the burdens of falling incomes, extravagant expenses and dated visions of their own might. Despite the lean times, many had refused to kick their luxurious habits, and their credit was running low. Rory O'Moore was an old Gaelic patriarch of Leinster stock with lands in Antrim, and when he first tabled his plan for a Gaelic uprising in February 1641, he found sympathetic ears. The old Irish way of life could not survive for much longer; if Scotland could rise up, defeat the crown's forces and demand that its concerns be taken seriously, then why not Gaelic Ireland? The three kingdoms were in the eye of a perfect storm and, to O'Moore and his rapidly widening circle of conspirators, it was time to act.

After dark on 22 October Phelim O'Neill, who was a kinsman of the old Earl of Tyrone, led a small band of soldiers in surprise attacks that seized the garrisons of Charlemont and Dungannon, some twelve miles apart in central Ulster. Almost a hundred miles south, in the capital, a plan to snatch Dublin Castle, the nexus of royal authority in Ireland, was foiled on the same night. However, within twenty-four hours, Gaelic bands across Ulster followed O'Neill's cue and began a wave of localised attacks on

English settler communities, capturing several towns and forcing others, such as Derry, Lisburn and Belfast, to bar their gates. Without any organised royal force to oppose them, the rebels effectively took control of Ulster in a few hours. It was a shocking success. Word of the lightning raids swept through the north, and soon hundreds of armed Catholic bands joined the uprising. Ulster, which had been mechanically twisted by three decades of plantation and religious bigotry, was now a province of 'men whose minds are exasperated by the remembrance of former injuries'. Now, with most of the north falling into Gaelic hands almost overnight, the natives who had suffered under the yoke of English control began to violently settle old scores. The small stones that start an avalanche began to tumble.[1]

Few of the Gaelic conspirators truly believed that their rebellion would be so successful so quickly. Phelim O'Neill caught the scent of imminent carnage and desperately tried to take control of what had become a spontaneous popular uprising. On 24 October O'Neill issued a declaration insisting that the rebels refrain from violent excesses. It was wasted breath. Gangs of rebel militia armed with knives, pikes and crude old matchlock muskets began to round up English settlers and a series of tragic, unforgivable atrocities took place. Throats were slit with impunity; entire families were stripped naked and driven from their homes into the cold. The slaughter at the bridge of Portadown in Armagh, where eyewitnesses later reported seeing some one hundred Protestants drowned in the River Bann, was perhaps the most gruesome of the 'barbarous and inhuman massacres' that were now spreading through Ulster like wildfire. Vicious reprisals against Catholics by English settlers were also reported. Word of the sudden storm reached Westminster, where tempers were already hot. First hand reports of the rebellion became twisted and inflamed as they travelled, and by the time they reached London members of the House of Commons were told of Protestant women having babies cut from their wombs and children being forced to slit their parents' throats. The truth dissolved in the frenzy, and it became a matter of accepted fact to many that all Irish Catholics were murderous traitors. Several members of the commons, including an MP for Cambridge named Oliver Cromwell, were listening carefully.[2]

With Ulster under rebel control, Phelim O'Neill marched south in late October. After laying siege to the royalist garrison at Drogheda and scattering some of the king's soldiers outside Dublin, the Gaelic rebel leaders confronted the Catholic Norman gentry of the Pale, who had so far kept their hands clean. The old aristocrats and the heirs of Henry II's first settlers were no longer the crown's gatekeepers in Ireland. Protestant lords and landowners had strong-armed them out of key government posts and also now had a firm grip on both houses of the Dublin parliament. All the Old English Catholic gentry had left was royal favour – titles, lands and prospects derived directly from Charles I, who had come to see Ireland as a useful breadbasket for wealth and soldiers. Now, however, the kingdoms were slipping into civil war, and Charles's favour might soon be worth little. Despite their shared Catholic faith, the Norman gentry had always turned their noses up at the boisterous, unpredictable Gaelic lords with O and Mac in their names. But the sands were shifting quickly. The king they relied on was tottering. A hard, puritanical parliament in Westminster was spitting flames about Irish Catholics and gathering its strength. And now, a ragged army led by Gaelic lords they never trusted was camped on the outskirts of Dublin, demanding their allegiance. With little alternative, the Catholic gentry of the capital allied themselves with the rebels. They publicly professed continued loyalty to the crown but claimed that uniting with their fellow Catholics was the only way to protect their religion and property in the dangerous times ahead. It was a decision that would condemn them all.

*

In April 1642, seven months after the rebellion had begun, the Irish lord justices – the administrators of the royal government – sent a panicked letter to London. The kingdom, they warned, was in the midst of anarchy. The royal army had 10,000 troops, but little more than half of them were in any condition to fight. Most had spent the winter sick, hungry and without pay, holed up in freezing garrisons near Dublin. There was hardly a shilling left to purchase fresh supplies. 'The rebellion has now overspread all parts of the kingdom ... the rebels are generally masters of the field.'[3] A few weeks earlier, the mayor of Derry wrote that only a handful of towns in west Ulster were still holding out against the rebels, and all were living in fear of 'a most cruel and merciless enemy'.[4] The rebellion had shone a hot light on the cracks in this new Irish kingdom. King Charles's government, which was preparing to make war against parliament at home, could no longer enforce its will on the island. The Protestants of Ulster were forced to realise that they were outnumbered, vulnerable and could only rely on themselves. In the south, the spirit of rebellion continued to stir: in March 1642 as many as 12,000 rebels had encircled the city of Cork and threatened to take the town by force or 'starve up his Majesty's forces in it'.[5]

In June, as England staggered on towards all-out civil war, a number of Irish Catholic nobles discussed a plan to form a pseudo-government to defend their lives and property, independent of the royal administration. The main thrust of the rebellion had fizzled out over the winter: despite the tacit support of the Old English gentry, the rebels did not have the strength to storm the capital and were driven out of the Pale piece by piece by royalist troops under the command of James Butler, the Protestant Earl of Ormonde. In late April, just days before the lord justices sent their frantic dispatch for help to London, Ormonde's forces scattered the rebel forces in county Kildare. But the Catholics' ambitions did not end there. Between November 1642 and January 1649 an independent Catholic Confederacy met in Kilkenny nine times and effectively became an alternative government to Dublin Castle. It absorbed some of the leaders of the 1641 rebellion, such as the military commander Owen Roe O'Neill, and engaged with foreign emissaries such as the powerful papal nuncio Archbishop Giovanni Rinuccini. It cloned many of the functions of a working government, appointing its own sheriffs and constables to police the law in areas under its control. Its troops scuffled with the royal forces under the control of Ormonde, who was subsequently appointed lord lieutenant of Ireland. It was the strange product of a perilous time: a Catholic assembly that swore continued loyalty to Charles but was in direct conflict with the king's Irish administration. Both sides ultimately entered into an alliance after long, torturous negotiations. Their common enemy was about to lift its head.

In 1647, 2,000 parliamentary soldiers landed in Dublin, and after Charles's execution in January 1649 Cromwell gave Ireland his undivided attention. Cromwell personally led an expeditionary force of some 12,000 troops, and after briefly laying siege to the royalist port town of Drogheda, thirty miles north of the capital, his soldiers unleashed their cruelty. On 11 September, Cromwell's soldiers sacked Drogheda in one of the most horrendous incidents in Irish history. Seeking to set a brutal example for the rest of the kingdom, Cromwell forbade his soldiers to spare the lives of any man or woman found carrying a weapon. It was taken as an invitation to slaughter. Every crevice of the town was searched and pillaged, and thousands of soldiers and civilians were butchered in the streets. Hundreds fled into the town's church seeking refuge; Cromwell's men barred the doors and burned the building to the ground. The garrison commander who had at first refused to surrender was beaten to death with his own wooden leg. It was a hellish and brutal episode that claimed the lives of as many as 2,800 people. Somewhere in the carnage a young royalist soldier named Richard Talbot, a son of Catholic gentry from Kildare, barely out of his teens, narrowly escaped with his life. Half dead and horrified, Talbot fled to the continent with an iron grudge.

With Drogheda in ashes, Cromwell marched south to Wexford and repeated the butchery. Unrepentant, he defended his brutality as divine revenge for the Irish massacres of Protestants in 1641, labelling his work 'a righteous judgment of God upon these barbarous wretches'.[6] Cromwell was a cold Puritan who believed that to be a Catholic in Ireland was to be a traitor without the right to life, mercy or the protection of the law. Cromwell's authority in Ireland quickly became absolute: Ormonde fled with the last remnants of the royal government in 1650, while Limerick and Athlone surrendered on terms the following summer. The western port city of Galway was the last garrison to submit to parliament in April 1652. Cromwell had stalked and bled Ireland until its carcass lay slumped at his feet. He reached into his knapsack, pulled out a knife and began to carve.

*

Parliament had been making plans for Ireland's estates as early as March 1642, when horrendous rumours about the massacres in Ulster were whipping London into an anti-Irish frenzy. The commons passed an act inviting members of the public to invest in bonds that would go towards the cost of sending an army to crush the Irish rebellion. Investors were told that their money would later be repaid in confiscated Irish land. Over a thousand English subscribers known as 'adventurers' fronted more than £300,000 towards the war effort, and ten years later they handed parliament their final bill for over one million acres of prime

Irish property. Other accounts now had to be settled too. With hard currency evaporating, Cromwell had enticed his troops to fight by offering Irish estates in lieu of wages. With the war finally finished, some 35,000 parliamentary soldiers were now waiting with their hands out. Cromwell's long and exhaustive war effort had left parliament in debt to the tune of £2.5 million. Dismembering Ireland became a matter of fiscal urgency.

In 1652 the victorious parliament passed an act that effectively forced every Catholic landowner in Ireland to share blame for the war. From the rebels of 1641 to the members of the confederacy, thousands were informed that their lives and estates were no longer their own. Hundreds were executed, such as Phelim O'Neill, while thousands more either fled to the continent or were deported to English colonies in the West Indies. Rory O'Moore, one of the instigators of the 1641 uprising, slipped into obscurity before dying in 1655. Everyone else with a shred of property to their name was forced to take part in a crude land exchange programme, whereby their estates would be confiscated in return for a two-thirds equivalent holding in the western province of Connaught, where the earth was mostly mountainous, boggy and worth a pittance. A series of hurried and inaccurate land surveys took place, and the entire process sank into a pool of threats, confusion and legal wrangling. In Munster and Leinster, where the land was most valuable, more than three-quarters of Catholic estates were forfeited and carved up among subscribers, soldiers and parliament's other creditors. It was cold victor's justice and another brutal outing for the Tudor art of mass confiscation. Cromwell's experiment would ultimately fail, and after his death the realm would seek the familiar comfort of a king. But by 1660, when Charles returned to England in glory, Catholics, who had held 60 per cent of Ireland's land before 1641, now held as little as 9 per cent. The Old English gentry had fallen the hardest. If the Nine Years War had been the moment of reckoning for the Gaelic warlords of the north, then it was Cromwell who had severed the Normans from their past glory. Stripped of their wealth, identity and access to power, they were left to rue how they had gone from being the bannermen of Henry II to exiles in their own kingdom. More than anyone else in Ireland, it was the old Catholic gentry who rejoiced in the restoration of the monarchy and the return of Charles II in 1660. After a decade in penury, they were convinced that the lands and favour they had lost would be returned. They were wrong.

4

Oliver's Shoemakers

On 14 May 1660, two weeks after Westminster had declared Charles Stuart the new king, a headless carcass was hauled through the streets of Dublin. Propped up on a hearse and surrounded by candles and emblems of state, it was towed through the damp avenues of the city followed by a line of mourners with blackened faces. As the cortège passed, men and women lining the streets of the capital took turns to stab and wallop the headless dummy, which had been stitched together as a parody of Cromwell's deceased republic. When the procession finally reached the mayor's residence, sweet cakes and ale were passed among the jubilant crowd. The dummy was set on fire and then 'trod to dust and mortar'. Cromwell's time was finally over, and a relieved and bloodied Catholic Ireland had come to dance on its corpse.[1]

The return of the king thrust the conundrum of Irish land immediately onto the agenda. Within weeks of Charles's restoration, the petitions and lobbying on behalf of dispossessed Catholic landowners began on both sides of the Irish Sea. To the Old English gentry, who felt they had suffered the most during the civil war, the right to satisfaction seemed clear: they had fought against Cromwell to preserve the Stuart line and had lost their wealth, property and lives because of it. Charles owed them. However, they were not the only voices in the new king's ear, and they were far from the loudest. In the Declaration of Breda, which had crucially won over the army, Charles had promised General Monck and the rest of the troops that he would not interfere with their lives or possessions – possessions that included, thanks to Cromwell, huge tracts of confiscated estates in Ireland. Charles knew that the army's consent was the only reason he was no longer shuffling about in exile. Now that he was king, he could not start charging about snatching deeds from soldiers' hands. In the first months of Charles's reign the royal court at Whitehall became a hive of intrigue, and it soon became obvious where the king's immediate loyalties lay. In the Act of Indemnity and Oblivion, which trawled its way through parliament in the summer of 1660 and gave some legal meat to Charles's promises from Breda, a clause was inserted excluding those 'who have had any hand in the plotting, contriving or designing the great and heinous rebellion of Ireland'. No distinction was made between the Gaels who had first risen up in 1641 or the confederates who had tried to make hay in the mess afterwards. They were all accused of betraying royal authority, and none would be entitled to any 'estate, liberties, franchises' or other property. The spectre of further punishment was left to hang in the air. It was a swift and stunning setback for the Irish Catholic gentry, who had effectively been told by the new king that they were guilty until proven innocent.

In November 1660, after intense lobbying and legal counsel, Charles made his first attempt to untie the Gordian knot of Irish land ownership. In a long-winded declaration, the king confirmed that all Cromwellian soldiers and investors who had received confiscated property could keep it. Those Catholic nobles and gentry who could legally prove that they 'had never acted against our royal father or ourself' would get their lands back, as would particular favourites who had fled Ireland and served with the royal court in exile. Charles spoke of his 'natural inclination to mercy' but fudged the chance to add any more detail by stating that a long-term fix for Ireland 'is not now before us'. With the king's ambiguous wishes before them, it fell to the Irish parliament in Dublin to turn them into law. In 1661 the Protestant-dominated assembly sent their first draft bill to London for approval, and the intense lobbying in Whitehall and Westminster resumed. The Protestant interest in Ireland, who controlled the Dublin parliament and the king's Irish privy council, seemed to hold every card. In order for the Irish Catholic gentry to make their case in the cutthroat halls of the royal court, they would need a lobbyist able to manhandle his way to the king's ear. It was in this circus of whispers that the rise of Richard Talbot would begin.[2]

After surviving the massacre at Drogheda, Talbot had escaped Ireland and served stints with the French army in Spain and Flanders. He spent his twenties living the clandestine life of a royalist agent abroad, a world of coded letters and daggers hidden in sleeves. In 1655, when he was just twenty-five years old, Talbot was arrested in connection with a failed plot to assassinate Oliver Cromwell. He was questioned in Whitehall by the lord protector himself but managed to escape out an open window and fled back to France. Through his older brother Peter, a Catholic theologian and prominent member of Charles's court-in-exile, Talbot made the acquaintance of James Stuart, Charles's younger brother. James quickly became fond of the Irishman, who was two years his senior and dazzled him with stories of intrigue, duelling and his 'great experience of the world'. Talbot had all the talent and instinct needed to thrive at court. He was a man 'of very good sense, very obliging, but immodestly vain and full of cunning'.[3] Letters describe him as a charming but disagreeable sort, and he never failed to turn heads when he entered a room. Talbot was tall, broad and thickly set, with a gruff manner and a fondness for brandy, swearing and grudges. Later on in life, as gout began to cripple him, he developed a slow and almost menacing limp. He was crafty, short tempered and sly – qualities that the pliant young James found fascinating. James granted him access to his inner circle and 'took him into his family'.[4] Talbot built a close bond with the exiled young prince and learned the power of royal intimacy. Talbot was James's fixer, arranging visits with his mistresses, and was also a custodian of another, more explosive secret. James Stuart, who was next in line for the throne after his brother, was a Catholic.

When Charles was restored in 1660 Talbot's friendship with James, who was now the Duke of York, brought him into the decadent circles of Whitehall. Talbot chased the hand of Frances Jennings, a beautiful young attendant to James's first wife, Anne Hyde, and though Jennings rejected his affections and chose the Irish officer George Hamilton – a nephew of the Irish lord lieutenant, the Duke of Ormonde – the pair eventually married after Hamilton was killed in Luxembourg. Talbot's favour with the king's brother gave him clout at court, and his ego gave him reason to use it. He became a conduit for the petitions and flattery of the Irish Catholic gentry who wanted their land back and reckoned that a solid word from Richard Talbot would bring their case to the Duke of York's ear, and perhaps even the king's. Over time he became an unusual hydra of minister, spokesman and lobbyist for the Irish interest in London, and he was always eager to sharpen his own status and wealth. One writer described Talbot as 'a man of stately presence … naturally proud and passionate', but driven by 'an unbounded ambition'.[5] Like all men who wrestled for influence in the restoration court, Talbot made enemies quicker than he made friends. But he had a knack for the sport of it all, and even though the legislation on Irish land that finally emerged in 1662 created more problems than it solved, it would keep Richard Talbot glued to the centre of affairs.

*

The Act of Settlement of 1662, which was returned to Dublin and passed into law, was a mess that failed to dilute Ireland's toxic cocktail of land and religion. In an attempt to find a compromise where few people wanted one, the law stated that all former Irish landowners deemed innocent of rebelling against the crown would have their estates returned, and any English soldiers or adventurers forced to make way would be compensated with estates elsewhere in Ireland. All Irish land that had belonged to the regicides – well over a hundred thousand acres – was personally given to James, the Duke of York. A new civil court of claims would be set up to decide who had actually rebelled against the crown during the war. Any Irishman who was found innocent and had their estates confiscated by Cromwell but did not receive anything in Connaught in return would be first in line to get their land back. Waiting with them at the top of the queue would be the 'ensign men' who had fled overseas with Charles. But no one would get anything until the new Cromwellian owners were compensated and relocated first. Charles would take his cut by way of 'quit rents', a property tax equivalent to one year's rent per estate. The law was dense and layered with murky clauses, and the entire act was built on the idea that Ireland was a bottomless basket of land, which needed only to be indexed and divided up until everyone had a chunk. Obviously, it was a disaster.

The court of claims began to hear cases in Dublin in January 1663. It had been stacked with English judges, and Irish applicants claiming that they had never rebelled would have to satisfy an agonisingly strict definition of innocence to have any hope of success. The Dublin establishment quietly expected that the court would dismiss practically every Irish application and stick firmly to the Protestant status quo. To their astonishment, it did not. Over the eight months that it was in session, the court of claims ruled that 566 Catholics were innocent of rebellion and should have their lands restored. The court, it turned out, was easily swayed by influence, favours and hard cash. Well-connected courtiers regularly leaned on the judges to secure the right results for their families, friends and anyone else willing to part with enough money. Richard Talbot earned a small fortune in this way, taking on individual clients and lobbying hard in return for pieces of restored estates or eye-watering lump sums. The court stank of corruption, and several members of the Protestant nobility cried foul. Sir Audley Mervyn, the speaker of the Protestant-dominated Irish House of Commons, swore that 'Hannibal was at the gates'.[6] The Duke of Ormonde himself wrote that many of the 'extraordinary' decisions of the court would only serve to whip up 'mischiefs and inconveniences'.[7]

Ormonde had a better feel for Irish politics than most. Returned to the post of lord lieutenant and elevated to a dukedom in the early days of the restoration, Ormonde was not a fool. In April 1663, as verdicts of innocence from the court of claims began to pile up, he wrote to a friend expressing concern that land disputes had the potential to drag Ireland back into war. 'Many of the English had said they would not quit the possession of what they held' no matter what the court ruled, he warned. If sheriffs then had to be sent to execute orders by force, Catholic deputies would inevitably have to assist them, as no Protestant would take arms to force another off his land. 'To the common people ... it would look like, and for ought anybody knows, may prove a war'.[8] Word of the trouble brewing in Dublin travelled as far as the royal embassy in Istanbul: 'The English conceive the Irish to have too much favour, and the restitution of so many of them to their estates to be destructive to the English interest … what may be the result thereof, we are not without some fears.'[9] The stinking legacy of 1641 was dragged up. In one case, a lawyer objecting to an Irish applicant's ruling of innocence mocked the court's logic. 'Sirs, if you judge this man innocent we must believe the English cut one another's throats and that there was no Irish rebellion.'[10]

The Act of Settlement did not clear up Cromwell's wreckage but simply shovelled it around. Those Irish landowners who had accepted property in Connaught under penalty of death complained bitterly at now having to wait at the end of the queue. The new Protestant landowners, meanwhile, resented having to give back anything at all. Confusion was rife, as many chose to ignore rulings. The court of claims had become such a thorn that it was wound up after only eight months, despite the fact that many Irish applicants were still waiting to make their cases. Charles and his government tried to cut through the muddle with another law in 1665, dubiously titled the Act of Explanation. This law stated that all soldiers and investors who had received confiscated Irish estates must now give back one-third of them, in order to create a surplus pool of land to settle outstanding claims. The decrees of innocence were controversially rubber-stamped, and a number of well-connected Catholics were awarded their old estates in full, as well as a sweetener of 2,000 extra acres. The Act of Explanation almost brought the roof down on the Dublin parliament. On 16 December 1665, as the bill was being debated, tempers became so hot that swords were drawn and furious Protestants swore 'that the lands they had gotten with the hazard of their lives should not now be lost with ayes and no's'.[11] Ormonde barely managed to steer the bill through, but the tangled web of rivalry and protest only grew thicker. Five years, two laws and one crooked court later, all that the Irish land settlement had achieved was to remind Protestant settler and Catholic native that they were in each other's way.

Aside from the handful that could afford to buy a lobbyist like Richard Talbot, hundreds of members of the old Irish Catholic gentry were left with nothing. In 1660 Catholics held 9 per cent of Ireland's estates, but by the end of Charles's reign in 1685 this had only crept up to 20 per cent. The new order, it seems, was not so different from the old. One writer later described Restoration Ireland as a kingdom full of penniless Catholic heirs, wandering Dublin with heavy and resentful feet. Out of as many as eight thousand families who claimed a right to restitution, 'there was not above five hundred restored'.[12] Rightly or not, the luckless majority felt a cold sting of betrayal. The Old Catholic gentry clung to their belief that they had suffered for their 'constant loyalty and unshaken fidelity'[13] to the Stuarts and now felt abandoned and slighted. The king's decision to grant a colossal estate to his brother James, for example, instead of dividing up the Irish lands taken from the regicides, was just one notch on a list of grievances. Charles's attempts to repair the damage of the Cromwellian settlement was 'universally looked on as a most ungrateful return',[14] while one Irish account labelled it the 'greatest injustice' done to a people 'from the first day of the creation'.[15] The grumbling would only grow deeper and more spiteful in the years to come, as Ireland and the rest of the kingdoms began to grow prosperous in a time of peace. Those with land revelled in a new era of wealth and credit, while those without it watched enviously from outside, their faces pressed hard against the window.

*

Restoration Dublin was a city of fortune. It had once clung to the River Liffey like a child to its mother's coat, but now it was enjoying a poised and breathless adolescence. Waves of migrants arrived in the city every week, many of them investors from England drawn by rumours of endless opportunity. New suburbs were built and knitted together by grand avenues such as Aungier Street and King Street. A walled park on the southern edge of the city, St Stephen's Green, was where the fashionable classes came to disappear. The royal hospital in Kilmainham, finally completed in 1684, was one of the most splendid buildings in the kingdom. Dublin had a colourful pulse, from the taverns and slaughterhouses of the Liberties to the new Theatre Royal on Smock Alley, where boisterous productions became the talk of the city. The capital turned on a great medieval axis between Christchurch Cathedral and Dublin Castle, barely 200 yards apart from each other, their spires and turrets looming above the rooftops like lanky twins in a playground. The castle, in particular, was the heart of the kingdom – the seat of government and home to the viceroy's court, where opulence and connections were the price of admission. A French writer who visited Dublin during the reign of Charles II described it as 'one of the greatest and best-peopled towns in Europe'.[16]

Dublin was not a lone star. In the years following the restoration, Ireland's economy put on a lot of weight. Its ports were crammed, its tastes grew finer and the root to all wealth was land and produce. The Irish Sea became a highway for livestock exports, and tens of thousands of cattle each year were crammed into merchant vessels and shipped to the meat markets of London and the English north-west. When Westminster passed a series of laws to protect English farmers from Irish goods, Irish produce simply went elsewhere. Butter and wool exports surged, and shiploads of Irish goods began to crop up in ports as far away as the Caribbean, where regulations were lax. Ireland's agricultural economy remained as vulnerable as any other to wobbling prices, currency values and bad harvests. But in a new era of peace at home, Irish wealth found a sturdier footing. For the old Irish landowners squeezed out by Cromwell and the bungled land settlement, it was tough to watch. The mostly Gaelic-speaking peasants who farmed the land saw nothing of prosperity, surviving on a 'very mean and sparing' diet of milk, whey, potatoes and oatmeal.[17] But for the landlords collecting ever-rising rents, it was a wonderful time to be alive. Property values soared, making it easier for landlords to secure cheap credit and enjoy the fruits of high society in Dublin. They jostled to be seen at the most exclusive functions, spent fortunes on fine brandy and tobacco, wore tailored cravats and waistcoats made from the most expensive silk and linen and were a constant eyesore to the old Catholic gentry who believed that all this should be theirs. 'Oliver's soldiers, poor bakers, shoemakers, tailors ... lord it in their coaches throughout the kingdom of Ireland, while the true lords and gentlemen of those lands are going a-foot', one Irishman wrote with gritted teeth.[18]

The Protestant landlords, merchants and clergy of Ireland were not blind to this envy. Jealousy over wealth and property was 'the matter most capable of combustion, and it hardly can be expected it should be otherwise', the Cork-born Protestant diplomat Robert Southwell predicted.[19] The simmering religious tensions of the kingdom, which ran all the way to Whitehall, did little to cool the mood. King Charles was a Protestant, but his private sympathies towards Catholics were a source of suspicion. His queen, the Portuguese Catherine of Braganza, was a Catholic. So was his brother. Charles did not share Westminster's zeal for rooting out religious dissent, but every time he tried to soften restrictions against English Catholics that had lingered from the days of Queen Elizabeth, parliament pushed back hard. There was, after all, more than just a king's conscience at stake.

5

Forever Incapable

In the latter half of the seventeenth century, with the shocking cruelty of the wars of religion seemingly in the past, the princes of continental Europe found a new reason to blow each other to pieces. His name was Louis XIV, *Le Roi Soleil*, the man who had been king of France since he was four years old and was as accomplished at critiquing ballet as he was at plotting the mass movements of troops and artillery. In 1667 the twenty-nine-year-old Louis personally led his armies into the field as they overran the Spanish Netherlands and the Franche-Comté. He was reluctantly forced to hand back almost of all his new territory the following year when a triple alliance of Sweden, England and the Dutch United Provinces threatened to attack. The chastened king of France clenched his fists. Convinced that the upstart Dutch Republic that had violently broken free from Spain was the architect of the move against him, Louis began a decades-long obsession with grinding them into the earth. To succeed, he would first have to isolate The Hague from its allies. He began in England.

The key to it all, it seemed, was money. Charles II enjoyed a famously decadent lifestyle and was always open to finding new ways to pay for it. Of all of the Dutch Republic's allies, he was also the most likely to be tempted by a good offer from France. England and the Dutch had recently been at war with each other, after all, and Louis was also Charles's first cousin. The Houses of Stuart and Bourbon were knitted together through marriage, and Charles had likewise spent part of his continental exile under Louis's protection. In 1670, Louis and Charles agreed a controversial deal. The Treaty of Dover saw Charles agree to swap sides and support Louis in his war against the Dutch in return for an annual pension. English brigades were to be loaned to the French army on a rolling basis, and many Irish Catholics who were barred from holding commissions at home under the penal laws left to fight on the continent. Among them was a young man named Patrick Sarsfield, the idle yet boisterous second son of Old English gentry from County Dublin, whose mother was also the daughter of Rory O'Moore, one of the Gaelic conspirators of the 1641 rebellion.

The Treaty of Dover did not go down smoothly with the English public. Many voices wondered aloud why Protestant England had chosen to ally itself with Catholic France against the Protestant Dutch Republic. Had they known the full truth, Whitehall Palace might have been torched. Beneath the military and economic chaff of the treaty there was an explosive secret clause: in return for a French pension, Charles promised that he would publicly convert to Catholicism before the end of his life. Many historians suspect that he had privately resolved to do so long before agreeing to Louis's treaty. The clause was never committed to paper, and its existence was not revealed until years after Charles's death, with good reason. Much of English public opinion, and its violent mouthpiece in Westminster, was ferociously anti-Catholic. Charles understood that a Catholic sitting openly on the English throne could spark an insurrection. One day, in a not so remote future, he would be proven right.

*

Richard Talbot strode into the privy council chamber and gave a deep and exaggerated bow. The fourteen men sitting across from him ran their eyes over his clothes, manners and intentions. Talbot's reputation had begun to precede him. To his enemies, he was a troublesome insolent. To his Irish kinsmen, Talbot was their *de facto* leader and agitator at the royal court, the 'agent general of the Roman Catholics of Ireland'. And he was about to stir the pot like never before. In 1671 Talbot presented a formal petition to the king and his privy councillors in London claiming that the land settlement in Ireland was being obstructed and asked Charles to personally intervene. Talbot did not care if he was trampling on the status quo – he was convinced that his favour with the Duke of York gave him cover. 'I have forgot the part of a courtier as to fear offending any man in power in speaking the truth,' he told his brother Peter, who had since been appointed archbishop of Dublin.[1] Charles was intrigued by Talbot and his petition and ordered that a new committee be set up to explore the Irish land settlement, some six years after the Act of Explanation of 1665 had drawn a crude line under it.

In 1672, with his secret pact with Louis still lingering on his conscience, Charles sought to loosen the penal laws against Catholics, Presbyterians and other religious dissenters with a declaration of royal indulgence. He hoped to build a broader coalition of public support before finally going to war with the Dutch later that year. Westminster erupted. The House of Commons lashed out at the king for pandering to Catholics and pointed to the 'great insolences of the papists in Ireland',[2] particularly Archbishops Peter Talbot and Oliver Plunkett, who had been permitted to practice relatively freely under Charles's administration. Parliament decided that it was time to show its teeth. In 1672 it passed the first of the Test Acts, which demanded that men in civil and military office, or anyone who wished to live within thirty miles of London, had to swear an oath denouncing the Catholic Holy Communion. The law effectively outed James, the Duke of York, who resigned his post as lord high admiral rather than take the oath, thereby admitting that he was a Catholic. The dam had burst, and the first great flood of anti-Catholic hysteria since Charles took the throne was unleashed. In 1673 the House of Commons demanded that the king abolish the new committee on Irish land created at Talbot's request. It also called for Charles to expel every Catholic bishop and priest from Ireland, confiscate every Catholic-owned gun, shut every Catholic school and personally forbid Richard Talbot from ever showing his face at court again. Charles took the hint, and although the wilder of the demands were ignored, Richard Talbot and his brother Peter were forced into temporary exile in France, while Oliver Plunkett and most of the Irish Catholic clergy were driven underground.

In the autumn of 1678 London was gripped by a rumour that Catholic conspirators were plotting to assassinate Charles, who had never fathered a legitimate son, thereby allowing his Catholic brother James to take the throne. The man who apparently uncovered the plot, a fantasist named Titus Oates, testified before the House of Lords and gave a long, rambling narrative of a conspiracy that apparently ran from London to Spain and involved dozens of agents, lords and members of Catholic religious orders. Oates claimed that, as well as wishing to poison the king, the plotters intended to overthrow the royal government in Dublin and open the door for France to invade England. The conspiracy was a complete farce, invented entirely by Oates and a fellow madman named Israel Tonge, driven by nothing more than bigotry and mischief making.

Nonetheless, their claims swept through England like a plague. The 'Popish Plot' sparked a wave of beatings, arrests, show-trials and public executions of Catholics on imaginary charges. Archbishop Peter Talbot, who had returned from his exile but was in poor health, died while in custody in Dublin Castle. Archbishop Oliver Plunkett was accused of treason, went on trial in London in 1681 and was hung, drawn and quartered. By the time it was discovered that Oates and Tonge had made the whole thing up, the damage had been done. A deep and violent English suspicion of Catholics had been stirred once more and no one – not even the king's brother – was able to escape intact.

In November 1680, when the fury of the Popish Plot was razor-sharp, the House of Commons passed a bill that tried to remove James from the line of succession. The bill demanded that the Duke of York be 'forever incapable to inherit, possess or enjoy the imperial crown of this realm' and called for him to be banished from the kingdoms immediately. If he ever set foot in England again, the bill warned, 'he shall be deemed and adjudged guilty of high treason'.[3] The bill died in the House of Lords, but its message was shrill. 'Popery is too strong to be subdued,' one MP declared during a furious debate in the commons. 'After this king's life, the Protestant religion must either be overcome by popery, or defend itself by the sword.'[4] The commons was threatening James with a civil war like the one that had claimed his father's head. The Duke of York prudently withdrew himself to Brussels and Scotland until things had calmed down.

*

Charles was growing sick of parliament and its continuous outrage and dissolved it for the fourth and final time during his reign in 1681. The trouble did not disappear with it. In 1683 several former members of parliament were implicated in an aborted plot to assassinate the king and his brother and hand the crown to the Duke of Monmouth, Charles's illegitimate Protestant son. Eleven men were arrested and executed, while Monmouth was forced to flee to Holland and seek the protection of William of Orange, a Calvinist and the titular head of state of the Dutch Republic, and a man with more than just a passing interest in English affairs. William was both James's nephew and his son-in-law: his mother was Mary Stuart, James and Charles's younger sister who had died in 1660; and his wife, also named Mary, was James's eldest daughter with his first wife, Anne Hyde, who died in 1671. As a result, the thirty-three-year-old William also found himself tangled up in the messy weave of Stuart succession. He gave Monmouth refuge in Holland and quietly continued to watch events unfold.

The Monmouth scandal had given England something different to be horrified about. By now, the turmoil of the Popish Plot had soothed sufficiently for the Duke of York to return to court and re-take his place as Charles's accepted heir. However, James did not forget how suddenly his future had almost been snatched from him in 1680. He began to gather his strength, fearful of the day when parliament might sink its jaws into him once more. Luckily, there was one person already within the duke's close circle who had displayed a knack for survival. Richard Talbot began to convince James that, should he need its support, Ireland would be a powerful ally. Its brisk economy produced solid customs revenues, which were paid directly into the king's privy purse. By the same token, however, Talbot warned James that Protestant interests had firm control of Ireland's army, courts and government, epitomised by the grand old aristocrat of Irish politics, the Duke of Ormonde, who had become Talbot's bitter enemy. Prodded by Talbot's advice, James began to tinker with Irish affairs. In October 1684 Ormonde received news that he had been fired. The Irish viceroy was already aware of plans to appoint a new tranche of Catholic army officers and magistrates in Ireland and could feel Talbot's fingerprints all over it. He received permission to remain in office until the following spring and spent the weeks in between scrawling letter after letter complaining about Catholics being parachuted into 'more than half the army, and a like proportion of the privy council, judges and magistrates'.[5]

Then, in February 1685, the kingdoms were suddenly wrenched from one era into the next. Charles suffered a stroke and died four days later in Whitehall Palace. He was just fifty-four years old. In his final hours, as he gasped and struggled to speak, the king finally fulfilled his promise and converted to Catholicism. For a quarter of a century, Charles Stuart had struggled to chart a new course for his kingdoms. In Ireland, he left behind a realm where the Catholic and Protestant gentry were bitter rivals to each other's ambitions. In one of his final acts as viceroy, the Duke of Ormonde proclaimed that the Catholic Duke of York was now King James II. As he gathered his papers and effects in preparation for his retirement in England, Ormonde stumbled across a copy of an old letter he had written to the late king almost four years earlier. Back then Ormonde had wistfully stated that 'this kingdom improves visibly' and that nothing except 'a civil war, or some other of God's notional judgements' would shunt Ireland from its new 'career of prosperity'.[6] As Ormonde sailed away from the kingdom for the final time, he wondered what would become of it now that men like Richard Talbot found themselves in the company of the king.

6

Jacobus Rex

It was a strange place to crown a king. The village of Taunton, tucked away on the road between Exeter and Bristol, was more used to seeing hens being bartered as currency or farriers trimming hooves like sculptors. It was a no-frills coronation. There was no incense, nor any great emblems stitched into banners with gold weave. There were no emissaries from foreign palaces, nor any great lords or leaders of the Church. Instead, the new King James was presented with a small flag made by local schoolgirls, as a few hundred townsfolk watched awkwardly. The local aldermen, it is said, were only present because the King's soldiers threatened to have them shot. But the man they were paying homage to at gunpoint was not James Stuart, the King of England, Ireland and Scotland, who had been crowned in Westminster Abbey over a month earlier. This was James Scott, the thirty-six-year-old Duke of Monmouth, the illegitimate son of the late King Charles who had returned from his exile in Holland to overthrow his uncle. Monmouth staged his farcical coronation in Taunton, near the coastline where he had landed with a tiny invasion force, and had sent messengers to spread word across the English south-west, hoping to provoke a massive uprising.

Monmouth had been on the fringes of power all his life. Born to one of Charles's mistresses in Rotterdam before the restoration, he was raised as a prince in all but name. His father doted on him with wealth, titles and a good marriage. He was a handsome, popular figure in the royal court and had a stout reputation as a soldier, rising to the rank of captain general of England. He was the heir to the throne that many hard-line Protestants dreamed of. Just how deeply he was tangled up in the failed plot to murder Charles and James in 1683 was never firmly established, but Monmouth had felt enough heat to flee England in disgrace. After learning of his father's death and his uncle's succession, Monmouth and a small cohort of supporters had begun to scheme. They landed in Dorset on 11 June 1685, and within weeks they had raised a rag-tag army of some 4,000 suggestible peasants. Monmouth gambled that he could whip up the old fury of the Popish Plot and use it against his uncle. He believed that the gentry of southern England would flock to his banner with men and arms and money the second a viable alternative to the Catholic king appeared. He would be proven utterly, viciously wrong.

On 6 July Monmouth's poorly armed and ill-disciplined troops were scattered by a small but highly motivated force of royal soldiers at Sedgemoor in Somerset. Hundreds of rebels were cut down as they fled the battlefield, while Monmouth himself was captured and dragged to London in irons. In Scotland, an almost simultaneous rebellion led by Archibald Campbell, the Earl of Argyll, was crushed with even greater ease. Monmouth was condemned for high treason. From his cell in the Tower of London, he wrote a letter to his uncle begging for his life, pleading with James to accept 'how heartedly I repent of what I have done' and insisting that 'some horrid people' had manipulated him.[1] It is claimed that the letter was hidden from the new king, perhaps to spare him an awkward decision. Monmouth was beheaded on 15 July, and his disastrously misjudged power play came to a predictable end. Monmouth, his conspirators and perhaps even his uncle had expected a violent outcry when England was asked to crown a Catholic king. To all of their surprise, they heard nothing.

*

The moment James Stuart was told that his brother was dead and that he was now *Jacobus Rex*, he immediately withdrew to his private chamber alone. No one will ever know what words he spoke to himself in the dark, as grief and joy and fear welled up in his heart. He had stood at Charles's side on that historic day in Dover in 1660, as had poor Henry, their youngest brother, who had succumbed to smallpox before that year was out. The twenty-five years since then were like the wall of a great gallery, where scenes of torture and lust and doubt were arranged in an orderly line towards an orderly conclusion. The Duke of York had suffered but God, he believed, now saw fit to reward him with a crown. He was fifty-one-years-old. He prayed, rose from his feet, wiped his eyes and opened his chamber door to the world waiting outside. There were instant problems, naturally: James was a Catholic, he had no legitimate son to call his heir and the whispers had it that his second wife, Mary of Modena, the new queen, was barren. After the furore of the Popish Plot and the exclusion crisis, James feared that he might have to fight to secure his throne. But the outpouring of love and affection he received from the people of England in the weeks after Charles's death was beyond unexpected. 'The world stood astonished to see the metamorphoses in a manner of a whole kingdom,' a biographer wrote years later. 'The Prince, who so little a while before had been persecuted, banished … to see this same Prince welcom'd to the throne with such universal acclamations of joy … was what history has no example of.'[2]

James was not alone in thinking that his ascension might not go down well. When word of Charles's death reached Ireland, the Duke of Ormonde, now in his final hours in office, put the army on high alert in case pockets of hard-line Protestants, most likely in Ulster, took arms against the succession. 'I considered it possible, that upon such a change, some endeavours might be used to raise disturbance in opposition to his present Majesty's accession to the crown,' Ormonde wrote a month later, relieved that nothing had happened.[3] For this helpful swell of calm, James owed a lot to his late brother. In the later years of Charles's reign, after he had accepted that he would not produce a legitimate heir, Charles worked hard to safeguard his brother's inheritance. The prickliest voices in parliament had been gerrymandered out of Westminster, and the Stuart brothers regularly rehearsed what James would have to do when the time came. After Charles's death, James immediately issued a proclamation that he would not trample on parliament and rule arbitrarily like his cousin Louis XIV, who was reviled in much of England as the worst sort of Catholic dictator. James also swore that, even though he was a Catholic, he knew that 'the principles of the Church of England are for monarchy, and that the members of it have shown themselves good and loyal subjects'. He voiced admiration for the established Protestant Church, and promised that 'I shall always take care to defend and support it.'[4]

His sentiment cut well. The mood of the English public had soothed considerably since the days of the Popish Plot, and a kingdom barely a generation removed from the civil war had no stomach for deposing another Stuart. Parcel after parcel of letters, addresses and tokens of fealty flowed into Whitehall. Over 12,000 people signed one message of loyalty from the tin workers of Cornwall, while another from the gentry and chief subjects of Norfolk carried 6,000 signatures.[5] Town magistrates, Protestant clergy, merchants and men of every standing in every crevice of the realm poured their hearts out. Even those who had lobbied hardest for James to be banished in 1680 now flung their arms around him. 'Whatever my opinions were when I delivered them … they are altered now I am become his subject,' the MP Ralph Montagu wrote, his tail wedged between his legs.[6] James immediately convened parliaments in England and Scotland, and the members of both clamoured each other to profess loyalty and service. In Ireland, meanwhile, there was no need to doubt the mood. The Catholics of the kingdom rejoiced in the coronation of a man of the Roman Church, and the old Irish gentry still struggling to reclaim their wealth and status 'exulted in the assured hope' that James would restore the estates 'of which they had been, for so many years, so unjustly despoiled'.[7] The Catholic clergy of Ireland sent the new king a congratulatory message, to which James replied with an assurance that they would receive 'royal protection and favour … upon all occasions'.[8]

*

As James rose, so did Richard Talbot. By the summer of 1685 James had elevated his old fixer and confidant to the nobility, granting him the symbolic title of Earl of Tyrconnell. He also instructed Talbot to return to Ireland and take a long, hard look at the Irish army that the Duke of Ormonde had assembled. Talbot, who from now on was addressed in letters and conversation as Lord Tyrconnell, was rarely subtle. On arriving in Ireland he began to methodically pick apart the army and its command structure, which was dominated by Ormonde's Protestant appointments. He made a public show of calling for the investigation of any officers who had fought for Cromwell, despite the fact few – if any – of those old veterans were still in the service. He pushed for a new oath of allegiance that would be more agreeable to Catholics seeking to enlist and sought fresh commissions that he could distribute to new officers of his choosing. Tyrconnell even sought a law that would allow Catholics – specifically, him – to sit on the king's Irish privy council. James was happy to oblige his old friend to a point but was wary of giving Tyrconnell too much, too soon. His reign was in its infancy, and Richard Talbot's name was still dirt in Westminster. James had to think smart. When it came to naming a new lord lieutenant and viceroy of Ireland – the position that Tyrconnell coveted most – James appointed the English Protestant nobleman Henry Hyde, the Earl of Clarendon, who was the younger brother of James's late first wife, Anne. Lord Clarendon was a safe choice: a pliant English conservative who would not rock the boat or take a sledgehammer to the Irish land laws. James, of course, had received more than 100,000 Irish acres through his brother's land settlement. He had a personal interest in the status quo.

Clarendon was a prodigious man of letters and devoted sizable chunks of his day to reading, writing and compiling correspondence. When he received a long written briefing from a companion about Ireland just as he was preparing to take up his new post, Clarendon studied it carefully. 'It will be a matter of great difficulty to steer a right course,' he was told. 'It is natural and necessary to believe that the Irish will have an aversion to the English, and their government; and if ever they have it in their power, they will shake it off.'[9] Tyrconnell was on army business in Dublin when he was informed that a plump English courtier was coming to take over the Irish administration. He could not hide his disgust. 'Clarendon's nomination as governor terrifies the Catholics,' he wrote to the king.[10] James quietly ignored his friend's protests. Tyrconnell had packed up his belongings and sailed back to England in a huff before Clarendon arrived in

Dublin in January 1686. But he did not intend to be out of the picture for long.

*

By the summer of 1686, Clarendon's administration was already wobbling. The new lord lieutenant had arrived in Ireland with an open mind and was willing to share some degree of power with the Catholic gentry, provided that it did not greatly bother the way of things. But Dublin had a fierce appetite, and the city was rife with gossip about an imminent overhaul of the army, government and judiciary that would see Catholics placed in powerful positions. The speculation seemed to always trickle back to one man, whose name was now on everyone's lips: Lord Tyrconnell. Clarendon became irritated when he received word that Tyrconnell had spent the spring in England speaking against him mischievously. Each time Tyrconnell's name appears in Clarendon's letters from this period, words like 'insolence', 'contempt' and 'monstrous vanity' are always close by. Tyrconnell returned to Dublin in June and cranked up his overhaul of the royal army. He was personally appointed to the rank of lieutenant general, effectively making him Irish commander-in-chief. Two Irish Catholic veterans of Charles's French brigades were also appointed to the senior staff: the Cork native Justin MacCarthy and Richard Hamilton, brother of George Hamilton, the man who had first beaten Tyrconnell to the affections of his wife. With James's implicit blessing, Tyrconnell began to dismiss Protestant soldiers from army regiments. The business was sudden and dramatic: by September 1686 there were over 5,000 Catholic soldiers enlisted in an army of some 7,500 men. Catholic priests began to replace Protestant clergymen as regimental chaplains. It was all starting to give Clarendon a thumping headache. Mounds of petitions of protest piled up on his desk from angry ex-soldiers, which in turn sparked a series of heated arguments between Clarendon and Tyrconnell, who was doing his best to undermine the lord lieutenant at every turn.

The fabric of the armed forces in England was also changing, as James sought to relax measures such as the Test Act and other restrictions intended to bar Catholics from serving at home. Patrick Sarsfield, the young Irish soldier who had enlisted to fight in Charles's French brigades, had been in London looking for employment in the early summer of 1685 when word arrived that his old commanding officer, the Duke of Monmouth, had launched a rebellion. When a royal force was being mobilised to march on the south-west in response, Sarsfield had eagerly volunteered. When the king's troops clashed with Monmouth's rebels at Sedgemoor, Sarsfield had been in the thick of the action, narrowly surviving after charging the rebel lines and being knocked off his horse and left for dead. Word of Sarsfield's reckless bravery travelled all the way back to Whitehall, and James saw fit to reward him with an officer's commission. By July 1685, aged around twenty-five years old, Sarsfield was a lieutenant colonel; by May the following year he was the colonel of his own cavalry regiment under the command of a charismatic and well-connected young Protestant general named John Churchill.

Back in Dublin, the quiet surge of Catholic influence was gathering speed. Catholics were appointed to all three levels of the judiciary, and in 1686, after originally deciding against allowing Catholics to serve as royal counsellors, James admitted Tyrconnell and General Justin MacCarthy to his Irish privy council. Catholic sheriffs, magistrates and justices of the peace were appointed across the kingdom, while town and city corporations – which were instrumental in electing members to the parliament in Dublin – were told to admit Catholic members. Penal laws restricting open Catholic worship were relaxed, and Irish priests began to repair their churches, hold conferences with their peers and say mass with little fear of punishment. Clarendon mumbled under his breath as he was forced to oversee James's reforms. To the lord lieutenant and the Irish Protestant gentry, the king's sudden and detailed interest in the prospects of Catholic Ireland reeked of Tyrconnell's influence. They took heart, however, in knowing that James had no apparent interest in tearing up the Irish land settlement, which kept the real wealth and power of the kingdom in their hands. 'The king's resolution not to have the acts of settlement shaken … does much please people here, for such discourses run like wildfire through the town,' Clarendon wrote in 1686.[11] However, Robert Southwell, the Irish-born Protestant diplomat, could see thunder on the horizon. In October 1686 he wrote to a friend that if the land settlement did remain intact, it would not be 'by the goodwill of others'.[12] Southwell, Clarendon and anyone else with a nose for court politics could see that Tyrconnell's ambitions were gathering momentum. It now seemed only a matter of time before he was strong enough to run his fingers over the seams of the Irish land settlement and start to unpick them one by one.

7

All Prudent Courses

James could not have wished for a better start. The three kingdoms had revelled in his coronation with songs and colour, and Monmouth and Argyll's uprisings had been crushed. The new king's days took a pleasant routine: meetings with counsellors, discussions with secretaries about the day's correspondence and walks in Hyde Park when time allowed. He received regular dispatches from Clarendon in Dublin, mostly about petty things like rent disputes in Tipperary or Kildare. James wrote pleasant, inconsequential letters to William of Orange, his son-in-law in The Hague, telling him things like how the queen of England had hurt her shoulder in a fall or how the weather made for good hunting. He signed off each note to William with a promise that he would always be 'as kind to you as you can desire'.[1] As king, James was at the centre of an infinite system of cogs and gears, each one reacting to his every turn. He was comfortable with his new position, and by the autumn of 1685 he was ready to start taking a direct role in the running of his kingdoms. He did not expect any trouble.

However, things slowly began to crack. In the aftermath of Monmouth's rebellion, James had directed that anyone with even a tenuous connection with the uprising be placed on trial. Some 1,400 men and women were sentenced to death for treason in court proceedings known as the 'bloody assizes'. Many had their sentences commuted or were exiled to the West Indies, but around 250 people were gruesomely executed. An elderly noblewoman named Alice Lisle, who had allowed two rebel fugitives to rest overnight on her property, was found guilty of harbouring the enemy and beheaded. The grisly execution of the king's justice began to leave a sour taste in the mouths of the English public, particularly in the south-west. At the same time, the rebellions had convinced James that rural militiamen were not strong enough to serve as his first line of defence. With concerning haste, he began to build up the size of his standing army in England – by December 1685 it had risen from 8,500 to 20,000 men, almost unheard of in a time of peace. There was not enough barrack space to house this sudden surge in troops, and many towns and villages were forced to let soldiers into their homes. Widespread reports of drunken brawls, promiscuity and other lewd behaviour inevitably followed. Army training camps were held at Hounslow Heath and Blackheath, conspicuously close to the city of London, leading many to wonder if the king was trying to make a point. Then parliament discovered that several of the army's new officers were Catholics whom James had exempted from taking the oaths required under the Test Act. James tried to play down the issue, insisting that the Catholic officers 'are most of them well known to me … having formerly served me on several occasions, and always proved the loyalty of their principles'.[2] Parliament did not take the king's word for it. One member of the commons who spoke up against the king's new army was sent to the Tower of London. When Westminster refused to cease its complaints, James suddenly prorogued the English parliament – a way of shutting it down without formally dissolving it – in November 1685. It would not sit again for the rest of his reign.

*

Perhaps it was his belief that God had led him this far and would lead him further. Maybe it was the pieces of his father that lived on inside him, convinced that a king should only be answerable to heaven. Perhaps he simply did not care. As 1685 drifted into 1686, James began to provoke the people of England. The *London Gazette*, the paper of record that was typically crammed with bulletins from overseas, became curiously devoid of any reports of the massacres of the Huguenots, French Protestants who had been stripped of their legal protection under the Edict of Nantes by Louis XIV in the summer of 1685. Later that year, James re-established diplomatic ties with the Vatican and even received a papal envoy at court. In April 1686 he helped finance a new Catholic chapel on Lime Street in London, flagrantly in breach of penal laws that had banished the Roman Church from the capital. Whitehall tried to cover its tracks by insisting that the church was attached to the diplomatic mission of the Elector Palatine and therefore exempt from English law. London was having none of it. Angry crowds manhandled priests and parishioners as they passed in and out of the chapel, and when things got too rowdy James sent soldiers to provide protection. Meanwhile, anti-Catholic riots were suddenly being reported as far north as Worcester and Coventry. Protestant clergymen began to rail from their pulpits against the spectre of arbitrary rule and military dictatorship. James struck back by issuing a directive warning Protestant ministers to be careful about what they said. When Bishop Henry Compton of London refused to discipline a rector who spoke out publicly against the king, James had Compton suspended by an ecclesiastical commission he had set up to keep an eye on the Protestant Church. The Protestant fellows of Magdalen College at Oxford University, who had repeatedly blocked James's attempts to install a Catholic president, were dismissed amid widespread outrage. James's carefully worded promise to respect the Protestant Church in the spring of 1685 was not aging well.[3]

James had surrounded himself with advisors like Robert Spencer, the Earl of Sunderland, and Father Edward Petre, his Jesuit confessor, who assured him that he was right. With their perfumed encouragement, James chose to make his boldest move yet. In April 1687 he published a declaration of indulgence that suspended the penal laws, nullified the demands of the Test Act and offered complete religious freedom to Catholics, Presbyterians and all other Christian churches that did not conform to the established Anglican faith. He even went so far as to publicly admit that he 'cannot but heartily wish … that all the people of our dominions were members of the Catholic Church'.[4] Even if his intentions were noble, his declaration showed a frightening lack of political tact. James had effectively decided that he had the power to overrule the laws of parliament. To a slowly deepening pool of opponents, James was starting to stink like a tyrant. He had raised a standing army stuffed with Catholic officers; he had imprisoned political opponents and prorogued parliament and had now stated publicly that England's laws were just apples on a tree that he could pick, ignore or discard as he chose.

In James's mind, his motives were honest and simple. Without a son to inherit after his death, the crown would pass to his Protestant daughter, Mary, the wife of William of Orange. So long as the penal laws remained in existence, all the royal protection and favour that James could currently offer his Catholic subjects would die with him. He was fifty-two years old, about to turn fifty-three. His brother had died at fifty-four.

Who knew how long he had left? With little reason to hide his hand, James officially dissolved parliament in July 1687 and began a murky strategy to pack England's councils and boroughs with men on whose support he could rely. Mayors were fired and corporations were warned that their charters would be torn up, all so that James could manufacture an election that would give him a House of Commons willing to erase the penal laws once and for all. It was a dangerous game.

*

Lord Clarendon was fed up. On 13 August 1686, nine months before James issued his declaration of indulgence, he had had another blazing row with the Earl of Tyrconnell, who was now about as welcome in Dublin Castle as a toothache. Clarendon realised that it was now only a matter of time before the Irish land settlement was exhumed and so decided to do some pre-emptive digging. He met with Tyrconnell and proposed setting up a new commission that would rubber stamp the existing arrangements but would also provide a financial package to former Catholic owners seeking compensation. Tyrconnell scoffed at the idea, flanked by two close allies: Stephen Rice, one of Ireland's new Catholic judges, and Richard Nagle, a sharp and ambitious barrister from Cork who had also just been named to the Irish privy council. Tyrconnell and his cohort stormed out, and Clarendon was left alone with the knowledge that he had become a lame duck viceroy. The following day he lashed out with his sharpest weapon – his pen. Writing to the king, Clarendon warned that Irish Protestants had watched the 'great alterations made in the army' with deep concern and were now talking once more of that terrible winter of 1641. '"When we see", say they, "all our countrymen disarmed, and that the arms and the power are in the hands of the Irish, how can we forget the barbarous murders committed on us by their fathers?"' Clarendon added that the Irish Catholic gentry were now so convinced that land settlement was on its last legs that they had begun roguishly touring their old properties and even forbidding their former tenants from paying any more rent to the current landlords. Clarendon advised James that a public declaration promising that he had no desire to tear up the Irish land laws 'would have a great effect'. That same day Clarendon wrote another letter, this time to his brother the Earl of Rochester, in which he was far more frank. Lord Tyrconnell, he morosely predicted, would not stop until he had been booted out of Dublin Castle. 'I never knew I stood so much in any man's way before: it is very probable … he may get the better of me.'[5]

At the end of August 1686, Tyrconnell made his move. Alongside his fixer, Richard Nagle, he sailed to seek an audience at Whitehall. Clarendon saw what was about to happen and desperately whisked ahead letters to the king and queen in a bid to scupper Tyrconnell's plan. It was no use. Tyrconnell was received at court, and during a series of private discussions with James and his senior secretary, Lord Sunderland, he demolished Clarendon's character and competence. The Irish viceroy, he said, was weak, easily manipulated by Protestant interests and lukewarm about the king's pro-Catholic reforms. Tyrconnell presented his alternative candidacy as a fait accompli: he had the support of much the Irish Catholic clergy, the army high command and the native Irish gentry. Lord Sunderland was unsure. Other potential replacements for Clarendon were mooted: William Herbert, the Marquis of Powis, or perhaps even a puppet administration under the eldest of the king's illegitimate sons, the sixteen-year-old James FitzJames, whom the king had fathered with his mistress Arabella Churchill. But Tyrconnell was a man of crude and captivating energy. After weeks of hard manoeuvring, brinkmanship and even a whiff of blackmail, his selection was settled. Tyrconnell would be sent back to Dublin to take over as viceroy and the head of the Irish government, albeit with the slightly reduced title of lord deputy instead of lord lieutenant. The handover, however, would have to be delicately done.

Sunderland suggested that Tyrconnell's appointment, which was bound to ruffle Protestant feathers, be announced alongside a royal declaration confirming that the Irish land settlement was going nowhere. Richard Nagle laid out a famous counter argument. Writing from Coventry in late 1686, while negotiations between Tyrconnell and Sunderland were taking place in London, Nagle made an eloquent case for the entire system of land ownership in Ireland to be shredded. The land acts of Charles II, he wrote, were a woeful mess, and the failure by the court of claims to hear dozens of petitions before it was abruptly wound up had rendered the entire project invalid. If James truly wished to improve the lot of his Irish Catholic subjects, Nagle said, he could not morally 'confirm the most considerable interest there in the hands of the Protestants'.[6] Nagle's letter was widely circulated throughout Ireland, and the popular appetite for change became insatiable. James refused to budge on the land question, but he was prepared to sign off on the new administration in Dublin Castle. On 1 January 1687 Lord Sunderland sent a four-line letter to Clarendon in Dublin, informing him that he was being recalled and that the Earl of Tyrconnell was returning to take his place. One half of Clarendon was crushed; the other was utterly relieved. Tyrconnell left London with a parting message of luck and kindness from his old friend the king. 'We doubt not but you will pursue all prudent courses,' James wrote.[7]

Tyrconnell was greeted like a conquering prince when he returned to Dublin on 6 February 1687. Church bells rang out across the city, and thousands of ordinary Catholics rushed to the dockside to watch the new viceroy disembark. His appointment to the most powerful post in Ireland stirred firm feelings in his opponents too: two weeks earlier, rumours had cut through Dublin of an apparent plot by Protestant students of Trinity College to assassinate Tyrconnell on his arrival in the capital. The reports were investigated and shown to be nothing more than cranky fantasy. With nothing left to fight over, Clarendon and Tyrconnell, the man who had manufactured his downfall, held two brief and apparently cordial meetings before Clarendon finally handed over the sword of office on 12 February. Soldier, spy, courtier, plotter, lord, viceroy – Richard Talbot's ascension had been steep and ruthless. He was only just beginning.

8

Nineteen Parts of Twenty

Louis's ascent was endless. His armies had asked questions, and his enemies had no answer. The Treaty of Nijmegen in 1678 had stretched France's borders and influence. Louis had left the clutter and stink of Paris behind and moved to the magnificent Versailles, the finest palace on earth. His line was secure in the lives of his son and grandson. Louis XIV was forty-seven years old in 1685, standing proudly as the 'dread of Europe'. When the great Voltaire later wrote his history of Louis's reign, he described these days as 'the very pinnacle of his greatness'.[1] But in climbing so high, Louis had fundamentally changed the nature of things. Before, Europe went to war over religion. Now you were either with France or against her.

Louis revoked the Edict of Nantes in 1685, clearing the way for the brutal persecution of France's Protestant Huguenots. The following year the Catholic Holy Roman Emperor, Leopold I, formed a new defensive alliance against France known as the League of Augsburg. The architect of the project was William of Orange, whose Dutch republic had been invaded and almost overrun by France in 1672. William knew that Louis coveted the lucrative ports and merchant cities of Flanders. The emperor in Vienna, meanwhile, was wary of French ambitions in the Rhineland. The new alliance also drew in Spain, Sweden and a necklace of German princely states that all knew that, individually, they would have little chance of survival if France turned its guns on them. Louis's ministers would argue a different point, stating that French aggression was the only defence for a kingdom surrounded by enemies. The pieces were being arranged for another all-consuming continental war. The only variable now left in play was England. Louis had managed to turn Charles's head with the Treaty of Dover in 1670 and was now intent on doing the same with James. Since being crowned king, James had been too tangled up in his clunky domestic affairs to discuss picking sides in a foreign war. However, neutrality was a fragile luxury in seventeenth-century Europe. James might not have been interested in war, but war was interested in him.

*

In Dublin Castle Lord Tyrconnell attacked his new position as lord deputy with force and expected his aides to do likewise. Richard Nagle was named attorney general, a key post that would not only allow him to sculpt the sought-after new land laws but also meant that he would sit as speaker of the Irish parliament in Dublin that would eventually have to be convened to debate the laws. Elsewhere, more Catholics were appointed to the judicial benches, ensuring a Catholic majority in every court. Radical alterations to the Irish army continued, which Tyrconnell justified as being entirely necessary for 'the preservation of the peace of this kingdom'.[2] Tyrconnell began to distribute new commissions to Irish Catholic gentlemen, who would in turn raise and pay for their own regiments and revel in the social prestige that came with an officer's uniform. The Catholic primate of Ireland was appointed chaplain-general of the army, with the power to attach a priest to every regiment.

Recruitment gathered pace in every nook of the kingdom, and a major training camp was organised at the Curragh in Kildare in the summer of 1687. Tyrconnell was determined to give shape to this new, vigorous Catholic army.

Tyrconnell shared James's intention to chop up and reform the electorate to his liking. Privately, Tyrconnell's vision extended beyond rewriting a few thousand deeds of ownership – he intended to craft a kingdom where property, credit, commerce, political capital and legal authority were vested entirely in Catholic hands. He wanted Ireland to emerge from under Westminster's boot and become a vibrant, wealthy, independent kingdom, loyal to the Stuart line through choice, not force. His efforts before and after being named viceroy of Ireland hardly disguised his intent. In May 1686 the Duke of Ormonde, now retired in London but keeping an eye on Irish affairs, wrote ominously that 'the Protestants of Ireland are afraid'.[3] William Petty, an old Cromwellian army doctor who had settled in Ireland after the civil war and invested in a number of commercial ventures, wondered if he might have been better off sticking to his medical practice in England rather than 'meddling with forfeited lands'.[4]

Sunday sermons were a solid thermometer for the public mood. As Tyrconnell began to disturb the texture of Ireland, the reaction among the Protestants of the kingdom was firm. Tyrconnell's eyes and ears throughout the island told him of 'false reports and malicious insinuations' against his government in many circles. The viceroy felt pressed to issue a public declaration in February 1687, insisting that while he would respect the 'just rights and properties' of all men, he did not intend to put up with 'undutiful or irreverent expressions' against the king's government, which he blamed on 'some few fiery spirits in the pulpits'.[5] Fearmongering was not his only cause for concern. The Irish economy stuttered through 1687, mostly due to a wet harvest and heavy French taxes on imports. But a slow trickle out of Ireland of Protestant wealth and commercial expertise did not help. Weighing their prospects in a kingdom heading in a blunt direction, many Protestant shipping agents, bankers and traders simply decided to leave. 'A great many of the richest trading citizens removed themselves and their effects to England,' the Protestant deacon William King later wrote.[6]

In August 1687, Tyrconnell was summoned to Chester to meet with James during the king's summer progress. Nothing irritated a Stuart more than a lack of money, and with the Irish economy wobbling, rumours began to swirl that Tyrconnell was to be reprimanded or even dismissed. Tyrconnell travelled to Chester as instructed and met with James in private. No direct record of their conversation exists, but it is easy to imagine the bombastic Irish lord deputy making a firm defence of his record and intentions. When the meeting was over, Tyrconnell emerged a vindicated man. Not only was his own position secured, but he also received James's blessing to return to Dublin and begin work on a bill to finally dissolve the Irish land settlement. James had not given Tyrconnell a free hand, and any new land bill would have to be approved in London first. But James's decision to finally place Irish land on the butcher's block was immediately noticed. The French ambassador wrote to Louis that 'the reversal of this settlement is regarded as a matter of great importance, and if it can be effected without opposition, will mean an entire separation of Ireland from England. This is the general opinion of the English.'[7] Gossip would fly years later that James and Tyrconnell had discussed another, more volatile issue at Chester: Tyrconnell had apparently received the king's blessing for a plan to place Ireland under the protection of France in the event of James's death, so as to provide a sanctuary for all of James's Catholic subjects. Rumours of the deal – unconfirmed, unacknowledged, fleeting as a whisper – never went away. It is not difficult to imagine that James, who was still without a male heir, was keeping his options open.

But soon the entire narrative of the succession would take a dramatic, unbelievable turn.

*

In February 1688 Tyrconnell despatched the Irish Catholic judges Stephen Rice and Thomas Nugent to London with two different versions of a new land law. One bill proposed a fresh court of claims that would hear all outstanding petitions and recommended that anyone found innocent of rebellion during the civil war should receive their old estates in full, provided the present owners were compensated with the equivalent of six years' rent. The second bill would simply divide every disputed estate in Ireland in two, with the new and old owners both keeping one half. As Rice and Nugent made their way through London to their audience with James, crowds of commoners mocked and taunted them. The poisonous stew of Irish land and the rising influence of Catholics were becoming sharp talking points throughout the realm. Earlier in his reign, when James still had a smidgen of caution, he might have dismissed Rice and Nugent as radicals. Instead, the Irish judges found the king in an assured and attentive mood. The explanation was simple – the queen was pregnant.

From the fishmongers of Billingsgate to the shipyards of Newcastle, everyone had thought they knew how the next royal succession would unfold. The queen was obviously at fault – her marriage to James had produced a litany of miscarriages and children who did not survive infancy. The king would die in his bed at some random hour, like his brother before him, and the crown would then pass to Mary of Orange, wife of William, the great champion of Protestant Europe and the titular head of a republic founded on the principles of devolved power. At the very least, William of Orange would be prince-consort of England; at best he would be king in all but name. James's determination to shout down the law would die with him. But then, like a clap of thunder in a clear sky, it was announced just before Christmas in 1687 that the queen was with child. Heads turned and brows crumpled. James ordered a day of public thanksgiving, but few in England were in the mood to rejoice. If the queen gave birth to a son, then the prospect of a new Catholic dynasty would become cold fact. Englishmen of all ranks did not hide their unease. The Earl of Clarendon, back in London after his sour time in Dublin, wrote in his diary of people openly wondering if some cruel trick was being played. 'It is strange to see, how the Queen's great belly is every where ridiculed, as if scarce anybody believed it were true.'[8]

James was overcome with joy. He threw himself once more into his controversial project of reform, certain that God had chosen to reward his work with a son. On 27 April 1688 he issued a fresh declaration of indulgence, this time ordering that England's Protestant clergymen read it aloud in their Sunday sermons. Seven Protestant bishops petitioned the king to change his mind. James snapped and warned them 'that they had raised a devil they could not lay'.[9] The Anglican clergy held firm, and the king's declaration was largely ignored. Meanwhile, the kingdom's Presbyterian and other dissenting faiths chose to throw their lot in with the established Protestant Church that was used to trampling on them, believing that Catholicism was the greater of two evils. Pamphlets were printed and dispersed in every county, accusing James of disregarding the law and wishing to invite blasphemy, adultery and even Jews and Muslims into the realm. Humiliated, James had the seven Protestant bishops who had stood up to him arrested and demanded that they be placed on trial for seditious libel by speaking against the king's wishes. The heat and hostility engendered by the queen's pregnancy and James's hardening stance was pushing England towards the edge. Then, on 10

June 1688, the cannons of the Tower of London roared in unison over the city. Church bells rang for hour after hour on royal orders. The queen had given birth to a son.

*

The rumours were hilarious. The queen had never been pregnant, it was said; pillows had been stuffed under her dresses every morning for months, and when the time came some other woman's infant was smuggled into St James's Palace in a warming pan and presented as a prince. James had expected that there would be slanders and took steps to cut the whispers off at the source. On the night of the birth, he set aside the usual practice of confinement and had his privy counsellors and 'diverse ladies of quality' personally witness his son arriving into the world, bloody and screaming. It still did not do the trick. James's youngest daughter, Anne, from his first marriage, expressed doubts about their new half-brother's legitimacy to her sister Mary. 'Where one believes it, a thousand do not,' she wrote.[10] In Dublin, the birth of the new Prince of Wales was celebrated like a religious feast. On 1 July, the anointed day of public thanksgiving, a grand procession wove through the Irish capital, led by 'all the troops in the town', who rapped on their drums as Tyrconnell, the Irish privy counsellors and members of the nobility rode past in opulent six-horse carriages. After a celebratory Mass was heard, the dignitaries attended a banquet at Tyrconnell's vice-regal lodge in Chapelizod on the outskirts of the city. From there, they had a clear view of a grand fireworks display that lit up the sky over the River Liffey.[11] Catholic Ireland raised a toast to the infant prince and dreamed of a new vision of the future, which was already growing lucid and rich before their eyes.

The day before, London had also erupted in celebration, but for a vastly different reason. After two days of evidence in front of a packed court, the trial of the seven bishops charged with seditious libel against James drew to a close. The verdict – and perhaps James's entire reign – now hung on a point of law. The bishops did not deny that they had defied the king's wishes. However, it was argued that as James did not have the power to arbitrarily suspend the penal laws – or any laws for that matter – the bishops could not be found guilty for disobeying an illegal order. On 30 June the jury at Westminster Hall returned a verdict of not guilty. The roof almost came down. 'There was a most wonderful shout, that one would have thought the hall had cracked,' an eyewitness wrote.[12] Bonfires were lit across the city, and word whistled from town to town as fast as messengers could ride. James, who had spent the day visiting an army camp on the outskirts of London, was just sitting down for dinner when the soldiers outside 'gave up a great shout' in celebration of the verdict.[13] The bishops' acquittal was heralded throughout England with far more passion and relief than the birth of the Prince of Wales. It was an ominous sign.

The same day that the seven bishops walked out of Westminster Hall, seven men each signed their names to a piece of paper: Lords Danby, Shrewsbury, Lumley and Devonshire, Henry Sidney, Edward Russell and Bishop Compton of London. It was a secret letter inviting William of Orange to invade England, force James to admit that his infant son was a fraud and that Mary of Orange remained the right and lawful heir. The seven signatories assured William that 'nineteen parts of twenty of the people throughout the kingdom … are desirous of a change'. England had been living with 'infinite exasperation' and was 'so generally dissatisfied with the present conduct of the government', they added.[14] William was assured that if he landed with troops somewhere on the English coast, the bulk of the English army and navy would desert James and flock to his side. The letter was treason, and the seven signatories knew it. But this was not a time for half measures. Within a year, they believed, James would be able to summon a crooked parliament that would wipe away the penal laws that secured the Protestant ascendancy in the land. William, meanwhile, was already making his own calculations. In the spring of 1688, as Europe was inching closer to another war, James had spurned Dutch overtures to join the continental alliance against France. It now seemed inevitable, William believed, that James would follow his brother's path and side with Louis. He had already begun preparations for a pre-emptive strike against England when the seven signatories' infamous invitation arrived in The Hague. The summer grew warm and fragrant. The wind began to change.

9

Invasion

A good war was rarely an accident. It required months, perhaps years, of intricate planning: raising and staffing regiments, hammering out supply contracts, hauling around heavy artillery and, if possible, finding a reason to fight. William of Orange knew the mathematics well. In the Dutch United Provinces, with its curiously modern separation of powers, the States General took care of domestic matters while the defence of the republic was the duty of the titular head of state, the *stadtholder*: a hereditary post vested in the House of Orange-Nassau. In the late summer in 1688 its current patriarch, who was now almost thirty-eight years old, was preparing to stretch every syllable of his job description. A famous image of William of Orange, painted by the great portrait artist of the time, Peter Lely, captures a stern young prince with little time to smile. His eyes are deep and pinched, as if every curtain in the room is being scrutinised and evaluated. His hair is dark and wavy, and his nose is thick. Standing in black plate armour, William's right hand clutches a field marshal's baton – a military insignia with no practical use, of course, other than the visual drama that comes with holding a big stick. It was not an idle image.

William's concerns about his father-in-law's intentions had been bubbling since the winter of 1687, even before it was revealed that James's queen was pregnant. That November he had sanctioned a pamphlet stating that he and his wife Mary – who was still at that point the heir to the English throne – believed that the penal laws of the three kingdoms should be upheld. William and James's personal correspondence, which had once been amiable and chatty, began to turn sour. In March 1688, James decided to recall 3,000 of his soldiers who had been serving in the Dutch army as part of a long-standing diplomatic agreement. The Dutch States General was not happy, and a compromise had to be haggled that would allow the English officers the choice to remain in Holland or return home. Roughly a hundred officers travelled back to England, most of them Catholics. In any other time, their religion would have made it illegal for them to hold commissions in the English army. But these were unusual days, and James ordered the creation of three new infantry regiments specifically for the returning officers to command.

James's attempt to recall the Dutch brigades raised William's suspicions further. The English king had already refused an invitation to join the alliance against Louis, the League of Augsburg, which by now also counted the explicit support of Pope Innocent XI, who resented Louis's desire to control church affairs in France. In April 1688 London and Paris reached an accord that would see Louis help finance the cost of James's naval fleet in the English Channel. It was not a formal alliance, but in William's eyes it was not far off it. The Prince of Orange saw England drifting ominously towards France and decided that he would not allow it. William began to refit the Dutch fleet for war and began to make overtures to Brandenburg, Waldeck and other allies to support a pre-emptive strike against England. Either through arrogance or ignorance, James still believed that he could remain neutral in the coming war between France and the rest of Europe. He later claimed, naively, that he intended to stay out of it all and make a fortune selling supplies to everyone once the war sent prices through the roof. James still could not see how vulnerable his disastrous politics at home had made him. Many disaffected and well-connected English Protestants began to defect to Holland, providing William with a valuable trickle of intelligence.

James's continental diplomats began to raise the alarm, but the king swatted their concerns away. Bevil Skelton, an English envoy in France, sent back report after report about Dutch intentions. When James seemed to ignore him, Skelton became so frustrated that he gave his support, without permission, to a French warning to William that any move against England would be an act of war. James was furious and Skelton was recalled and briefly gaoled in the Tower of London. Elsewhere, the Irish diplomat Ignatius White, the Marquis of Albeville, became so anxious with events that he left his posting in The Hague without permission to warn James about Dutch activity in person. Rather than heed his ambassador's fears, James was more concerned with the breach of diplomatic protocol and scolded Albeville for leaving his post. James eventually decided to take some minor precautions: in June 1688 he instructed the navy to keep an eye on the English north coast, where it was assumed any Dutch fleet would attempt to land. But even at this hour, James would not believe that William would play such a bold hand. He rejected another offer of French military aid. In August, even Lord Tyrconnell was writing to James to warn him of a reported plot to overthrow him being hatched in Holland. The Earl of Sunderland, James's chief minister, dismissed the Irish viceroy's alarm. 'The king is very well assured that whatever the [Dutch] design may be, it is not against him … I believe there never was in England less thoughts of rebellion.'[1]

By the early autumn of 1688, however, something suddenly seemed to change. Lord Sunderland's daily correspondence became dominated by military logistics. Dozens of new commissions for regiments of cavalry and infantry were dispersed like confetti. On 24 September the Earl of Clarendon wrote that James was now openly talking of war and the prospect that his own people might take arms against him. 'He told me the Dutch were now coming to invade England in good earnest ... "Now my Lord", said he, "I shall see what the Church of England men will do."' Having earlier dismissed Tyrconnell's anxieties, Lord Sunderland now sent a message to Dublin requesting that four regiments of Irish cavalry and infantry be sent to Liverpool at once, in order to fatten out the new force staffed by Catholic officers who had returned from the Dutch brigades. Whitehall was now receiving letters from lords and gentry across England, promising their support against 'the design of the Hollanders'. At the end of September the imperial ambassador to London reported back to Vienna that large chunks of the Protestant clergy and nobility – and even much of the armed forces – were preparing to break their loyalty to James. War was the prattle of coffee houses, and the topic of nervous prayers.[2]

*

Dublin skipped from one rumour to the next in the spring and summer of 1688. A Catholic heir to the throne had been born just as the seven Protestant bishops were on trial in London, and it was all overtaken by whispers of a Dutch invasion. Tyrconnell took steps to ensure that whatever happened next, the new royal administration in Ireland would not tumble in a time of crisis. When William of Orange invaded England, as it was now accepted that he would, Tyrconnell believed that the powerful Protestant minority of Ireland might be inspired to take arms. This was not to be taken lightly – one estimate in 1688 claimed that there were up to 20,000 Protestants with access to firearms in Dublin. The potential for trouble in Ulster, meanwhile, was just as acute. Over the winter of 1687 Tyrconnell had billeted troops in the north, and by the following summer the Irish army's total strength was roughly 8,000 men. When Tyrconnell received the order from Sunderland that he send some 5,000 of those troops away to shore up James's strength in England, Tyrconnell feared that it would drastically weaken his own hand.

Tyrconnell spent the summer of 1688 chained to his desk, poring over details about an army that he needed to bulk up more than ever. Commissions and recruitment manifestos were signed off on, as were details about uniforms, salaries, provisions and discipline. By the end of August materials were already running low, forcing Tyrconnell to tighten controls on exports to keep as much wool and other victuals as possible from leaving Ireland. In September, as James finally moved to a war footing and the invasion was now looked on as imminent, Tyrconnell issued an order banning all Irish officers from leaving their posts without permission. New military governors were appointed in the strategic cities of Limerick and Cork. In October, Tyrconnell sent an urgent request to James for weapons, ammunition and cash, expecting that he might have to mobilise his troops soon. 'No time is to be lost,' he warned.[3]

*

When James belatedly recognised that one arm of his family was moving against him, he tried to pull the other arms close. It was common knowledge at court that James had fathered two sons with his mistress Arabella Churchill while he was Duke of York. By 1688 the boys, James and Henry, were approaching adulthood and James FitzJames, the elder of the two, was beginning to be noticed. At the age of sixteen, in 1686, FitzJames had travelled to the continent to begin his military apprenticeship in the Habsburg Imperial army. He had made a solid first impression on Emperor Leopold, and within a few weeks he was fighting against the Turks on the frontlines at Buda. FitzJames was wounded in battle and returned to London for the winter, where his father rewarded him with the title of Duke of Berwick. He returned to the continent in the summer of 1687, and after being promoted to major general in the imperial army he was summoned back to England to enter his father's service full time. Berwick's first domestic posting was the governorship of Portsmouth, the bustling southern harbour that was about to become the centre of a gathering storm.

Portsmouth was James's back door to France. When he finally began to make preparations for a fight in the late summer of 1688, James knew that he would have to hold Portsmouth at all costs, particularly if the tide turned against him and he needed to smuggle his wife and infant son out of the country. When Tyrconnell's Irish troops arrived in England as requested, James duly sent one regiment to Portsmouth to buttress the Duke of Berwick's royal garrison. The Irish troops did not take long to settle in. Portsmouth became an oven of drinking, brawling and violent excesses. One Irish soldier almost started a riot when he fired his musket into a Protestant church. The teenage Berwick tried to divide and conquer by splitting the Irish soldiers up between his existing English regiments. It did not work. Five English officers refused to accept Irish troops into their command, with one snarling that 'it was a dishonour to the subjects of England to have recourse to foreigners... to fill up their companies'.[4] The dissenting officers were court martialled, and the controversy put a heavy dent in army morale. Disaffection with James's policies seeped all the way into the senior command. John Churchill, the soldier, diplomat and close advisor to the king who had risen to the rank of major general, was ready to commit to another prince. By August 1688 Churchill had secretly informed William of his willingness to swap sides when the moment came.

As summer faded into autumn, James began to panic. On 25 September he issued writs to summon parliament early in 1689, despite the fact that his plan to gerrymander it to his liking was not complete. The prospect of a fair and free assembly outlining its grievances, the king hoped, might be enough to turn down the volume of the crisis. Three days later, James received a delegation of senior Protestant clergy, led by the Archbishop of Canterbury, and agreed to a sweeping package of concessions: his meddling in the Church of England's affairs would end, all vacant posts in the church hierarchy would be filled and Catholics would be excluded from parliament and government as demanded under law. It was a startling climb-down for James, but it had come far too late.

*

Wheels were turning with relentless force. Roughly 15,000 soldiers from the Dutch Republic, Denmark and the German princely states were gathering near the shipyards of southern Holland. A fleet of 53 frigates and 400 transport ships was being fitted out to sail. On 30 September, William published a pamphlet explaining to the Dutch people why he was embarking on this dangerous expedition so late in the year. The pamphlet was William's first strike to secure the moral high ground. It presented the *stadtholder* as a Protestant crusader intent on restoring the right and just government of England. It insisted that William's true target was not James nor his crown, but rather 'those counsellors, who have chief credit with the king' and had pushed him dangerously towards 'arbitrary government'. William described Tyrconnell's Catholic resurgence in Ireland as a dangerous omen: 'The dismal effects of this subversion ... appear more evidently to us, by what we see done in Ireland; where the whole government is put in the hands of Papists' while Protestants are forced to remember 'that cruel and bloody massacre which fell out in that Island in the year 1641'. William also cast doubt on the legitimacy of the new Prince of Wales and insisted that the bulk of England's lords and gentry were on his side. He conveniently left out any mention of his true aim to force England's army and navy into his alliance against Louis, aware that the pamphlet would also be circulated in England. William knew that if the English public saw him as a foreign warmonger, his campaign would not get far. Time and events were marching against him, and William had little space for failure. On 8 October, after Louis's armies had marched into Alsace and seized the city of Philippsburg, William made his final pitch for support to the Dutch States General, who would have to agree to front him the money for the plan. If England could be brought into the war on the side of the alliance, the United Provinces 'would be preserved in its freedom and welfare'. If not, William warned, 'the King of England and the French would try to ruin this State once and for all'. His speech had the desired effect. The invasion of England was approved.[5]

Across the sea, James's own preparations had become frantic. Army units were mobilised to secure central London and the Thames estuary, while potential landing sites for the Dutch, including Hull, Chester and Carlisle, were garrisoned. Troops were dispersed to Rochester, Gravesend, Dartmouth and Maidstone to wrap a defensive ring around London. Frigates stationed in the Caribbean were recalled to help patrol the coast. If war arrived in the morning James could hypothetically call on 40,000 soldiers and would be fighting with home advantage. But his fragile nerves and fluctuating moods dragged him down like a dead weight. 'You will all find the Prince of Orange a worse man than Cromwell,' he mumbled to his privy councillors, morbidly contemplating his own defeat.[6]

On 15 October the Prince of Wales was christened James Francis Edward Stuart. A week later, the king called a special congress in London to try and finally dispel the slanders about his son's parentage. Awkward, embarrassing and graphic details about the child's birth were laid out to an assembly of privy counsellors, Protestant clergy, noblemen and the lord mayor of London. James was firm in his reasons. 'I have taken this time to have the matter heard and examined here, expecting that the Prince of Orange with the first fair easterly wind will invade this kingdom,' he stated. 'I am king, and do intend to go in person against him, whereby I may be exposed to accidents.' However, if he was to die in battle, James insisted that he wished to make it plain that his infant son was the lawful heir to the throne.[7] The conference took place amid a thickening wave of scandal. On 26 October London was rocked by the news that the Earl of Sunderland, the king's chief minister, had been dismissed, and rumours tore through the capital that Sunderland and his wife had been in secret correspondence with conspirators in Holland, working to cripple the royal regime from within. Five days later, an army officer returning from Holland was discovered carrying a copy of William's pamphlet outlining his reasons for invading England. It was passed on to the king, who now seemed to be flirting with a nervous breakdown. James hauled in Bishop Compton, the Earl of Clarendon and several other lords and counsellors, demanding to know what they knew about William's claims that Englishmen had been plotting to bring down the king. He heard nothing but pleas of ignorance and fealty.

William had attempted to embark with his fleet on 19 October but had been driven back by a storm. Eight days later the weather broke, and the wind shuffled abruptly to the east.

William's vast, incredible flotilla – twice the size of Philip II's doomed Spanish Armada – took to the sea. The swift breeze drove the ships hard along the southern coast of England, past the mighty silhouette of Dover Castle. Sentries raced back to London with reports of a fleet stretching almost the entire width of the channel. James knew that the moment had come. He ordered that security be tightened at Portsmouth and issued a general summons for the army to rally at Salisbury, some eighty miles south-west of London. William had intended to land near Portsmouth, but thick fog forced him further down the coast until he was able to make landfall in the small harbour of Torbay in Devon. On 5 November 1688 the Prince of Orange set foot on English soil as an invader. He was barely forty miles from the place where the Duke of Monmouth had done likewise little over three years earlier. Back then, the invader from Holland had been shunned by the people of England and dragged to a brutal death. This time, England was willing to listen.

Part Two

Revolution

'You may my glories and my state depose, but not my griefs; still am I king of those.'

William Shakespeare, *Richard II*, Act IV, scene i.

10

Villainy upon Villainy

James could not hide his nosebleeds. They would strike without warning, often as frequently as four times a day, and usually when he was wrangling anxiously with his generals and counsellors. James's physicians blamed stress and instructed that he keep to his bed. But there was no time to waste on rest. England had been invaded, and every hour seemed to heap on some new calamity or concern.

*

William's huge fleet had spent two days unloading 15,000 Dutch, German and Huguenot soldiers, dozens of pieces of artillery and thousands of pounds of rations and ammunition. Seasick but in a bright mood, the army then set out for Exeter. When the town's magistrates, mayor and Church of England bishop received word of William's approach, they decided to flee rather than risk having to pay homage to an invader. On 9 November William entered Exeter on horseback to a thunderous reception from the ordinary people. An old carving of his arrival shows trumpets blaring, flags catching the autumn air and lines of ecstatic townsfolk tossing flowers and reaching out to touch William's hand. The prince is seen lifting his hat to the crowds, as bodyguards and soldiers circle about him on foot. But in the background, there is a hint of something else. As William's horse wades through the crowd, several gentlemen watch from a balcony high up to his right, their faces mute and expressionless. Before the invasion, English conspirators in The Hague had assured William that the nobility and gentry of the land would rally to his cause if he appeared. However, in the days after landing at Torbay, this did not happen. William could not bury his concern. For all the adulation the public might scatter his way, William knew that without the support of men with property, money, weapons and influence, his prospects were thin. In Exeter, and throughout the rest of England, the nobility were biding their time. Choosing the wrong side in a conflict still yet to add flesh to its bones could cost everything.

One-line notices announcing the arrival of the Prince of Orange were scattered across the three kingdoms on 6 November. Lord Middleton, who had replaced the Earl of Sunderland as James's chief minister, spent the next few days buried in military orders. The realm was officially under attack. On 7 November John Churchill, the charismatic thirty-eight-year-old commander who had already secretly aligned himself with William, was promoted to lieutenant general and commander-in-chief of the army, answerable only to James. There was still no whiff of doubt about Churchill's loyalty. Elsewhere, Tyrconnell received another request for Irish soldiers to be sent to England immediately. Garrisons in the north of England were ordered to remain on high alert should 'any disturbances happen'.[1] The tension in London became unbearable. The city's bishops and lords, who feared that the slightest disturbance could engulf the city in riots, drafted a petition calling on James to convene parliament immediately.

James's youngest daughter, the twenty-three-year-old Princess Anne, became withdrawn and refused to visit her father. James was making his final preparations to link up with the army at Salisbury when, suddenly, the narrative of the crisis was snatched from his hands. He would never get it back.

On 14 November Edward Hyde, Viscount Cornbury, the eldest son of James's former Irish viceroy, the Earl of Clarendon, marched out of the royal army camp at Salisbury, trotted over to William's lines and swore loyalty to the Prince of Orange. The defection of Cornbury, who was a first cousin of James's daughters, Mary and Anne, was a shocking embarrassment that rattled James's reign right to its keystone. A few weeks earlier the king had been ready to lead his army into battle like a medieval Plantagenet. Now members of England's high aristocracy were openly abandoning him. A great crisis of monarchy was unfolding and James was always one step behind, reacting to events instead of shaping them. It was no way to survive.

News of Viscount Cornbury's defection tore through England like a forest fire. It was the talk of every manor house and tannery. John Stevens, an English Catholic revenue officer who had formerly served in Ireland under the Clarendon administration, was on the road back to London from Wales when word of the defection arrived. Stevens noted an immediate change in the public mood, as if the news 'gave courage to many to rise'. Almost overnight, England became a dangerous and suspicious place. Armed men began interrogating travellers on the roads, while the homes of known Catholics were broken into and searched. Horses were seized, Catholic chapels were looted and 'leading men' in many towns and villages, particularly in the north, began rallying support for William.[2] Cornbury's defection had changed the rhythm of things. James was at last forced to realise that his enemies were not just the men who had climbed off William's ships. As far as he knew, there could be traitors everywhere.

The Earl of Clarendon was distraught when he heard of his son's defection. 'O God, that my son should be a rebel,' he wailed into his diary.[3] He immediately requested an audience to beg James's forgiveness, but the king was occupied. On the night of Cornbury's defection, riots had finally broken out across London and several people directly connected with the king were targeted: the Blackfriars home of James's official printer, for example, was ransacked by a crowd of over 1,000 people. The day before, a Catholic priory at Clerkenwell was targeted by a mob and soldiers had fired into the crowd, killing four people. James ordered that all Catholic chapels in London, except those directly connected to the crown or foreign embassies, be shut. It was of little use. The streets of the capital had been stirred by shouts of popery and tyranny, and they would not be easily silenced.[4]

On 15 November the Protestant bishop of Exeter, who had run for his life rather than submit to William, arrived in London to a warm reception from the king. Glad of such a rare and public display of loyalty from a Church of England clergyman, James rewarded him with the prestigious vacant post of archbishop of York, hoping to send a message. Cornbury's defection seemed to drop James into an invisible pool of quicksand. He delayed his planned departure for Salisbury by a few days to allow nerves to settle. He summoned a meeting of his senior army officers in London and promised them that if they stuck by him he would preserve their rights, privileges and religion. James was increasingly unsure about whom he could count on. Cornbury's betrayal 'seem'd to pull up all his hopes and expectations by the roots'.[5]

By 17 November James had relocated to Windsor Castle, from where he intended to depart for Salisbury the following morning. That night, however, a delegation of bishops and lords from London made an unexpected appearance. They presented the king with a petition calling for him to immediately summon parliament and give England a chance to clear the air. James was fraught, tired and unimpressed. He snapped at the delegation that he was 'not pleased' with their timing and refused to countenance calling parliament while England was being invaded.[6] He left Windsor the following morning in a huff and was now convinced that the capital he was leaving behind was no longer safe. James ordered that his infant son be taken immediately to Portsmouth in secret and instructed the Prince of Wales's minders to remain on standby to sail to France at a moment's notice.

*

The year was late, the roads had started to churn and information travelled slowly. It inevitably meant that when James received bad news, he received several days' worth of it at once. Since Cornbury had burst the dam, more and more of James's subjects had begun to declare for William's campaign of Protestant liberty and the rule of law. In Chester, Derby, Birmingham and Worcester petitions in support of William began to circulate. The city of Nottingham became a rallying point for dissent in the north. Some 60,000 copies of William's grand pamphlet, originally published in Holland, were now being read aloud in English churches and nailed to the doors of town halls. The commoners of England were increasingly captivated, and thousands of men without weapons or military experience declared a desire to enlist with the Prince of Orange. In Nottingham, the gentry and nobility issued a joint declaration outlining nine grievances against James's 'Jesuitical Privy Council' and declared their support for William's quest against 'Popery and slavery'.[7] The sudden stirring of religious passion in the ordinary people was timely. To biased observers like John Stevens, who no longer felt safe on the road, the slogan of Protestant liberty was just a convenient cloak for a kingdom that was fed up with its king. He scoffed that Protestant men who once had little time for faith suddenly 'began to lament the danger [of] losing their religion'.[8]

James reached Salisbury late on 19 November, and early the next morning he climbed on his horse and rode about the sprawling camp that was now home to some 19,000 soldiers. Countless wagonloads of bread, biscuits, gunpowder and cannon shot were being stockpiled. Captains and lieutenants barked at their men as they marched out on patrols or took part in firing drills. On the surface, the army was braced for war. But beneath the skin, its morale was jelly. Every day brought more news of defections to William – fifty miles away in Gloucestershire, for example, the local militia had caught one nobleman attempting to defect with a hundred men, and a violent scuffle had broken out. Reports of Englishman fighting Englishman conjured all sorts of dark and weary images. James had sought to strike first and ordered his navy to sail to Torbay and attack William's fleet at anchor. However, hard winds and a stormy winter current prevented the royal fleet from getting close enough to land a single shot. The stress continued to tear at James from the inside. After the king had arrived at Salisbury, his nose started to bleed.

*

The distance between the two armies was shrinking. Scouts from both sides rode about the green and gentle countryside of the south-west, canvassing locals and trying to discover as much as possible about the other army's movements. On 20 November, their arms finally became tangled. A party of twenty-five Scottish veterans of the Dutch brigades who had declared for William were spotted near the village of Wincanton in Somerset, some thirty miles west of Salisbury. The Irish cavalry colonel Patrick Sarsfield was sent to investigate. The Scots were tipped off at the last minute and quickly set up an ambush on a tiny country lane outside the village. Sarsfield's column crept up the road. The Scots' senior officer stepped out, exchanged a few awkward words with Sarsfield and then opened fire with his sidearm. The royal troops scrambled for cover. The lane was swallowed in a fog of carbine smoke, screams and bursting grenades. Sarsfield's greater numbers slowly began to tell, and just as the Scots were about to be flanked a cry came up from Wincanton that Dutch reinforcements had arrived. It was a ruse, and it worked. Sarsfield's troops pulled back, and the surviving Scots slipped away to safety. Dead and wounded men were littered along the road and knotted in the ditches. Three royal troops had been killed and another badly wounded, while as many as twelve of the Scots were dead, with six more taken prisoner. William's invasion was no longer a bloodless exercise. The survivors from Wincanton raced back to their camps, anxious to report the news.[9]

The day after the skirmish, William's army began to chug out of Exeter like a bear waking from hibernation. The Prince of Orange did not want to rush into battle, as he knew he had to win the publicity war first. Fresh copies of his pamphlet and new declarations professing a desire to liberate the people of England were distributed to massage public opinion and, crucially, draw more of the gentry and nobility to his cause. James was just as keen to postpone the fight, but for a different reason. The king was falling apart. Nosebleeds, anxiety attacks, 'anguish' over riots in London and worries about mounting defections among the aristocracy had left him 'in a very ill state'.[10] On 23 November James held a council of war in Salisbury with his advisors and general staff. The mood was bleak. When a defensive plan to pull back behind the line of the Thames was suggested, James was keen. The order for a general retreat to Reading was issued, and the king decided that he would return to the capital. What little chance James had left of taking control of his own destiny had been tossed away like a rotten turnip. The decision to retreat decimated the army's fragile spirit. The road was now open for William to march unmolested into the Thames Valley, within striking distance of London. Then, just when it seemed that things could not get any worse, they did.

Before dawn on 24 November, barely a few hours after James's council of war, John Churchill, the commander-in-chief of the royal army, finally made good on his promise and defected to William. Henry FitzRoy, the Duke of Grafton, who was another of Charles's illegitimate sons and a senior officer, went with him. It tore the army's heart out. 'Villainy upon villainy', the Earl of Middleton wrote, his pen almost snapping with the strain of betrayal.[11] The following day Princess Anne's husband and James's other son-in-law, George of Denmark, also defected to William, as did the twenty-three-year-old Irish nobleman James Butler, who had inherited the title of Duke of Ormonde after the death of his grandfather, the old warhorse of Irish politics, that July. James was left with nothing but dry quips as his kingdom disintegrated around him. A few weeks earlier, in the days after the invasion, as the names of each new defector were read to the king, George of Denmark had taken to gasping '*Est il possible*?' like a startled matron. When James was told that George himself had finally split, he smirked. 'So, *est il possible* is gone too.'[12]

*

The Earl of Clarendon was keeping his head down in London. Still mortified by the defection of his son, Viscount Cornbury, he gingerly called to Whitehall on 20 November to visit his niece, Princess Anne. Since suffering a miscarriage a few months earlier, Anne rarely spoke a spare word to anyone. Now, however, she was unusually frank. When Clarendon spoke of the shame of his son's actions, Anne responded that 'people were so apprehensive of popery, and that she believed many more of the army would do the same'.[13] Anne clearly knew something her uncle did not. On 18 November, before James had arrived at Salisbury, she had secretly sent a message to William informing him that her husband, George of Denmark, would defect shortly. On the night of 25 November, just hours before her father was due back in London, Anne snuck out of her chamber with two ladies-in-waiting and into a carriage, to be whisked away to Nottingham. The following morning, startled maids found the princess's room empty and London was briefly snatched by rumours that she had been kidnapped or murdered. But by the time James returned to Whitehall later that day, the cold truth had set in. 'Even my children have forsaken me,' the king was reported to have sighed.[14]

Blow after blow, defection after defection – James seemed as helpless as a man whose roof is torn off in a hurricane. The king had lost his chief minister, the commander of his army, a litany of noblemen and his daughters. In the darkest hour of his reign, which had begun in 1685 with such startling promise, James began to dwell on the fate of Richard II. The last pure Plantagenet to reign before the line was torn into the Houses of Lancaster and York, Richard was a tyrant who was overthrown by his cousin, imprisoned and left to starve to death. Despite all the pamphlets insisting otherwise, James was now convinced that William was coming to take his throne. Cornered and alone in Whitehall, the king found a final shred of defiance. On 27 November James told his privy counsellors that 'he had read the story of King Richard II', but he would not share his fate.[15]

11

Nothing Less than Despair

As far as William knew, he was marching to war. It was not the ideal outcome. After all, he had come all this way to seize control of England's army, not blow it to pieces somewhere between Windsor and Yeovil. The English conspirators who had held his ear in Holland had assured him that it would not come to that. But William was not a man who liked to bluff. As his army marched out of Exeter on 21 November, it moved with dreadful expectation.

For the cattle farmers and blacksmiths of gentle Somerset, the sight of a continental army on the move was almost mythical. Thousands of infantrymen with long muskets slung over their shoulders shuffled to a menacing rhythm of drums. Dozens of heavy cannons mounted on wheels were dragged through wet and soupy roads. Hundreds of wagons creaked along under the weight of barrels of flour, brandy and other victuals. The colours of each regiment were caught in the wind and rain, hoisted beneath the great flags of Brandenburg, Waldeck and Orange-Nassau. At the tip of the column were hundreds of soldiers in blue coats trimmed with orange sleeves, sashes and stockings. Their faces were strict and beaten by the weather – the hallmarks of a lifetime on the front lines. These were the Dutch blue guards, the elite shock troops who served as William of Orange's personal bodyguards. As this great arsenal of men and materials began to lumber eastwards towards London, it offered England a rare glimpse of the pageantry of European war.

The army trickled up through Sherborne, Wincanton and on towards Salisbury. William took his quarters in village inns or local manor houses, provided that one could be found and kitted out at such short notice. Every day he pored over maps of southern England, pointing and conferring with a close cabal of generals. His second-in-command was the gruff Frederick Schomberg, a seventy-two-year-old Protestant German who had spent most of his career in the French service but was forced out when Louis revoked the Edict of Nantes in 1685. Others invariably found huddled around the table at William's daily briefings included the thickset Dutchman Godard Van Reede, the Baron of Ginkel, and the Scotsman Hugh Mackay, commander of the remnants of the royal brigades that had stayed behind in Holland and declared for William. But in the bustle of William's travelling headquarters, there was one man who held the Prince of Orange's attention tighter than any other: William Bentinck, his best friend.

Born to a Dutch noble family loyal to the House of Orange, Bentinck had been close to William for most of their adult lives. In 1675 during the first war with France, William had caught smallpox and spent over two weeks in bed, drifting in and out of consciousness and clinging to life. Bentinck never left his side. William would later remark that although most of those two weeks were a blur, he remembered that every time he called out for help it was Bentinck's voice he heard in reply. Their friendship grew strong, and Bentinck became one of William's most trusted counsellors and diplomats. He regularly travelled to England as William's envoy, and the prince came to rely on his friend's instincts and advice on English affairs. They signed their correspondence to each other with the letter 'G', for Guillaume – a token of mutual affection. In the months before the invasion Bentinck was William's point man, negotiating loans with the financiers of Amsterdam and thrashing out deals for mercenaries with the princes of Germany. Bentinck had a knack for politics and was one of the chief architects of William's invasion narrative of Protestant liberty and law. Snippy, blunt, warm in certain company but also a bit of a hothead, Bentinck was, in many ways, very like his master. It was Bentinck who typically stood between a visitor and an audience with William. As the army moved east through England, Bentinck found himself with more and more visitors to screen. After James had fled the field at Salisbury, even more aldermen and gentry began to flock to William's camp. The Prince of Orange had become the kingmaker, the old Earl of Warwick reborn. Riding on horseback through the small hamlet of Berwick, William waved to a cheering crowd and proclaimed, 'Thank you, good people; I am come to secure the Protestant religion, and to free you from popery'.[1] William disliked public ceremony, and playing to the crowd was never something he enjoyed. Nonetheless, he stuck to the message. England, after all, was beginning to like what it was hearing.

*

The day after he had returned to London to find that his daughter had abandoned him, James called the nobles and senior clergy of the capital to a summit at Whitehall. He knew that the defections could not be shrugged off any longer, and he needed to plug the leak. The great northern city of York, the seat of James's former dukedom, had declared for William on 24 November. It did not matter if this was a war or a publicity contest. James was losing either way. He sought to clear the air by issuing a general pardon for anyone who had defected, provided they immediately laid down their arms. He was also finally willing to call parliament at once.

Some forty nobles and clergymen arrived at Whitehall for James's summit on 27 November. The discussion was frank. Everything from the current crisis to old sore points like James's apparent abuse of powers was raked over in a blunt and testy debate. James tried to present himself as calm and in control, even though he was sick to his bones with worry. He stressed that, despite all the propaganda to the contrary, William wanted the crown. He also claimed to have discovered a plot by John Churchill and the Duke of Grafton to kidnap him. Passions began to spill over. Many lords, including the Earl of Clarendon, openly spoke out against James's pro-Catholic reforms for the first time. Others suggested that James offer an olive branch and hold talks with William. The king reluctantly agreed. A few days later Lords Halifax, Nottingham and Godolphin were dispatched as envoys to try and broker a deal with the Prince of Orange. As an opening gambit, James offered to call parliament immediately, provided that William keep more than thirty miles from the capital while it was in session. It appeared to many that James was finally willing to take a smack on the knuckles. Instead, he was just playing for time.[2]

On 29 November James had a secret message delivered to his naval commander, Lord Dartmouth, asking him to put his infant son on a ship to France immediately.

It was no longer safe for the boy to remain in England. ''Tis my son they aim at, and 'tis my son I must endeavour to preserve, whatsoever becomes of me,' James wrote.[3] Dartmouth agonised over the instruction but refused to carry it out. In an emotional reply to the king, Dartmouth wrote that shipping away the heir to the throne without a formal order would leave him vulnerable to accusations of treason. Besides, Dartmouth said, sending away the prince 'looks like nothing less than despair' and would give heart to James's enemies.[4] When he received Dartmouth's reply, James was stunned. The Prince of Wales was stranded in Portsmouth with just a small retinue of lords and nurses, and William's army was creeping over the horizon. The roads were being watched. If the baby prince were to fall into the enemy's hands, he would be a priceless hostage. James sent a panicked order for the child to be brought back to London immediately. 'My son is not safe,' he wrote.[5]

*

England was restless. The king had agreed to summon parliament, but it had not been enough to break the fever. William's campaign was growing more magnetic the closer he marched to the capital. Among the latest wave of defectors to join the Prince of Orange was a surprising face: the Earl of Clarendon, who suspected that his days at James's court were numbered. His son's defection had cracked the glass, and Clarendon himself had since spoken up passionately against the king's policies at the Whitehall summit. The former Irish viceroy decided that the law would be a safer haven than James's mercy. And now, in the eyes of much of the kingdom, the spirit of the law resided in William. Arriving at William's camp in the first week of December, Clarendon quickly became familiar with the twisting cogs of the continental army. He ate breakfast with Schomberg, chatted with John Churchill and was reunited with his son. Clarendon even managed an audience with William himself, who 'received us very obligingly' and began to politely interrogate him. Why had James left Salisbury so quickly? What was discussed at the summit in Whitehall? The prince was cordial and stuck to his message of parliament, religion and law. But Clarendon could not forget James's claim that William had a deeper desire to seize the throne.

Clarendon spoke with the prince's brusque confidant, William Bentinck, on 4 December. Bentinck snapped that any suggestion that his friend wanted the crown was a 'most wicked insinuation'.[6] Clarendon was glad to hear it. Later, however, he mentioned his conversation with Bentinck to Gilbert Burnet, a Scottish clergyman who had fallen out with James years earlier. Burnet began to speculate about who might and might not receive postings in William's future government. Clarendon thought it was odd to hear men close to the prince's circle discussing jobs at Whitehall if William truly had not come to seize the throne, as he and so many others still claimed. Everything was not what it seemed.

*

James's three delegates reached William's camp near Ramsbury, some seventy miles from London, on the evening of 6 December. After two days of sitting on their hands, Lords Halifax, Nottingham and Godolphin were finally granted a brief audience with the Prince of Orange. They asked William to begin formal negotiations with them, but they were waved away. Instead, any talks would have to take place through a chain of proxies, with offers and counter-offers passed back and forth like parcels. After two days of haggling, William's panel of negotiators presented James's envoys with an offer: all Catholics employed in the army and government in breach of the Test Act must be fired; all proclamations made against William since his landing at Torbay were to be withdrawn; the keys to the Tower of London were to be handed over to the city; Portsmouth was to be placed under joint control; and James would have to settle William's expenses for the expedition. Finally, William stipulated that he and his father-in-law would either both preside over the coming parliament together or neither of them would. It was a bitter pill, and William knew that James would reject it. He sent the delegates away and informed them that he would wait at Oxford, sixty miles from the capital, while James drew up a response. Meanwhile, blood was still being shed: on 9 December Dutch troops captured Reading, killing somewhere between thirty and fifty Irish soldiers who had been instructed to hold the town. Lords Halifax, Nottingham and Godolphin arrived back in London to present William's terms to the king. To their horror, he was nowhere to be found. James had vanished.

Before dawn on 10 December, the Queen of England snuck out of Whitehall palace disguised as a laundrywoman. The baby Prince of Wales was with her. With a small party of servants and nobles led by a French courtier, the count of Lauzun, the queen and the prince crossed the Thames under the cover of darkness. They piled into a line of waiting coaches and raced downstream to Gravesend, from where they boarded a ship and fled to Calais. The following night James sat in his privy chamber in Whitehall as servants ruffled about packing his clothes, letters and keepsakes into chests. The king's anxiety had swallowed him at last. James was convinced that his army was full of traitors and that there were hardly ten men left in England whom he could trust. A few hours earlier, the Catholic chapel in the Tower of London had been ransacked by a mob. The net was closing. He remembered the fate that his father had suffered after he fell into his enemies' hands. Before sneaking out of Whitehall in disguise at 3 a.m., James wrote two final letters – one to Lord Dartmouth, the commander of his navy, and the other to the Earl of Feversham, the Frenchman who was now in charge of the army. James explained that he was fleeing for his life. The 'ambitious Prince of Orange' and his cohort of 'rebellious lords' were unlikely to show him mercy when the capital fell. James instructed Feversham to disband the army and told Dartmouth to instruct any captains who remained loyal to sail to Ireland, 'where there are still some that will stick to me'.[7] Accompanied by just two Catholic courtiers dressed in plain clothes, James rode towards Kent, from where he intended to escape to France. In one final act of defiance, James took the great royal seal – one of the most symbolic artefacts of kingship – and threw it into the Thames.[8]

The sudden disappearance of the royal family threw the realm into a panic. Anti-Catholic mobs continued to carve through the capital, this time targeting the homes of the Florentine and Spanish ambassadors. Catholic chapels in Lime Street, Lincolns Inn Fields and elsewhere were ransacked or torched. Crowds of commoners marched through the streets of London waving oranges impaled on swords and staves, rejoicing in the collapse of James's regime. Government officials were beaten up in the streets. Outside the city, the homes of Catholic gentry were looted. False rumours spread that Irish soldiers, suddenly unemployed after Feversham, had disbanded the army and were rampaging towards the capital, which 'did very much fright and terrify people'. London was now the howling centre of a kingdom in chaos.[9]

*

William was quartered in the village of Abingdon, near Oxford, on 12 December when he was told that James had fled. 'He could not conceal his satisfaction at the king's being gone,' Clarendon wrote.[10] The pretence of the invasion began to melt away, and preparations began for the final march into London. The following day, however, William's mood swung back when he received word that the royal army had been scattered by Lord Feversham, acting on James's orders. Another frustrating message soon followed. On the night of 11 December a rowdy bunch of sailors keeping an eye on the ports for any fleeing Catholics had caught three men hiding on a ship being loaded up with supplies. One of them, whom they thought to be a priest, was heckled and strip-searched for money. The three prisoners were dragged back to a nearby inn, where someone made the startling discovery. The priest whom they had tossed about like a cabbage was in fact the King of England. Word swept up to London and within hours an armed escort was on the road to escort James back to the capital. The hapless monarch could not even manage to flee his own kingdom successfully. James's re-entry into the narrative made things tricky for William. The capital was too volatile for him and James to be present in the city at the same time. With cold efficiency, William decided that James had to be removed. Like every other action in his invasion so far, disposing of the king would have to be spun correctly.

James returned to London on 16 December, five days after his bungled escape. He had been briefed on the road about the riots, beatings and destruction of property that had engulfed the capital since he'd left. It was to his great surprise, therefore, that he received a rapturous welcome on the streets of London, with 'bonfires, ringing of bells, and all imaginable marks of love and esteem'. The words of songs heralding 'England's joyful welcome to the King' were printed and circulated among the crowds. To James, who was convinced that his people had abandoned him, it was a moving embrace. Many Londoners were simply relieved that order might now be restored after successive nights of rioting. If James hoped that this was a fresh start, however, was about to receive a firm rebuke. William, who was now camped at Windsor castle on the outskirts of the city, had sent his ambassador, William Nassau de Zuylestein, to intercept James before he reached London and instruct him to go straight to Rochester, some twenty-five miles down the Thames. Zuylestein was late, and by the time he reached the capital James was already back at Whitehall. A terse conversation took place between king and diplomat. James asked for a face-to-face conference with William; Zuylestein refused and said that James would have to order all of his troops out of London first. James protested about the imprisonment of Lord Feversham, whom William had thrown into the cells at Windsor. The ambassador replied that Feversham's release was not up for discussion. Zuylestein bowed, spun on his heels and hurried back to Windsor. James could not shake the feeling that he had just been given an order, not a request.[11]

At eleven o'clock the following night, just as James was preparing for bed, there was a knock on the door of his privy chamber. A stark-faced official stood in the doorway and told the king that Dutch soldiers had just marched into the palace grounds, had attempted to block the entrances and were now in a tense stand-off with the royal guards. The king was furious. He summoned the Dutch commander Hendrick Trajectinus, the Count of Solms, and demanded an explanation. At first, James suggested that a mistake had been made and that the Dutch had confused Whitehall with St James's Palace, where it was expected that William would camp next. Solms, who spoke barely a word of English, politely shook his head and showed James his orders, which specifically mentioned Whitehall. The colour drained from James's face. He ordered the royal guards to stand down and allowed the Dutch soldiers to take their place. Whitehall was no longer a palace. It was a prison.

One hour later, there was another knock on the door. James's chief secretary, Lord Middleton, who was keeping watch in the privy chamber, turned the handle and peered out nervously into the corridor. Standing there were three noblemen carrying an urgent letter from William. James held a candle up to the hastily scrawled note. William had written to his father-in-law suggesting that 'to avoid the disorder' that would result if they were both in London at the same time, James should pack his things and get out of Whitehall by ten o'clock the next morning. William offered to send Dutch blue guards to escort the king from the capital and 'secure him from any harm'. James read between the lines and told the messengers that he would comply. At first light the next morning, the king's effects were quickly repacked and loaded onto a barge in the river. A small party of officials and diplomats waved a tearful goodbye to the king from the side of the Thames, and James sailed upstream towards Rochester, watched all the way by the strict eyes of his Dutch escort.[12]

Later that same morning, William finally entered London to triumphant scenes. The sound of hundreds of church bells rang out across the rooftops, and thousands of people scrambled for a glimpse of the prince and his staff. Men and women wrestled each other out of the way to kiss the hands of William and his generals as they rode towards St James's Palace. The grey plumes of dozens of bonfires could be seen in the chill winter air. Effigies of the pope were burned. Almost every nobleman, lawyer and clergyman in the capital clamoured to try and get into St James's for an audience. Bishop Compton of London returned from Nottingham waving a banner embroidered with the words 'we are unwilling to change the laws of England' in Latin. Meanwhile, out of sight and mind in Rochester, James's Dutch armed escort had thinned out. It was as if someone, with careful and detailed planning, was telling him to flee England once more. James took the hint. Convinced that his life remained at risk if he stayed, James snuck out of Rochester unimpeded on 22 December. Within twenty-four hours he was on a ship to France, rocking and thrashing his way across a winter sea.

The luckless flight of the King of England, Ireland and Scotland from his own realm was met with more than just a little pity. The Earl of Clarendon, who sensed that this might have been William's plan all along, wrote that James's plight 'moved compassion even in those who were not very fond of him'.[13] Others tried to smuggle letters through to Rochester before the king left, begging him not to run away. However,

James was certain that he had no choice. 'How can I hope to be safe,' he wrote in a parting message, 'so long as I was in the power of one who had … invaded my kingdoms without any just occasion' and had cast 'the greatest aspersion … that malice could invent' by doubting the parentage of his son.[14] James was now a refugee on the water. William had planted himself in St James's Palace and began to catch up on a month's worth of correspondence and news. The French had laid siege to Maastricht, spies had been arrested and whipped in The Hague and Louis' son, the Dauphin, had arrived in Luxembourg, intent on blasting his way to the Dutch border. Thousands of decommissioned royal soldiers, many of them Irishmen, were now unaccounted for across England. In London, the messy legal business about what to do with the crown was only just beginning. In Ireland, there remained a Catholic army and government stoutly loyal to James. William would need to start finding solutions, and he would need to find them quickly.

12

House of Fear

Bundles of letters were criss-crossing the Irish Sea in packet boats every day, but Dublin was still struggling to keep up with the news. On 29 December an Irish Protestant judge in Dublin named John Keating sent a message to John Temple, an acquaintance in London. Keating was well placed to take Ireland's temperature: he was a member of the Irish privy council, had solid connections in the capital and had a reputation as a fair and impartial judge, which is probably why Tyrconnell let him keep his job. In his letter to John Temple, Keating described Ireland as a kingdom suddenly gripped by paranoia. All their news of the invasion was outdated or untrustworthy, while Catholics and Protestants were now living in open fear of each other, 'or at least pretending to be'. Afraid that another 1641 was only hours away, many Protestants had crammed onto ships with all the plate (small segments of valuable metals that were of higher value than coins) and baggage they could carry and fled Dublin. Thousands more Catholics had begun to enlist in the royal army, as rumours swirled that the Prince of Orange would be sending 'a considerable army' to invade Ireland before Candlemas. In the north, Protestants had started to band together in armed associations, seizing weapons, horses and entire towns. Bandits preying on the disorder were prowling the country, stealing entire herds of cattle at a time. Famine and civil war seemed certain. Men of all creeds were gripped by 'anxiety and sorrow', and the kingdom of Ireland, Keating wrote, was 'ready to fall into ruin'.

However, Keating's letter was not an idle lament. Halfway through, he dropped a startling piece of information about Lord Tyrconnell that he knew would grab John Temple's attention. In between his increasingly manic efforts of ordering out commissions and gathering army supplies, the Earl of Tyrconnell had begun to mutter 'in both public and private' about his willingness to hand Ireland over to William if James gave his blessing. If this was true, it was astonishing news. Keating reasoned that the 'moderate men' of Ireland – with Tyrconnell among them, apparently – had no desire for a civil war that would reduce the kingdom to 'ruins and rubbish'. The message tucked away in this letter to London was clear. If the Prince of Orange offered decent terms to Ireland, Ireland might be willing to accept.[1]

Keating had chosen his words with care. He knew that John Temple's brother William had served as English ambassador to The Hague and had access to the Prince of Orange's court in St James's Palace. Keating also knew that his revelation about Tyrconnell's desire to do a deal would be passed through the back channels of court all the way to the prince himself. At that moment, William, his advisors and the members of parliament now arriving in the capital were more concerned with settling affairs in England. When they were finished, Ireland would not take long to bludgeon its way to the top of the agenda. As of now no one, William least of all, had any great notion of what to do about Tyrconnell and his army. Keating hoped that the Prince of Orange was open to ideas.

*

As James was scrambling away from Salisbury in late November, he sent a cautionary letter to his viceroy in Dublin. England was lost, his army had betrayed him and the people were rallying to William, the king wrote. Tyrconnell should now take whatever steps were necessary to preserve Ireland.[2] The viceroy was hardly surprised. Like so many others, he had seen the Dutch threat coming long before James felt any sting of danger. As soon as he received the king's dispatch, Tyrconnell called a meeting of the Irish privy council where it was agreed that new regiments would have to be raised immediately to maintain order in the kingdom. The Irish regiments that had been sent to England earlier in the summer had been disbanded and scattered – some soldiers were arrested and interned on the Isle of Wight, others managed to slip away to France. Hundreds more were making their way north to try and barter passage back to Ireland from Chester or Liverpool. Several officers, including Patrick Sarsfield, had their commissions paid up and were now lying low in London as tempers raged. In early December, William was told that most of the Irish soldiers at large in England would gladly 'lay down their arms' in return for safe passage home. The whole situation was a mess.[3]

Back in Dublin, Tyrconnell knew that finding thousands of new recruits for the Irish army would not be a problem. The issue would be figuring out how to clothe, arm and feed them. The ports were virtually on lockdown, and Dublin Castle's treasury was almost empty. Tyrconnell suspected that it would not be long before Protestants in Ulster and the capital began to agitate once word of William's march into London arrived. He was not wrong. A plot to seize Dublin Castle and arrest Tyrconnell was only abandoned after one of the few influential Protestants left in the army command, William Stewart, Lord Mountjoy, spoke against it. Mountjoy was a charismatic Ulsterman who sat on the privy council and was respected as 'a good officer and a man of spirit' with 'a very large authority throughout the north of

Ireland'.[4] To the ever-suspicious Tyrconnell, a Protestant leader of Mountjoy's calibre was someone to worry about.

As 1688 drew to a foggy close, Ulster became a house of fear. Protestant innkeepers, merchants and gentry began meeting in churches, market houses and manors. Men who had survived 1641 or had grown up listening to tales of butchered cousins and uncles believed that another massacre was looming. Within a matter of weeks, armed defence associations began cropping up in Down, Antrim, Armagh and elsewhere. In the town of Hillsborough, just a few miles south of Belfast, a 'council of union' was formed among Protestant gentry who began to raise their own troops, seize weapons and stockpile supplies. The council chose a leader, the Earl of Mountalexander; they quickly gathered together several thousand cavalry and infantry and began preparations to send an envoy directly to William to seek help.

Tyrconnell sensed the mood. On 7 December he issued a declaration condemning the 'perverse humour' of the north, where many were now behaving in a 'warlike manner'. He stated that rumours of another 1641 were an 'evil design to disturb the peace', and though promising protection for all loyal subjects regardless of their religion, Tyrconnell immediately banned all 'malicious' public meetings, which were now taking place across Ulster almost every night.[5] The viceroy was playing several hands at once. As he was preaching calm to armed and anxious Protestants, Tyrconnell was simultaneously overseeing a massive build-up in the Catholic-dominated army. Dublin Castle had originally planned to raise 20,000 new soldiers following the privy council meeting in December, but within two months the number had reached 40,000 and was still climbing. It was a staggering surge, and it gave the viceroy a crippling workload. For the first time since he took office, Tyrconnell seemed despondent and unsure. As Judge Keating had reported, the lord deputy began to cut a moody figure in the corridors of the castle or in the dining-rooms of the viceregal lodge at Chapelizod. He began to complain of ill health and was heard openly stating that he would gladly hand over his sword of office if there was someone to give it to. Tyrconnell's cold feet became the subject of ripe gossip in the capital, but soon the city was gripped by a more pressing crisis. As passions in Ulster continued to bubble, one town was about to shut its gates and become the epicentre of a war: Derry.

*

Back in 1608, when the broken arms of Gaelic Ulster were still flailing in the aftermath of the Nine Years War, the small town of Derry in north-west Ulster was attacked and burned. The following year James I granted the town to the city of London, handing it the unenviable task of carving a new English settlement from the flesh of the old Tyrconnell heartland. London did not shirk the task. Over the next forty years, through grants and subscriptions, it built Derry up piece by piece into a bustling market city with rich fisheries and sturdy defences. Sitting on a ridge overlooking a kink in the River Foyle, which flows down into Lough Foyle and then out into the sea, the new Derry was guarded by walls over twenty feet high and more than twelve feet thick in places. It had all the teeth and bones of a modern fortress: nine bastions – thick, angular structures jutting out of the walls from which cannon and musket shot could be poured in all directions; a wide and deep ditch that turned the ground before the walls into a killing zone; and four great gates carved into the walls like the points of a compass. The city within was little more than a square mile in size, and rising up over the skyline was the great spire of St Columb's, the first Protestant cathedral built in the three kingdoms since the reformation. Derry was tough, but it was not invincible. High ground loomed over the city on both sides of the river, from where cannons could be pointed down over the walls. The River Foyle, meanwhile, was an exposed artery. If an enemy fleet managed to blockade it, the city could be starved to death. These were hypothetical concerns, however. Derry was not designed to endure a siege by a Habsburg or Turkish army. It had been built with one specific purpose in mind: to keep out restless Gaelic natives. Derry had survived both the 1641 rebellion and the civil war. In that sense, it had already proven itself entirely fit for purpose.[6]

In late 1688 the city was gripped by panic. In the first week of December an unlikely mix of luck, lies and opportunity turned Derry into the hinge on which the fates of two kings and a large chunk of history would turn. On 3 December a discarded letter was found in the streets of the village of Comber in County Down, far away on the other side of Ulster. In the letter, an anonymous writer warned a local gentleman about a Catholic plot to launch a co-ordinated massacre of Ulster Protestants on 9 December. With gruesome echoes of 1641, the letter claimed that the Irish planned to 'kill and murder man, wife and child' without mercy. The letter was a hoax, but lies always run faster than truth. Within days thousands of copies had been printed and were being dispersed from town to town across the province. On 7 December, the letter reached Derry. At that moment the city was unguarded, as Tyrconnell had just withdrawn Lord Mountjoy's mostly Protestant regiment that had been billeted in the area. Mountjoy's men were to be replaced by new Catholic recruits under the command of Alexander MacDonnell, the Earl of Antrim. The text of the Comber letter whipped through the cramped streets of Derry like floodwater. Frantic shouts went up that the incoming Catholic garrison was part of the plot. Then, with fateful timing, a messenger arrived in the city with word that Antrim's troops were almost there.

At noon, as the town's aldermen and bishop argued over what to do, the first of the royal soldiers began to cross the Foyle, unaware of the ferocious panic unfolding inside the city. In a moment of historic frenzy, thirteen teenage apprentices sprinted down to Ferry Quay gate and raised the drawbridge before the soldiers could enter. The troops were stunned and confused. A shout then came down from the wall warning the soldiers to retreat or be shot. The troops turned away, unsure what in God's name had just happened. A public meeting took place inside the walls. The bishop and several local officials pleaded with the people of the city to open the gates before they were all lynched for treason. A cry of refusal went up, as if 10,000 people were trying to speak at once. The following day the city armoury was broken into, and 150 muskets and a small barrel of gunpowder were seized. The day after that, as Antrim's puzzled soldiers remained camped a short distance away from Derry waiting for orders, the cannons fixed to the city walls opened fire. The city was saluting the news that George of Denmark, *Est il possible*, had defected. However, the novice soldiers outside the city feared that they were under attack and fled. Lord Antrim himself arrived to try and work things out but was rebuffed. With no idea what to do next, Antrim sent word south to Tyrconnell. The city of Derry had taken care to declare their 'duty and loyalty' to James but stated that they were defending themselves against 'a general massacre of the Protestants in this kingdom'. When word reached the capital, Tyrconnell was livid, but he knew that the situation would have to be handled gently. He dispatched Lord Mountjoy to break the impasse, aware that the people of Derry would listen to him. Mountjoy was firm and authoritative to all sides. The city of Derry was told to reopen their gates, hand over the weapons they had stolen and accept a military governor named Robert Lundy, one of Mountjoy's lieutenant colonels. In return, Mountjoy secured several concessions from Tyrconnell, including a pardon for the entire city, a promise not to arrest any man who attended the outlawed 'tumultuous meetings' and an assurance that only Protestant soldiers would be garrisoned within Derry. Tyrconnell bit his lip, agreed to the terms and marked Mountjoy's card with thick ink.[7]

13

We Shall Never See Each Other Again

Two men walked up the gangplank of a ship lolling at anchor in Dublin harbour. Both were carrying secret messages bound for Paris. One was Lord Mountjoy, who was being sent as an envoy by Tyrconnell to seek James's permission to surrender Ireland to William. The other was Stephen Rice, one of Tyrconnell's Catholic judges, who was on a more sinister mission. Rice had been told that the moment their ship arrived in France, Lord Mountjoy was to be placed under arrest and sent to the Bastille. Rice carried out his orders to the word. With Shakespearian efficiency Tyrconnell disposed of Mountjoy, 'the most leading Protestant of Ulster', before he could become the figurehead of a Protestant rebellion or a threat to his own authority.[1] If there had been doubts about the viceroy's intentions as he sulked and moaned at the turn of 1689, he had just provided a ruthless response. The betrayal of Lord Mountjoy – who would remain locked up in the Bastille for three years – provoked an outcry among the Protestants of the kingdom, who had just seen a potential leader snatched from them. In Derry, Sligo,

Hillsborough and Dublin they spat fire about the 'falsehood' of 'Lying Dick Talbot' and swore never to trust him or his government again.[2] Tyrconnell knew that hatred was the price of control. By the end of January 1689, he and the rest of James's supporters in Ireland had steeled their attitude. If the Prince of Orange wanted the kingdom, he would have to come and take it by force.

*

It had been a cold and tense Christmas in London. The Thames had frozen over, and traffic on the river had been choked to a standstill. Most of England's bishops had taken up residence in town, keen to be as close as possible to St James's Palace, the new centre of the world. Parliament was preparing to hold a grand convention to decide 'the settling of the government', and delegates were arriving in the city every day. From the rank and slippery avenues of Cheapside, up through the merchant houses of the old city and into the courtyards and prim gardens of the west end, London whispered and wondered. William's soldiers, with their foreign tongues and strange uniforms, were an awkward presence in the streets. Danger and suspicion was rife. A Dutch soldier had been found with his throat slashed in Long Acre, while letters were full of talk that all Catholics were about to be expelled from the city. Correspondence was being opened and inspected before delivery – when people complained, postmasters simply shrugged that they were under orders.[3] One man was arrested in the street for handing out pamphlets calling for a new republic; another was dragged away to gaol for threatening to assassinate William. Many people – mostly those sympathetic to the vanished James – felt that London was an occupied city, where the streets swarmed with menacing foreign soldiers. And all the while, concerns about the 'unsettled posture' of Ireland dominated letters, conversations and arguments.[4] The city of London, of course, had commercial interests in Derry, while many members of the Lords and Commons had money tied up in Irish estates. For them, protecting their investments was becoming a creeping priority.

Back at St James's Palace, William was not wasting time. He sent for his wife in Holland, aware that she would be a calming and legitimising presence at his side for the public. The parliamentary convention had not even begun, but William was already urging the delegates to hurry up so he could get on with his real work, chiefly 'the preservation of Holland … against the threats of France'. The prince had quickly drawn together the regiments of English cavalry and infantry – some 8,000 men in all – that were to be sent to the continent 'early this spring', once parliament had tied up its loose ends.[5] William's days were long and exhausting, and securing an audience with him was tricky. He devoted every Tuesday and Friday solely to his correspondence and often sent away unscheduled visitors. This became a particular problem for the steady trickle of lords and gentlemen arriving from Ireland, hoping to press William into taking action there. Many had to wait for days before being allowed a word with the prince; others had no luck at all. Frustrated, some turned to courtiers like the Earl of Clarendon, who shared their sympathies and thought that William needed to take 'earnest' steps against Lord Tyrconnell, his old foe, under whose administration Irish Protestants 'have suffered great hardships'. William, however, remained elusive, save for a vague assurance that he would 'take care' of Ireland in due course.[6] He may have seemed uninterested, but William was quietly gathering his thoughts – he had, for example, requested a list of all Protestants who had been removed from the Irish army by Tyrconnell. As court chatter began to mount that William was about to make a public declaration on Ireland,

Clarendon and the Irish peers clicking their heels in London grumbled about their lack of input.

By this stage, the suggestions about Tyrconnell's plans that had been tucked away inside John Keating's letter to John Temple had, as hoped, been brought to William's attention. The prince, who already had too much to do, was intrigued by the prospect of settling Ireland without much fuss. Noblemen kept arriving at St James's Palace offering to sail with several regiments and bring Ireland to heel by force, but William kept turning them down. He knew better than most that war was never a clean, affordable or quick way of doing things. If he could avoid it, he would.

*

As the River Seine twists north-west out of Paris, it skirts the ankles of a great palace of pale stone. Wrapped in a garden of five-and-a-half million trees, the palace of Saint Germain-en-Laye is a daunting, majestic marriage of gothic and renaissance craft. Dozens of vaulted windows are stacked up towards a high flat roof, from where a terrace provides stunning views of Paris upstream. Inside, the palace's main courtyard resembles a cathedral without a roof, tightly cloistered within storeys of high arches and peach stone. This was where Louis XIV was born, and though he had long since been occupied with the renovations at Versailles, he ensured that St Germain was kept in pristine condition. It was here that James II, wrecked and humiliated, was reunited with his wife and son on Christmas Day 1688.

As James and his exiled retinue were approaching St Germain, he sent his bastard son, the eighteen-year-old Duke of Berwick, on an important detour. In those frantic final days before fleeing England, Berwick had been given orders to quit Portsmouth, join his father at Rochester and travel to

France at his side, along with a close group of royal advisors, servants, bodyguards, nobles and his own younger brother and fellow bastard, Henry FitzJames. As they neared Paris, James told Berwick to ride to Versailles and pay homage to Louis on his behalf. James expected that this would be an awkward conversation: in the weeks before William's invasion, he had ignored French warnings and waved away their offers of support. He did not have that luxury any more. With no money, few possessions and only a skeleton household, James knew that his immediate comfort now depended on the warmth of his cousin's welcome. Luckily, the King of France was in a welcoming mood. On arriving at Versailles Berwick was received with 'politeness and friendship' by Louis, and Berwick felt that the king 'spoke from his heart' when he offered sympathy and support for his father. Louis undoubtedly felt a duty of care for his luckless relative and fellow monarch and gave James his blessing to take up residence at St Germain with an annual stipend of some £50,000.[7] But he was also working the angles. If James expected Louis to pay for his shelter and hospitality, Louis was determined to get value for his money.

A trickle of harassed and weary supporters followed James to France in the first weeks of 1689. Many of them were cashiered Irish officers given passports and permission to leave by William, who did not like the idea of them hanging around London. Others were ordinary English and Scotsmen – government officials, gentry, clerks; most of them Catholics, all of them unwilling to trade their allegiance to William like a pawned trinket. Together they would be known as Jacobites, taken from *Jacobus*, the Latin for James. Among them was John Stevens, the revenue officer-turned-refugee who had snuck into London and found William's soldiers 'in quiet possession of the royal palaces' and the city's gossips churning with 'villainous reflections' on James. Stevens, like hundreds of other Jacobites in the city, decided that England was no place for them any more. Escaping would not be simple.

The Thames was clogged up with ice, and the few ships able to make it through became caught up in the murky business of human trafficking. With no alternative, Stevens and 'a multitude' of other Jacobites were forced to take their chances with crooked ship captains who charged steep fares and crammed passengers into 'barbarous' conditions below deck. Stevens's ship only made it as far as Gravesend before running aground on ice on 11 January. When they finally made it out into the Channel four days later, the ship was thrown about in rough, violent winter waters before limping into Calais. Stevens and the other exiles stumbled onto French soil seasick and frozen. With little idea of what to do next, they began the 140-mile march south to St Germain like dazed pilgrims.[8]

At first, James tried to secure support from the other Catholic princes of Europe, putting out feelers to Madrid, Vienna and Rome. He quickly learned that friends of France had little support beyond Louis's borders. Emperor Leopold snubbed James's envoy; Pope Innocent politely fudged his requests for aid. James and his stream of itinerant supporters arriving in Calais by the day were firmly France's problem. As he settled down to his life as an outcast, James cut a lost and withdrawn figure. He had been on the verge of a nervous breakdown and was now living with the shame of being run out of his father's kingdoms. The talk in London had it that James was idly enjoying the charms of Paris in winter, attending operas and riding with the Dauphin. In truth, he was dazed and reeling. His letters from St Germain are numb with indifference: writing to Tyrconnell, who had pleaded for money to pay and equip his 40,000 new recruits, James stated deadpan that his viceroy would have to make do with 8,000 French muskets and find a way 'to defend yourself … till summer at least'. Instead of hard cash, James offered Tyrconnell a faint hope that Louis might 'press the Hollanders' enough on the continent so that William 'will not have men to spare to attack you'. The exiled king sent a similarly hollow message to his old privy counsellors in London, warning them that William would not be an easy king to serve.[9]

James seemed to have given up. England was lost, his regime had collapsed and his household was in disarray. But even in the wreckage of the Jacobite court there were opportunities for men seeking influence. As James's ministers began to jostle for position at St Germain, the man with the sharpest trajectory was John Drummond, the Earl of Melfort, a Scottish noble who had travelled to France ahead of the royal entourage and helped lay the groundwork for James's arrival. Melfort was almost forty years old, tall and lean, with ebony hair and subtle but firm features. He was 'a well-bred gentlemen' with a solid family: he and his brother, the Earl of Perth, had both converted to Catholicism and secured key posts in James's Scottish administration – Melfort as secretary of state and Perth as lord chancellor. Melfort excelled in the artistry of court politics and was renowned as 'very handsome and a fine dancer'. A smooth talker but also quietly ruthless, Melfort was seen as 'very proud, not able to bear a rival in business'. When he had first arrived in Paris, Melfort had made a solid first impression on Louis. Such things counted for a great deal.[10]

*

In the middle of January 1689 three ships set out on different courses over the dark and foamy seas between Ireland, England and France. Each carried little messages of war, peace, death and power. In London, William had chosen to ignore the warmongering of the Irish peers and decided to send an envoy to Dublin to seek terms with Tyrconnell. In Versailles, Louis and his ministers of war and the navy had been mulling over sending French officers, weapons and money to Ireland to open a new front against William and his alliance. However, Louis first wanted to send scouts to Ireland to determine if war would work. Finally, far away in Dublin, Tyrconnell had sent Lord

Mountjoy and Stephen Rice on their infamous voyage. As well as his clandestine mission to remove Mountjoy, Rice had also been given a bundle of letters for James and was instructed to personally urge the king to travel to Ireland with all the supplies and money he could find. The respective success and failure of these three diplomatic missions from three capitals would set the kingdoms on a carefully laid path to chaos.

In London, Whitehall Palace had been fitted out for Mary's imminent arrival from Holland. The parliamentary convention was due to start within days, and though it was now openly agreed 'that the Prince and Princess of Orange will be crowned', this would not be the end of it.[11] William was pushing for parliament to cover the costs of his invasion, and then there would be the matter of Ireland. From this distance it was impossible to know how solid the reports of Tyrconnell's wavering were, but William wanted to find out. He decided to open dialogue with Dublin Castle but knew that he would need the right envoy. The message had to be firm enough to appease the peers – Tyrconnell's removal from power was a must – but William also knew that concessions to Catholics on matters of religion and property would help. After some wrangling he agreed to send the Irish major general Richard Hamilton, whom Tyrconnell had previously elevated to one of the top posts in the Irish army. Hamilton had travelled to England with his regiment after James's request for Irish soldiers, and when the army was disbanded he and his men had been interned on the Isle of Wight. Hamilton did not remain a prisoner for long thanks to his connections at St James's Palace, most notably the new Duke of Ormonde, who was his cousin. Hamilton's character as a potential envoy to Ireland was vouched for by John Temple, whose uncle of the same name had received Judge John Keating's coded letter. Hamilton was brought before William, given instructions and allowed to sail to Dublin with 11 of his officers and 140 of his men. The plan backfired in spectacular fashion. The moment Hamilton arrived in Dublin he tore up his orders and immediately defected back to Tyrconnell. He and his troops barrelled into a tavern in Ringsend, toasted James's health and chuckled at the ruse they had just pulled. Richard Hamilton's return was a huge jolt for Irish morale. 'The Papists in Dublin made bonfires when Dick Hamilton came over, saying he was worth 10,000 men,' the House of Lords in Westminster later heard.[12] The young John Temple, who had vouched for Hamilton with William, was disgraced. A few weeks later he took a small boat out onto the Thames, jumped into the water and drowned. In his suicide note, Temple begged William's forgiveness for his 'folly'.[13] The prospect of a deal between London and Dublin, if it ever really existed, was finished.

On 10 January, Mountjoy and Rice sailed out of Dublin. Before he left, Mountjoy wrote an open message to his Protestant kinsmen which spoke of his desire for peace and his belief that all Irishmen, whatever their religion, 'must do our work without blood' and avoid 'the misery of the kingdom'.[14] Five days later a team of French scouts, led by the Marquis de Pointis, a naval engineer, arrived in Ireland. For one month Pointis poured over army recruitment lists, took notes on training drills, held discussions with Tyrconnell and generally sniffed out how fertile the kingdom was for war. Pointis also brought over a fresh batch of correspondence from St Germain, including a letter addressed to Tyrconnell that had been dictated by James and signed by Lord Melfort, an indication of just how quickly the Scottish courtier was rising. In the note, James asked for a detailed account of the politics, army and geography of Ireland. Tyrconnell was more than a little miffed. In his reply, he reminded the king that he had kept him 'very well informed' about Ireland ever since he took office.[15] James, it seems, had either forgotten everything he had been told or had not bothered to pay attention in the first place.

The fact that Melfort's name was suddenly appearing on royal correspondence was also an ominous hint to Tyrconnell about who was really asking the questions.

Tyrconnell's reply to St Germain was grim. He stated that although he had managed to raise some 40,000 recruits, they were 'all unclothed and the greatest part unarmed'. The exchequer was broke, and the only salaries being paid to soldiers were coming out of their officers' pockets. The Irish army was gargantuan, but in reality it was unfit for action. Most of the kingdom's Protestant nobles, meanwhile, were already in England 'soliciting the Prince of Orange to invade'. Tyrconnell then provided a summary of the throbbing headache that was Ulster. The city of London, he said, had already loaned William £300,000 to invade Ireland, and his troops were now thought to be gathering in Chester, Bristol and Liverpool. Louis could send all the muskets he wanted, but without cash Tyrconnell feared that he could not prevent his soldiers stealing supplies from the common people, which would likely lead to 'a famine before midsummer'. As politely as decorum would allow, the viceroy demanded money. He even suggested offering the commercial ports of Galway and Waterford to France as collateral for a loan. 'Money must be sent out of hand, Sir, or all is lost.' Finally, Tyrconnell begged James to come to Ireland in person and asked how the king could 'continue where you are when you may possess a kingdom of your own'. The viceroy was convinced that if James arrived in Ireland, the rebellious agitators in Ulster 'will submit to you' or be crushed within a month.[16]

Pointis's report to Louis on Ireland's fitness to fight was a mixed bag. Of the roughly 40,000 soldiers now in the army, less than 6,000 had any experience. About half were armed with 'worthless' muskets; the rest carried around rotten pikes or clubs with nails stuck in them. But what they lacked in supplies and training, Pointis stressed, they made up for in zeal, and the Irish Catholics 'are resolved to perish rather than submit to Protestant domination'. He was likewise impressed with the recruits' enthusiasm to train and learn despite receiving little food, clothes or pay. Perhaps most curiously for Versailles, Pointis teased out an interesting endgame. With French assistance, the Irish army could subdue Ulster, invade Scotland and feasibly march down into England. Even if the Irish army simply stayed put, its existence alone would demand that William send the bulk of his own forces over to Ireland to deal with it. This would naturally weaken the *stadtholder*'s already 'great efforts' to resist French ambitions on the continent. The key to the whole package was James: if the exiled king could 'regain his confidence' and travel to Ireland, he would give heart to his Catholic subjects and potentially inspire 'malcontents' in England and Scotland to rise up against the Prince of Orange. It was an enticing prospect.[17]

Louis's minsters were already quibbling about Ireland before they received Pointis's report. The fierce and combative war minister, the Marquis of Louvois, thought little of James's mettle and questioned the sense of diverting military resources away from Flanders and the Rhineland. If French officers did have to go to Ireland, he said, they should be among 'the most mediocre' in the service. The naval minister, the Marquis of Seignelay, framed a different argument. The French navy had recently undergone a huge expansion, and Louis's desire to be master of the sea could now be put to the test. Seignelay stressed that a major expedition to Ireland had almost limitless potential to harass and sap William's energy. Louis agreed. By February the preparations had begun; soon Seignelay, Louvois and even Louis himself were writing with curiously identical phrases about how James had 'resolved to go to Ireland', as if he had actually had any say in the matter.[18] The heavy and intricate gears of the French military machine began to turn. Versailles decided that it would fund a war in Ireland and would send a number of senior French officers to oversee the campaign. James would be going too. According to one account, the exiled king 'could barely conceal his disappointment'.[19]

The Jacobite driftwood that had been gathering in Paris for weeks now needed to be rustled into an invasion force. All refugees able to fight were drafted into regiments; captains, chaplains, surgeons and engineers began to march towards the northern port of Brest, where the French fleet that would ferry them to Ireland was gathering. For experienced soldiers like Patrick Sarsfield, who had made his way to France from London, a new commission and the prospect of frontline action in his homeland was enticing. For others like John Stevens, who was now a soldier marching to war, it was an introduction to a life they thought they would never know. In the middle of February 1689, Stevens and his fellow volunteers began the 'tedious' march north through Brittany, barely aware that they were the newest and tiniest pieces in a great European game. Stevens noted in his journal that his first taste of army life had left him 'excessively tired' and his feet 'very sore'. He would suffer a great deal more before it was all over.[20]

*

In London and Dublin, the weeds on the road to conflict were being cut away. The parliamentary convention finally opened in Westminster on 22 January, and the Lords and Commons began to haggle over the legal interpretation of James's decision to run away. During the exclusion crisis almost a decade earlier, the rival Whig and the Tory factions in Westminster had argued bitterly over James's right to inherit the crown. Now they were simply debating the proper way to take it from him. Complaints about the abuses of his reign were tossed about like wedding rice; words like tyranny, antichrist, slavery and abdication flew through the air. After one week of legal arguments, the convention agreed that a Catholic king was 'inconsistent' with Protestant law and deemed that James had effectively abdicated when he fled England. On 12 February Mary arrived from Holland, and the following day she and William were declared co-regents of England, Ireland and Scotland as part of a compromise between the Lords and Commons. A 'declaration of right' was passed that secured the dominance of the Protestant faith and the laws of parliament. Though William and Mary were to have equal standing as monarchs, the regal powers of the crown were vested in William, now King William III, who swore to uphold the 'very great trust' that had been placed in him. A day of thanksgiving was proclaimed across England, and as the news skipped joyously from town to town it was met at every turn with bonfires, fireworks, trumpets and musket salutes.[21]

If the Prince of Orange had been willing to broker a deal with Ireland through back-door diplomacy, the King of England had to take a firmer hand. After being awarded the crown, William had apparently inherited a *de facto* right to the kingdom of Ireland, which stretched all the way back to Henry VIII. On 22 February he issued a declaration demanding that Ireland surrender and submit to his government by April. He promised religious tolerance to all Catholics who obeyed but warned that he would invade and confiscate the property of anyone who did not. His demands were ignored. Two days after William's threat, bands of Irish soldiers went from street to street in Dublin seizing all privately owned weapons, ammunition and horses. The following day, Tyrconnell issued his own declaration stating that he was disarming the general populace to prevent their weapons falling into the hands of William, who 'intends to invade'.[22] Tyrconnell's true motive, barely concealed in the text, was to disarm the Protestants of Dublin before they could rise up in William's name. According to one Protestant account, some 3,000 muskets and pistols were seized in the capital, as well as countless more 'swords, bayonets and pikes'. The confiscations continued across the rest of the kingdom over the following days, except in Ulster, where Tyrconnell dared 'not yet attempt it'. Any Protestants who refused to comply with the order were warned that they would suffer 'the disorders of the soldiers' now roaming from house to house like bailiffs.[23] Tyrconnell issued further orders banning any coinage from leaving the country and forcing innkeepers – again, mostly Protestants – to provide quarters for soldiers. With James and the French due to sail for Ireland within days, Tyrconnell had no reason to be subtle. Battle lines were being carved into Ireland's skin, and the viceroy's knife was sharper than most.

On 15 February, a forlorn James boarded a coach at St Germain, his temporary asylum, and set out for Brest. It is said that in bidding farewell to his cousin, Louis told James 'the best I can wish you is that we shall never see each other again'.[24] With that, the king without a crown trudged off to war on an island he had no interest in. After reaching Brest, James's departure was postponed by several days due to storms and an accident at sea. It was not a good start.

14

Now or Never, Now and Forever

One by one the great ships turned into a crevice on the Cork coast and crept up towards the port of Kinsale. From the seaward batteries of Charles Fort, which guarded the harbour, the Irish sentries watched in awe as the enormous hulls of *Le Faucon, Le Furieux, L'Apollon* and the other frigates passed by. James, who had travelled with his two illegitimate sons aboard the *Saint Michel*, was greeted 'with all imaginable joy' by a crowd of townsfolk as he climbed ashore.[1] It was all rather like that famous day in Dover, now lost in another lifetime. On 12 March 1689 James Stuart became the first English king to set foot in Ireland since the doomed Richard II almost three centuries earlier. He would have been hoping that the similarities ended there.

Louis had sent James to Ireland with twenty-two ships – a fleet grand enough to make an entrance, but too small to carry over his entire force. As such, James arrived first with a core contingent of some 200 Jacobite officers, noblemen, secretaries and senior clergy, as well as several French officers sent to add their continental nous to the raw Irish army. The rest of the Jacobite fighting force, including conscripted refugees like John Stevens, would have to wait in Brittany for the fleet to complete its round trip. For two days the dockside in Kinsale was in noisy motion as the French ships unloaded tonnes of muskets, ammunition, uniforms and supplies, as well as the men who would have their say in the war to come: the young Duke of Berwick and the ambitious Earl of Melfort; Judge Stephen Rice, back from his voyage to banish Lord Mountjoy; colonels Simon and Henry Luttrell, brothers from a famous Old English family near Dublin; Colonel John Wauchope, a Scottish veteran of the Dutch brigades; and Patrick Sarsfield, whose reputation for turning up in the thick of the action was beginning to precede him.

Then, of course, there were the French – the bristly and aloof counts and marquises sent to direct Versailles's new war of convenience. There was the Marquis de Boisseleau, a grumpy veteran of the sieges of Luxembourg and Valenciennes; the Marquis de Pusignan, a major general; and the Marquis de Maumont, a favourite of Louvois's, who had been discreetly told to work his way into Tyrconnell's confidence and keep his eyes open. The titular leader of the French mission was the sixty-year-old Conrad de Rosen, a thick-jawed German native who had fought in both of Louis's Dutch wars and had been handed the prestigious new title of 'Marshal of Ireland'. However, the real powerhouse in the French delegation was not a soldier but a diplomat: Jean-Antoine de Mesmes, the count d'Avaux, who had been appointed as Louis's personal ambassador to James. D'Avaux was the French king's eyes and ears in Ireland, and his letters would keep Louis, Louvois and Seignelay constantly briefed on James's movements and moods. He was also the custodian of a war dowry of 500,000 livres. Part-counsellor, part-treasurer, part-spy, d'Avaux was instructed to make sure that when, as expected, rival factions began tussling for James's attention, the king-in-exile would remember that France's interests must come first.[2]

Two Irish delegates formally received James at Kinsale. The first was Thomas Nugent, the Catholic judge who had been heckled on the streets of London on his way to present a draft Irish land bill to James in February 1688. The other was Lieutenant General Justin MacCarthy, one of the most senior commanders in the army, who had arrived at Kinsale after a colourful detour through the nearby walled town of Bandon. Inspired by events in the north, the Protestants of Bandon had shut their gates on the royal garrison but quickly backed down when MacCarthy arrived with enough cannons, cavalry and furious intent to burn them to the ground. A local Protestant minister, Nicholas Brady, struck a deal with MacCarthy that spared the town in exchange for handing over the ringleaders, knocking down its walls and paying a cash bond to ensure future obedience. Rather than keep to standard practice and hang the rebel leaders on the spot, MacCarthy had them hauled off to the city of Cork, where James could decide what to do with them later.

The royal cortège arrived in Cork on 14 March to 'demonstrations of extraordinary joy' from the people of the city. James took up residence at the Bishop's Palace on the southern bank of the marshy harbour town and began to receive a string of visitors. With one eye on his public image, James personally pardoned the 'begging' rebels of Bandon and held a cordial audience with the city's Protestant clergy.[3] The Earl of Tyrconnell, who had been kept in Dublin on government business, was notably absent during his king's first days in Ireland. However, James's viceroy had a decent excuse. After months of threats, manoeuvring and public warnings, Tyrconnell had finally decided to end the rebellion in Ulster by force.

*

Tyrconnell's ruthless gaoling of Lord Mountjoy had left Ulster furious. Tricked into a false mission of peace, the one man who could have united the Protestants of the north had fallen victim to mischief. To them, it was final proof of Tyrconnell's true intentions to divide and conquer them. In Derry, Enniskillen, Coleraine, the Connaught town of Sligo and every other corner of the north where rebel associations had sprung up, the only thing left to do was take arms against 'great and imminent danger' and pray that William would send help.[4] In early February, as James was preparing to embark from France, they received a lifeline.

William had begun preparations to invade Ireland when an envoy from the rebel council in Hillsborough, County Down arrived in London. After several detailed discussions with William and his counsellors, the messenger departed on 10 February with an assurance from the man about to be crowned King of England that he would 'rescue' Ireland from 'the oppressions and terrors' of a Catholic regime that had 'usurped' lawful Protestant power. The envoy returned to Hillsborough on 9 March with a promise that William would support 'the Protestant nobility and gentry in the north of Ireland' with cannons, gunpowder and 15,000 soldiers. William also sent several blank commissions legitimising the rebel leaders as his officers. They were now Williamites, soldiers formally recognised by the new king. Put simply, William had declared war on Tyrconnell's government.[5]

In the early spring of 1689, the uprising in Ulster was still scattered and disorganised. Without the dominant leadership of a man like Lord Mountjoy, the temper of the rebellion varied from place to place. Sketched on a map, the flashpoints of the rising were like the tips of an awkward triangle: Derry in the north, Hillsborough in the east and Enniskillen in the west, with Sligo jutting out from Connaught like a sharp tooth. The north had become a patchwork quilt of resistance – some Williamite raiding parties, particularly in the east, struck out to seize weapons, villages, crossroads and large chunks of the countryside. Elsewhere in places of strength like Enniskillen, the rebels dug in and watched the horizon. Isolated causeways and thick bogs became tiny battlegrounds, as Williamite patrols and Irish army units scouted and stumbled across one another. Each skirmish would leave a few men shot or stabbed to death, their bodies stripped of clothes and valuables and abandoned to the elements.

Young and bellicose rebel leaders like Arthur Rawdon from County Down began to emerge – emboldened by William's promise that his army was coming. At the end of February the rebels launched an attack on the coastal town of Carrickfergus, just north of Belfast and home of one of the most intimidating Norman castles in the land. After a brief and muddled attack the Earl of Antrim, the Jacobite commander, struck a truce. Protestants within the town were allowed to arm themselves in self-defence, and a portion of the Catholic garrison was disbanded. Antrim requested to send an account of the events to Tyrconnell in Dublin. Williamite officers vetted the message to ensure it did not contain any secret nuggets of intelligence. However, the Catholic priest who was sent to the capital to deliver it did not dilute his words. The rebel Williamite forces, he told the viceroy, were ragged, disorganised and without 'all ammunition and necessary provisions for appearing in the field'.[6] Until now, Tyrconnell had been forced to grind his teeth and wait. Once he received word of the brazen rebel attack on Carrickfergus, his patience snapped. On 7 March he publicly announced that he was sending Lieutenant General Richard

Hamilton north with an army of some 2,500 men to crush Ulster's 'high treason ... by force of arms'. Derry, Sligo and the other centres of 'wickedness' were given one final chance to surrender or face ruin. Arthur Rawdon, Lord Mountalexander and other men named as 'principal actors' in the rebellion were politely told that they would receive no mercy.[7]

Tyrconnell wanted the north dealt with quickly, and the speed with which Hamilton struck into Ulster took the Williamites by surprise. On 14 March Arthur Rawdon was posted with some 500 troops in the small village of Dromore, just south of Hillsborough, when his scouts brought word that a small chunk of Irish cavalry had been spotted galloping up the road ahead. Assuming that they were Hamilton's first scouts, Rawdon set a trap. He drew up his soldiers across the main street of Dromore and sent his own cavalry around on a loop to cut off the scouts' retreat. Rawdon had been disastrously misinformed. What had been mistaken for a small cavalry company was in fact the first tip of Hamilton's entire army, now bearing down menacingly on Dromore. When the true nature of the Irish force just a few hundred yards away became known, the village was thrown into hysterical panic. The Williamite soldiers threw down their muskets, abandoned their posts and ran. Hamilton's cavalry set out after them, like hunters chasing deer. Hundreds of fleeing rebels were trampled under hooves or slashed and stabbed with sabres. Rawdon thrashed his horse up the road towards the rebel headquarters at Hillsborough, where a 4,000-strong Williamite garrison was waiting. By the time he arrived, word of Hamilton's charge had already 'struck such a terror' that the town was being abandoned.[8] Rawdon and the bulk of the Williamite soldiers fled north towards Coleraine, stripping the countryside of any food or useful materials along the way to prevent them from falling into Hamilton's hands. Many rebels were captured, while Lord Mountalexander – the titular head of the Ulster uprising – jumped into a boat and fled to the Isle of Man. The first strike of the war in Ireland had been a swift and brutal victory for Tyrconnell's forces. Hillsborough was captured, the rebels were on the run and within a few days almost half of Ulster was in Hamilton's hands.[9]

*

It was to be the pinnacle of his career in royal service, a moment of true glory. When Lord Tyrconnell finally arrived in Cork to meet James, he rode into the city at the head of a column of 'a hundred gentlemen on horseback'. When he reached the Bishop's Palace, James shocked the assembled dignitaries by walking forward to embrace Tyrconnell rather than wait for the viceroy to walk to him, as was custom. The king clearly did not mind – after months of being failed by circumstance and wallowing in self-pity, James seemed refreshed to be in the company of an old friend who had stood by him. He praised Tyrconnell's 'unshakeable firmness' and immediately elevated him from earl to duke, the highest rank in the nobility. At a banquet that evening Tyrconnell sat at James's right, a position of immense prestige, with the Duke of Berwick sitting on the king's left. James presented Tyrconnell with the *Cordon Bleu* – the insignia of the French chivalric Order of the Holy Spirit. Tyrconnell felt caught in a whirlwind of pride, vanity and esteem and firmly believed that he was closer to James's confidence than ever before. But court politics is a fat beast dressed in layers of finery. As James publicly pulled Tyrconnell close with one hand, he was preparing to push him away with the other.[10]

James reached Dublin on Palm Sunday, 24 March, four days after departing from Cork. The road between the two cities 'was like a great fair', as Irish Catholics treated the travelling king like 'an angel from heaven'. Every town held its own reception, where young maidens danced and local dignitaries lined up to proclaim their 'staunch loyalty, profound respect and tender love' for James.[11] Not to be outdone, the capital gave the king the most lavish welcome. The roads were freshly gravelled and lined with soldiers; lush, colourful tapestries were hung overhead, and musicians performed on open-air stages all along the king's route. Flowers were thrown into the street until the cobbles disappeared under a blanket of stems and petals; crowds of people ten-deep tiptoed for a glimpse. Church bells, instruments and a symphony of cheers rose up over the alleys and rooftops of the capital.[12] It was spectacular. When James's procession finally reached Dublin Castle, the cannons fired a tremendous salute. Magistrates, nobility, gentry, judges, city officials and aldermen waited in full regalia to receive the king. After James had climbed off his horse, the lord mayor presented him with the freedom of the city. A delegation of Protestant clergy, led by the influential Bishop of Meath, swore loyalty to him as their sovereign. James was reportedly moved to tears by the 'loud and joyful' welcome of Dublin, a city that believed something historic was about to happen. As he entered the castle, James passed under a banner with a heavy and prophetic message: 'Now or never, now and forever'.[13]

The royal apparatus immediately set to work. On 25 March James formally summoned the Irish parliament to sit in the capital in May. He was briefed on the progress of the northern campaign, where Richard Hamilton was now charging north towards Coleraine along the eastern shore of Lough Neagh. James appointed a raft of new Irish privy councillors, including the Duke of Berwick and Patrick Sarsfield, and issued a declaration promising freedom of religion to all people in the kingdom. Likewise, James declared it illegal for anyone outside the army to carry weapons, a threat ostensibly issued against 'robbers, thieves and plunderers', but one that also had the Williamite rebels in Ulster in mind.[14] Meanwhile, Tyrconnell sensed the new texture of the king's inner circle and began to manoeuvre accordingly. D'Avaux wrote to Louis that

Tyrconnell had put him up in a house in 'a beautiful area' of Dublin, and on the morning of James's first formal court at Dublin Castle, Tyrconnell personally collected d'Avaux with a decadent fleet of twenty horse-drawn carriages. The viceroy clearly understood that the French ambassador was a man he needed on his side.[15] On 15 March, meanwhile, Tyrconnell had written to Lord Melfort's brother, the Earl of Perth, expressing his hope that the new Irish army would be fighting in Scotland by July. It was a fanciful idea, of course, but it was what the Scottish Jacobite faction – and, by proxy, the Earl of Melfort – wanted to hear. After all, Lord Melfort now had a firm grip on James's ear and was guarding it closely.

Another decision James made in his first days in Dublin was to create a powerful inner council to advise him with daily briefings. It had three members: Tyrconnell, Melfort – who had recently appointed as secretary of state for Ireland – and d'Avaux. The council became a courteous battlefield as each man sought to advance the rival interests already tugging at the chains of the Jacobite cause. Lord Tyrconnell's priority was the forthcoming Dublin parliament, which was due to convene on 7 May. His years of legal and administrative ditch-digging ensured that it would return a Catholic majority and would finally be able to re-write Charles's hated land settlement. Lord Melfort, who did not have the faintest interest in Irish affairs, made no secret of his wish for James to take Tyrconnell's army and depart for Scotland as quickly as possible. He expressed this sentiment in a letter to Louvois in March, prompting the French minister for war to write back and warn him that setting his sights on Scotland before Ireland was fully subdued would be a dangerous wager. D'Avaux, meanwhile, measured the Irish expedition in terms of how much it could rattle William with the least possible strain on the French purse. D'Avaux also frowned on Melfort's plan of shipping the army to Scotland, not least because it would be expensive.[16]

The wrangling between James's closest advisors was given a new colour in April when the king revealed his decision to travel north 'to visit and encourage' the soldiers in Ulster.[17] Tyrconnell had already briefed him: although the Williamites were currently in retreat, they were expected to make a stand at Derry. Tyrconnell and d'Avaux both protested that James should remain in Dublin and leave the war to his generals. James batted away their concerns. He and Lord Melfort had already agreed that his presence in the north would help bring matters to a swift conclusion, clearing the way for the invasion of Scotland. Preparations for the king and his retinue to march into Ulster began. Tyrconnell, however, would not be going with them. Marshal Rosen and the French officers had decided that the 40,000-strong Irish army was too big to train and equip, and therefore Tyrconnell was told that he was being sent away on an administrative errand to travel around the kingdom, disband regiments and reduce the army by some 10,000 men. Tyrconnell saw Melfort's fingerprints all over it. The Irish viceroy and his contrary opinions were being conveniently shoved out of earshot.

By the first week of April, Jacobite Ireland was on the move. Tyrconnell had left the capital accompanied by Patrick Sarsfield to begin trimming the fat off the army in Munster and Leinster. The Duke of Berwick and the French major generals Maumont and Puisignan rode north to link up with Richard Hamilton for his final push towards Derry. On 8 April James, Melfort and Marshal Rosen set out for the garrison of Charlemont in Armagh. D'Avaux trudged north with them, grumbling at how being 'of a contrary opinion' to Lord Melfort now meant finding yourself on the wrong side of the king.[18]

15

To Derry

With every piece of lost ground, the rebels' world was shrinking. Coleraine was captured, and Sligo had been abandoned under orders from Robert Lundy, the military governor of Derry and now *de facto* commander-in-chief of the Williamites in Ulster. Enniskillen still held out, but its soldiers were dug in tight. As Richard Hamilton's army rumbled across north Ulster, capturing great chunks of scavenged and scorched countryside as it went, the epicentre of the conflict shifted west towards Derry, the 'rebellious nest' of Protestant defiance and the old scar on Gaelic Ulster.[1] Refugees fleeing the Jacobite advance had been flooding through the city's gates for weeks, and despite dwindling supplies and harsh conditions, the mood inside the walls was fierce. On 20 March the officers and leading men of the city signed a proclamation swearing to resist the enemy at all costs, which was read aloud in the main square 'to the great satisfaction' of the people. The following day, the first ships carrying supplies and money from William arrived in Lough Foyle. The citizens of Derry responded by openly declaring allegiance to William and Mary for the first time. Later, when the first Jacobite scouts were spotted in the distance, another declaration calling on every man in the city to fight was nailed to the door of the market house and read to every company of soldiers in the garrison, who responded with 'loud acclamations' and furious cries.[2] The wet earth and hard stone of Derry was about to be the scene of a great and terrible battle. Or so it seemed.

*

The war had barely begun, but Ulster was already a wasteland. As James, Rosen, Melfort and d'Avaux marched north from Dublin, they passed through miles of ravaged countryside. In one of his frequent letters to Versailles, d'Avaux described the north as 'a complete ruin' where nothing of worth remained. There was no bread, flour, oats or straw for the horses; those farmers who had not already had their livestock stolen 'do not dare' put their animals out to forage, as soldiers and bandits 'have their way' and seize what they want. The province was lawless – since James's arrival in Kinsale alone, d'Avaux wrote that 'more than 5,000 oxen' had been stolen. The town of Omagh in County Tyrone had been picked clean before the Williamites had abandoned it: the windows and chimneys of every house had been smashed, and the locks had been ripped out of the doors. 'No one has ever seen a country so sorry, so stripped of all things,' d'Avaux declared.[3]

Despite the stark surroundings, James was enthusiastic and determined to press on, coaxed all the way by Lord Melfort. From Charlemont he marched to Omagh and then announced that he would go to Strabane, just a few miles downstream from Derry and worryingly close to the front lines. D'Avaux counselled discretion and patience but grew increasingly frustrated at hearing that James and Melfort had already made their decisions. Melfort, he believed, was pushing the king down a reckless path. Rosen and Maumont were sent ahead to Dungannon with several hundred cavalry, dragoons and infantry, but they only had enough powder to fire 'five shots each'. Supply lines were already overstretched. D'Avaux wrote to Louis that 'all those in the king's confidence' had begun to approach him and quietly express their doubts and qualms about Melfort. 'He thinks only to get the king of England to Scotland,' d'Avaux wrote.[4]

Tyrconnell would have been a useful ally in these discussions, the French ambassador admitted. Despite all his vanity and grumpiness, the lord deputy tended to see things from a French perspective. But Tyrconnell was out of sight, milling around the south of the kingdom dissolving wide-eyed and ragged regiments. Wherever Tyrconnell and Sarsfield went on their errand, captains proudly drew up their men in formation only to be told that they were all being sent home. The disbanded officers, many of whom had paid for the upkeep of their troops out of their own pockets, 'were struck to the very heart' by the news, as their 'uncommon zeal for the cause' would now come to nothing.[5] With his pride bruised and his place at James's side gone, Tyrconnell completed his tour and returned to Dublin. He drifted between the vice-regal lodge at Chapelizod and his family estate at Talbotstown, complaining in his letters of 'how ill I have been of late' and writing correspondence to his old friend Richard Hamilton, who was inching closer to Derry every day.[6]

*

The burning mood in the city was being stoked from the bottom up. Driven by the frontier spirit of their fathers, the common folk of Derry were ready to fight and die. There was lingering unease within the walls between those of the Presbyterian and Anglican faiths, both were quietly distrustful of the other. But as the city swelled with refugees and tempers began to sharpen, ministers from both churches preached the same message: God will deliver us. In this quickening current, one clergyman in particular began to turn heads – George Walker, an Anglican rector from Tyrone who had recently arrived among the crowds of refugees. Described by his enemies as a 'fierce minister of the gospel', Walker and his peers helped preserve morale in Derry as Hamilton's army closed in.[7]

One man who did not seem to share the pious enthusiasm of the streets was the governor, Robert Lundy, who had become the leader of the Ulster rebellion by accident. Lundy, as his rivals were not shy in pointing out, had received his original commission from James and had been awkwardly thrust into the fold after his commanding officer, Lord Mountjoy, was thrown into the Bastille. As the next most senior army officer in Ulster, Lundy took charge by default. He was prudent and cautious and had been unwilling to charge out and fight Hamilton's army in the field. He had ordered the Williamite garrison in Sligo to pull out and reinforce Derry, despite the fact that Sligo was 'a solid defensive post, with a new stone fort'. When Hillsborough fell, Lundy decided that Coleraine was too weak to hold and did not send reinforcements to prevent its capture. Lundy had signed each declaration of defiance that Derry's council of war put before him, but there were whispers about his nerve. On 21 March, when William's first shipment of supplies reached Derry, a commission from the new king formally recognising Lundy as his governor also arrived in the cargo. According to one account, Lundy swore his new oath to William and Mary 'very privately', away from the ears of senior officers and Protestant gentlemen of the city. When he was asked to repeat the oath in public to boost popular morale, Lundy 'absolutely refused'.[8] William's secretary in London had sent Lundy a personal message from the new king, assuring him that two regiments of soldiers would be arriving in Derry soon, and that in the meantime he must hold the line and inspire 'a more than ordinary vigour' in the people.[9]

*

There would be one last chance to block the Jacobites' advance before they reached Derry. Hamilton's army was marching hard from Coleraine some thirty miles to the east, while Berwick and Maumont had been ordered to take their regiments and link up with him for the final assault. But before they could surround Derry, the Jacobites would have to find a place to cross over onto the west bank of the river, before the Foyle became wide and impassable. Both sides' maps converged on the same spot – the open ground between the villages of Clady and Lifford, fifteen miles south of the city, just where the River Finn joins the Foyle like a branch on an oak tree. If the Jacobites crossed the Finn, they could swing north and march on the city unimpeded. On Saturday 13 April, after yet another council of war, Lundy and the leaders of Derry issued a rallying cry for every man 'that can or will fight for their country and religion against Popery' to appear at Clady by ten o'clock on Monday morning, armed and ready. With no time to lose, the arches on the bridge over the Finn at Clady were demolished, and the Williamites piled up rubble and earth to build makeshift defences on the western bank. On Sunday 14 April, the day after the call to arms, Jacobite scouts were spotted on the opposite side of the Foyle, just a few miles from Derry. The time to fight, it appeared, had finally come.[10]

The attack began at eight o'clock on Monday morning, just as the Finn was shaking off its dawn mist. Hamilton, Rosen, Berwick, Pusignan and the other Jacobite generals had left the main army near Strabane and marched on Clady with a strike force of 600 cavalry and some 350 infantry. The timing of the attack took the Williamites by surprise – more than 7,000 troops had been mustered at Derry, but they were still several miles up the road when the attack began. Hamilton spread his cavalry out to probe several points along the Finn, testing the rebel defences. The Williamites posted near the shallowest points of the river fired their muskets furiously from across the water, forcing the Jacobites back. The barrage was thickest at Clady, where a few dozen men under the command of captain Adam Murray, the son of a Scottish settler, fired again and again until the river was choked in gunpowder smoke and 'all their ammunition was spent'.

As the first of Lundy's reinforcements began to arrive from Derry, they were immediately pinned down by Jacobite shots from across the river. Hamilton seized the moment and told his cavalry to dismount and swim. The Jacobites waded into the icy water, holding their muskets and pistols up over their heads as the current began to lick their shoulders. One Jacobite lost his footing and was dragged under. Noise and confusion baffled the small knot of defenders on the other side. Soon the first of the soaked Jacobite soldiers staggered up onto the opposite bank. Marshal Rosen, arriving with his troops at Lifford a short time later, plunged into the river and began to wade across. The isolated Williamite defenders upstream had been bunkered down under heavy fire but were suddenly thrown into 'such a panic' when they saw enemy soldiers crossing the river. A messenger raced up the road to warn Lundy, who had still yet to arrive with the bulk of the army. The governor halted, as if all the air had been snatched from his lungs. He told his men to turn around and retreat back to the city. Lundy did not know that he had an overwhelming numerical advantage and that barely a few dozen Jacobite soldiers had so far struggled across the river with damp muskets. All Lundy could see ahead of him was disaster. Adam Murray and the rest of his company struggling to beat the Jacobites back at Clady were told to abandon their posts. Word of the Jacobites' crossing filtered down the line and Williamite soldiers began to break, shouting 'To Derry, to Derry!' Richard Hamilton caught whiff of the panic and told his cavalry to mount up and charge. Timber planks were thrown down across the broken arches of the bridge at Clady, and hundreds of Jacobite horsemen thundered across. They tore up the road for almost five miles, cutting down hundreds of Williamite stragglers caught in their path. Dozens more flung themselves into bogs and 'marshy places' along the roadside to avoid being trampled or skewered. After several hours of gruesome pursuit, Hamilton told his cavalry to halt and regroup. There was now nothing but fresh air between them and the gates of Derry.[11]

16

No Surrender

On the morning of 15 April, as the faint popping of gunfire could be heard drifting downstream from Clady, thirteen ships were anchored in Lough Foyle. The soldiers William had promised to send to Derry had arrived from Liverpool, with seemingly perfect timing. Commanded by Colonel John Cunningham, the ships had brought with them two full regiments of troops, 1,000 muskets, £2,000 in cash and a fresh batch of letters and instructions from London. But Cunningham did not have the latest news from the city just a few miles upstream. He did not intend to charge in blindly. Cunningham sent a messenger ashore with a note for Governor Lundy, and when he heard no reply he sent another. Finally, after hours of pacing his cabin, Cunningham received a message from the governor, who had just scrambled back into the city from Clady and locked the gates behind him. Lundy's tone was bleak. He informed Cunningham that the Jacobites had overrun Clady 'with great vigour' and were now marching on Derry. He added that without an immediate reinforcement of men and provisions 'this place must fall very soon into the enemy's hands'. Lundy wrote that he was holding a council of war the following day and asked Cunningham and a few of his officers to sit in. But they would have to move fast. Lundy was convinced that the Jacobites would have the city surrounded within twenty-four hours, and unless Cunningham moved immediately, 'it will not be in your power' to make it ashore. Leaving his soldiers and supplies with the main fleet, Cunningham climbed into a dinghy and set out for Derry under the cover of darkness.[1]

*

There were now roughly 20,000 people crammed inside the walls of Derry, many of them without food, possessions or shelter. Less than half were able to fight – the city garrison comprised some 7,000 men and 341 officers, some better armed than others. Aside from Enniskillen, tucked away in harsh countryside fifty miles to the south, Derry was the last refuge of the Williamite cause in Ireland. Governor Lundy estimated that there was only enough food and ammunition to last the city 'for above [*sic*] a week, or ten days at most'. Others would later insist that Lundy was crying foul, claiming there was enough fish and grain to last the garrison for three months.[2] Either way, Lundy felt the need to start making hard decisions. His every action seemed cagey, reserved and defensive.

The day after Clady, Cunningham and his senior officers sat in on Lundy's council of war as requested. Lundy painted a desperate picture: the enemy were thought to have as many as 25,000 men – in truth they had less than a quarter of that number – and were led by veteran French commanders with an arsenal of heavy cannons. Derry, by comparison, was overcrowded and poorly stocked. Lundy was convinced that if the city was besieged it would starve to death and that surrender was now the only feasible option. Before the meeting, Lundy had made sure that only military men would be in attendance. As he laid out his version of the facts to Cunningham and his staff, there was no one there to contradict him. In fact, the only Derry native present was the town clerk. Cunningham, who had been given direct instructions by William to follow Lundy's orders, was not in a position to challenge the governor. One English officer did point out to Lundy that 'in quitting the town, they were quitting the kingdom'. But there was no real dissent. The officers agreed that as 'the enemy will soon possess themselves of this place', there was no point in Cunningham bringing his reinforcements or supplies ashore.[3]

Lundy's thinking was straightforward. He and his officers had sworn loyalty to James when they took their original commissions. Having since taken new oaths to William and Mary – reluctantly or otherwise – they rationally expected that if they fell into Jacobite hands, they would be tried by court martial and shot. James would probably offer mercy to the common folk of Derry, but treason amongst officers was a matter of army discipline. Lundy and several of his subordinates agreed that it would be safest if they 'privately withdraw' from Derry before the city was taken. They also knew that their decision would have to be kept quiet. The town clerk, shuffling awkwardly in his chair, was sworn to secrecy. Outside, the anxiety within the cluttered city was growing thick. After Lundy had locked the gates hundreds of stragglers from Clady were forced to sleep outside the walls. The following day, tempers spilled over. One soldier stuck outside fired his musket at a sentry and warned that if the gates were not opened immediately he would burn them down. Despite orders to the contrary, the portcullis was raised and hundreds of cold, angry and confused soldiers poured into an already paranoid city.[4]

*

D'Avaux's mood had not gotten any better. Annoyed at being dragged across a warzone only to have his advice ignored, the ambassador took it out on his pen. Writing to Versailles, d'Avaux said that James's decisions were becoming increasingly odd and that the king had developed a frustrating habit of forgiving 'without reflection' captured rebel leaders, despite French demands that they be executed.[5] D'Avaux could not understand what others would describe as James's 'over-great indulgence' of the Protestant rebels. Still scarred by accusations that he was a Catholic tyrant, James became 'infatuated with this rotten principle' that showing mercy to Protestants in Ireland would win back the loyalty he had lost in England.[6] It did not go down well with his generals. Pusignan griped under his breath after James refused to let him hang two rebel leaders. D'Avaux wondered why James was so afraid of delivering justice and if his leniency would come back to haunt him.

The king and his cavalcade had reached Omagh when a scout arrived with news that thirteen English ships had been spotted in Lough Foyle. James's optimism received a crack over the head. He suddenly decided that perhaps it was not so wise to be a few miles from the front and chose to ride back towards Charlemont and Dublin 'with what haste he could'. However, on 17 April the Duke of Berwick arrived at his father's retreating camp with some curious intelligence. For some reason, the English reinforcements in Lough Foyle had not come ashore. Having held back his advance from Clady in order to scout the land ahead, Richard Hamilton now felt confident enough to press on and surround Derry. Believing that the city was in no state to survive a siege, Hamilton was confident that the city would agree to terms. If James himself were present at the negotiations, he was sure that the citizens would 'infallibly surrender' without much fuss. A delighted James turned his convoy back around towards Derry. The swift solution to Irish affairs that James and Lord Melfort were banking on seemed to have appeared.[7]

*

Unaware of the fear and fury bubbling up within the walls of Derry, Hamilton decided to open dialogue with the city. A captured Protestant minister was sent through the gates with a message for Lundy; the governor responded by sending out three delegates to the Jacobite camp to discuss formal negotiations. The citizens and local volunteers itching for a fight were not impressed – when the three delegates returned to Derry later that day, the sentries on the walls initially refused to let them in. At the same time, two Protestant gentlemen captured at Charlemont were sent into the city on a Jacobite errand to spread exaggerated rumours about the size and strength of James's army. Both of them were arrested. Meanwhile, some of the garrison's senior officers began to try and sneak out of Derry, with mixed success – one was shot dead by soldiers from his company; another was reportedly chased down to the river and fired on as he scrambled into a waiting boat. Just a week earlier, the city's council of war had issued a declaration stating that any man who refused to fight should be 'deemed a coward'. The rank-and-file took the message seriously. Many began to question the governor's stomach, while others later 'expressed themselves in a ruder manner', calling for Lundy and his officers to be hanged.[8] Colonel Cunningham was secretly approached to replace the wavering Lundy as commander but refused. On 18 April, Cunningham and the rest of his troops sailed out of Lough Foyle accompanied by a number of officers from Lord Mountjoy's old regiment, to the shock of the city folk. Arthur Rawdon, the young rebel commander, had fallen seriously ill and departed with them. When word of Cunningham's withdrawal reached London, there was a gutting realisation that William's ambitions in Ireland – for the foreseeable future, at least – were finished. The new king ordered that no more shipments of weapons or supplies be sent to Derry. There was simply no point.[9]

After sending Cunningham and his reinforcements away, Lundy had stayed behind in Derry to take charge of the surrender. Richard Hamilton had offered straight terms:

if Derry handed over its weapons and horses and opened its gates, the city would be spared. Lundy was given until noon on 18 April to respond; in the meantime, Hamilton promised that his soldiers would not come within four miles of the walls. This was dressed up as an act of clemency, but in truth it was a bluff – Hamilton did not want to reveal how few men, mortars and siege cannons he really had. With a solid offer on the table and a governor intent on surrender, it seemed that the most formidable garrison in Williamite Ulster was about to fold. Then, just hours before Hamilton's deadline, a sequence of sudden and unpredictable events dragged Derry back from the brink.

As the cramped streets began to sweat with arguments about surrender, shouts were heard from the walls that the Jacobite army was approaching, despite Hamilton's assurance that he would keep away. James, unaware of the terms of the truce, was marching towards the south wall and Bishop's Gate with a great body of officers and men, their banners raised high and their drums thumping. From the walls, it looked like Jacobite treachery. Amid panicked cries that the Irish had broken their word, the gunners on the walls opened fire. Cannon and musket shot rained down on the king's vanguard, tearing up earth and ripping through flesh. James had wisely chosen to keep out of firing range but watched in horror as one shot killed an officer just a few yards ahead of him. Confused and afraid for their lives, the king and his host 'took to their heels' and ran away 'in some disorder, and much surprised'.[10] James had been told that Derry would surrender the moment he appeared – his later claim to have been 'baffled' and 'affronted' by the city's violent response was putting things mildly.[11] Berwick later blamed Marshal Rosen for failing to warn the king about the terms of Hamilton's truce. Either way, a breakdown in communication somewhere in the Jacobite command convinced Derry that the Irish could not be trusted. Lundy was indoors preparing to send another delegation to meet with Hamilton when he was told what had happened. He dispatched two riders to the Jacobite camp to beg James's forgiveness. Then, as news of the commotion outside the walls was still rippling through the town, the clerk who had been present at Lundy's secret council of war two days earlier finally broke his silence. The officers' plan to abandon Derry to its fate and send away William's reinforcements was revealed. A riot almost broke out, as the 'great uneasiness and disorder' of the city finally spilled over.[12]

Adam Murray, the officer whose few dozen men had fought hard to hold the bridge at Clady, had since been posted at Culmore Fort, a village a few miles downstream from Derry at the mouth of the Foyle. On 18 April, as the city was shaking with hysteria, Murray and some 400 of his cavalry arrived at Ship Quay Gate, over at the opposite end of the city from where James had been fired on. Murray had heard about the ruckus and had come to investigate. Despite Lundy's orders that no one be allowed into the city, the sentries opened the gate and Murray marched through. Crowds of desperate townsfolk rushed through the streets to greet him, and Murray began to shout with 'vigour and resolution' that he would defend the city. It was at this moment that Murray is believed to have shouted what would become Derry's epitaph: 'No surrender'. According to one account, Murray stormed into Lundy's council meeting and had a furious exchange with the governor about his plans to hand the city over to the enemy. Murray stormed out of the room and refused to return to his post at Culmore. That night, just a few hours before Lundy's delegation was due to ride out and officially offer Derry to the Jacobites, Murray's soldiers posted new sentries on each of the four gates and seized the keys to the city. Murray had effectively staged a coup. His actions were later described as 'the only thing that prevented the surrender of the city to King James'.[13]

Lundy had been deposed and was now afraid to show his face in the street. With the old governor barricaded into his quarters and refusing to have anything more to do with Derry, a council of war was held the following day to select a new leader. Adam Murray was offered the position but turned it down, stating that his place was with the soldiers. Two governors were selected instead: Major Henry Baker, who would command the city garrison, and George Walker, the firebrand Anglican minister, who was put in charge of the city's supplies and civilian population. Locked up in his room, Lundy knew that if he stayed in Derry any longer he would be lynched. Disguised as an ordinary soldier carrying a bundle on his back, he slipped away under the cover of darkness and sailed for Scotland. Baker and Walker, who clearly had enough on their hands, were content to let him escape. When Richard Hamilton's deadline for surrender passed without reply he sent Lord Strabane, a Jacobite nobleman who had travelled with James from France, to offer terms. Adam Murray, who had now been promoted to colonel, met with Strabane outside the walls. As well as a full pardon, freedom of religion and protection for anyone who chose to hand over their arms and leave Derry, Strabane said that James was personally willing to offer Murray £1,000 and a senior commission in the Jacobite army. Murray rejected the offer. Roughly 1,000 ordinary Protestants, most of them women and children, took advantage of the change in government and left Derry, unwilling to be caught in the carnage that was about to begin.

James set up a new field command post at St Johnston, far away from the city cannons, and held his own council of war. D'Avaux, Melfort, Berwick, Rosen, Hamilton, Pusignan and Maumont were all present. The king, still shaken by his disastrous episode before the walls, announced that he was returning to Dublin to prepare for the upcoming parliament. He instructed that Derry be placed under siege. As Rosen would be returning to Dublin with him, James left Lieutenant General Maumont in charge of the siege instead of Richard Hamilton, because he was the elder of the two. Hamilton, who had successfully led the Ulster campaign so far, would now have to take orders from a Frenchman. With that, James departed for the capital. Throughout the Jacobite lines, soldiers spoke with confidence that Derry was 'a place of no strength ... full of divisions and subject to no command' and would fall quickly.[14] Higher up the chain, however, the mood was not so sure. The Jacobites had barely 5,000 men, and their lack of weapons, artillery and experience was a problem. The army, Berwick later admitted, was 'not prepared for a siege'.[15]

*

Four hundred miles away from the scorched glens of Ulster, William was buried in paperwork. James's name was currently being scrubbed from every official prayer for the king's health; likewise, all mentions of the monarch in the courts, parliament and legal papers were being amended to refer to the new co-regents. William's letters, meanwhile, were still eating up the better part of his time. Messages of congratulations were flowing in from the likes of the Prince of Brunswick, and these all had to be acknowledged; from Berlin the ambitious Elector of Brandenburg, Frederick Hohenzollern, sent praise for what 'all Protestants, indeed all Europe, have received by your means'. Then, a messenger arrived unannounced at Whitehall with startling news from Ireland. The people of Derry had deposed Robert Lundy for the 'treachery' of sending away William's reinforcements. The town had chosen new leaders who were 'resolving to defend the place'.[16] With the instinct of a general reacting to some sudden twitch on the battlefield, William immediately ordered that fresh soldiers and provisions be sent with all speed to Derry. Written instructions flew down the chain of command like a condor – officers were selected, supplies were sourced and the admiralty began pulling ships together for the voyage. The demand for urgency was hammered in at every turn. William knew what the consequences would be for Ireland, England and his war in Europe if Derry were captured. But even with this dramatic turn of events, the odds were harsh. The Earl of Nottingham, who had defected from James and was now one of William's secretaries of state, wrote that despite the renewed resolve to rescue Derry, he feared 't'will be too late'.[17]

17

Cruel Consistency

They started by pulling up the streets beneath their feet. Before the impact of Jacobite mortars and bombs could start blowing paving slabs into shrapnel, the city governors ordered that they be taken up. There was now nothing between Derry and the earth below, waiting to swallow it. Elsewhere, cannons were mounted on the tower of St Columb's Cathedral and the central market house, while extra guns were fixed on each of the city's four gates. Every square yard of the walls was divided up between different companies of soldiers who were given orders to defend their post to the death. Makeshift timber parapets were lashed together to provide cover from bullets and grenades. The surplus paving slabs were passed up to the walls and smashed, ready to be flung down on any enemy head that came too close. Derry was a hive of terrified activity as soldiers and civilians rushed past each other carrying bullets and gunpowder to the walls or stuffing away furniture and possessions in cellars. Every house and outbuilding beyond the city walls had been torched to prevent the Jacobites from taking shelter. All life had retreated inside the walls, and in that crowded square mile of space thousands of people now wrestled with defiance and terror. No one knew how, where or when the Jacobite attack would begin. All they could do was pray and prepare.

*

Maumont rolled out his map and studied the twists and turns of the Foyle. Every pathway, every mark of high ground and every tricky inlet was noted. Finally, he tapped his finger on Culmore Fort, which guarded the mouth of the river some five miles downstream from Derry. Adam Murray and his regiment had been guarding the post, but since Murray's return to the city it was effectively unguarded. Maumont knew that control of Culmore would allow him to cut off the mouth of the river and deny Derry its only lifeline. He quickly drew up over 1,000 cavalry and infantry and marched north to the fort with Berwick and Pusignan in tow. Isolated from the city garrison and startled by such a sudden show of Jacobite force, the senior officer at Culmore surrendered without firing a shot.

The Jacobites were thinking on their feet. The army had first marched into Ulster expecting a few victories in the field, followed by a relatively tidy surrender. They did not expect to have to lay siege to a city and were ill equipped for the task. Maumont had no heavy cannons to batter down the walls, and the Irish troops had no experience of the mathematical attrition of siege warfare, save for the handful that had fought on the continent. Maumont did not have sappers or tunnelling equipment; even if he did, the marshy flood plain that Derry was built on would make it next to impossible to dig a path up to the walls. Maumont had been promised that heavy weapons and fresh supplies would be sent from Dublin quickly, but until then he would have to improvise. He set up a battery of small cannons and field mortars across the river, opposite the city's Ferry Quay Gate. When the bombardment began on Sunday

21 April, it barely made a dent. One man inside the city was killed by an exploding shell, while some brickwork on the market house was damaged. Incendiary bombs were fired over the walls, but many landed harmlessly after their fuses were blown out by the wind in flight. The only real damage to the city was psychological – the whistle of incoming mortar fire and those terrifying few seconds before impact were 'frightful to our people', one eyewitness wrote.[1]

After capturing Culmore, Maumont had drawn up his lines in a wide arc around the landward west bank of Derry, roughly two miles long. The same day that the bombardment began from across the river, a party of over 1,000 infantrymen and cavalry sallied out from the city and clashed with Jacobite soldiers who had just dug in around the village of Pennyburn, just outside Derry on the road to Culmore. The Jacobites were caught off guard. Most of the Irish cavalry had set their horses out to graze; the only mounted troops nearby were Maumont and his senior officers, who were out scouting the terrain when the alarm was raised. The French commander, the Duke of Berwick and a party of colonels and lieutenants raced towards Pennyburn and the Foyle shoreline, their stomachs in knots. Murray's cavalry were looping around behind Pennyburn and were about to overrun the Jacobite positions when Maumont and his horsemen crashed into them. Horses screamed and tumbled, muskets cracked and sabres sliced into metal and flesh, all hidden by a blinding fog of gun smoke. The shouts of pain and fury were terrifying. Murray and Maumont were swept towards each other in the confusion, swinging and wrestling. The Jacobites were outnumbered, but Maumont's unexpected charge had rattled Murray's advance. The Williamite horsemen begin to pull back. Then, somewhere in the madness, a bullet flew into Maumont's head and killed him instantly. Unaware that their commander was dead, the Jacobite officers chased Murray's horsemen back towards the wall. They were riding into a trap. Murray had left lines of infantry to cover his retreat, and as the Irish cavalry flew after him they were caught in a sudden hail of shot. The Jacobites were forced to turn back with heavy casualties. The Duke of Berwick escaped but later wrote that every last man who rode into the trap was either wounded or had his horse shot from under him. Murray, who had been cut off from the rest of his cavalry, narrowly made it back into the city alive. Accounts of the death toll at Pennyburn vary, with the Williamites claiming to have killed as many as 200 men while losing only nine or ten of their own. Berwick, as was his style, later downplayed the whole thing, claiming that fewer than ten of his troopers had been killed in a 'not considerable' skirmish.[2] But the loss of Maumont, who had led the charge and fought 'gallantly' before his death, was a disastrous blow to the Jacobites. The siege was barely a few hours old, but their general was already dead.[3]

Pennyburn had been a vicious introduction for the Jacobite troops. They now had to assume that their every move was being scrutinised from the walls and that the Williamites would pounce on the slightest weakness and strike out from the gates. Four days after the skirmish that claimed Maumont's life, Adam Murray rode out from Butcher's Gate once more with a large party of soldiers to attack Pennyburn again. The fighting dragged on for hours, and about 500 Jacobite troops who had been billeted in the hamlet were driven from ditch to ditch. They were 'in danger of being totally routed' until Robert Ramsay, a Scottish brigade commander, charged into Murray's flank just before dusk. Murray and his men were forced back towards the walls again, chased all the way by the French major general Pusignan and his cavalry. During the scramble Pusignan was shot and died from his wounds a few days later. The Duke of Berwick also had to be carried from the fray after suffering a serious bruise to his spine that had to be bled with a knife. Pennyburn remained in Jacobite hands, but once more it had claimed the life of a French commander. Both Maumont and Pusignan had been killed in less than a week, 'the first sacrifices of quality' at Derry.[4] Having been passed over for command just a few days earlier, Richard Hamilton was now in charge by default. For all his luck and popularity with the Irish troops, Hamilton had no experience of directing a siege. He would have little time to learn on the job.

*

The mortars kept screeching over the river, but now the bombs were starting to explode. One blew through a roof and killed an old woman upstairs in her home. Another struck a house where several officers were dining on the ground floor, killing the landlord and blowing a massive hole in the wall. The cannons on the city walls fired back across the river, killing one Jacobite artilleryman and damaging several mortar guns. As the bombardment of the city intensified, the civilian governor George Walker ordered that all barrels of gunpowder be stashed in cellars or at the bottom of dry wells to prevent a lucky shot from blowing up half of Derry. The city leadership did what they could to keep discipline intact. Patrols and watch duty were kept on rigorous schedules, while homes were searched and all surplus food was taken to the central storehouses. Rations of salmon, beef and oatmeal were divided up, while Anglican and Presbyterian ministers took turns using St Columb's Cathedral for their daily services. However, life under siege began to blacken spirits. Presbyterian ministers grumbled that they received no extra pay or rations for their services, while the Anglican ministers did. Tempers also began to fray in the city command – a 'tedious' argument between the military governor Henry Baker and the hot-headed English colonel John Mitchelburne, a veteran of Mountjoy and Lundy's regiment, turned into a scuffle and

Mitchelburne was briefly confined to his quarters.[5] All the while, the mortars kept falling, and the Jacobites continued to trundle around menacingly beyond the walls. On 5 May, they finally made their move.

Half a mile outside Bishop's Gate on the south wall, there was an old windmill on a small hill 'half a cannon shot' from the city. Windmill Hill, as the locals knew it, was a tempting prize. If heavy cannons could be mounted on it, the Jacobites would have almost the entire city in their line of fire, including the great symbolic spire of St Columb's. Back when he still had some shred of fight in him, Robert Lundy had ordered the construction of a large fort, known as a ravelin, just beyond the south wall as an extra line of defence between the windmill and the city. However, in the pitch dark early hours of 6 May, as Robert Ramsay and a small group of Jacobite soldiers crept up to capture the hill, the place was unguarded. Richard Hamilton was still waiting on the siege cannons that had been promised from Dublin; he already knew where he wanted to put them when they arrived.

As the sun rose a few hours later, the sentries on the city walls looked out in shock and saw Ramsay's men drawn up along the hill, digging trenches and piling up earth. With the river to their right and some inky marsh on their left, the Jacobites would be almost impossible to dislodge if they were allowed to dig in. It was a worrying thought for Baker and Walker, who needed to move quickly. Ten men from every company in the city were called up, and at 4 a.m. the next morning 1,000 soldiers silently snuck out from Bishop's and Ferry Quay gates, crept up towards Windmill Hill and launched a surprise attack. Many of the Jacobites were asleep in half-dug trenches when the gunfire erupted. Musket shots came first, then the thuds and screams of men wrestling, stabbing and gouging each other 'from ditch to ditch'.[6] Faced with a furious assault from what seemed like 'the whole town sallying out upon him', Ramsay's lines broke.[7] As Ramsay tried to rally his men, he was shot and killed. The fighting was close and gruesome – clubs, bayonets, pikes and a thick wave of musket shot. Between 150 and 200 Jacobites were killed, most of them 'shot through the breast or head' at close range.[8] Up to 500 more were wounded, and roughly 300 who were too mangled to crawl or limp away were left on the hill to bleed to death for days, moaning with pain and thirst. As well as Robert Ramsay, the Jacobites lost 'several officers of distinction' in the fight who were either 'mortally wounded' or dragged into Derry as prisoners. The Williamites, meanwhile, claimed to have suffered as few as three fatalities, as well as capturing five Jacobite regimental banners – prized trophies of war. In their flight the Jacobites had also left behind dozens of shovels and pickaxes, which the city garrison immediately put to work by building earthworks and digging trenches of their own. They were going to need them.

*

Three skirmishes, three dead commanders: the deaths of Maumont, Pusignan and Ramsay rattled the Jacobite army, which had previously charged across Ulster with barely a scratch. With still no sign of any heavy artillery coming up the road, Hamilton decided to hold his lines and regroup, content to blockade the city and keep peppering mortars onto its rooftops. The Duke of Berwick admitted that they had been taken aback by the 'obstinacy, number and bravery' of the city's soldiers in the opening days of the fight.[9] For the rest of May, the siege slipped into a rotten stalemate coloured by potshots and sniper fire. Every now and then there would be a sally from the gates and a small skirmish; shots and curses would be exchanged and the Williamite troops would race back into the city. The Jacobites threw up tons of earth, moved massive stones and lashed together timber beams to build up defences around their own lines. Hamilton pushed his headquarters to within two miles of the city to tighten the blockade. The smaller cannons and mortars kept firing.

Behind the walls, the traumatised people of the stinking city found shelter from the bombs and the wet summer wherever they could – in cellars, doorways, pantries and outhouses. Food was scarce, and sleep was a luxury. Dysentery – the dreaded 'bloody flux' brought on by foul drinking water – began to claim its first victims. With the street slabs pulled up, Derry's muddy thoroughfares began to fester with waste, bringing a river of sickness to every door. Wells inside the city became 'muddy and troubled' from damage and overuse, forcing many to take their chances with three public wells just outside the walls.[10] With Jacobite snipers and patrols everywhere, fetching water became a dangerous game: one man had a bottle shot out of his hand as he was drinking from it. As rations began to dwindle, hunger ate away at people's patience. Arguments and scraps broke out, often between mutually distrustful Presbyterians and Anglicans. At the end of May 'above a hundred officers' – many of them Presbyterians – approached Governor Baker with accusations that his civilian counterpart, George Walker, had been hoarding supplies, sending secret messages to the Jacobites and indulging in unnamed 'personal vices'.[11] There was probably little truth to it, but Baker did not want a revolt on his hands. He took control of the city's supplies away from Walker and handed it to a new fourteen-man council. Baker then told the agitators to leave it at that. The 'contagious distemper' rotting away behind the walls was doing more damage to Derry than any Jacobite bombs.[12]

*

In the first week of June, the heavy cannons that had been painstakingly dragged up from Dublin finally arrived at the front lines. Hamilton immediately ordered the construction of a new battery in an orchard on the east bank of the Foyle, and the shelling of the city across the water intensified. Bombs stuffed with gunpowder weighing as much as nineteen stone each began to pulverise buildings day and night, driving terrified people out of their homes for the cover of the walls. The shattering explosions 'ploughed up our streets, and broke down our houses'.[13] Cannonballs ripped through roof beams and bricks, and the horrific cries of maimed men and women became the chorus of Derry. One single bomb blew fourteen men to pieces and set fire to two barrels of gunpowder; another blast killed seven men in an instant. Explosions and shrapnel killed two officers and a surgeon. Dozens of civilians died in the barrage. In the first thirteen days of June, a total of 217 Jacobite artillery rounds landed on Derry with cruel consistency. It was the most ferocious shelling of the entire siege.[14]

Galvanised by the arrival of the heavy cannons, Hamilton decided to re-take Windmill Hill. Since the first battle a month earlier, the Williamites had built a new network of trenches from the bogside to the river, guarded by earthworks so high they could only be scaled by ladders. On the morning of 4 June, thousands of Jacobite soldiers drew up in three sections beyond the windmill and began to march. With the river at low tide, Jacobite cavalry galloped along the edge of the water and 'charged furiously' at the defenders' left flank.[15] The bulk of the Jacobite infantry sprinted straight up the road towards the hill in the middle with 'pikes in hand', while the crack grenadier assault troops attacked the Williamites' right flank by the bog, flinging crude metal explosives into the trenches and firing until the air was choked with powder.[16] The Williamites replied with volleys of musket fire from behind their thick and stubborn defences. All across the line, the Jacobites roared 'dreadful shrieks and howlings' as they flung themselves at their enemy.[17] Down by the water, the Jacobite cavalry raced towards the high lip of the Williamite trenches. Edmund Butler, the son of an Irish nobleman, led the charge and drove his horse up over the ditch but was knocked off his mount and captured. Another officer from Tipperary charged after him, but his horse was shot dead as it leapt through the air and he barely scrambled away alive. The Jacobite cavalry failed to fight their way over the ditch. Having beaten back the first wave of attacks by the river, the Williamites roared in defiance, climbed out of their trenches and chased the enemy cavalry away with pikes and muskets. Further up the line, the Jacobite infantry had reached the earthworks in the centre but were pinned down by rapid and ceaseless gunfire. The mounds of earth were too high to climb, and any man caught without cover was shot to pieces by the defenders above them. The Jacobite grenadiers by the bog, meanwhile, were 'vigorously repulsed'.[18] The fighting dragged on for several blood-soaked hours until the Jacobites finally withdrew. It had been a grizzly day's work for both sides. The attackers lost anywhere between 200 and 400 men. The Williamites, bracketed by tall and thick earthworks, survived with far fewer deaths but some sickening injuries: one captain had his arm shattered by a cannonball and died three weeks later; another soldier had all the flesh torn from his calf by an explosion but somehow survived. A bullet grazed another colonel's cheek; while a captain survived despite being shot in the back and having a bomb explode in front of him. Hamilton and his troops were starting to run out of ideas. 'The tradesmen of Londonderry have more skill in their defence than the great officers of the Irish army in their attacks', one Jacobite grudgingly noted.[19]

News of the failed assault on Windmill Hill was met with irritation in Dublin and Paris. James, who had confidently expected Derry to be captured by now, decided to send the senior French commander Marshal Rosen north with fresh troops to speed things up. A downhearted Lord Melfort wrote to Richard Hamilton expressing sympathy for 'the loss of so many brave men' and reassured him that he would soon find a way to be 'master of that rebellious town'.[20] In Versailles, Louvois smacked his fist on his desk as d'Avaux's letters arrived with news about Maumont, Pusignan and the lack of progress. Having always doubted if James was worth so much French effort, he sent a pessimistic reply. 'If Londonderry cannot be reduced it would be as well not to leave the troops to perish before it.'[21]

*

Of all the things Derry was being starved of, information was what it craved the most. A messenger to London had managed to make it out of the city just before the siege, but since then there had been no news from Enniskillen, Whitehall or anywhere else. What little intelligence the Williamites did receive came from enemy prisoners or letters rummaged from the pockets of dead Jacobites. Since William's last promise of support, there had been nothing. Then, on 7 June, three English sails appeared on the horizon in Lough Foyle. The messenger who had snuck out of Derry before the Jacobites surrounded the city had told William about Lundy, Baker, Murray and the city's defiance. William immediately ordered that a relief force be sent to Derry as quickly as possible. The logistics were not easy – the royal army had been scattered during William's invasion and the better part of what remained, including Lieutenant General John Churchill, now the Earl of Marlborough, had since been sent to the fight in Flanders. Nevertheless, by the end of May four battalions of English troops had been rustled together and were ready to sail for Derry under the command of Major General Percy Kirke. Rough seas had delayed their departure, but by early June Kirke had rounded the Isle of Man and the ships were heading towards the Ulster coast. Three small scout vessels were sent ahead into Lough Foyle before Kirke's main fleet of twenty-four transports and three frigates arrived. On 7 June the three scouts sailed towards the mouth of the Foyle but came under fire from Jacobite cannons at Culmore. Word raced down to the main Jacobite camp, and pieces of heavy artillery were hauled up to Culmore to brace the river mouth. The English scout vessels limped away. Hamilton knew what was coming next. If scouts were suddenly appearing in Lough Foyle, a full relief fleet would not be far behind. The Jacobite commander diverted several of his heavy cannons away from the city to fatten up the battery at Culmore and ordered the French military engineer, the Marquis of Pointis, to drag a great timber boom, lashed together with ropes and chains, across the river as a floating barricade halfway between Derry and Lough Foyle.

The sight of three sets of sails on the horizon was a vision of hope for Derry, which was growing more decrepit by the day. Food was now so scarce that horses were being eaten, while rampant disease had 'destroyed many of the garrison'.[22] In one day alone fifteen officers had died of fever and dysentery.[23] The military governor, Henry Baker, who had worked so hard to keep Derry's rival factions from each other's throats, fell ill and began to deteriorate rapidly. By early June the city's standing army of almost 7,500 men and officers had fallen to just over 6,000 and was shrinking every day. The Jacobite army had yet to make a dent in the walls, but Derry was dying on its feet. Then, on 13 June, almost two months into the siege, thousands of tired and bloodied men on both sides of the walls were gripped by a 'mighty consternation' as they looked down river and saw dozens of sails in the distance. Kirke had arrived.[24]

18

Dividing the Skin

On the banks of a different river the days did not pass to a melody of mortars and screams, but rather the clop and rattle of carriages, the bows and ruffled chatter of gentlemen and the scraping of quills on historic, wishful pieces of paper. Dublin was full of gossip about the latest news from Derry, but it was a world away from its sewers of dysentery, its charred ruins and its hillsides decorated with corpses. Before the gates of Derry James had survived a violent and awkward exchange with one part of Ireland. Almost 140 miles south, in the capital, he was now preparing for another. After a meticulous power grab under the Duke of Tyrconnell, the stage was finally set. The parliament of 1689 was about to begin.

On 7 May, just hours after Robert Ramsay and the Jacobites had been beaten back in the first battle of Windmill Hill, the doors of the great hall at King's Inns on the north bank of the River Liffey swung open, and a procession of royal footmen strode towards the head of the room. James followed in lush ceremonial robes, wearing a new crown that had been made for him in Dublin. The floor was thronged with gentlemen and lords in pristine formal attire, and when the king reached the speaker's chair he began to read a carefully worded address. Scanning the hall, he thanked the delegates for 'the exemplary loyalty which this nation express'd to me, at a time when others … so basely betrayed me'. Conscious that his words would travel further than just the back of the room, James spoke of himself as a tortured liberator, a man whose desire for religious freedom had seen his enemies 'set themselves up against me'. Gathering himself, he then addressed the reason why most people were here – the land settlement of Ireland. James could sense the itch for retribution in the room but urged restraint. He stated that he would approve any laws that would be 'for the good of the nation', provided they were also 'consistent with reason, justice and the public good'. Despite the king's obvious call for caution, if someone had thrown copies of the Acts of Settlement and Explanation onto the floor at that very moment, they would have been trampled on and thrown into a fireplace. This was Tyrconnell's parliament, packed with Old-English Catholic lords and gentry who had waited a generation to get their lands back. Restraint was going to be a tough sell.[1]

It seemed as if every step in Tyrconnell's political career had led to this moment. He had elbowed and charmed his way into high office, chopped up the Irish judiciary, handpicked sheriffs, redrawn charters and flexed his muscle everywhere he could. This was to be his zenith – a gerrymandered Catholic parliament in Dublin that could not only tear up the land settlement but also completely sever Ireland's legal, economic and moral submission to England. With more than a hint of historical gravitas, the session of 1689 would be remembered as the 'Patriot Parliament'. Tyrconnell was not alone in picturing what would emerge at the other side: an independent Irish kingdom, free from penal laws and English tariffs, loyal by choice to James Stuart and his Catholic heir. Ironically, one of the biggest obstacles to this vision would be

James Stuart himself. With Lord Melfort in his ear and a firm belief in English power in his heart, James would spend the parliamentary session grumbling, protesting and fighting to keep Irish passions in check.

The timing, of course, was delicate. Derry and Enniskillen were still holding out, and rumours began to swirl that William and his army commander, Frederick Schomberg, were preparing to invade. One week before parliament opened the French fleet that had ferried James to Ireland had completed its round trip and returned to the Cork coast with some 3,000 Jacobite soldiers, a fresh batch of officers and more muskets and money. However, just as the French fleet of some thirty-two frigates and transports was nearing Kinsale, a knot of English sails was spotted in the distance. A fleet of twenty-two ships sent by William to patrol the Irish coast had stumbled upon the French. Admiral Chateaurenault, the commander of the French expedition, took the wind and sailed away around the south-west tip of Cork and up into Bantry Bay. The French ships deposited their cargoes and waited. The English fleet, under the command of Arthur Herbert – the man who had delivered to The Hague William's famous invitation to invade England – spent two days scouring every nook in the coast before finally creeping into Bantry Bay on 1 May. The French immediately opened fire, and the English shot back. Cannonballs cracked into hulls, and sharpshooters skimmed musket fire across their enemy's decks. Outmanoeuvred and unable to match the French firepower, Herbert withdrew. Neither side lost any ships, and the result was inconclusive. By body count alone, it had been a French victory: Chateaurenault had lost forty men; Herbert had lost ninety-six. It was a strange skirmish that captured the jumbled nature of this new conflict: even as their sailors were murdering each other in Irish waters, England and France were still technically at peace with each other. Likewise, the only man in Dublin who did not celebrate the reports of a French victory was James, whose heart still belonged to the English navy from his time as first lord of the admiralty. James publicly ordered a *Te Deum* to be sung in celebration but was privately miffed. He had become obsessed with avoiding anything that might offend English opinion – he had a gut feeling that the battle of Bantry Bay had just stirred up offence again, days before parliament began in Dublin.[2]

*

The parliamentary session ran from 7 May until 20 July, straddling some of the most crucial weeks of the conflict. Later, when the men who survived it all sat down to write their stories, the timing of the parliament was not lost on anyone. As the siege of Derry sank into stalemate, the better part of Ireland's gentry, lords and many officers were tied up 'wrangling about settling the kingdom' before it was theirs to settle.[3] Both the Commons and Lords had Catholic majorities, but this did not mean that their business would be concluded quickly. Arguments and 'vain consultations' went on for hours[4] while behind the scenes d'Avaux and Melfort tried to bend James's opinions about debates on the floor. For James, the context was clear: he was completely broke and needed the Irish parliament to grant him a subsidy. But in return, the parliament wanted a great deal. Tyrconnell did not take up his seat in the House of Lords, citing illness, but it was whispered around town that he was sulking, unhappy at being kicked out of James's circle. It mattered little. The lord deputy had planned things so minutely that parliament would do what he wanted without him. The attorney general and Tyrconnell's close ally, Richard Nagle, was speaker of the commons and controlled the flow of the debates. Lieutenant General Justin MacCarthy, another Tyrconnell man, was named Viscount Mountcashel and took up a seat in the House of Lords. Thomas Nugent, the Catholic judge, was granted the title of Baron Riverston and did likewise. The House of Commons, meanwhile, was jammed with men who had seen their fathers' lands confiscated after 1641 and were baying for retribution. Patrick Sarsfield was chosen as a delegate for County Dublin but did not attend, as he had been sent north to occupy Sligo and harass the Williamite lines near Enniskillen. Ulster, meanwhile, was a batch of empty seats – there were no delegates at all from counties Londonderry, Fermanagh and Donegal. But despite the majority of Catholics from old Norman families, dissent still found a way to creep in. Many 'new interest' Catholic gentry who had bought property from Cromwell's adventurers now worried that land reform would see them lose everything; likewise, a handful of Protestant delegates in both houses spoke up whenever they could. The respected Bishop of Meath, for example, made 'a long and elaborate speech' against repealing the Act of Settlement, claiming that it would disturb the kingdom and injure the Protestant merchants and landowners who 'paid the greatest part' of the king's taxes. James quietly shared his opinion. The bishop likewise warned that arguing over property rights while Derry was not subdued was like 'dividing the skin before the beast was catched [*sic*]'.[5]

As the weeks passed and the floor of the Commons became a battleground between the moderate and the extreme, James's conservative opinions tugged away at the edges. He blocked an act that would have done away with Poynings' law, the old medieval corset that required all Irish legislation to be approved in London. James's fingerprints could also be seen on the laws dealing with religion: freedom of worship was enshrined and the oaths of allegiance were scrapped, and although Catholics would no longer have to pay tithes to Protestant ministers, Protestant bishops would be allowed to keep their churches and property. Unsurprisingly, this did not go down well. James and his advisors also came up with a novel solution to the wartime currency shortage: on 18 June he issued a decree that coins should be minted out of brass and copper, instead of silver and gold. These new shilling, sixpence, crown and half-crown pieces were to carry James's face and insignia, and their value would fluctuate wildly in the months ahead. Years later, the 'brass money' was derided as 'an utter and unavoidable ruin' and a fitting symbol of James's reign.[6]

Then there was the Act of Settlement: the great curse of the Irish gentry, forged by Cromwell and sealed by Charles. In the early summer of 1689, it was a vice squeezing James from both sides. As well as his reluctance to give up his huge personal portfolio of Irish estates, James could not shake his deep belief that Ireland was a subject kingdom and that its wealth belonged to England. It was thought that James had planned to publicly declare his support for the land laws shortly after arriving in Kinsale but had been wisely talked out of it by d'Avaux and Tyrconnell. Now, as the settlement was being dismembered on the floor of the Commons, all James could do was shake his head and quietly support the Bishop of Meath and other dissenters. He was too weak to do anything else, and it showed. A law repealing both the Acts of Settlement and explanation was passed through both houses, despite some qualms in the Lords. D'Avaux urged James to sign off on the repeal, most likely because Versailles believed that France would become Ireland's main trading partner if the kingdom's wealth and laws were placed in Catholic hands.

The repeal act returned all estates to whoever owned them prior to the rebellion of October 1641. The worried 'new interest' Catholics who had bought confiscated property were to be compensated with lands taken from a long list of Williamites named in a separate act of attainder. If the repeal act was built on old grudges, the act of attainder was a much fresher sort of hatred. It named a host of defectors, such as the new Duke of Ormonde, as traitors. Other Protestants who had simply fled Ireland out of fear were told that if they did not return by 1 October and affirm loyalty to James, their property would be confiscated. It was rough justice built 'to satisfy the humours' of an angry, buoyant Catholic majority.[7] James had no choice but to approve both acts, as the belief that they would have their family's lands restored was the main reason almost every Catholic gentleman in Ireland had stood by him. James's biographer later claimed that if he had not agreed to the Act of Repeal, 'the whole nation would abandon him'.[8] The Act of Attainder, meanwhile, was not a million miles from James's own sentiments. On 28 June, in order to harden the message, he issued a new decree against William and all his supporters, labelling his son-in-law a 'usurper' backed up by a 'pretended parliament' filled with 'rebellious men'.[9] The Dublin parliament granted James a subsidy of £20,000 a month for the next thirteen months. It was more than he had asked for, but the new taxes levied to pay for it would prove difficult to collect in wartime. Tyrconnell, meanwhile, was granted his own annual stipend of £20,000 from the proceeds of confiscated Williamite estates. The Irish parliament had been hot, drawn out and provocative, but as it closed on 20 July its members had agreed – at least in theory – that they would all be richer for it.

*

It had taken years of divisive work, driven at the last by Lord Tyrconnell, for Catholic Ireland to finally wash away the land laws. But now, in this moment of apparent triumph, no one could have predicted what came next. Instead of rallying to the front lines at Derry to finish the job, many gentlemen soldiers in the Commons scattered away from Dublin and returned to their ancestral estates. Officers began touring and inspecting their old properties instead of returning to their regiments. Some even settled in and took up residence in vacated or confiscated manors. 'Every one quitted his command to enter upon his estate, to settle his house, and improve his fortune,' noted a disgusted John Stevens, who had arrived in Ireland with Chateaurenault's fleet.[10] Most members of the Catholic gentry had taken commissions in Tyrconnell's army to fight for their family's inheritance. Now that this seemed to have been won back, many of them lost interest. Captains who might have been leading patrols at Pennyburn, defending the river at Culmore or otherwise leading the fight at Derry instead chose 'the actual enjoyment of an estate, without hazard to life'.[11] As the siege dragged on miserably, many disillusioned Jacobite soldiers began to desert without officers to stop them. John Stevens, who arrived at the front lines in Derry after an exhausting march north, wrote in his diary that he and the other reinforcements 'only made up for those that daily deserted'.[12] On 24 July the lack of discipline had become so rank that Lord Melfort was forced to issue a decree on James's behalf warning that all officers who were not back at their posts within fifteen days would be hanged.[13]

The ripples continued. For a man who had been so sensitive to Protestant opinion, it was odd for James to approve the fierce terms of the act of attainder. Even if he did wish to punish those who had deserted him, the clauses affecting Protestants who had simply fled Ireland in fear were stark. If there were truly any Irish Protestants still sympathetic to the deposed king, their loyalty no longer made sense. In reality, most had already switched their allegiance to William. However, the Act of Attainder had made it irreversibly black and white. The Dublin parliament had sought to alter the destiny of a kingdom. Its delegates had sketched a future where Ireland's Norman gentry would reclaim their historic place of wealth, status and power at the king's side. But as the lords and leading men of Jacobite Ireland spent more than two months staring wishfully at the horizon, they did not see the chasm opening at their feet. The siege of Derry was allowed to drift on with 'neither cannon to batter down the walls, nor mortars to demolish the habitations, nor ladders for scaling, nor any attempt made for undermining'.[14] General Kirke's relief force had sailed into Lough Foyle, and from across the Irish Sea the rumours of a full invasion by William's army gathered speed. Precious time and effort had been spent arguing over legal syntax when there was a war to be won. Jacobite historians would rue the lost opportunity. The Protestant clergyman William King later wrote that if James and his men had chosen to press their advantage and crush Derry, 'nobody can tell what might have been'.[15]

19

This, I Hope, Will be Your Destiny

When the sun rose in the morning it looked down on a wasteland of filth and starvation, cut apart by craters and trenches. On both sides of the walls men were living from hour to hour, wondering when fever or hunger or a bullet would take them. At night the weary sentries at Butcher's Gate and Windmill Hill would grip their muskets, stare out into the dark and wait. In the morning the sun would rise over the wet desert and the cycle would begin fresh. Derry was locked in a brutal impasse, and somewhere in those trenches and piles of burning rubble the future of Ireland was waiting to be claimed, cloaked in the stink of gunpowder and half-buried corpses.

Kirke's fleet had arrived in Lough Foyle on 13 June, but the Jacobite blockade had prevented him from getting any messages through to the city. Unsure of what was happening inland, and unwilling to attack the timber boom across the river, Kirke decided to hold tight. It was a decision that 'extremely troubled' the sick and starving city.[1] Rosen reached the Jacobite camp on

20 June but his attempts to whip the lethargic siege into action had little success. The Jacobite lines were pushed forward, their cannons were rearranged and their trench digging was stepped up, but the thick walls and marshy ground were tough obstacles. On 28 June 1,500 Jacobite reinforcements led by the Earl of Clancarty assaulted Butcher's Gate and managed to storm a cellar beneath one of the bastions. Before they could pack it with gunpowder and blow it to pieces, the defenders replied with a counter attack and the Jacobites were beaten back with heavy losses. Inside the walls, men were dying briskly. The military governor Henry Baker succumbed to his illness, leaving a void in the city command. A 'prudent and resolute' man, Baker had helped keep Derry's rival factions from lynching each other during the first two months of the siege.[2] The English colonel John Mitchelburne, who had once come to blows with Baker but had since reconciled, was named deputy governor in Baker's final days and took temporary charge of military affairs after his death. Mitchelburne would find his own place in history, most notably through his defiant hoisting of a red flag on the walls in full view of the Jacobite lines. But he would pay the cost: his wife and seven children would all perish during the siege. After Baker's death the city commanders planned to meet and elect a new permanent governor, but they never got the chance. Survival was a far more pressing matter.[3]

At the end of June Richard Hamilton, who was still technically in charge of the siege despite Rosen's arrival, fired a written message over the walls inside an empty shell. He promised the garrison that they would keep their lives and property and would enjoy religious freedom if they surrendered. When no reply came back, Rosen sent an ultimatum. Furious with how the siege of this small and starving city had been allowed to linger on for over two months, the French marshal sent another message over the walls on Sunday, 30 June. If the city had not agreed to start negotiating by 6 p.m. the following day he would seize every Protestant man, woman and child he could find in Ulster – whether they had accepted James's protection or not – and herd them up to the walls of Derry like cattle. If the garrison did not open their gates and let them in, they would 'be forced to see their friends and nearest relations all starved' in front of their eyes. Rosen then warned that he would burn every house, mill and farm in the north, and when the city of Derry was finally broken he would show 'no quarter, or spare either age or sex'. He meant every word of it.[4]

Inside the city the exhausted soldiers had to watch Kirke's fleet sit just out of reach downriver, like a dying man staring at an oasis. The garrison tried desperately to communicate with the relief fleet but failed. Flags were waved from the top of St Columb's, but Kirke's ships did not know the code. Adam Murray along with over twenty men tried to sneak upstream in a boat but were intercepted on the water by Jacobites. A miniature sea battle took place in the middle of the Foyle, as dinghies clattered into each other and soldiers were shot and hacked over the sides. Murray had a lucky escape after two bullets hit his helmet but did not pierce the metal. Elsewhere, a volunteer from the city snuck out into the countryside with a message and disappeared; two days later the Jacobites hung a man in full view of the walls, laughing that the messenger did not get far. When messengers did manage to run the gauntlet and sneak into the city, it was almost impossible to find a way back. Every twist of the river was being watched, and Jacobite patrols covered every scrap of ground between Derry and Culmore. Without dialogue with the city, Kirke could do little but wait.[5]

On 2 July, after Rosen's deadline had passed without a reply, the old general made good on his threat. With faint echoes of Portadown in 1641, crowds of Protestant men, women and children that had been rounded up from the local countryside were corralled together and driven up towards the walls at gunpoint. The exact numbers are disputed – one Williamite account claimed there were 'some thousands of them'; others saw fewer. It did not matter. Bawling masses of people 'under great distresses' were forced up to the gates at gunpoint.[6] Some edgy and confused sentries on the walls, unaware of what they were seeing, opened fire on the crowd but missed. Rosen watched in the distance, believing that if hundreds of people were driven into the city, its food stocks would be exhausted quickly. The acting governor, John Mitchelburne, called Rosen's bluff and ordered that the gates remain closed. The crowds of half-clothed and moaning people outside the walls were caught in a game of poker and were forced to spend the night shivering in wet trenches.

The following day, when hundreds more Protestants were shepherded up towards the gates, the city defenders began to construct a gallows on the walls in full view of the Jacobite army and threatened to start executing prisoners. Their threat was echoed in letters sent out by Jacobite prisoners to the main camp. One Irish soldier who had 'lost the fingers of his right hand' dictated a letter to Richard Hamilton after a message to Marshal Rosen went ignored. In it, the prisoner states that the driving of Protestants before the walls had 'so incens'd the governor and others of this garrison that we are all condem'd by a court martial to die tomorrow, unless these poor people be withdrawn'. Richard Hamilton refused to budge and sent back a reply that the prisoners' executions would be avenged with the deaths of 'many thousands of those people … within or without that city'.[7] However, in the tense few hours that followed cool heads seemed to somehow prevail. By 4 July Rosen had permitted all the Protestants before the walls to return to their homes, and the city took advantage of the confusion by smuggling out some 500 'useless people' into the crowds and taking in some new able-bodied men in return.[8] The gallows on the walls was taken down, and the Jacobite prisoners were spared. Nonetheless, the bitter aftertaste of the episode would linger. When word of what Rosen had done reached Dublin, James thought that the old general had gone mad. He dictated a letter to Rosen scolding him for actions 'so contrary to our intentions' and demanded that the Protestants be sent back to their homes at once.[9] When the news reached Whitehall, William sent a letter to Kirke demanding that he take firm action in response to 'these barbarities'.[10]

*

All that was left now was to starve the city to death. As the siege entered its third month, the Jacobite bombardment softened as Hamilton's army began to run out of shells. Morale in the Jacobite camp was plummeting. Many of the soldiers did not have tents and were forced to sleep outside during a cold and sickly summer. The scourges of fever and dysentery struck the squalid camp. At Windmill Hill, the Jacobite and Williamite trenches were so close that the soldiers on either side could talk to each other. The ordinary Irish troops, the Derrymen learned, held 'great prejudice and hatred of the French', who strutted about in their jack-boots, scooped up all the battlefield promotions and ate their fill of rations. The Marquis of Pointis, meanwhile, wrote to Versailles that, while the timber boom across the river had been constructed as planned, he himself was barely able to move from his tent due to injury and illness. Pointis would not, he admitted, be able to oversee the last of the trench digging, mining and other works that would attempt to squeeze the last life out of the city.[11]

Inside the walls, disease and distrust were rampant. Walker was once more suspected of hoarding rations, and his house was searched in secret. Walker admitted that the garrison faced 'a great danger of mutiny'. Sickness continued to decimate the city's fighting strength: at the turn of July, Derry could call on 5,709 soldiers from its original garrison of roughly 7,000; by the middle of the month, this had fallen to 5,114. Disease was so rife that the smallest wound could fester and prove fatal – during a small skirmish near Windmill Hill on 6 July, a Williamite captain was nicked on the hand, but in the next few days he caught a fever and died. Those who could still fight were 'weakened with hunger', and the civilians they were defending were little better. Food was so scarce that people were buying and eating rats, mice, salted hides and dogs that had grown fat from picking at rotten corpses. Traders sold quarts of horse blood and weeds for making soup. The hunger was so acute that 'a certain fat gentleman' reportedly locked himself in his house for three days, afraid that if the city turned to cannibalism he would be in danger. It was a wretched time and place to be alive.[12]

On 11 July the Jacobites called for a ceasefire to discuss terms of surrender. Kirke's fleet had sailed away out of Lough Foyle to try and make a landing in Lough Swilly, some fifteen miles west on the other side of the peninsula. To the watching Jacobites it seemed that another English fleet had abandoned Derry and that the city might finally make terms. Mitchelburne, Walker and the rest of the city command agreed to the offer, if only to give Derry a chance to draw its breath and buy some time. There was 'great rejoicing' in Dublin when word of the ceasefire arrived, and the capital began to hope that victory, at last, was at hand.[13] On Saturday 13 July two mid-level delegations from both sides met halfway between the city and the Jacobite camp. For almost a full day they bargained over the details of surrender. The Jacobites offered a pardon for the officers and soldiers, freedom of religion for the city and a promise that any man who wished to leave for England or Scotland would be free to do so. They added the caveat that the city would have to surrender no later than 12 p.m. on Monday and that only officers and gentlemen would be allowed to keep their weapons. The Derry delegation took their leave and returned to the city. While the talks were taking place, a young boy snuck into Derry carrying a hidden letter from Kirke, who had successfully landed at Inch Island in Lough Swilly. When a council of war took place in the city the following day to discuss the Jacobite terms, Kirke's letter was brought up. The city commanders decided to play for time.[14]

A long, written message was sent back to the Jacobite camp asking that the deadline for surrender be pushed to 26 July, the date at which the city expected to finally run out of food. The council stated openly that it was waiting for a relief force, but if none arrived by that date they agreed to surrender. The Jacobites broke off the talks without a deal. On 15 July the mortars started firing again, and the following day the Jacobites launched simultaneous attacks on Windmill Hill and Butcher's Gate, only to be driven back once again. Adam Murray's luck almost ran out – during the fighting he was shot through both thighs and barely made it back into Derry. A few days later, as Murray lay in agony in his sickbed, an officer stormed into his chamber and began to search the room for saddles and equipment. A soldier sitting at Murray's bedside took offence, and a vicious fight broke out. The officer drew his sword and lashed the soldier who had been at Murray's side. The bloodied soldier fell to his knees, picked up his gun and shot the officer dead. Derry had been driven demented by hunger and want and was now clawing at its own eyes.[15]

*

In Dublin and London the kings of England waited. William and James were separated by a gulf of land and water, but Derry was the shared pivot on which their ambitions now turned. In Whitehall, William's correspondence was full of breathless updates about the war in Flanders and the Rhineland – a war in which his absence was felt. As the French were burning the suburbs of Brussels the imperial commander, the Duke of Lorraine, was preparing to punch through Louis's defences at Mont Royal. Every dispatch from the continent was a reminder to William that time was against him. In late July the Duke of Lorraine wrote to the Prince of Waldeck, another senior commander in the grand alliance, expressing deep concern about the damage the French army might do if 'the affairs of Ireland' delayed William any longer.[16]

In Dublin Castle the Earl of Melfort's letters to Derry began to bubble with worry. James and Melfort had staked everything on a quick exit from Ireland and linking up with the Scottish Jacobite rebellion led by John Graham, Viscount Dundee, before the end of summer. Every hour that Derry held out seemed to push James further away from the throne. In early July, Melfort wrote to Richard Hamilton stating how he and the king 'cannot, at this distance, understand' why Derry had still not been taken. He told Hamilton to ignore reports of a coming English invasion and press ahead with everything he had. 'All the king's affairs depend ... on this one place.' Melfort urged Hamilton to seize his place in history as the man who won Ireland for King James. 'This, I hope, will be your destiny.'[17]

In the shipyards of Chester another man was keeping a close eye on the patchy updates from Derry. The Duke of Schomberg, William's seventy-three-year-old field commander, had been delegated to lead the invasion of Ulster and was now trying to scrabble together soldiers, weapons and ships for the expedition. However, everything was behind schedule, and Schomberg was in a stinking mood. He had been given £20,000 to pay his soldiers' wages, but he needed more. He complained about a lack of urgency from the navy. As his recruits sat idle, many soldiers simply decided to sneak off – in a letter to London, Schomberg reports how he had to shoot and hang a number of deserters. The latest intelligence from Derry was hardly soothing. Schomberg was not at all impressed that Kirke had not tried to break through the timber boom and relieve the city directly, more than a month after his fleet had arrived in Lough Foyle. Schomberg's own plan was to land in east Ulster with between 6,000 and 7,000 men and march west to link up with Kirke, who had been expected to break the siege weeks ago. But it was now almost August, and the city was still holed up and starving. Schomberg wrote to Kirke demanding that he sail back into Lough Foyle and do his job. Kirke, the old general told William, was showing himself up to be 'a capricious man'.[18]

*

Derry had only a few days left. After dark on 25 July, a small group of soldiers ran out from Butcher's Gate and started firing wildly at the Jacobite lines. They had hoped to create a ruckus and draw their enemy away from Windmill Hill, where another band of men had crept out to try and steal some Jacobite cattle. The plan failed. In a final act of desperation, the last cow left in Derry city was tied up outside the walls and set on fire. The starving soldiers hoped that the animal's cries would instinctively draw the Jacobite herd of cattle to the gates in a panic. The flaming cow broke loose and ran off into the night. The siege of Derry had begun with a defiant refusal to place their lives and faith in Jacobite hands. It was ending as a struggle to find the next meal. According to the diary of civilian governor George Walker, the garrison was down to 4,456 men by 27 July. In the previous two days alone 436 men had died of hunger and disease. All that was left to eat in the city were nine thin horses and a ration of one pint of grain per man. This is what oblivion looked like.[19]

On 28 July, the end finally came. Kirke had received Schomberg's angry correspondence, and after depositing his troops in Lough Swilly he sailed back around into Lough Foyle with three fully loaded supply vessels. Kirke had finally decided to run the gauntlet. Culmore Fort, Pointis's boom and the muskets of hundreds of Jacobites lining the river stood between him and Derry. If he failed, the city would starve to death within hours. At about 7 p.m., just after the evening sermon in St Columb's, the three transports entered the mouth of the river downstream. Two of the boats, the *Mountjoy* and the *Phoenix*, sailed up towards Culmore covered by the huge frigate HMS *Dartmouth*. The Jacobites had moved their heavy cannons away from the walls for this very moment, but as the huge hulk of the *Dartmouth* sailed into range, the Jacobite gunners inexplicably missed their target. The *Dartmouth* unleashed a deafening broadside against the fort, tearing up earth and mortar and pinning the Jacobites down. The *Mountjoy* decided to try and break down the boom. Charging straight at it, its hull recoiled against Pointis's great chain of timber and iron. The boom held firm, and the *Mountjoy* ran aground. Gunfire from the riverside began to lash its deck and hull. The *Phoenix*, the smaller of the two transports, was forced to stay back from the typhoon of shot. The Jacobites roared 'a loud huzza along the shore' and rushed to board the stricken supply ships, which were now stranded without the wind to escape.[20] But just when everything finally seemed lost, luck took Derry by the hand. A longboat manned by nine men from the HMS *Swallow* rowed up to the boom and started to hack away at its ropes and chains. The great barrier began to sag and limp; the rattle from the *Mountjoy*'s cannons shook it free from the rocks and onto a rising current, which then lifted her up and over the boom. The *Phoenix* followed her through.

It took almost three hours for the two battered vessels to reach the city. The wind was so faint that the longboat crew from the *Swallow* had to physically tow the *Mountjoy* up the river, with musket shots whizzing overhead all the way. The ships crawled so slowly that the Jacobites had time to set up two gun batteries along the way, but their shots somehow did 'no damage' to the boats.[21] The *Phoenix* finally reached Derry's quay to cries of 'unexpressable joy' from the city.[22] Soldiers rushed down through Ferry Quay Gate and began to unload her cargo of grain. The *Mountjoy* reached the dock shortly afterwards but its captain, Michael Browning, who had been born and raised in Derry, had been shot in the attempt and did not survive. The sight of two supply ships reaching Derry after months of a vicious and filthy siege shattered what morale was left in the Jacobite lines. Rumours later spread that the gun crews at Culmore were 'drunk with brandy' or had even been bought off by English gold. Either way, their failure to hold the river was attacked by Jacobite historians as 'a neglect of duty' that had blunt consequences for this war and so many others.[23]

For three days the ships' cargoes of flour, beef, peas and grain were deposited in Derry, with barrels stuffed with earth shielding the work from gunfire across the river. Starving Derry into submission was Richard Hamilton's last play, and it had failed. Hamilton and Rosen 'judged it in vain to remain there any longer'.[24] On the night of 31 July, the Jacobite soldiers who had spent 105 days camped outside Derry burned whatever they could not carry and marched away to Lifford and Strabane. On 1 August the sun rose once more over a city tortured by disease, hunger and death. But after fifteen weeks under attack, Derry was finally free. It had survived the longest and most horrible siege in Irish history, but it had paid a terrible price.

No one knows for certain how many people fought and died at Derry. Rival accounts always inflate their enemy's dead and play down their own. George Walker wrote that a city roughly a square mile in size had survived a siege by 'near 20,000 men'.[25] The Duke of Berwick, however, later wrote that even after he and Rosen had arrived with their reinforcements, the Jacobites had less than half that number. Likewise, the exact number of men, women and children who perished in those cruel and desperate weeks will never be known. By Walker's count over 2,500 of Derry's garrison had been killed – one man out of every three. A further 7,000 civilians are thought to have died within the city walls. Walker also later claimed that roughly 9,000 Jacobite soldiers had perished during the siege, the vast majority as a result of fever, pox and dysentery. One Jacobite account, however, puts their losses as low as 2,000 men, but among them 'fine gentlemen, and several heads of families … worthy of lasting memory'.[26] Either way, the damage to James's cause was immeasurable. As had been the case again and again since 1685, James could not find a way through the will of ordinary Protestants who simply refused to give him what he wanted.

*

There are no diaries or letters that speak of James's immediate reaction to the news that the siege had failed. There are no accounts of him screaming at his advisors, sinking his head into his hands in anguish or pacing the halls of Dublin Castle with worry. He likely accepted the news with the same withdrawn self-pity that had plagued him for years. If anything, he had expected it: on 22 July, Melfort wrote another letter to Richard Hamilton, but this time there was no talk of destiny. With words that were probably paraphrased from James's own, Melfort spoke of retreat: 'I confess it's hard to leave a town so near starved and of so much consequence for the king,' Melfort wrote. 'But if it be so, that mortification must be swallowed.'[27]

20

Outlive the Day

As Derry starved and burned, there was another place in Ulster that the Jacobites could not break. Sixty miles south of the city, the country disintegrates into a breathtaking maze of water and earth, as the River Erne chops down through Fermanagh towards the coast. Before it reaches the Atlantic, the river passes through Lough Erne, a colossal natural moat that straddles the border between the north and the west of Ireland. Right at its centre, the lough is pinched in two by a chunk of land some six miles long, as if an ancient giant had grabbed both sides of the lake in one hand and then clenched his fist. This narrow land bank is the crossroads between Ulster and Connaught, and right on its edge is the small town of Enniskillen.

Enniskillen had been forged in the same fires as Derry. Sitting on one of hundreds of tiny islands carved out by the river, the town was a former Gaelic stronghold that had been confiscated and granted to Protestant settlers under James I. Like Derry, it had been scarred by its memories of 1641 and waited with dread for the day when the Gaelic Irish would bare their teeth again. Unlike Derry, however, Enniskillen did not wait behind thick walls and bastions. It sat on a small island, contained barely a few dozen thatched houses and its only fortification of note was a lanky castle with two short towers sticking up like tree trunks. It did not wear layers of armour like Derry. Instead, Enniskillen was a fortress of natural strength, shielded on all sides by water and hemmed in by almost impassable marsh. In the winter of 1688, when the Comber letter ignited panic among the Protestants of the north, refugees across south Ulster and north Connaught began to converge on Enniskillen, like the sanctuary at the heart of a great natural maze. It would become another place where the 'stubborn temper' of the Protestant north would scratch into the Jacobites' skin like a tick.[1]

With no gates to shut in their defence, the men of Enniskillen chose to attack. When two companies of Tyrconnell's infantry were marching to garrison the town in December 1688, some 450 local horsemen and volunteers with 'not twenty well-fixed firearms' between them drew up a mile outside the town to block the soldiers' path. The startled Jacobites turned and withdrew back into Cavan, twenty-four miles away. Enniskillen quickly set up its own rebel association, despite having 'not ten pounds of powder' in the garrison. Gustavus Hamilton, a local justice of the peace, was named as governor, and on 11 March Enniskillen publicly declared allegiance to William and Mary. Local Protestant gentry began to draw up and pay companies of soldiers from among their tenants; muskets and shot were rummaged together, and farmers' scythes were melted down to make pikes. Messengers whittled across the sparse and stunning countryside of south Ulster, smuggling dispatches between Enniskillen, Hillsborough, Sligo and Derry, desperately trying to avoid royal patrols. As Richard Hamilton's main army was cutting through east Ulster, a second army under the command of Pierce Butler, Lord Galmoy, was sent to subdue Enniskillen.

It would be a rough task. The spring of 1689 had been unseasonably wet, and the 'pitiful stormy weather' turned the Erne country into a swamp. When Robert Lundy ordered Sligo to be abandoned, much of its garrison trundled into Enniskillen along with hundreds of Protestant refugees. Among them was a young man named Thomas Lloyd, the son of a Roscommon settler who was barely in his mid-twenties but had solid army experience from his time serving with Richard Hamilton's dragoons before the invasion. Lloyd had energy, presence and ferocious courage and was quickly appointed lieutenant colonel of the Enniskillen armed forces. Lloyd and his new dragoons were about to make a name for themselves.[2]

Galmoy's Jacobite army did not get far. In late March he arrived at Crom Castle, a small frontier garrison on the edge of Upper Lough Erne, about sixteen miles upriver from Enniskillen. Galmoy had been sent north without any heavy cannons and was forced to improvise. He told his men to build two mock pieces of artillery out of tin and had them dragged up before the walls as a bluff. When his demand for surrender was ignored, Galmoy told his men to fire the guns. One of the fake cannons exploded, naturally, maiming an artilleryman. As Galmoy's troops fumbled about, the defenders at Crom sent word downstream to Enniskillen. Reinforcements from the town arrived and cut into Galmoy's lines, killing some forty Jacobites and driving Galmoy back to Belturbet in County Cavan. Humiliated, Galmoy went fishing for payback. During a parley with the Enniskillen troops, both sides had agreed to a prisoner exchange that would see a captured Jacobite captain swapped for the son of Dixie Dean, a local Protestant gentleman. The Jacobite officer was duly sent to Belturbet, but instead of keeping his side of the bargain, Galmoy had Dean hanged for treason. Rumours reached Enniskillen that Dean's head had been cut off and used as a football in the streets of Belturbet before being impaled on a pike over the market house. The war along the Erne was already becoming a vicious and spiteful affair.

*

After Galmoy had been driven off, the Enniskillen troops mounted their horses and struck out. Even though two new forts had been built on the eastern and western roads into the town, the garrison knew that if they were hit with a direct assault they would have little chance of survival. Attack remained the only defence. With their knowledge of the marshes, woodlands and causeways of the Erne country, the Enniskillen dragoons began to terrorise the soft edges of the Jacobite lines in south Ulster. Led by Thomas Lloyd, who had been dubbed 'Little Cromwell', they rode out into Tyrone and Monaghan, raiding Jacobite posts, burning buildings, rustling cattle and constantly probing for weaknesses. They ghosted through the countryside so quickly that Jacobite intelligence could not keep up. As the siege of Derry was just beginning to the north, the Jacobites already sensed that Enniskillen would be a dangerous thorn in their back. The task of subduing the town was therefore handed to Patrick Sarsfield, who had just marched into the abandoned town of Sligo unopposed.

Rather than risk charging into the watery maze around Enniskillen, Sarsfield decided to starve the town out by capturing Ballyshannon, the last port on the river downstream, from where he could cut off all shipping and supplies in and out of Lough Erne from the coast. Sarsfield's blistering reputation for action followed him into the unfamiliar country of south Ulster, but it did not do him much good. Ballyshannon refused to surrender, and when Sarsfield was forced to send much of his cavalry to check a Williamite force moving against him four miles upstream at Belleek on 7 May, his men were routed. Sarsfield was forced to retreat to Sligo with heavy casualties, perhaps as many as six hundred killed and sixty captured. Thomas Lloyd's dragoons also seized two small cannons, several horses and 'some good arms', which were all desperately needed.[3] It was an eye-catching day's work for the men of Enniskillen, who were now a violent threat to James's ambitions in the north. From Dublin, Lord Melfort wrote to Richard Hamilton at Derry, warning him to 'be watchful on your side', as Lloyd's men 'are much puffed up with their success against Sarsfield'.[4] There was no way of knowing when or where they would strike next.

*

James was furious. The rebels in Enniskillen had turned the Erne lake lands into a vicious frontier, and two attempts to wipe them out had failed. Lloyd's horsemen were now raiding with impunity – by the end of May they had struck out as far south as Kells in County Meath, barely forty miles from Dublin, before racing back to Enniskillen with 'above three thousand cows and oxen', as well as sheep, horses and a fresh batch of Jacobite prisoners. On 19 June Lloyd launched a lightning raid on Belturbet in Cavan, where the Jacobites were gathering supplies ahead of another push on Enniskillen. One account claimed that after a hot skirmish the raiders escaped with 'twenty horse-loads of biscuit, above fifty barrels of flour [and] a hundred barrels of wheat'. It was another criminal embarrassment for the Jacobites.[5]

James's first reaction was to send Conrad Rosen into south Ulster to clean up the mess, but as the French marshal was en route towards Enniskillen he received fresh orders to divert to Derry, where things had begun to fall apart. James's next move was to send his eighteen-year-old bastard son, the Duke of Berwick, to try his luck. On 21 June Berwick marched away from the front lines at Derry with orders to head south and join Sarsfield in a renewed two-pronged attack on Enniskillen. Berwick immediately showed his flair for the rough, pillaging style of combat in Ulster. On his march south with 400 cavalry and dragoons, Berwick attacked a Williamite outpost in Donegal, burned the garrison and seized 1,500 cattle and sheep. After rendezvousing in Cavan with fresh regiments of horses, dragoons and infantry from Dublin, Berwick looped around behind Upper Lough Erne and prepared to attack Enniskillen from the north. On 13 July at Trillick, some twelve miles outside the town, Berwick scattered roughly 300 infantry and cavalry sent out to block him by Enniskillen's governor Gustavus Hamilton. Berwick's riders hacked down the fleeing Williamites, leaving 'not more than five or six' of them alive. The road to Enniskillen was now wide open, but before Berwick could seize his advantage Rosen recalled him to Derry. Reports were coming through that Major General Kirke had landed troops in Lough Swilly, and Rosen ordered Berwick to return north to guard his flank. Patrick Sarsfield, who had launched another attack on Ballyshannon with some 3,000 infantry and horsemen, was left on his own and forced to withdraw. Enniskillen slipped through the Jacobites' fingers again.[6]

*

James kept trawling through his officers for someone who could finally crack Enniskillen open. After Berwick's recall, James finally turned to Lieutenant General Justin MacCarthy, the most senior Irish field commander in the army and a man whose swift suppression of the rebellion in Bandon gave him plenty of capital. James even considered travelling to Enniskillen himself in late July, but this time d'Avaux's objections prevailed. One disastrous march into Ulster was enough. A week after being routed by Berwick at Trillick, the commanders in Enniskillen received fresh reports that MacCarthy had arrived in Belturbet with some 5,000 soldiers from Cork. This time, they were prepared. After Kirke had landed his troops at Lough Swilly, he had sent supplies of muskets, gunpowder and grenades to Enniskillen, as well as eight small cannons and a bundle of new commissions to raise extra companies of cavalry and dragoons. Kirke also sent several officers led by the firm English colonel William Wolseley. Their timing was excellent. For all of Thomas Lloyd's disruptive success in poaching food, Enniskillen had 'not much more than three barrels' of gunpowder left at the start of July.[7]

On 28 July a breathless messenger arrived in the town with news that Justin MacCarthy had reached Crom Castle. The following day the Jacobites began 'to batter the castle' with shells and musket fire. The commander at Crom, David Creighton, pleaded with Enniskillen for reinforcements. On 30 July several hundred cavalry and infantry under the command of one of Wolseley's officers rumbled out of Enniskillen and down along the east shore of Lough Erne towards Crom. MacCarthy was expecting them. He sent out brigadier Anthony Hamilton, Richard Hamilton's brother, with 'most of his horse and dragoons' to block the Williamites' advance.[8] MacCarthy gave Hamilton strict orders to dig in, drive the relief force back and hold tight. The plan almost worked.

On the morning of 31 July, Anthony Hamilton's Jacobites were dotted around the roadside as the first of the enemy troops marched into view. There was a sudden torrent of gunfire and the English and Enniskillen soldiers began to stumble back. Hamilton ignored his orders and told his men to break cover and chase after them. It was a fatal mistake. Five miles up the road, in a bog just beyond the village of Lisnaskea, the English troops had set a trap. The road pinched to barely a few yards wide as it passed through a patch of churning marshland. Hamilton led his troops in a charge up the road, straight into the ambush. Williamite soldiers hidden on either side of the causeway fired into the crowd, killing a dozen men on the spot and badly wounding many more. Hamilton was shot, slumped to the ground and was carried away. Barely able to speak, he handed command over to one of his captains, who ordered the Jacobite troops to fall back. As the Jacobites broke away on foot, the Williamite troops hurtled after them, slashing and stabbing and pummelling any man who lost his footing or was too hurt to escape. One Williamite account claimed that as many as 200 Jacobites were killed in 'a very great slaughter' along the road.[9]

*

When word of the success at Lisnaskea reached Enniskillen a few hours later, Colonel Wolseley held a council of war with his officers. With Governor Gustavus Hamilton laid up with fever, Thomas Lloyd represented the Enniskillen troops. The meeting was prompt and decisive. When Wolseley asked the room if they wished to hold firm or ride out and attack the main Jacobite force immediately, the reply was unanimous. A few hours after the ambush at Lisnaskea, Wolseley was marching out of Enniskillen with some 2,000 cavalry, dragoons and infantry to confront Justin MacCarthy himself.

The wounded Jacobite survivors of the ambush limped back to their lines at Crom and briefed MacCarthy on the bungled disaster. The Jacobite commander's instincts told him that a major attack was coming, and he decided to pull his troops back to better ground. He marched away and arranged his lines on a hillside near the village of Newtownbutler. It was an impressive post. The road heading up the steep slope before them cut through some pockets of dense and seemingly impassable woodland. MacCarthy set up two gun batteries either side of his lines and aimed his artillery straight down the road where Wolseley and his men would have to march. When the first of the Williamite cavalry finally came into view, the Jacobite guns roared into life. Cannonballs began to pound the narrow causeway, hurling mud and violent noise into the air. Wolseley's troops 'could not advance one step'.[10] However, with their instinctive feel for the local landscape, the Enniskillen troops were able to pick their way through the woodlands on either side of the road and overrun the Jacobite batteries. The gunners were immediately shot and stabbed to death, and the cannons fell silent. The road was suddenly clear, allowing Wolseley's cavalry to race up the hill like a tidal wave. The Jacobite horsemen spun and fled, leaving their infantry to briefly hold the line before being swallowed in the cascading enemy charge. Hundreds of Irish soldiers threw down their long muskets and fled into a marsh more than a mile long to their right. Seized by a cocktail of bloodlust and adrenalin, the Enniskillen soldiers plunged in after them.

One by one, the fleeing Jacobites were picked off in the marsh and put to death with swords, clubs and muskets. Throughout the night parties of Enniskillen soldiers combed the bog an inch at a time, beating bushes and shaking trees to find more men to kill. When one officer found a Jacobite soldier hiding, he struck him with his sword so hard that the top half of his skull came clean off, 'with not so much as a bit of skin' left to hold his brains in. Of the 500 or so Jacobite soldiers who had scattered into the bog, 'scarce a man' was said to have survived the massacre. Many of those who managed to elude the search parties lost their way in the marsh and drowned. In the aftermath of the battle of Newtownbutler, the Williamites claimed to have killed 2,000 Jacobite soldiers and captured some 4,000 officers. It was their most brutally decisive victory to date in this unusual civil war.[11]

When his lines had broken, Justin MacCarthy and half a dozen of his officers fled on horseback into a nearby forest.

As the world around them was consumed by gore and rage, MacCarthy contemplated his defeat. At that exact moment, the Jacobite camp at Derry was being burned as Rosen and Richard Hamilton were preparing to abandon the siege. MacCarthy hid and listened to the laughter and songs of victorious Englishmen and Enniskilleners. He could smell the wet, swampy earth and the sharp scent of gunpowder. He could hear the faint screams of his men being hacked to death like dogs in the marsh nearby. King James's cause seemed to be dying all around him. With nothing else left, MacCarthy decided to die as well. Grasping the reins of his horse in one hand, he took a deep breath and drew his pistol. With a dig of his spurs, he charged out of the wood firing at a small group of Williamite soldiers nearby. After a split second of surprise, the soldiers raised their muskets at MacCarthy and fired. Bullets tore through the general's flesh, and his horse crumpled to the ground with a sickening thud. MacCarthy's twisted form was thrown to the earth, more dead than alive. A Williamite soldier walked towards him with the butt of his musket raised, ready to bash his skull to pieces. But just then, one of MacCarthy's officers cried out that he was their general and pleaded for quarter. The soldier lowered his gun, and MacCarthy was carried away to Enniskillen a broken and bloodied prisoner.[12]

*

The Jacobite campaign in Ulster was in shreds. The siege of Derry had been broken, and their final push against Enniskillen had drowned in the marshes of Newtownbutler. The Jacobite army had faced walls, trenches, bogs and causeways, but Ulster's hardest armour had been its refusal to accept defeat. The spirit of the frontier had been mixed into the mortar of Enniskillen and Derry, and their people had inherited memories of 1641 like pocket watches and dinner cloth. James promised mercy and tolerance, but the Protestants of the north did not think his Irish troops would keep their king's word. Believing that they were staring at their own genocide, they simply chose to say no. The Jacobite army had marched into the province without heavy artillery, experience or luck and could not beat the door down. In the first week of August, Rosen, Richard Hamilton, Berwick and the remains of an army that had been 'reduced almost to nothing' were trudging back towards the south.[13] Patrick Sarsfield had retreated to Sligo. The mood within the senior command was cracking. The youthful Berwick, still buoyed by his success at Trillick, remained keen to attack Enniskillen, despite the Jacobites having 'few, if any, cannon balls and scarce any ammunition'.[14] Rosen was having none of it. The old general huffed that if he thought Enniskillen could be taken he would have taken it himself.

Back on the shores of the River Erne, the garrison at Enniskillen rejoiced in victory. The vicious raids of Thomas Lloyd, the timely intervention of William Wolseley and the hostile landscape of the lake lands had combined to ensure that 'the name of Inniskilling men became a terror to the Irish'.[15] But there was no time to reflect. Schomberg and his fleet were expected to land in east Ulster any day, and soon it would be time for the Williamites of the north to go on the offensive. Meanwhile, Justin MacCarthy lay captive in his sick bed, having somehow survived his charge into the jaws of death. James was so concerned for the health of his general and privy counsellor that he sent his personal physician to Enniskillen to treat him, along with a few hogsheads of wine to lift his spirits. MacCarthy's recovery would be long and painful. Some time later, when his strength began to return, one of his captors asked him why he had chosen to charge out of the woods that day at Newtownbutler, rather than surrender and seek quarter. MacCarthy replied that the siege of Derry had failed, and James's army in the north appeared at that moment to be 'much broken'. He knew what the failure to subdue Ulster would mean. Huddled in the woods of Newtownbutler, MacCarthy had believed that James's kingdom had just been lost. With the heavy guilt of a broken soldier, he said that he was 'unwilling to outlive that day'.[16]

Part Three

War

'Cry woe, destruction, ruin and decay:
the worst is death, and death will have his day'.

William Shakespeare, *Richard II*, Act III, scene ii.

21

A Noisy World

Life in London did not agree with William. When Mary arrived in the capital back in the spring of 1689, she found her husband exhausted and 'in a very ill condition'. In their first private moment together since the invasion, they had held hands and wept 'tears of joy' at being reunited, but also spoke with sadness about the happy lives in Holland that fate and opportunity had forced them to leave behind. At first, the new king and queen had resided at Whitehall, but as William spent his days chained to a desk wading through mountains of correspondence, he became ill. William suffered from asthma, and the damp mist rolling off the Thames aggravated his condition. Tired, overworked and in need of fresh air, William withdrew to Hampton Court Palace, fourteen miles south-west of the city. The queen was glad to go with him. Unlike her father and uncle, Mary had little time for the lush pageantry of the Stuart court. In Holland she was content to spend most of her hours at prayer and writing notes in her diary, but now, as queen, she had been thrust into a life of public engagements, banquets and theatre. 'My heart is not made for a kingdom', she lamented, describing London as 'a noisy world, full of variety'.[1]

London had its issues with the royal couple as well. The coarse and divisive way that they had come to power left a lot of people uneasy, and it showed. The Earl of Clarendon, who was out of the loop with the new regime and now spent his days idling about town, noted in his journal that someone had torn the sceptre and crown off William's official portrait at Guildhall. On the odd occasion that the king and queen did return to London on business, they held a muted court with little colour and scandal. Mary wrote in her diary that William's moods and bad health seemed to 'put people out of humour'.[2] But in these dangerous days, with Whigs and Tories squabbling in parliament and Jacobite conspirators plotting to retake the throne, the new king and queen grudgingly accepted that they had to remain visible in the capital. So, like every other couple trying to put down roots somewhere, they decided to buy a house.[3]

In late 1689 William and Mary paid £20,000 for the Earl of Nottingham's manor and gardens in the suburb of Kensington and immediately began work to turn it into a palace. Gardens and architecture were two of William's keenest hobbies, but with wars to manage he left it to the queen to oversee the improvements. Mary relished the task. Meticulous plans for new apartments and annexes were drawn up, and the queen personally oversaw every detail of the design and decoration. She frequently visited the site in order to 'hasten the workmen'. It was a habit that almost proved fatal. One Sunday in early November, just a short while after Mary had been poking around in one of the new extensions, the building 'suddenly fell flat to the ground', killing seven or eight workers.[4] It was a dramatic near miss for the devout queen, who may have probed it for signs and omens. But to William, it was simply more bad news.

The war in Europe was grinding on, and cracks were starting to show in William's grand alliance. His allies squabbled over tactics, provisions and the quartering of troops in each other's lands. In London, William was furious after his campaign plans for the next twelve months were apparently leaked by one of his counsellors. Meanwhile, he had been caught up in a domestic squabble with the city of Amsterdam and felt obliged to send his best friend and fixer, William Bentinck, back to Holland to sort it out. And then there was Ireland, which was still an unresolved mess. The Duke of Schomberg had arrived in Ulster with his army at the end of August, but despite all his regiments and supplies he had failed to attack the Jacobite army and was now bunkering down for the winter. William was tired, frustrated and sickly, but he knew that unless his fortunes changed quickly, much more than just plaster and brick would come crashing down around him.[5]

*

On 13 August 1689, less than two weeks after the siege of Derry had been raised, Schomberg's invasion fleet landed at Bangor, some ten miles from Belfast. It contained close to 10,000 men, including regiments of Dutch blue guards and Huguenots from France. The majority of the soldiers, however, were Englishmen who had been 'raised, armed and clothed in less than six weeks'.[6] Combined with Kirke's relief force and what remained of the garrisons of Derry and Enniskillen, Schomberg's arrival brought the Williamite forces in Ireland to roughly 20,000 men. However, if the buoyant and furious Protestants of Ulster had expected the seventy-three-year-old duke to immediately charge towards Dublin, they would quickly be disappointed. Schomberg was a prudent and cautious veteran of European battlefields. He was not about to be rushed by anyone.

After unloading his troops and victuals, Schomberg's first move was to attack the nearby Jacobite garrison of Carrickfergus, the mighty old Norman fortress. On 28 August, after a few days of brisk fighting, the vastly outnumbered Jacobite forces agreed to surrender, provided that Schomberg allowed them to march away south and link up with the rest of their army. As the disarmed Jacobites filed out of town in full procession, they had to run a gauntlet of Ulstermen baying for revenge for Derry. Curses were tossed about; sabres and muskets were raised. Schomberg himself had to personally ride up and down the lines with his pistol in his hand to prevent his troops from letting their blood lust get the better of them. It soon became clear that Schomberg was a stickler for protocol. At some point during his first few days in Ireland, he received a letter from the Duke of Berwick, who had been sent back into Ulster with 1,600 troops to harass the Williamite lines. Was it a taunt, a notice of affairs or just a polite communiqué from a fellow gentleman? Schomberg never found out. He refused to open the letter on principle, as the young Berwick had addressed Schomberg as a count and not by his new and more prestigious title of duke. Berwick was hardly fiddling with his buttons awaiting a reply. While Schomberg was 'amusing himself' at Carrickfergus, the young Berwick was busy turning the road south into an obstacle course.[7] He moved his troops into the town of Newry, about thirty-five miles south of Belfast, and began to dig in. After Schomberg had wasted precious time scouting the town, consulting his maps and arranging his regiments to attack, Berwick simply pulled out and burned Newry to the ground.

*

The Duke of Tyrconnell spent the summer of 1689 in the shadows. His poor health gave him cover to avoid the parliament or any official functions where he might have to face up to public embarrassment. Gossip in Dublin was razor-sharp, and the viceroy had a reputation to protect. As it turned out, Tyrconnell's spell in the wilderness was perfectly timed. As the Jacobite army limped out of Ulster, the scramble to find someone to blame began. Having been forced out of James's inner circle at the start of the campaign, Tyrconnell was not tarnished by its failure. The man widely thought to have been the architect of his downfall, the Earl of Melfort, was not so lucky. The Scot had been an unpopular figure from the moment he set foot in the kingdom, and he had never concealed his desire for James to rush into Scotland as quickly as possible. Their mutual loathing of Melfort was one of the few things that the French and Irish factions in the Jacobite leadership could agree on. Melfort's character and competence were questioned at every turn, with Rosen going so far as to write that he 'did not speak a word of truth'.[8] After the debacle at Derry, James came under intense pressure to make Melfort the scapegoat. In September, Melfort was dismissed and returned to St Germain, from where he would later be sent away to serve as Jacobite envoy to the Vatican. James later admitted that he had cut Melfort loose out of 'necessity'.[9] Writing from Saint Germain that October, Melfort grumbled that he had been a stooge for Rosen, d'Avaux and 'a knot of Irish' that had all hated him from the start. He warned James to be wary of his advisors, believing that they had the poisonous potential to start 'a war in your own court'.[10]

*

As Schomberg's army trundled south in a winding column of flags, drums and gun carriages, one of the men in its ranks was keeping a diary. George Story was an English chaplain who had joined the army in the 'late hurry of affairs' before it sailed to Ireland and was now soaking up the sights and sounds of a kingdom at war. Like d'Avaux before him, he was taken aback by the ghostly scenery of Ulster, which had been pillaged, burned and carved to pieces by soldiers on the move. As the army marched towards Newry, Story saw deserted thatched cottages with crude iron crosses above their doors and fields filled with rotting corn. At Newry he walked through the charred skeleton of a town that had been stripped of almost everything of use. He saw cannons dumped in the river. He saw barrels of salted beef and herring that no man would touch out of fear that they had been poisoned. By the second week of September, Story and the rest of the army had crossed into Leinster and made camp near Dundalk in County Louth, some fifty miles north of Dublin. Story wrote that while the army had seized what it could from the barren countryside – including about 2,000 sheep – bread and grain were already scarce, and some soldiers were beginning to collapse with sickness.[11]

Schomberg's was not the only army marching into County Louth. Twenty miles to the south, about seven hours away on foot, thousands of Jacobite soldiers were beginning to gather near Drogheda, the last major garrison between the Williamite army and Dublin. James, it seemed, was finally ready for the battle he had run away from at Salisbury almost a year earlier. The reverses at Derry and Newtownbutler had dented Jacobite morale, but on paper relatively little appeared to have changed. If James could defeat Schomberg, his army could theoretically march back into Ulster unimpeded and finish what it had started in the spring. Rosen and the French officers had tried to convince James that Louth and Dublin would be 'impossible to defend' and that he should instead retreat back to the garrison town of Athlone on the river Shannon and dig in until next year.[12]

But James was undeterred. By the end of August a bustling Jacobite camp was coming to life at Drogheda, swollen every day by the arrival of hundreds of new Irish recruits with knapsacks over their shoulders, a skip in their step and barely a working musket between them. John Stevens, who rarely had a good word to say about his Irish peers, described the new soldiers as 'ragged and ill shod'. D'Avaux, who had once again been dragged away from the comforts of Dublin to follow James up to the front lines, wrote to Louvois that the new recruits at Drogheda were cheerful and 'very animated'. But without guns, powder, training and good officers to keep them in check, d'Avaux doubted that high spirits would get them very far.[13]

The army camp at Drogheda was also the place where Lord Tyrconnell made his public return to favour. With Melfort dismissed, the lord deputy of Ireland suddenly recovered his health, and within weeks he was back in the engine room of the Jacobite government, ordering out fresh commissions and sending dispatches to Paris. The 'knot of Irish' that Melfort had blamed for his demise had lobbied hard for Tyrconnell's return, but James's decision was more than just a publicity gesture. After a summer of indecision, poor management and bad luck, James accepted that Richard Talbot, who had built his career on getting things done, would be useful to have around. The Duke of Tyrconnell did not disappoint. By the middle of September, almost two-thirds of the 20,000 Jacobite soldiers at Drogheda were fresh recruits that Tyrconnell seemed to have unearthed almost overnight. Many had belonged to regiments that Tyrconnell and Sarsfield had dissolved just a few months earlier. Their wretched lack of weapons and supplies aside, it was a staggering piece of recruitment. There were now tens of thousands of armed men in County Louth, split between two camps half a day's march from one another. But somehow, the horrific battle that the kingdom was holding its breath for did not take place.

*

On the surface James seemed eager to fight. After first making camp at Drogheda, he pushed his army ahead to Ardee and then up to the River Fane, barely half a mile from Schomberg's lines. James personally scouted the Williamite positions with 'a great body of horse' and found his enemy dug in behind lines of earthworks and trenches on the outskirts of Dundalk.[14] On the morning of 21 September, the Jacobites tried to pick a fight. As the English sentries peered out into the hazy distance, they saw thick lines of enemy troops drawing towards them in attack formation. The Jacobites marched until they were within a cannon shot of the Williamite earthworks. Then they began to feint and shuffle around, trying to goad the Williamite officers into ordering their men out of their trenches. Schomberg held his nerve. 'Let them alone, we will see what they will do,' he repeatedly told his officers.[15] A tense stand-off between the two armies continued all morning. Both sides stared nervously at each other with their stomachs in knots, waiting for the sudden blast of cannons and drums that would signal an attack. But Schomberg refused to take the bait. At 2 p.m., after what must have felt like a lifetime, the Jacobites were ordered to fall back. The armies of the two kings had squared up to each other, but neither had been willing to fire the first shot.

Versions of what actually happened that day are mixed. On the Williamite side, it is accepted that Schomberg had simply refused to order his men to leave their trenches and attack, believing that sacrificing his tricky defensive line would play into the enemy's hands. The old general had also refused to let his troops chase and harass the Jacobites as they retreated, just in case they stumbled into some invisible trap down the road. Many of his subordinates grumbled that an army sent to Ireland to destroy a shirtless and ill-equipped enemy had allowed themselves be stared down, like a playground brawler. But George Story came to Schomberg's defence, insisting that the duke had acted 'according to the rules of the art, and prudence' by refusing to fight on James's terms.[16]

On the other side of the trenches, James's biographer painted him as a buccaneer spoiling for a fight. He claimed that James had driven his men right up to the enemy lines, despite Rosen's nagging, and that in the end it was the scraggy old Schomberg who did not have the stomach for it. Other Jacobite accounts, however, claim that Rosen and Tyrconnell had urged James to attack the trenches, but the king had clammed up and refused, fearing that 'the victory would prove too dear'.[17] No one knows for certain. Either way James pulled his army back from Dundalk, and after several idle weeks camped out in the elements he ordered his men to disperse for the winter. The Jacobite rank-and-file celebrated Schomberg's refusal to fight as if it was a victory, and the novice Irish recruits began to sing and beat their chests for having 'braved the enemy'.[18] Schomberg had avoided a gruesome battle, but his lines were still thinning. There were, after all, many ways for a soldier to die.

*

The Williamite camp at Dundalk sat near the roots of the Cooley Mountains, a rugged peninsula of moors and peaks that juts out into the sea like a bent elbow. Summer had limped away, and in the 'extremely violent' wind and rain that followed the camp became a hostile place. Thousands of soldiers sat around in flooded trenches and slept in shabby tents and huts. By the first week of October, fever was rampant. George Story's diary became a grim account of men collapsing and dying every hour. Disease festered in cramped trenches and earthworks, while filthy drinking water allowed the dreaded 'bloody flux' of dysentery to sneak into the camp like a thief. Doctors and surgeons struggled to fight the outbreak. Sick men were loaded up onto ships offshore that became grim and stinking hospitals. When the lower levels of the ships filled up, tents were erected on the top decks. When the top decks became overcrowded, the sick were loaded up onto carts and dragged away to the nearby town of Carlingford. Many did not survive the journey. Regimental chaplains spent their days walking from tent to tent, praying with weak and delirious men who would be dead by the next time they visited a few hours later. The plague was not just confined to the ordinary soldiers: Story's diary began to fill up with laments for officers like Thomas Gower, a popular young gentleman with 'a quick and ready wit', and Colonel Wharton, an infantry commander whose regiment 'would have followed him anywhere'. Men scrambled about looking for answers. Some began to accuse the soldiers from Derry of bringing illness into the camp; others blamed the 'carelessness' of the new English recruits who did not know much about shelter and hygiene. Story noted that the veteran Dutch soldiers in the camp built sturdy huts on good ground, and as a consequence 'not above eleven of them died'. The death toll in the camp rose so quickly that Schomberg had to prohibit the firing of three-gun salutes whenever a man was buried. He did not want the enemy in the distance to hear how many of his troops were dying.[19]

The soldiers that were deemed fit for duties were so weak that they could barely hold their muskets straight. Some began to mutter that Schomberg was at fault for choosing such a sodden place to camp. The duke did his best to raise spirits and was frequently seen riding about the camp and talking to his men. But there was little anyone could do. Doctors with basic field kits had to carry out crude amputations of toes and feet, which almost always became infected afterwards. Medicine and other victuals were terribly limited. On 23 October, as the death toll in the camp soared past 1,000 men, Schomberg ordered his army to withdraw towards Newry, believing that the very earth they were standing on was now soaked with disease. In early November he wrote two letters to William in which he tried to explain how awful things had become. The terrain, he said, was boggy and hard to navigate; supplies were low, and many of his troops could barely stand. Schomberg said that his own health was failing and that his doctors had urged him to return to England. He told William that he would stay at his post but warned that, unless the weather changed, his men recovered or new supplies were found, 'it will not be possible to sustain this war'.[20]

The pestilence was not confined to the Williamite camp. A few miles away, Jacobite soldiers were also being stung by the elements. Storms that would rage from morning to night flooded their huts and tents with as much as a foot of water. The Jacobites did enjoy access to local markets and regular supplies of beef, mutton and game. But almost every acre of crops within a day's ride had been burned or stripped, and a diet heavy on red meat but low on bread began to weigh on the soldiers' health. Knotted with the effects of the wet weather, the conditions 'bred much sickness' in the Jacobite lines, albeit on a far smaller scale to the epidemic pummelling their enemies a few miles away.[21]

By the first week of November, Schomberg and James had both pulled their armies out of the field. The Enniskillen dragoons rode home, while the rest of the stricken Williamite units trudged off to Armagh, Antrim and Newry, where many would face a long winter sleeping in charred houses or lying on thin beds of straw in barns. Some 1,700 men had died of disease in Schomberg's camp in the space of a few weeks that autumn, with roughly 800 perishing aboard the dreaded hospital ships offshore. A ghastly 3,800 more men slowly and painfully succumbed to sickness in Belfast over the winter. Thomas Lloyd, the 'Little Cromwell' of Enniskillen, was among the dead. In all, an estimated 6,300 Williamite soldiers died without firing a shot after the siege of Derry had been raised. There were few words to describe the slow, relentless, tragic march of death through the army. George Story called it 'the most lamentable sight in the world'.[22]

*

The Jacobites returned to Dublin triumphant. The new Irish recruits told stories of how the Dutch and English mercenaries of the usurper had hid in their trenches at Dundalk and refused to meet their challenge. After the crushing failure at Derry, the Jacobite rank-and-file celebrated the absence of another defeat. As James departed the capital to spend the winter at Kilkenny Castle, he left behind a city filled with soldiers in the mood to revel. Unlike most of the Irish recruits who could just return home, the French, English and Scottish soldiers in James's army needed quarters. The new governor of Dublin, Simon Luttrell, came up with a neat solution. He marched into Trinity College and threw the resident academics out into the street. Although the provost's private quarters and the university library were placed under James's protection, the rest of the grounds were seized and turned into a makeshift barracks. The university's Protestant chapel was re-consecrated as a Catholic church and then loaded up with barrels of gunpowder, biscuit and other supplies. From Trinity College, Dublin's maze of taverns, theatres and brothels were comfortably within reach for the troops.

King James II, whose brief reign was the catalyst for revolution and war. Indecisive and short on political skill, he did not see his throne slipping away until it was too late. (National Portrait Gallery, London)

William of Orange, stadtholder and later King William III. Moody, reserved and asthmatic, William was invigorated by the fresh air and activity of the campaign. (National Portrait Gallery, London)

Richard Talbot, Earl (later Duke) of Tyrconnell. Brash, calculating and fierce, Talbot came to dominate Irish politics as lord deputy and viceroy until his death in 1691. (National Portrait Gallery, London)

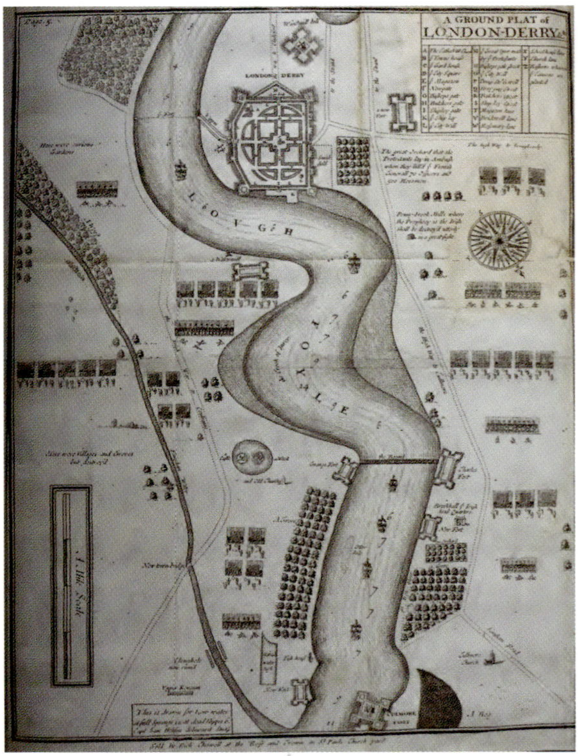

The Williamite chaplain George Story's map of the Siege of Derry. The city sits at the top of the map, with Windmill Hill to the west. Culmore Fort is visible near the mouth of the Foyle.

The view to the sea from Charles Fort, Kinsale, Co. Cork. It was along this path that James arrived in Ireland in splendour, and later escaped in ignominy.

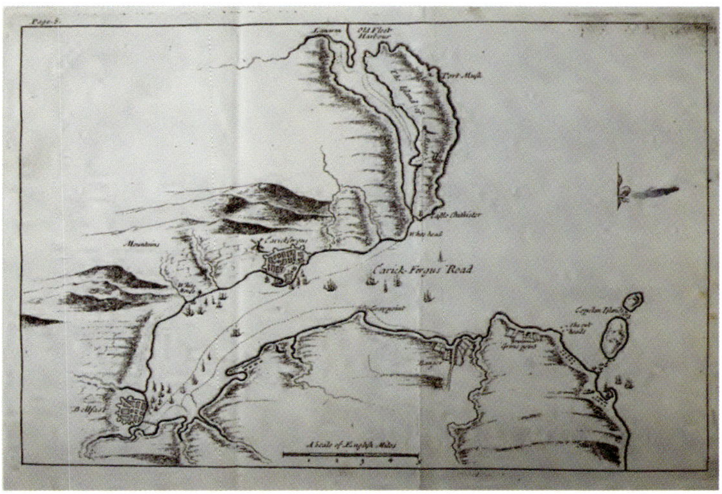

George Story's sketch of the route from Carrickfergus to Belfast, which William followed on arriving in Ulster in 1690.

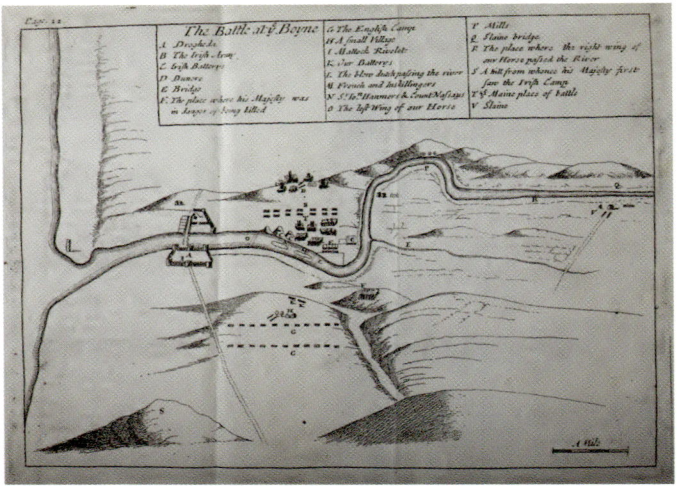

George Story's sketch of the Boyne battlefield. James's failure to block his son-in-law from crossing the Boyne was a devastating psychological blow.

The Battle of the Boyne between James II and William III. (Jan van Huchtenburg)

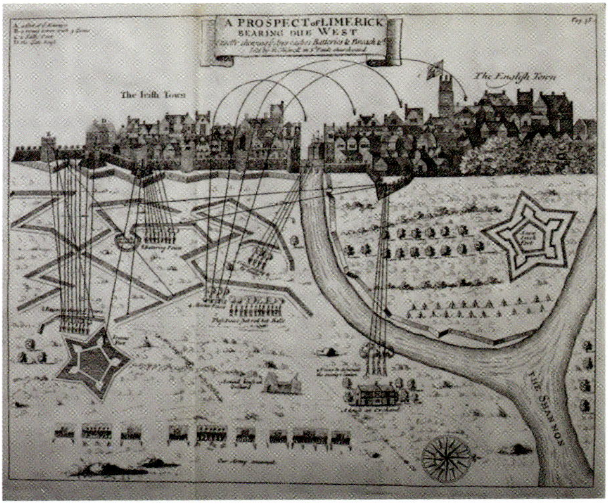

George Story's depiction of the first Siege of Limerick. English town is on the right, with its silhouette of St Mary's Cathedral. Baal's bridge provides access to Irishtown.

King John's Castle, Limerick. (Monica Kub)

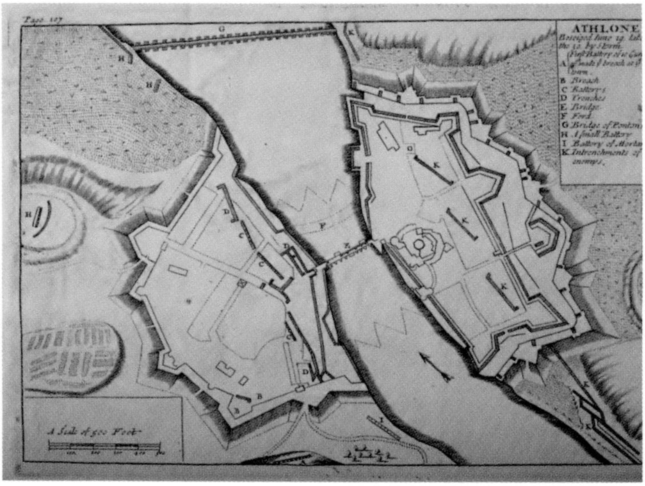

George Story's map of the Siege of Athlone 1691. The Williamite batteries were driven as close to the river's edge as possible, with frightening impact.

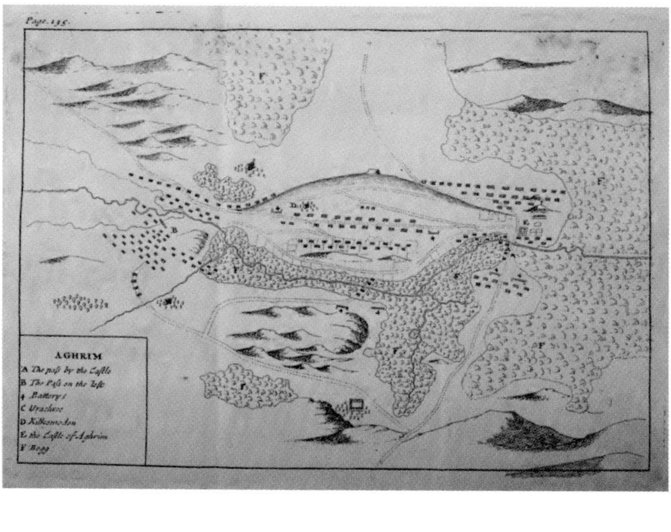

George Story's map of the battlefield at Aughrim, July 1691. Some 7,000 men are believed to have lost their lives at Aughrim, making it the bloodiest battle in Irish history.

The Battle of Aughrim. (John Mulvany)

The Treaty Stone, Limerick, just metres from where the Jacobites were massacred on Thomond Bridge. (Michael Cowhey)

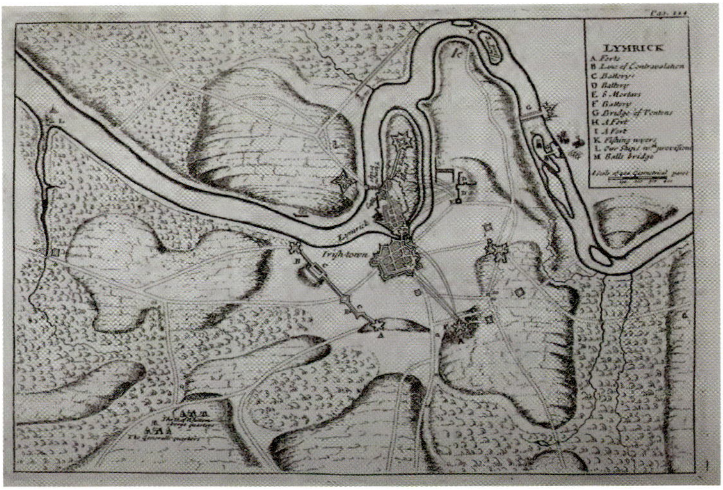

George Story's depiction of the second Siege of Limerick, 1691. Thomond Bridge, Englishtown, was the scene of the final, gruesome confrontation of the war.

Statue of Patrick Sarsfield, Earl of Lucan, in Limerick city. Sarsfield's character and competence are disputed, but his fame as a soldier endures. (Michael Cowhey)

Over the winter of 1689 Dublin croaked and brawled as thousands of quartered soldiers and officers indulged in 'the fooleries of gaming, drinking and whoreing'.[23] The pockets of barmen and purses of prostitutes were stuffed with army wages. Discipline within the ranks collapsed spectacularly. D'Avaux wrote to Versailles in December that the piecemeal success at Dundalk had puffed up the spirits of the army, while John Stevens accused his comrades of shirking their duties for 'pleasure and ease'.[24] Soldiers fought in the streets at all hours; empty houses were stripped, looted and trashed; Protestant churches were broken into and subjected to 'disorderly' behaviour.[25] The riotous and lazy mood seemed to creep out into the rest of Jacobite Ireland, where little attempt was made to fortify or restock garrisons over the winter. 'This was not the way to secure Ireland and conquer England,' one Jacobite wrote.[26]

One man who was not wasting his time, however, was Lord Tyrconnell. With a spring campaign to organise, the viceroy spent the winter in meetings and writing communiqués to St Germain, where James's wife, Mary of Modena, was a useful diplomatic back channel to Versailles. Writing on 12 December, Tyrconnell told Mary – and by proxy Louis – that the French navy needed to get involved in the Irish war and stressed how urgently he required bulk copper to mint coins and cover expenses. Plans were already in motion for regiments of French infantry to arrive in the spring. The wait for the next campaigning season would not be an uneventful one for Dublin Castle. Patrick Sarsfield recaptured Sligo from a combined force of Enniskillen and Huguenot troops after the town had briefly changed hands. The recovering Justin MacCarthy, meanwhile, bribed a guard and managed to escape his captivity in Enniskillen just as the idea of swapping him for Lord Mountjoy, who was still locked up in the Bastille, was being discussed. Tyrconnell narrowly avoided an embarrassing family disaster after a young relative, Colonel Walter Dungan, the son of the Earl of Limerick, picked a fight with the seventeen-year-old Henry FitzJames, James's other illegitimate son, during a drunken argument in Dublin. The Duke of Berwick's younger brother became so enraged that he smashed a glass in Dungan's face, but the row was broken up before swords or pistols could be drawn. It was a violent season.[27]

*

Westminster was starting to breathe down William's neck. Wars were an expensive business, and after Schomberg's failure to confront the Jacobites at Dundalk, it became clear that this one was going to drag on. Parliament was now demanding to know where its money was going. On 1 November the House of Commons appointed two committees to look into military expenses and possible 'miscarriages of war', giving them authority to pull records, request invoices and question witnesses.[28] The Commons then sought permission to send its own inspectors to Ulster to gather untarnished intelligence about conditions on the ground. On 29 November the parliamentary committee on Irish affairs launched a scathing attack on the army supply officer, John Shales, accusing him of a mix of incompetence and treason for failing to prevent the disastrous loss of life at Dundalk. William tried to get parliament off his back by dragging them into the game. He invited the Commons to nominate seven of its members to take over the provision of supplies for the army in Ireland. The Commons refused, politely reminding William that it was his business to manage the war. With the heavy sigh of a man with too much to do, William grudgingly accepted that if this sideshow in Ireland were to end, he would have to go there and end it himself. It would mean putting even greater distance between him and the real battle with France on the continent, which had been Louis's plan from the moment he staked James in this game of royal roulette. 'It is a terrible mortification for me,' William wrote to his ally the elector of Bavaria. 'I am obliged to go to Ireland, where I will be out of knowledge of the world.'[29]

22

Fishing with a Golden Hook

On 2 June 1690 a letter arrived from Rotterdam addressed to Robert Southwell, the Irish diplomat in London who had just been named one of William's secretaries of state. By now Europe was full of chatter about William's plan to travel to Ireland, and more than a handful of people were speculating about what might go wrong. Southwell's correspondent in Rotterdam was one of them. What would happen, he wondered, if William were hit by a cannonball, kidnapped in an ambush or died of fever? How hard would Westminster, Paris and Vienna shake if William did not survive? At this unsure moment in history, the new King of England was the axis on which a great continental struggle was turning. His personal intervention in Ireland, Southwell was warned, could be like 'fishing with a golden hook, where more is ventured than like to be gotten'.[1] As William set sail from Hoylake near Liverpool on 11 June 1690, at the head of a fleet of 300 ships crammed with 15,000 soldiers, siege guns, ammunition, noblemen, officers and £200,000 in silver, he may have been wondering the same thing.

*

A few weeks earlier three Protestants from Dublin – a lawyer, an officer and a clergyman – arrived at the Duke of Schomberg's headquarters in Armagh and requested an audience. It had been an eventful few months in the capital and the three men, who had fled north in secret, had a lot to tell. The winter of 1689 had been a lazy, drunken hiatus for much of the Jacobite army, which was now staggering out the door like a man with a stinking hangover. First, Schomberg was told something he already knew: in March, some 6,000 French troops had arrived in Kinsale under the command of the Count de Lauzun – a short, pompous fifty-eight-year-old black sheep of the Parisian court, whose career had been fast-tracked after he helped smuggle James's wife and son out of London. The French fleet had then returned home with a cargo of almost 5,500 Irish troops as part of a soldier swap that James had reluctantly agreed to in order to keep Louis and 'the great and powerful' minister for war, Louvois, onside.[2] Justin MacCarthy, the general who had been shot to pieces at Newtownbutler and then escaped from Enniskillen, had sailed away with them. No one is certain why, but the relationship between Lord Tyrconnell and MacCarthy had soured to the point that both men were happy to put a few hundred miles of sea between them. MacCarthy was not the only man of note to shuffle off to France in the spring of 1690. Rosen and d'Avaux had both been recalled to Paris and were glad to leave Ireland behind. With Melfort, Rosen, MacCarthy and d'Avaux all out of the picture, Tyrconnell and a small cabal of allies, including his personal secretary William Ellis and judges Thomas Nugent and Stephen Rice, now had a firm grip on the Jacobite government. They did not take long to make their presence felt.

Back in Armagh, the three messengers from Dublin continued to chew Schomberg's ear. Protestant-owned goods and valuables in the capital, they said, had been seized and sent to France as collateral for James's war loans. Their owners were offered brass and copper coins in compensation, but many rejected them or never received payment. Dublin Castle routinely ignored Protestant complaints, unless a well-connected Catholic could be found to lobby on their behalf. When Lauzun had arrived in the capital, he had stomped into Dublin Castle and demanded that the governor, Simon Luttrell, hand over the keys to the city. He had scoffed at the tatty uniforms of the Irish soldiers and demanded that thousands of new hats, shoes and jackets be made at a time when fabric was scarce and expensive. The bulk of the new supplies that had been shipped over from France were still stuck in Cork waiting for carts and wagons. Prices in the capital had risen sharply as French troops began to arrive with silver coins in their pockets, reducing the brass coins already in circulation to worthless shrapnel. Elsewhere, hundreds of Irish recruits levied the previous year had simply not bothered to report for duty in the spring. There were also troubling reports of Protestants in Dublin being interned in prison to prevent them stirring up trouble when William finally landed in Ulster. The lawyer, officer and clergyman had given Schomberg a curious glimpse at the underbelly of Jacobite Ireland. James's army might be sloppy, ragged and ill equipped, but his Irish government still had the power to injure and annoy. Dublin Castle, the nerve centre of Jacobite authority, would have to be captured first, and captured quickly.[3]

*

As the Jacobite army tried to shake off the effects of a sloppy winter in early 1690, Schomberg took advantage. The corridor of the Irish Sea between Belfast and the north-west of England became a highway as transports swept over and back with soldiers and huge stocks of grain and gunpowder. In March, 400 crack Danish mercenaries under the command of the German Duke of Wurtemburg arrived from Chester, instantly standing out as 'lusty fellows … well clothed and armed'. In early May they were followed by regiments of English, Dutch and German troops. On arrival most were sent straight into action at Charlemont, the last Jacobite garrison in Ulster, which was now under attack. After a short siege the eccentric Jacobite commander, Teague O'Regan, surrendered on terms and rode out in a tatty jacket, wrinkly boots and 'almost tipsy with brandy'. A nearby German colonel, getting his first glimpse of the enemy, shook his head and wondered why he had come all this way 'to fight against such scoundrels'.[4]

There was an itch under the Williamites' collars. Perhaps it was the disaster of the previous autumn or hot tempers stirred up by reports of what was happening to Protestants in Dublin. Either way, the army was anxious for work, and when it was confirmed in March that William was on his way, the anticipation spiked. George Story wrote that the news stirred 'great satisfaction' among the troops – partly because William would be bringing silver to finally pay their wages, but also because the chance to impress the king in person was enticing. Some did not wait until William had arrived. On April 18 Cloudesley Shovell, a veteran sailor who had fought at the battle of Bantry Bay the previous year, was in Belfast when he received intelligence that a Jacobite frigate was anchored near Poolbeg in Dublin under light guard. Shovell whipped together a small fleet, sailed into Dublin bay and snuck up the River Liffey with a strike team in longboats. The crew of the Jacobite frigate were busy loading up wool, hides and plate destined for France when a shrill cry went up that they were under attack. Shovell's men rowed hard for the dockside, blasting their muskets and whipping up confusion. Shovell signalled back downstream for a fire ship packed with gunpowder to sail up and ram the frigate. The Jacobite captain panicked and ordered his crew to abandon ship. Shovell's men scrambled aboard, seized the deck and began to steer the frigate out into the bay. Soldiers, city folk and even James himself rushed down to the dockside when they heard the commotion and arrived just in time to see Shovell making off with his new prize. One hot-headed French officer charged into the water on his horse, firing manically with his sidearm. The Williamites slipping away downstream shot back, blew the Frenchman's horse out from under him and sent him tumbling comically into the mud. Shovell's raid had snatched one of James's few warships out from under his nose. It was also proof that Dublin was dangerously vulnerable.[5]

*

With the loss of Charlemont and the raid at Poolbeg, the Jacobites began 1690 fumbling from one setback to the next. Something was amiss. The previous autumn, Tyrconnell had pulled off another masterstroke of military recruitment, but since then a malaise had crept into the Jacobite government. Soldiers were allowed to run amok in Dublin over the winter, while decent intelligence about the enemy's movements had dried up. There were costly lapses in planning: Charlemont, for example, had a stout arsenal of cannons, gunpowder, mortars, bullets and grenades, but hardly any food. In Dublin, there were reports of brass cannons being melted down into coins. It was only after Lauzun had barged into the capital in March that serious efforts were made to tackle the lack of bread and uniforms. For a man known as a frenetic administrator, Tyrconnell and his government suddenly appeared limp. His sharp and sudden fall from grace the previous summer seemed to have turned the viceroy into an old man. He and his cabal were back in charge, but with no rivals left to conspire against and blame, Tyrconnell would have nowhere to hide if things went wrong. He was coming up on sixty years old and was constantly pained by gout and an open sore on his leg. He was overweight and severely stressed, and his heart did not thank him for it. In early 1690 he wrote a letter to Mary, James's queen in St Germain, which was anything but confident: 'God … has not thought fit to shake this confounded Prince of Orange coming over to us with such power as will set us hard … that this country cannot possibly hold out longer than this year … is not to be in the least doubted.'[6] Tyrconnell being who he was, he never stopped working the angles. He knew that Mary would keep prodding Versailles for aid if she knew her husband's cause was desperate. But he was also managing expectations and probably getting his excuses in early.

In the third week of May, the Jacobite army finally began to gather on the outskirts of Dublin in preparation for a march north. Troops were reviewed, officers and companies were shuffled about and supplies were indexed. It had been a dry spring, and as the soldiers began to trudge up the road towards Drogheda they kicked up a cloud of dust that left them all 'stifled and blinded'. There was nothing much to see anyway. The countryside of Louth remained barren and bare, populated only by bandits and peasants scavenging from day to day. When the army arrived at Drogheda, the English Jacobite soldier John Stevens was appalled. He had visited the town in 1685 when he was an official working for the Clarendon government, and back then this bustling port on the River Boyne had been 'in a flourishing condition', crammed with trade ships and market stalls overflowing with vegetables and fish. Now it was a ghost town, 'its trade lost, most of its inhabitants fled, and the buildings ready to fall to the ground'. Like so much else in Ireland, the new epicentre of a European war, Drogheda was 'totally ruined'.[7]

*

The minutiae of running a war brought the best out in William. Since his arrival in London in late 1688, William had been buried in paperwork. On 28 February 1690, as he was drowning in petitions and treasury briefings, he wrote a downbeat letter to his close friend, William Bentinck. 'I do not know how it will end,' he sighed, insisting blankly that 'I shall not lose courage so long as I can keep it.'[8] This was William the administrator, a man who saw warrants and committees as a form of purgatory. William the general, who arrived near Carrickfergus at the head of an armada on 14 June 1690, was a different beast.

After being greeted by Schomberg, Kirke, Wurtemburg and the rest of his generals at the quayside, William boarded a coach and shuttled into Belfast, where he was met by an awestruck crowd and later received a delegation from Derry led by George Walker, the embattled old civilian governor. William was surrounded by a powerful tangle of dignitaries and officers, including George of Denmark, James's other son-in-law; James Butler, the young Duke of Ormonde; Robert Southwell, William's new secretary of state for Ireland; George Clarke, his secretary at war; the count of Solms, the Dutch commander of the blue guards who had seized Whitehall Palace in December 1688; Godard van Reede, the Baron of Ginkel, a stout Dutch general; and, of course, William Bentinck, the king's old friend and the new Earl of Portland. But despite his large and prestigious company, William was in no mood for pomp. After a short stay in Belfast he headed south to Lisburn and Hillsborough, setting a brisk pace for his sprawling ranks of soldiers and officers to keep up with. He scrutinised every detail, inspecting his troops up close despite fears that dust from the march would aggravate his asthma. He had brought a special timber cabin with him that could be dismantled and transported, allowing him to camp with his soldiers instead of wasting time looking for houses to sleep in. When he was politely asked why he was in such a hurry, William bluntly replied that he had not come to Ireland to let the grass grow under his feet.[9]

Some sixty miles to the south, James was driving his own army on with similar vigour. It had been a sluggish few months for the Jacobites, but now at last they had mobilised an army of some 25,000 troops, comprised of Irish, French, Walloons and even some German Protestants who had been captured in the Rhineland, conscripted into French service and then shipped over to Kinsale. As the countryside around Drogheda began to swell with tents, flags and the endless hum of wheels, hooves and feet, James gave off the air of a man with intent. He was still a bag of nerves somewhere beneath all his finery, but at a glance he seemed active and eager to take control of strategy. His army, he later admitted, was 'half disciplined, half armed ... with a weak artillery and very little money', but he was still keen to face his son-in-law on the field.[10] Despite the fact that England's politicians, Protestant clergy and senior army officers all seemed to be at ease with the new regime, James kept hearing whispers of plots and conspiracies to restore him to the throne. In May 1690, three weeks before William left London, an anonymous report claimed that many of the English nobles who had backed William's invasion had met in secret and decided that they 'could no longer support the Prince of Orange'. Pamphlets promising a full pardon for anyone who came back to James's side had been circulated to 'almost every member of parliament'.[11] It became accepted that James's new design was to block

William's march on Dublin, force him into a stalemate and drag out the war until some uprising began in England or the French navy was able to intervene. It was a wishful gamble, and not everyone approved. James's wife wrote to Tyrconnell and urged him to discourage her husband from giving too much credence to rumours of English plots. James, however, was determined 'to hazard a battle' here and now. Besides, he insisted, his soldiers 'seem'd desirous to fight'.[12]

*

The war had turned Louth into a carcass. Its villages were deserted and its fields were naked. It was now just a haunted corridor with two armies creeping through it. From Drogheda, James pushed his troops north to Ardee and then Dundalk. On 22 June scouts from both armies clashed at Four Mile Pass, close to where Schomberg had dug in the previous autumn. The horsemen swept around each other in a panic, charging, swinging and shooting before scattering back to their camps. The Williamites seemed to come off worst, losing somewhere between twenty and sixty men, with a just handful of casualties on the other side. The skirmish stirred James's anxieties back into life. He began to fear that William might send half his army south on a wide loop through County Armagh and then cut him off from behind. Terrified of being caught in a pincer, James told his men to retreat from Dundalk to Drogheda, where he could use the River Boyne as a shield. The day after the skirmish at Four Mile Pass, the Jacobite army was in full reverse.

The soldiers in both camps were on edge, and the tension of waiting for battle made men suspicious and violent. A former Jacobite officer who had deserted over to William was captured and hanged in front of his old regiment. Three Scottish Jacobites defected in the middle of the night, sparking fears that they had been spies all along. An Irish man and woman were caught pouring a strange substance into a well near William's hut. Believing they had uncovered a plot to poison their king, a crowd of frenzied soldiers attacked the pair. The woman was beaten and hung from a nearby tree, while the man was almost cut to pieces with sabres and bayonets. An Irish boy suspected of spying for the Jacobites was hanged. A French Williamite soldier who was sick with fever collapsed and pulled out a hidden set of rosary beads to pray. A nearby Dane, discovering that there was a secret Catholic in their ranks, walked over and shot him dead.[13]

There were only a handful of places where William's army could cross the Boyne. Drogheda had been garrisoned with 1,300 men, and attacking it would be tedious and time consuming. Two miles west, where the river cuts down through a lush and forested valley, there was a ford at the riverside hamlet of Oldbridge and then another at Rosnaree, about three miles further upstream. It would be an awkward bottleneck for William's army of 36,000 men to try and pass through, and James decided to trust the geography. Late on 28 June the Jacobite army reached the north bank of the Boyne, some two miles west of Drogheda, and set up camp. Their plan was to march over onto the south bank the following day and then dig in. Tents were pitched, campfires were lit and tired troops flung off their boots after another hard march. Then, at around midnight, the camp was jolted by an alarm. Something had been seen or heard in the dark, and the Jacobite troops stood in formation all night waiting for an attack that never came. Relieved, they crossed onto the south bank at first light and began to draw up along a hillside gazing down on the river. James set up his headquarters in the ruins of Donore church, about a mile south of the hamlet of Oldbridge where earthworks were now being dug and houses were being fortified with timber blinds and barricades. That night, two regiments of Jacobite infantry garrisoned in Oldbridge stared out into the shallow moonlit water in front of them, knowing that this was where William's hammer would fall. A few hours later, in the soft blue light of dawn on Monday 30 June, a crowd of Irish peasants were seen scrambling down the hills on the north bank of the river, as if fleeing from some great and invisible beast. The slow, menacing thud of 36,000 pairs of boots began to drift over the water, growing louder with every breath.

23

The Boyne

One of the first shots of the battle was almost the last. The Williamite army reached the north bank of the Boyne on the morning of Monday 30 June, but William was not in the mood to fight just yet. The Jacobites were dotted and stretched out along the opposite hillside like firs, but the crevices and crannies of the south bank needed to be scouted before William could make a move. He also tended to think that Mondays were unlucky. Instead of driving his men and artillery into battle immediately, William decided to have a look around. Gathering a party of officers and advisors, he rode down towards the riverside from where he could size up the barricades and earthworks across the ford at Oldbridge. He then rode west along the water's edge, making notes in his head about currents and distances and tree cover. Then, bizarrely, he decided to have a picnic.

Stopping in a small glen, William sat down on the grass and spent an hour eating and chatting with his retinue. The Jacobites watching on the opposite shore were amazed. William was wearing the blue sash and crest of the Order of the Garter and was dangerously visible. Two quick-thinking Jacobite gun crews hauled their cannons up to the riverside and hid behind some hedgerow. When William finished eating and mounted his horse to leave, they opened fire. The first cannonball clattered into one cluster of bodies, killing an officer and two horses. The second clipped the riverbank, spun up towards William and nicked his shoulder, ripping through his coat and tearing off some skin. There was a desperate gasp. An aide dashed over to William and stuffed his handkerchief into the bleeding wound. William, emotionless and in shock, mumbled that he was fine and was quickly rushed away. Across the river 'a most prodigious shout' went up; the Jacobite gunners were convinced that they had just killed the usurper. Within minutes rumours tore through both camps that William was dead. George Clarke, his secretary of war, turned white with terror. 'I could not bring myself to believe that he was alive,' he later wrote.[1] After William's shoulder had been dressed, he felt the need to get back on his horse and ride around the camp to let his men know that he was still there. It had been an unbelievably close shave. If the cannonball had struck three inches closer, it would have taken William's head off or blown a hole through his chest. The impact would have torn through Europe like thunder. 'It would have been of fatal consequence … if he had fallen,' the chaplain George Story wrote later, his heart still in his mouth.[2]

That evening, with his shoulder aching, William held a council of war with his general staff. It was a lively meeting. Rival battle plans were discussed, thrown out and criticised. Some suggested moving inland to find a better, flatter place to cross the Boyne. Others called for the army to charge right across the ford at Oldbridge and smash the Jacobites head on. William ultimately decided to compromise. The Duke of Schomberg's forty-nine-year-old son, Meinhardt, would take one-third of the army – roughly 12,000 men – and march inland to cross the river upstream at Slane. The rest of the troops would stay behind and attack Oldbridge. At some point in the discussion, someone wisely thought to ask how William's soldiers, with all their various languages, colours and banners, would recognise one another in the smoke and carnage of battle. Therefore, the order went out for every Williamite soldier to stick a sprig of green leaves in his hat. As many of the rank-and-file on both sides would be wearing almost identical red coats, that tiny piece of foliage was likely to be the difference between life and death.

Across the valley James was quietly wrestling for his soul, once more torn between his need to fight and his fear of disaster. He had slinked away from this battle twice before, at Salisbury and Dundalk, and at his own council of war on the evening of 30 June he tried to do it again. James decided that their current position would be too tricky to escape from if William managed to cross the river. The only decent road off the battlefield pinched over a bridge a few miles south in the village of Duleek. James, once more an anxious wreck, did not want to be caught with nowhere to run. He ordered that the army's baggage and twelve of its eighteen cannons be packed up and sent back towards Dublin that night in preparation for a full retreat the next morning. Two regiments of infantry were sent down to Oldbridge to cover the withdrawal, while a regiment of 480 dragoons under the command of Tyrconnell's nephew, Neal O'Neill, was ordered upstream to Rosnaree ford to guard their flank. James's council of war concluded, and the cannons on either side of the water that had been taking pot shots at each other all afternoon fell silent. When the mid-summer sky finally began to darken, quartermasters distributed satchels of powder and shot to Williamite troops who had been told to be ready to march 'at a minute's warning'.[3] Fear and adrenaline worked quickly under the skin. Hardly anyone slept.

*

The first of July was a beautiful summer's morning, warm and clear, 'as if the sun itself had a mind to see what would happen'.[4]

At around 5 a.m., just as dawn was breaking, the right arm of the Williamite army began to traipse off upriver. A long, loud and conspicuous train of infantry, horsemen, artillery and wagons began to shuffle away under Meinhardt Schomberg. Very soon scouts brought word that the bridge in Slane, their original target, had been sabotaged. The younger Schomberg adjusted and sent his cavalry to ride off towards Rosnaree instead, where Neal O'Neill and his small scatter of dragoons were waiting. As the first of Schomberg's horses came into view, O'Neill's men opened fire. For more than half an hour the dragoons held the Williamites back, blasting over and over again from behind cover. But as Schomberg's infantry and field cannons finally started to arrive at the ford, the weight of their fire became too thick. O'Neill was shot through the thigh and fatally wounded. His dragoons mounted up and staggered away. Schomberg's troops began to creep over the river.

At dawn, James looked out over the Boyne with a knot in his stomach. From his command post at Donore he could see thousands of Williamite soldiers moving inland towards Slane and Rosnaree, and he began to panic. With the enemy already on the move, he realised it was too late for him to retreat as planned. In a quick flurry of doubt and contradiction, he made a serious tactical error. James wrongly guessed that William's entire army was marching upstream to flank him and therefore ordered some two-thirds of his own force to march west and block them. As the tussle at Rosnaree ford was just beginning, some 17,000 Jacobite soldiers – including all of the experienced French infantry who had arrived in Ireland that spring – were shuffling away from their positions near Donore hill. James left Tyrconnell, Richard Hamilton, the Duke of Berwick and less than 8,000 Irish infantry and cavalry behind to guard Oldbridge against some 24,000 Williamite troops across the river. It was a fateful mistake, and William watched from across the river as his father-in-law stumbled into his simple trap. After 9 a.m.

the Williamite cannons and mortars opened fire and began to pummel the makeshift defences at Oldbridge. After an hour of deafening artillery work, William gave the signal for a full attack.

Hundreds of Dutch blue guards began to march down towards the river, their drums and fifes blaring with intent. When they reached the waterside the music stopped, and lines of men ten abreast began to wade in. As they inched forward their bodies formed a dam, and the current suddenly rose up to their chests. The blue guards lifted their muskets and satchels over their heads and continued to carefully pick their way through the water. The Jacobite infantry, dug in behind earthworks and garden walls and upstairs windows in Oldbridge, stared out at them and waited. Their hearts were pounding. Then, just as the first of the blue guards began to clamber out of the river, a scream went up and the Jacobite guns opened fire. A sudden storm of smoke and noise swallowed the riverside. Dead and wounded blue guards began to crumple as bullets cut into the water. The second, third and fourth lines of Dutchmen piled across and began to rush up towards the Jacobite positions. A violent and furious fight for the riverbank broke out as men stabbed and battered and shot at each other in a haze of fog. One Jacobite officer charged forward and drove his sword into one of the first Dutchmen across the river, but he was trampled and killed moments later as more blue and orange uniforms swarmed out of the water. Within minutes the Dutch had broken through and driven the first line of Jacobite infantry back, brutally seizing a foothold on the south bank of the river.

A few hundred yards behind, Tyrconnell was watching anxiously. Through the curtain of smoke and confusion he could now see thousands of Williamite infantry on the north bank preparing to cross. Masses of English, Huguenot, Danish and German soldiers were moving up to the river in formation. Somewhere in the crowd John Mitchelburne and George

Walker from Derry were preparing their troops to engage. A continent's worth of enemies were gathering in Tyrconnell's eye line, ready to overrun him. Unless the blue guards could be driven back into the river right now, the battle was lost. Quickly gathering together roughly a thousand Irish cavalry troops, Tyrconnell cried out for a charge. An avalanche of hooves came tumbling down the hill towards Oldbridge, where the blue guards had scattered the first line of defence. William watched from across the river in horror. The blue guards, his personal troops, were about to be trampled into dust. Frozen in a moment of despair, William was heard to mutter, 'My poor guards, my poor guards, my poor guards,' as the Duke of Berwick crashed into their lines. The world froze for a split second. But then, through the swirl of smoke, bodies and horses, William could see the blue guards huddled together in tight defensive squares. As the Jacobite cavalry swarmed around them, the Dutch held the lines and fended the enemy off with musket fire and thrusts from their bayonets. The blue guards had survived the charge. George Clarke, who was watching the battle at William's side, heard all the air leave his king's lungs, as one does 'after holding their breath upon a fright or suspense'. William was relieved and elated. He remarked that he had just watched his blue guards do something that he had never seen any infantry do before in his life.[5]

The horde of Williamite regiments on the north bank now began to push over the river towards Oldbridge. Richard Hamilton had tried to drive the rest of the Irish infantry up to engage them, but many of the raw and ill-disciplined recruits simply refused to charge into the hail of cannon shot flying at them from across the Boyne. With no time to scold or threaten, Hamilton simply pulled together more cavalry and led another charge into the Williamite lines. He clattered violently into a regiment of Huguenots, who had no pikes or bayonets to defend themselves, and then into lines of English and Dutch soldiers pushing inland from the river. It was loud, terrifying and cruel work. The Duke of Wurtemburg, the commander of the Danish troops, was leading his men over the river just downstream from Oldbridge when Berwick and his cavalry charged into them at full speed, thrashing their swords and firing their carbines at silhouettes in the smoke. Those Jacobite infantry who did stand and fight could be heard screaming for cavalry support as the Williamites began to overrun them. Again and again the Irish horsemen charged, rallied and charged again, desperately trying to beat back the advance 'with unspeakable bravery'.[6] Tyrconnell himself was near the heart of the storm, straining through age and illness to try and hold the enemy back. He was knocked from his horse in the melee and injured. But the momentum was irresistible. For every Williamite soldier killed after crossing the river, ten more scrambled over from behind him. The Jacobites, deprived of any reinforcements by James's decision to pull most of the army away, simply could not cope.

It was still not even midday, but the bright summer morning had been lost in a hurricane of noise and blood. 'There was nothing to be seen but smoke and dust, nor anything to be heard but one continued fire.'[7] Berwick and his exhausted cavalry charged the enemy ten times, and each time he looked around there were fewer and fewer of his men left alive. Berwick's own horse was shot out from under him, but he was rescued before he could be trampled to death. The Jacobite colonel John Parker's troop of 300 cavalry, who seemed to be constantly in the thick of the fighting, had only thirty men left by early afternoon. Many of the hardened Williamite soldiers from the continent later remarked that 'they never saw brisker work' than that morning by the Boyne.[8] Just before noon, the old Duke of Schomberg decided to lead his cavalry over the river and ride into the furnace. The old general was in his seventy-fifth year but was as keen as ever to prove his grit. Riding headlong into the swarm of Irish cavalry, he was hacked across the head with a sword before an Irish soldier named Brian O'Toole is claimed to have shot him through the neck. The corpse of William's second-in-command, one of the most renowned generals in Europe, slumped to the ground like a butchered carcass. George Walker, the governor who had helped lead Derry back from the abyss, was shot in the stomach and bled to death on the grass. Brian O'Toole, who supposedly fired the fatal shot at the Duke of Schomberg, was killed a few minutes later 'fighting like a lion'.[9] He was just one of hundreds of men who had rushed into that fog of war by the River Boyne and never returned.

With his army beating its way across the river at Oldbridge, William could smell victory. He decided to finish the battle himself. Mobilising regiments of Dutch, Danish and Enniskillen cavalry, he rode left towards a deeper ford at Drybridge, a few hundred yards down river from Oldbridge, and began to wade across. The current was fast, and the horses struggled to keep their feet in the thick mud of the riverbed. It was an exhausting ordeal for man and beast alike, and when William made it across he could barely breathe. He was forced to dismount and lie on the ground gasping for air, as attendants feared he was dying from an asthma attack. A few moments later, William's lungs began to relax. He sat up, slowly rose to his feet and then immediately mounted his horse again. The Enniskillen cavalry began to push up the sloping ground ahead on the Jacobite right, but Irish cannons pointing down at them opened fire, blowing thirty men to pieces in a horrific storm and scattering the rest. William personally rode into the Enniskillen troops scrambling away and called on them to prove their reputations and fight back. Galvanised and furious, they turned and charged back up the hill. Gunpowder smoke and dust were blinding. Shots rained into faceless shapes and crowds. The noise was terrifying. In the confusion, one Enniskillen soldier ran up to William with his pistol cocked, mistaking him for a Jacobite. William kept his cool and simply said, 'What, are you angry with your friends?'[10] The soldier lowered his gun and begged his king's forgiveness. By now, Williamite infantry and cavalry were pouring over the river, and the vastly outnumbered Jacobites were tumbling up the hill in retreat. The battle was done.

Three miles away to the west, James and Lauzun were idly sitting on their horses. Meinhardt Schomberg and his troops had forded the river at Rosnaree several hours earlier, but since then they had been stuck at the bottom of a marshy valley below the Jacobite positions. At the top of the slope, James waited with more than half of his army as scouts went ahead to try and pick a way through the bog. Shortly after midday, a breathless messenger arrived with word that Oldbridge had been overrun and the Jacobites' right flank had been beaten. At that moment, with the day seemingly lost, James finally found a scrap of his courage. Turning to Lauzun, he said that the only thing left now was to charge into the valley towards Meinhardt Schomberg before their men heard about Oldbridge and scattered. But it was too little, too late. Patrick Sarsfield, who had been scouting the marsh ahead, told James that it was simply impassable. In the distance, James could now see some of Meinhardt Schomberg's troops marching away south, as if trying to loop around behind him and cut off his escape to Dublin. James ordered a full retreat from the battlefield. Most of his men had failed to fire a single shot.

The Jacobite retreat from the Boyne was a muddled mix of heroism and panic. After James gave the order to fall back, his soldiers began to converge on the narrow lanes around the village of Duleek from different directions at the same time, igniting alarm and confusion. John Stevens, who had been in the reserve all day and was only just learning what had happened at Oldbridge, saw his comrades throw away their muskets and 'even their coats and shoes' in order to flee quicker.[11] Some

Jacobite cavalry came charging up a narrow laneway, knocking their own infantry out of their road. Jacobite soldiers everywhere began to scatter 'like sheep flying before the wolf'.[12] Back towards Donore, Richard Hamilton was desperately trying to protect his troops as they fled up the hill. Herding together all the able cavalry that he could find, he led one final charge into the Dutch and Enniskillen horsemen. Hamilton was wounded in the attack, captured and hauled before William, the man whom he had betrayed in January 1689 when he travelled to Dublin as his envoy and immediately defected. During a short and curt exchange, William asked Hamilton if the Irish cavalry would attack again. Hamilton replied, 'On my honour, I believe they will.' William snipped that Hamilton's honour was not worth much and rode away.[13] The Irish general who had let Derry slip through his fingers was taken from the battlefield as a prisoner. On the Jacobite left, some of the French infantry drew up in battle formation outside Duleek to ward off Meinhardt Schomberg's men, who had begun to catch up with and shoot Jacobite stragglers 'like hares among the corn'.[14] The Jacobites were in full flight, but William's army did not chase after them. William Bentinck offered to lead 3,000 cavalry into the maze of laneways and ditches around Duleek to butcher the retreating soldiers but was refused. The exhausted Duke of Berwick, who with the rest of the army was now staggering back towards Dublin, suspected that the enemy 'were very happy to facilitate our retreat'.[15]

By nightfall, the battlefield was an empty theatre littered with tents, baggage, discarded clothes and the corpses of some 1,000 dead Jacobites. The Williamites had lost between 500 and 750 men, including roughly 150 Dutch blue guards, their bodies tangled along the riverbed where they had punched through the Jacobite line. Given the monumental size of both armies, the loss of men and materials at the Boyne was relatively scant. The psychological damage, however, was catastrophic.

James had failed to hold his son-in-law back behind the river. A great gate had swung open, and now Dublin, Kilkenny and everything east of the River Shannon was William's to pluck. For the bulk of Jacobite officers and soldiers who had done nothing but stand around that afternoon, it had been a frustrating exercise. As they retreated to Dublin there were 'ill-suppressed murmurs' about how James had fudged his tactics and ordered that 'so many swords should be sheathed without a blow'.[16] The Boyne would be the last time that two contenders for the English throne would face each other on the battlefield. If it was an audition for the role, only one man had truly looked the part.

That night, at the end of a long and weary day, William, his generals and his army made camp near Duleek. Their tents, cabins and supplies were stuck on the other side of the valley, so for tonight at least they would have to rough it. Despite a successful day's work, William was mute, expressing 'neither joy nor any sort of vanity'. His shoulder and his chest were still burning. With no decent houses nearby, William spent the night sleeping in a coach. George Clarke, his secretary at war, found a soft square of grass, stretched out on his back and stared up into the night. Questions about Dublin and the aftermath could wait until morning. Clarke sighed, closed his eyes and 'slept very heartily upon the ground'.[17]

24

They Gave the Kingdom for Lost

James reached Dublin on the evening of 1 July, a few hours after scuttling away from the Boyne. He held an emergency meeting of his privy council in Dublin Castle, and by dawn the next morning he was tearing up the road south, having given orders for governor Simon Luttrell to abandon the capital. One account of that late-night council meeting has James launching a caustic attack on his Irish soldiers, claiming that they had 'basely fled the field' and left him with no choice but to run.[1] Other versions claim that James was typically nervous and unsure and only decided to flee on 'the advice of all his friends', including – apparently – Lord Tyrconnell. The viceroy was stuck somewhere on the road, but he sent his personal chaplain ahead with a message urging James to escape Dublin before it was overrun. The anxious king decided to flee Ireland entirely. After slipping out of the city a few hours later, James and a large mounted escort rode hard through Bray and Arklow, anxiously posting soldiers in every town to cover their retreat. From Duncannon in Waterford he sailed along the coast to Kinsale, where ten French ships that James's queen had sent as an insurance policy were waiting to smuggle him away. Before he climbed up the gangway, James scribbled an order to Tyrconnell, leaving him in command of all civil and military affairs in Ireland and also gave him the authority 'to use his discretion, either to make peace with the Prince of Orange, or continue the war'.[2] With that, the infamous episode that was James's brief, humiliating time in Ireland ended. Whatever happened next in this cursed kingdom, he believed, was Lord Tyrconnell's business.

The greatest immediate casualty of the Boyne had been the Jacobite army's discipline. In the confusion and shock of the retreat, hundreds of soldiers had simply run away. The Duke of Berwick set up a makeshift camp about five miles north of Dublin a few hours after the battle, and overnight on 2 July a long and slow trickle of exhausted and disorderly troops arrived, many of them unarmed after discarding their muskets in flight. When the sun rose the next morning, John Stevens saw only the 'shadows of regiments' huddled around waiting for orders from anywhere.[3] Inside the capital, Tyrconnell was just learning that James had ordered the city to be abandoned and that the army should retreat to either Limerick or Kinsale to 'make the best conditions they could for themselves'.[4] With most believing that William's troops would be breathing down their necks within hours, there was no time to dither. Tyrconnell quickly sent for his staff, gave instructions to pack up his belongings in Dublin Castle and the vice-regal lodge at Chapelizod and issued a general order for the army to retreat to Limerick. The following day, as John Stevens was trudging in a seemingly endless column of soldiers and carts through County Kildare, he watched Tyrconnell and his household tear past them on horseback. Although the nearest Williamite soldier was more than twenty miles away, the presence of the enemy army somewhere in the distance was a constant, nagging malice in the their minds. 'Fear never thinks itself out of danger,' Stevens wrote.[5]

*

William did not want to charge into Dublin like a bull. Just as it had been in London in December 1688, his arrival in the Irish capital would have to be carefully choreographed. On 3 July he received a letter from nine leading Protestants in the city, including the bishop of Meath, informing him that the Jacobites had bolted. Robert FitzGerald, the son of the Earl of Kildare, had set up an interim government to prevent looting, violence or destruction of property. The capital of Ireland, William was told, 'is absolutely at your majesty's repose'. On 5 July the Duke of Ormonde led his cavalry and dragoons to secure the city, and the following day William entered 'in great splendour', riding in procession through streets crowded with jubilant Protestants before attending a service at St Patrick's Cathedral, where a *Te Deum* was sung, giving praise to God.[6]

William had at first refused to get carried away, but in the aftermath of the Boyne it was impossible to not be infected by talk of victory. In a letter to the Earl of Nottingham, who was manning the fort back in London, Robert Southwell wrote that while the Boyne had barely been a skirmish in terms of lives lost, 'the consequence has been of great extent'. James had fled to France, while Lauzun and his French troops were expected to follow. Tyrconnell, his officers and the rest of the Jacobite flotsam were now expected to 'retire to a few places of strength' and 'capitulate in the best manner they can'. Some of Tyrconnell's papers had been found in the discarded luggage of the battlefield, and Southwell had discovered an unsent letter to St Germain in which the viceroy described his army as 'almost destitute'. The ordinary Irish people, Southwell added, 'were already sick of war', and thoughts among William's staff were turning to how Jacobite estates could be carved up 'to pay all arrears of the army'. It was only towards the end of his letter that Southwell seemed to pause and remember that this was still a war of many parts and that Ireland was just a means to a greater end. 'Our hope now all depends on the success of our fleet,' he wrote; the English navy was shortly expected to join the Dutch and attack the French in the English Channel. Southwell did not know it, but as the ink was still wet on his page, one-fifth of William's fleet was at the bottom of the sea.[7]

On 30 June, the day a lucky cannonball almost took William's head off, the combined Dutch and English navies had clashed with the French at Beachy Head, a few miles off the coast of Sussex. The French had snatched a brutal victory, sinking eleven of William's fifty-nine ships and forcing the rest to limp away to port. The defeat sent England into a frenzy. The French were now 'masters of the sea', and it would be nearly a month before the royal navy could be refitted and sent back into action. Until then, the English coast was defenceless. In an age when rumour travelled faster than news, talk of French invasion ships being sighted in the Channel flew up the coast like a condor. William's privy counsellors in London sent a flurry of letters to Ireland, desperately trying to contact their king. After Beachy Head, he was told, the French 'have it in their power to land where they please in England, and probably mean to do so'. Queen Mary, who had been left in charge of affairs in her husband's absence, was frantically trying to hold things together. Local courts of assize were suspended for a month as riders raced from town to town, ordering militiamen to take arms. To make matters worse, word also arrived from the continent that the French had smashed the alliance forces at the battle of Fleurus in the Spanish Netherlands on 1 July. Some 6,000 allied soldiers had been killed, while a further 8,000 had been captured. As William and his generals were busy chasing half-clothed Jacobites out of Dublin, France had struck two devastating blows on land and sea. It was the stuff of nightmares. On 15 July, as London anxiously waited for news from its absent king, Lord Nottingham sent another distraught letter to William. 'If the French should suddenly land, they might in a few days be masters of London … all of which makes his majesty's return so necessary that nothing should delay it.'[8]

*

Back in August 1684, six months before Charles II died, an engineer named Thomas Phillips was commissioned to write a report on the defensive strength of Ireland's main towns, cities and harbours. Phillips was one of the best surveyors of his time and had inspected fortifications everywhere from the Rhineland to Tangiers. For months he rode around Ireland poking at walls and sketching maps. He did not like what he found. With a handful of exceptions, he thought that Ireland was stuck in the wrong era, filled with crumbling old castles not built for the mathematic brutality of modern warfare. Limerick, the old Viking stronghold on the last crossing point on the River Shannon, was perhaps the most disappointing fortress of all. From its old walled town on a small island in the river, Limerick had spilled across into the county, creating a city of two halves: the medieval Englishtown on King's Island and the newer chunk of Irishtown to the south. Both were tightly packed with rickety tenements, wrapped in damp old walls and joined by Baal's Bridge, a stub archway over a tributary of the Shannon known as the Abbey River. Phillips explored Limerick's crowded warren of hidden laneways, taverns and priories. It had layers of music: the percussion of carts struggling up cobbled streets; the creaking of timber as ships crept in and out of the merchants' quay docks; the hum of traders arguing over prices; and the almost constant tapping of rain on leaky slates. Two towers rose up out of the harbour, while the thick bulk of King John's Castle and the sharp lines of St Mary's Cathedral loomed over the skyline. Thomond Bridge, the last crossing on the Shannon, was the gateway into Clare and Connaught beyond.

Thomas Phillips had been told that Limerick was the mightiest fortress in Ireland. The truth, he wrote, 'is quite contrary'. Limerick was the centre of all trade in the southwest, and after Dublin it was probably the most strategically vital city in the kingdom. But Limerick had been allowed to age and wither. Its walls were thin and had 'gone much to decay', while 'only a few small pieces of artillery' were mounted on its gun batteries. Phillips warned that every inch of the old walls would have to be demolished and rebuilt if Limerick was to survive any sort of attack.[9] His recommendations were ignored. In the hot and terrible summer of 1690, Limerick remained an illusion – an impenetrable fortress in the hearts of Irishmen but 'a heap of rubbish' in the cold light of day.[10] It was here that the scattered remains of the Jacobite army began to gather in the days after the Boyne, 'as if they were guided ... by some secret instinct of nature'.[11]

Tyrconnell reached Limerick on 6 July, the same day that William was entering Dublin like a grey-shirted Caesar. Limerick was bracing itself, and the 5,000 or so people who lived there watched with concern as thousands of hungry and irritated soldiers began to land on their doorstep. The journey from Dublin had been awful. Without food or provisions, many soldiers had simply seized what they needed from farmers and villagers. John Stevens and a few others had tried to steal some horses from a farm in Kildare but were chased off by a pack of locals waving pikes. Countless Irish peasants had to put up with having their homes looted. Things became so unruly that the Jacobite command had to issue a warning that plunder was 'forbidden upon pain of death'. But by then it had become too rampant to hold in check, particularly among the French, who 'plundered the country without any distinction of friend or enemy'.[12]

The days since the Boyne had been long and weary for Tyrconnell, and by the time he reached Limerick something in him was lost. Some secret part of him had feared the worst for some time; now it was becoming a cruel reality. His king had fled, the army had been scattered and the capital had been seized. He was already old, fat and sickly before being caught in the magma of a battle and being knocked from his horse. He was now exhausted and in a terrible funk and ordered that his wife and belongings be sent away to France. When he made it to Limerick, Tyrconnell began to lobby the army leadership to accept that the war was over. It would start an argument that would tear the Jacobites in half.

When the rest of the senior officers had reached Limerick, Tyrconnell called a council of war to discuss surrender. A few days earlier, on 7 July, William had issued a declaration demanding that the Jacobites lay down their arms by 1 August. He promised to pardon 'all poor labourers, common soldiers, country farmers … townsmen, tradesmen and artificers' who had sided against him but offered no clemency to the Jacobite gentry or noblemen.[13] The Duke of Berwick, who had sailed with his father to Kinsale but had been sent to rejoin the army at Limerick, does not appear to have been present at Tyrconnell's council. Instead, the old viceroy stared into a room full of headstrong young officers with no intention of giving up the game. Tyrconnell 'insisted that the town could not be held three days, and the country could not be defended, and recommended they capitulate with the Prince of Orange or accept what terms he offered'.[14] Lauzun and his French officers, Tyrconnell added, shared the same opinion. There was uproar in the room. Several officers stood up and began to shout 'with vehemency' that the Jacobites had enough men, territory and courage to keep fighting.[15] Fists were thrashed against tables as Tyrconnell shouted back. Looking around the room, he could see a rival faction forming before his eyes. There were colonels Gordon O'Neill of Tyrone and Nicholas Purcell of Tipperary; the Luttrell brothers, Henry and Simon; Viscount Clare, Daniel O'Brien; and then, standing at the centre of it all, was the man who would become the most serious threat to Tyrconnell's authority: Patrick Sarsfield, 'the darling of the army'.[16]

*

At this stage in his life, Patrick Sarsfield was the most famous soldier in Ireland. He was in his mid-thirties, tall, broad and energetic, his face anchored by a strong nose and chin. He could not have appeared any less like the fat and cranky old Tyrconnell. Tales of his reckless bravery at Sedgemoor in 1685 and Wincanton in 1688 had bubbled into little legends. His father was of Old English stock, while his mother was the daughter of Rory O'Moore, one of the leaders of the 1641 rising. Sarsfield more than likely spoke fluent Gaelic as well as English, which allowed him to mingle and become a popular figure with the Irish rank-and-file. He had gone off to fight in France in 1678 and had returned with fluent French and a short temper. In 1689, when he was travelling around Ireland with Tyrconnell, disbanding surplus regiments, Sarsfield had personally chased after and clattered two soldiers who had attempted to run away while their company was under review. D'Avaux had written that, although Sarsfield was not a pure aristocrat, he was 'distinguished by his merit' and had more clout among the ordinary soldiers than any man in the army.[17] Although he was fond of Sarsfield, James questioned his intelligence and dismissed him as being 'without a head'.

The Duke of Berwick colourfully described him as 'a man of an amazing stature, utterly void of sense, very good-natured and very brave'.[18] Sarsfield may not have been a scholar, but he had raw and unshakeable courage. His capture of Sligo the previous October – after he had occupied it, withdrawn and then attacked it again – was the only real Jacobite success of the miserable Ulster campaign. He was not a man to be ignored.

Tyrconnell's council of war in Limerick was the first moment that Sarsfield began to flex his muscle. More than anyone else, he would have felt cheated by the thought of surrender without having fired a shot at the Boyne. Some wondered if Sarsfield truly was a leader or simply a convenient front for other 'caballing gentlemen' in the army command who no longer wished to take orders from Tyrconnell.[19] The Duke of Berwick in particular believed that Henry Luttrell, who had served with Sarsfield for years, was 'one of the principal instigators' of the dissent, sliding from conversation to conversation 'perpetually speaking ill of Tyrconnell, and inflaming everybody against him'. Berwick accused Luttrell of massaging Sarsfield's ego 'by incessantly praising him' and working hard behind the scenes to 'render him subservient to his own designs'.[20]

But right now, the form did not matter. All Tyrconnell could see was the senior command of the army turning against him. The first council of war broke without an agreement. Some days later a second meeting took place, but this time the viceroy was not present. The army was starting to think for themselves. After the second council, Tyrconnell was approached with a demand that two delegates of the army's choosing be sent to France to brief St Germain and Versailles about conditions in Limerick and explain how the war was not over yet. Tyrconnell was then asked to hand over control of the army and appoint Sarsfield, who held the rank of major general, as commander-in-chief. Tyrconnell angrily dismissed both requests out of hand but accepted that there was no chance of convincing the army to surrender. William's demand for the Jacobites to lay down their arms was ignored. Limerick, with its divided leaders and rotten walls, would have to be defended.

*

Every hour William spent in Ireland was an hour wasted elsewhere. He had barely set foot in Dublin before he was off again, rejoining the army near the suburb of Finglas. His father-in-law had been driven away, but there were still a thousand things to do. Lieutenant General James Douglas was sent west with some 6,000 troops to attack Athlone, a stout fortified town on the Shannon some seventy miles upstream from Limerick. A new garrison was billeted in Dublin, and a commission was set up to explore how much money and property could be confiscated from Jacobite gentry who had 'at any time been in rebellion'. He shaved off pieces of his main army to garrison Waterford, Wexford and Kilkenny. By the second week of July, William knew that the Jacobite army was gathering at Limerick and would have to be dealt with one way or another. His own troops would need to stay sharp. As William was passing down through Naas, a subordinate informed him that one of his soldiers had been caught robbing an elderly woman. When the culprit was brought before him, William beat him with his own cane before having him hanged. There was no time for indiscipline.[21]

On 16 July William was a few miles outside Kilkenny when a bundle of letters from London arrived. As he read each of the dispatches, William felt like he had been shot in the gut. In one single packet of news he learned about Beachy Head, Fleurus, his wife's raising of the militia and England's 'being all in arms to oppose the French', who seemed certain to invade at any moment. He began immediate preparations to return to England before the French navy could sail into the Irish Sea and cut him off. The Dutch Count of Solms, who could barely speak a word of English, was appointed commander-in-chief of the army to replace him. William sent a hurried letter to his privy council in London promising that troops would be sent back from Ireland immediately and that he would follow in 'six or seven days', once his affairs had been put in order. The fizzy talk of victory that had filled the Williamite ranks since the Boyne came to an abrupt end. Robert Southwell's letters grew heavy with worry. William was leaving Ireland while Limerick, Cork, Athlone, Sligo and Galway were still in the enemy's hands. The Jacobites were rallying at Limerick with some 20,000 men. Southwell could not hide his fears about what might happen when William was gone. 'By his absence things may unravel,' he wrote.[22]

After his troops captured Duncannon fort in Waterford on 26 July, William decided that he had done enough and raced back to Dublin to depart. His shoulder was getting worse – in the days after the Boyne he had ridden everywhere on his horse, but the wound had begun to ache so much that he was forced to travel tediously in a carriage. William was lodged at Tyrconnell's old residence at Chapelizod and was signing off on the last of his Irish arrangements when another batch of correspondence arrived. A tremendous weight seemed to dissolve from around his neck. William was informed that since Beachy Head the dreaded French invasion had not taken place. Apart from briefly landing and sacking the village of Teignmouth in Devon – which William had never even heard of – Louis's navy had done nothing. A French privateer had been intercepted off the English coast, and among its cargo was a letter to Seignelay, Louis's naval minister, which revealed that the fleet had been confined to port due to bad weather and illness. As suddenly as it had appeared, the spectre of a French invasion of England had vanished. 'The fright was over,' a relieved George Clarke noted.[23] William abandoned his plans to sail back to England and decided to rejoin the army, which was now moving swiftly through Tipperary towards Limerick. By 31 July the army was camped around the village of Golden, barely thirty miles from the city. A deserter from Limerick brought word that 'the Irish were in division among themselves, and that there is a strong party who are opposite to the proceedings of the lord Tyrconnell'. It was encouraging news.[24]

*

After all the infighting, the Jacobites had at last started to prepare Limerick for the coming attack. Almost all the effort was concentrated on Irishtown, the southern half of the city, where it was expected that the Williamite army would hit hardest. Irishtown had four gates, three old towers, a gun platform known as the 'black battery' on the southeast corner and a wobbling old citadel that the engineer Thomas Phillips had wanted to tear down because it was so decrepit. There was barely a handful of small cannons mounted on the walls. To a harsh eye, the city's defences looked almost comical – a relic of medieval times when walls were built to guard 'against bows and arrows'.[25] The Jacobite engineers worked hard, but there was only so much they could do with rubble and earth. A deep, wide ditch with ledges carved out of the top was dug in an arc around the southern walls, and all the surplus soil was piled up to create improvised forts, which were then braced with 'stones heaped one upon another'. Every house and stable within a mile of the walls was stripped and burned. The work was carried out around the clock by shifts of soldiers. Many of them had nothing else to do, as they had thrown away their muskets on the march down from the Boyne. Brigadier John Wauchope, a gruff Scottish officer, had been so incensed when he saw one infantry regiment of 800 men line up with only 150 muskets between them that he threatened to have them shot.[26]

Limerick was restive. Every conversation seemed to become an argument; every argument became a fight. One afternoon three Irish soldiers were gathering timber from the rubble of an old building outside the walls when a French soldier accosted and beat them 'severely'. An angry stand-off took place, which was only ended when an Irish officer drew his sword and threatened to skewer the Frenchman on the spot. On another occasion, a French soldier shot and killed a Jacobite lieutenant who had confronted him about stealing a saddle. When the Frenchman was in custody awaiting court martial, his compatriots stormed the makeshift brig where he was being held and set him loose, so that 'his barbarous action passed unpunished'. The Jacobite army was splintering from the bottom as well as the top.[27]

*

The Duke of Berwick was alone in his quarters when he heard a knock on his door. Patrick Sarsfield stooped his head under the low doorframe and walked through. He bowed to the young duke and quickly shut the door behind him. What he was about to say could not be overheard. Berwick had been a late arrival in Limerick and was still getting a feel for the place. He did not know, for example, that on 16 July the anti-Tyrconnell faction had almost staged a coup during a march through the city when they planned to disarm the entire French corps by surprise and place the viceroy under arrest. Tyrconnell had discovered the plot at the last minute and quietly changed the arrangements for the march, throwing off the conspirators' plan without the dirty work of arresting officers for treason. Berwick was also unaware of just how deeply opposed to Tyrconnell most of the senior command was. He was about to find out. After swearing the young duke to secrecy, Sarsfield told Berwick that he and the others were 'convinced of the treachery of Tyrconnell' and feared that he was leading them to ruin. He asked Berwick if he would be willing to take command of affairs if Tyrconnell were arrested. The colour drained from Berwick's face. 'I was astonished,' he wrote several years later. He scolded Sarsfield, warning him that to plot against the viceroy 'was high treason'. Berwick warned Sarsfield that if he or anyone else continued to scheme against Tyrconnell, 'I should become their enemy.' Sarsfield left, and the army's hope to depose Tyrconnell before Limerick was attacked ended. It was probably just as well. Paris was already fluttering with rumours about how the cowardly Irish had run away from the Boyne and how their war with William was no longer worth French investment. If word had followed that James's viceroy had been arrested and Lauzun's men disarmed, Versailles would have washed its hands of the whole business. For better or worse, Tyrconnell would remain in charge.[28]

*

The servants and attendants of St Germain stood in full livery, their spines straight and stiff and their eyes following the carriage rolling up the long driveway of crunchy gravel. Its sides were decorated with opulent blue and gold panels; its roof was crowned with hand-carved *fleurs-de-lis*. The carriage came to a halt, and one by one the servants offered deep bows. The King of France had come to see his cousin. James had returned to St Germain on 15 July, carrying a year's worth of ignominy like a knapsack. Here he was again, back in Paris, about to ask his cousin for more money and help. Louis and James embraced and chatted pleasantly at first, but when the exiled king began to press the question of sending fresh troops to Ireland or possibly invading England, Louis turned his head. He had heard the dark rumours of how the Irish 'had abandoned their Prince and left him exposed to the enemy' at the Boyne and were now apparently huddling in Limerick waiting to throw themselves at William's feet.[29] He offered to send empty ships to Ireland to carry away the useful parts of the army, but no more than that. Louis le Grand, the great titan of Europe, would now apply his energies elsewhere. Ireland's war was no longer convenient.

Across the sea, Limerick was preparing to make its final stand without Lauzun and the French. Robert Southwell's prediction in the days after the Boyne that the French and Irish would quickly fall apart had come true. Unwilling to get caught up any longer in factional plotting, Tyrconnell and Lauzun were preparing to depart for Galway and leave the defence of Limerick to the army. Lauzun was delighted to get his men away from the Irish, 'who hate us so much that we fear they will play some dirty trick on us'.[30] From Galway, the French planned to leave Ireland as soon as possible, believing that there was nothing left there but death or captivity. 'They gave the kingdom for lost,' one Jacobite recalled.[31]

In the spring of 1689 it had been the Jacobites herding their enemies into an old riverside fortress, preparing to rip up the last roots of rebellion and claim Ireland for their king. Now they were the rebels, divided and outnumbered, hiding behind wet walls, waiting to spit on a monarch they refused to recognise. Unlike Derry, however, there was no one coming to Limerick's aid. Louis had turned off the tap. It would take some desperate gamble or hidden moment of chance for Limerick to survive. But as this strange war of three kings had already shown, everything was possible.

25

Sarsfield's Pyre

France's failure to attack England allowed William to snap his priorities in place. A swift conclusion to the Irish war was now all that mattered. Before leaving Dublin to return to the dust and blood of the frontier, William issued another public call for the Jacobites to surrender, this time extending the terms to those 'of superior rank and quality'.[1] It was still not enough. By 2 August William had caught up with his army in County Tipperary, where he plunged back into the logistics of the war. After waiting 'for a day or two' he pushed on towards County Limerick through another no-man's land of 'burned and levelled' countryside.[2] His strength in the field had been fattened since the return of Lieutenant General James Douglas, who had given up his attempted assault on Athlone after hearing rumours that Patrick Sarsfield and 15,000 troops were on their way up the Shannon. By now, William had been forced to sacrifice a chunk of the army that had fought at the Boyne – some regiments were returned to England, while others had to be left behind to garrison Dublin and other captured towns. But the army was still marching on Limerick with 25,000 men; a great lizard of noise and colour, its skin dotted with the banners and insignia of Denmark, Orange, Brandenburg and the cross of St George. Whatever the numbers, William's continental army remained a vivid and menacing pageant.

On 7 August the Williamites arrived at Caherconlish, a small village about nine miles south-east of Limerick. They had kept a brisk pace, and all along the road they had met Jacobite deserters leaking news of arguments and conspiracies inside the walls. William listened to it all with relish. In his impatience to reach Limerick before the city gathered itself from all its plotting, he had ordered his troops to move ahead without waiting for the supply train of siege cannons, ammunition, tools, gunpowder, grain and other supplies, which had been late setting out from Dublin and was now picking a slow path through Kilkenny and Tipperary. The roads were in decent shape after a dry summer, but the long lines of carts and carriages were still at least five days behind. William was not concerned. His shoulder had finally started to heal; he was fasting from dawn to dusk to try and earn the rub of providence; and his spirits were high. Robert Southwell wrote that as they approached Limerick William was 'as vigorous as ever I saw him'.[3]

An army is only as strong as its supplies, and the Williamites were towing a mighty cargo: twelve thousand pounds of gunpowder, three thousand cannonballs, eight heavy long-barrelled siege cannons, pontoons to build makeshift bridges, pickaxes and shovels to dig trenches, enough ingredients to make three days' worth of bread and countless other barrels of food, cloth and coins, all trundling along in carts in a line stretched out along the road for almost two miles. Its value was not just material: travelling alongside hundreds of bakers, craftsmen and traders was a Dutch engineer named Willem Meesters, who was 'an excellent artist' of siege warfare and had been specifically recruited for the Irish campaign.[4]

The supply train was a rich bounty. It was also dangerously vulnerable, packed with civilians and guarded by only a light cavalry escort. On 9 August a French Williamite soldier defected into Limerick and revealed its existence to the Jacobite command. It was like brandy from a faucet. Patrick Sarsfield immediately cobbled together a company of horses, struck out over Thomond Bridge and tore off into County Clare to find Lord Tyrconnell and the rest of the Jacobite cavalry, who had set up a temporary camp six miles outside the city. As he raced up the road, Sarsfield began to concoct a plan that was rash, dangerous and almost guaranteed to fail. There was no time to lose.

*

A week earlier, on 2 August, Lauzun and his 3,500 French infantry had marched out of Limerick towards Galway, exchanging spiteful glances with Irish soldiers and townsfolk as they left. Many had seen the great fortresses of Philippsburg and Namur; as they crossed Thomond Bridge they took one final look at the crumbling ruin behind them and scoffed. Lauzun quipped that Limerick's walls could be knocked down with roasted apples, while others took bets that the city would last three days. Despite the fact that they were losing thousands of experienced soldiers right on the eve of battle, the departure of the French was met with 'great satisfaction' among the Irish, who saw them as just another foreign army meddling in Ireland's fight.[5]

Before Tyrconnell uprooted his government from Limerick, he took care of some housekeeping. He appointed the Marquis of Boisseleau, a gruff thirty-nine-year-old French major general, as governor of the city. Boisseleau had been in Ireland since 1689, had briefly served as governor of Cork and had experience of commanding Irish troops at Derry and the

Boyne. He was a veteran of the Franco-Dutch wars and had more experience of siege craft than any other officer in the Jacobite army. He had the tact of a gentleman and the hard shell of a grenadier and was one of the few French officers who had rejected Tyrconnell's belief that the war was lost. Next, Tyrconnell and the senior officers had to agree on a battle plan. The army was split in two, with 14,000 infantry – many of them unarmed – billeted in the city itself while the 2,500 Jacobite cavalry withdrew into County Clare to cover the north bank of the river, keep the supply lines open and provide reinforcements for the city if needed. The Duke of Berwick had pitched a more aggressive plan, urging Tyrconnell to send the cavalry north, cross the Shannon at Athlone and burst out towards Dublin, burning every Williamite garrison along the way. The uproar would at the very least force William to send away troops to shore up his rear and slacken the siege. Tyrconnell would not hear it. It would be too easy for the cavalry to get bogged down or intercepted, he argued, and it would also leave the north bank of the Shannon wide open if William's troops could somehow make it across. Berwick was far from impressed. He was happy taking orders from his father, but being shot down by a career politician was another matter. Years later Berwick was still warming a grudge, snarling in his memoirs that Tyrconnell was 'heavy and fearful' and that 'neither his age nor bulk were accommodated to such an expedition'.[6] Tyrconnell and the cavalry withdrew as planned to a camp six miles from the city in Clare. Berwick went with them while Sarsfield, Henry Luttrell and the Scottish brigadiers John Wauchope and Thomas Maxwell stayed in Limerick to assist Boisseleau. Preparations for the arrival of the enemy were stepped up and every farmhouse, manor and hamlet within four miles of Limerick was torched.

The Williamites snatched their first glimpses of the city on 8 August, when William Bentinck led a party of 1,100 men forward to scout. Their king, inevitably, was not far behind – riding up to almost within firing range of the city walls with Ginkel, Prince George and other senior officers eager to have a look. Their party was spotted by a mounted Jacobite patrol, and although William managed to slip away from danger, a brief scuffle took place in which four or five soldiers were shot. It had been a worthwhile exercise. William already had a rough understanding of Limerick's features from maps and intelligence, but until now he had not seen the newly built outer defences nor the thick jumble of hedgerows that criss-crossed the fields and roads leading up to Irishtown that provided natural, unexpected lines of defence. 'We came to near the town and found all the hedges within a mile of the city lined by the enemy,' the chaplain Rowland Davies wrote.[7] William hastened back to his camp, and at a council of war that evening he gave the order for his troops to advance at first light. Everything now depended on speed.

Shortly after dawn on 9 August, the first Williamite cavalry and grenadiers began to pick their way through the fields and ditches east of Irishtown. They overran two old Cromwellian forts on Singland Hill, which gently rose up over the city half a mile away, and rooted out pockets of Jacobite infantry who fired 'several volleys' before running back to the cover of the walls.[8] The Dutch, Danish and English assault troops began hacking their way through briars and scrambling over ditches, creeping through 'the fullest of hedges and enclosures of any part of the kingdom' as pot shots skimmed past their ears.[9] As the Jacobites drew back within range of the walls, the cannons overhead opened up, tearing into small clusters of Williamite soldiers. One Huguenot officer had his legs blown off, and a handful more were killed. The skirmishing rumbled on throughout the afternoon, but by five o'clock that evening the spatters of gunfire began to end. The Williamites had pushed up to within a few hundred yards of the city's outer earthworks, losing somewhere between a dozen and thirty men for the effort. The Jacobites had lost even fewer. 'We lost but very few men, nor indeed could we spare them,' John Stevens wrote.[10] The soldiers had been close enough to taunt and heckle each other through the hedges, but the real fighting between them would have to wait. The handful of small cannons that the Williamites had brought with them were dragged up to Singland Hill and began to pepper the city with shells, sending two or three cannonballs through a chapel during Mass, but otherwise causing little mischief.

After the fighting died down, William sent a trumpeter to summon the city to make terms. Boisseleau sent back a note written in French to Robert Southwell – not William, whom he refused to recognise as king – stating that he intended to earn the Prince of Orange's esteem with a vigorous defence of the city. 'I am, Sir, your very humble and very obedient servant, Boisseleau,' he sarcastically concluded. Southwell was indignant and angrily predicted that when the heavy cannons and ammunition arrived in a few days, Boisseleau 'will be content to treat with the King of England, tho' he now refuse to do it with the Prince of Orange'.[11]

*

As Boisseleau was picking a fight with his pen, Patrick Sarsfield was rocketing through County Clare towards Tyrconnell's headquarters. When he reached the viceroy, Sarsfield told him what he knew about the Williamite supplies and immediately laid out his plan: he would lead a large and light cavalry force on a long sweep around behind the enemy lines and destroy the baggage train before it reached Limerick. He reckoned he would need around 600 men, which would still leave Tyrconnell with a healthy reserve of cavalry in Clare. No one knows for sure if there was a quick agreement or a testy debate between two men who were beginning to loathe each other. But within a few hours, Sarsfield was on the move with a large strike team, each of them carrying only their carbines, sabres and a handful of rations. Tyrconnell had weighed the odds and decided that Sarsfield's risk was worth taking. Sarsfield's first stop was Annaghbeg, 'a very rapid and dangerous' ford just upstream from Limerick, where the Jacobites had posted a barricade on the north bank.[12] On 9 August, after their army had seized the eastern approaches to Irishtown, Williamite scouts snuck up to Annaghbeg and saw companies of Jacobite infantry and cavalry dug in around a large manor on the other side. A few hours later, just before dawn on 10 August, Ginkel and Kirke approached the ford with a large assault but discovered that it had mysteriously been abandoned. Ginkel scratched his head and suspected that something was up.

In his eagerness to force Limerick into capitulation, William drove his lines right up to within sight of the walls on 9 August. 'The Prince of Orange … was informed that we were weak … that we had few arms and that our soldiers lacked everything necessary, which was for the most part literally true,' Sarsfield later wrote.[13] William hoped that the ominous vista of his army camped before the walls would scare Limerick straight. His confidence was misplaced. While still waiting for the trench-digging tools and heavy cannons in the supply train, the Williamite soldiers spent the next few days sitting idly outside the walls as shot after shot from the city's artillery dropped on their heads. Cannonballs skimmed off the dry ground, blowing off arms and legs. A member of William's king's guard was blasted to pieces by a direct hit, as were two of Prince George's horses. A tent right next to William's was hit by a shell, which forced William to pull his headquarters back out of range. The city's cannons 'played … most furiously' on the Williamite lines. 'We have not as yet our great guns nor mortars … we do nothing but lie and receive their shot,' one frustrated soldier wrote.[14]

On the afternoon of 11 August a Protestant landowner from Tipperary named Manus O'Brien arrived at William's camp and demanded to speak to someone in charge. O'Brien claimed that he had just seen some 600 Jacobite cavalry cross the Shannon near Killaloe, ten miles upriver from Limerick, and then disappear into the Silvermine Mountains, a thick ridge that straddled the border between counties Limerick and Tipperary. O'Brien knew that the Williamite supply train was somewhere on the other side of those mountains and feared that 'something extraordinary' was unfolding. His pleas were ignored. 'The messenger … was not much taken notice of at first, most people looking upon it as a dream.'[15] But after refusing to leave the camp, O'Brien eventually stumbled across an officer he knew, told him his story and was quickly brought before William himself. The king, who had other things on his mind, sent scouts up to Killaloe to verify O'Brien's story. When they returned a few hours later confirming that tracks were found snaking up into the Silvermines, William asked Bentinck to look into it. Bentinck passed it on to John Lanier, a one-eyed colonel who had defected from James in 1688, telling him to send out extra cavalry to escort the supply train. In the commotion and distraction of the camp, the instruction lost all urgency. Lanier did not ride out with his party of some 600 horsemen until 'after twelve of the clock that night, or rather two in the morning', several hours after William had given the order.[16] By then, it was already too late.

Sarsfield and his men had spent that day hidden in the forest that covered the Silvermines like a blanket. Small teams of scouts had ridden ahead, and by nightfall they had learned that the Williamite artillery train was camped near the ruins of Ballyneety Castle on the road between Pallasgreen and Tipperary town, sixteen miles from the city of Limerick. Irish lore has it that, with the guidance of a local bandit named Michael 'Galloping' Hogan, Sarsfield and his men took off after sunset on 11 August and rode hard for several hours, aware that the enemy was probably looking for them by now. After a tough and tiring sprint of more than twelve miles, Sarsfield and his party rode up onto the slope of a stubby hill overlooking the camp, less than a mile in the distance. From there, they could see the silhouettes of dozens of wagons stretched out carelessly along the road, while the flicker of campfires illuminated rows of tents and grazing horses. The camp was lightly guarded: it was being escorted by some eighty cavalry from the regiment of Colonel Edward Villiers, but after the wagons had halted for the night the officers had ridden ahead to the village of Dromkeen to find quarters.

Sarsfield's cavalry stretched out in a wide line and began to trot slowly down the slope, their fingers clenched tight around their pistols and sabres. The sound of their approach was lost in the late and lazy bustle of the camp. Some accounts claim that the Jacobites had discovered the password to sneak past the outlying sentries. Others claim that Sarsfield himself had thrown off their cover and given the order to attack by shooting in the face the first sentry they found. Either way, when the raiders were within a few dozen yards of the camp there was a sudden and violent burst, and their horses charged. The chaos was quick. The Jacobites ripped through the camp like hornets, slashing and shooting at half-sleeping men scrambling for safety. The riders swarmed over and back through the unguarded wagons, cutting down any soldier who broke cover or tried to shoot back. The screams and roars and crashes of gunfire were horrendous. Several merchants and a few of their wives were killed in the frenzy. Willem Meesters, the artillery engineer who would have been a useful prisoner, flung himself into a bush of nettles to hide. In just a few minutes the rout was finished, and somewhere between fifty and eighty people lay dead or dying in the grass.

With the camp secured, the Jacobites immediately got to work spoiling and destroying as much of the materials as possible. The pontoon bridges were stabbed full of holes, wagons of grain were flipped over and set alight and the horses were rounded up as loot. The shovels and pickaxes were used to dig a line of pits in the ground, into which each of the heavy siege guns was flipped muzzle-first, their chambers stuffed to the brim with explosives. With their fuses pointing up towards the stars, a line of gunpowder was poured between the half-buried cannons, while the wagons of cannonballs and musket shot were piled around them like a bonfire. The gunpowder was lit and Sarsfield's raiders swept away, their night's mischief almost done. Then, like a star falling out of the sky, a tremendous fireball lit up the night and sent a tremor through the earth that was felt for miles in every direction. A Williamite chaplain quartered with the officers in Dromkeen wrote that the explosion 'made our house shake and all within it startle',[17] while just over the horizon 'they saw a great light in the air, and heard a strange rumbling noise'.[18] An hour later, a survivor of the attack staggered into Dromkeen and told the officers what had happened. They raced back to the campsite but found only carnage: the wagons and supplies were burning, while dozens of dead and wounded shapes were littered on the grass. The cannons and ammunition were in a smoking heap. 'All the powder was blown up, the match and instruments of the guns, and wagons and corn were all burned, and great pieces of each blown over the fields.'[19] Sarsfield's pyre had blasted William's supply train to pieces. The only saving grace was the fact that the explosion had been so violent that it had thrown two of the eight heavy cannons out of the ground, breaking the line of gunpowder that was supposed to blow them to pieces in synchronised succession. Six of William's heavy siege guns therefore survived the attack, but almost everything else was reduced to ashes. The stunned officers looked around for any trace of the culprits, but Sarsfield and his men had disappeared into the night like ghosts.

*

Somehow, Sarsfield had pulled it off. The raid had been a stunning piece of improvised warfare: a mission of courage, desperation and superb carelessness. It was Sarsfield in a nutshell, and in the immediate aftermath it seemed to breathe new life into the Jacobite cause. On 13 August Robert Southwell sent a blunt update to London. 'We have had a considerable misfortune,' he explained.[20] On the night of the raid, John Lanier and his troops had been finally riding along the road towards Ballyneety when they saw the sky explode, and by the time they wheeled around to cut off Sarsfield's retreat he was already flying up the Shannon towards Portumna, a small crossing forty-five miles upstream from Limerick. When the news reached the city it 'gave such an encouragement to the Irish, that they laid aside all thoughts of capitulating'.[21] On the other side of the walls, it was a brutal blow. 'The greatest loss is the loss of time,' one soldier wrote. 'Without fresh guns we can do no good against Limerick.'[22] Southwell seethed as he thought about the dismissed warning signs and delayed orders. 'It was in our power to have prevented it all,' he grumbled.[23]

The attack shook the narrative of things. William immediately ordered fourteen new siege cannons and thousands of pounds of gunpowder and ammunition to replace everything that had been destroyed, but it all meant wasted time. William's troops would now not be able to fully invest the city until late August, dangerously close to autumn. His men were already going days without bread, and many began to wonder if wind and rain and scarcity might yet be the ruin of them. 'Limerick holds out resolutely, and hourly kills with their random shot,' one soldier scribbled in a letter, adding that many of the men now feared that taking the city 'will be both a bloody and tedious task'.[24] For now, at least, Sarsfield's raid had shaken the inevitability out of the siege. It had rattled Williamite morale and bought Limerick precious time. It was also the moment that Sarsfield's name was burned into Irish folklore. A Gaelic poet would later eulogise that this 'pillar of valour' with 'white handsome body and fair glossy hair' had sent William's hopes of victory 'like the smoke of a candle up into the sky'.[25] But William had too much at stake to let the loss of powder and guns break him. His hands were still wrapped around Limerick's throat, and he was about to squeeze.

26

Thirty Paces Wide

The days had been sucked into the same helpless rhythm. Hundreds of exhausted soldiers would march out through the gates of Irishtown and relieve the men who had spent hours huddled in the trench or on one of the huge new forts of mud and brick. They would find somewhere to squat, tuck their necks in and wait for mayhem. There had been a quiet few days after Patrick Sarsfield had blown the Williamite supply train to smithereens, but like a rough tide or a bad harvest, some things were inevitable. On 16 August the six heavy cannons that had survived the ambush at Ballyneety were finally hauled up to the front lines and put to work. Cannonballs weighing eighteen and twenty-four pounds each began to pummel the eastern wall of Irishtown, showering the defenders with shrapnel and razor-sharp bits of brick. The Williamites managed to scrounge new shovels and pickaxes, and after an immense night of digging on 16 August their trenches were now only 150 paces away from the outer defences. Thick sacks of wool lashed together with rope were stacked up to deflect Jacobite pot shots and grenades. The contest was becoming very close. At midnight on

17 August, Williamite shock troops overran one of the Jacobite earthworks, using ladders to climb over the rim before driving the defenders out with grenades and bayonets. Meanwhile, the main Williamite battery on Singland Hill to the south-east was working round-the-clock to keep the city sleepless and under fire. Shells smashed randomly into houses, draperies, butcher's shops and storehouses. William was only sleeping three or four hours a night and constantly demanded progress. Everything had to be quicker, quicker and quicker. He knew how little time he had. 'The king must soon be master of this place,' Robert Southwell wrote.[1]

Governor Boisseleau did not have enough troops to give his men more than a day's rest in between their shifts in the outer defences. The infantry were regularly drilled and inspected to keep them sharp, but fatigue and restlessness quickly began to set in. 'Alarms … were frequent,' John Stevens wrote as the bombardment of the city grew heavier and nerves frayed.[2] The high and narrow rooftops of Irishtown were clear targets for Williamite gunners, who were unleashing everything from red-hot cannonballs that would start fires to cluster bombs designed to spray explosives and shrapnel on impact. One night a heated shell crashed over the wall and started a fire in a stable that quickly spread, sending a tower of flames up into the sky. The Williamite soldiers outside the walls cheered in celebration, watching with relish as the fire 'burnt all that night, destroying a great quantity of hay, with several houses'.[3] William's strategy was simple. After scouting the city for himself, he decided that 25,000 or so troops would not be enough to attack Limerick from both sides. He had captured the crossing at Annaghbeg, but only as a precaution. William and his general staff agreed that they would concentrate all their firepower on Irishtown – capturing its outer defences, blowing a hole in the walls and then fighting their way in. There was no time for feints or intricacy, and it was too late in the year to starve Limerick out.

The Williamites' plan gave a brutal simplicity to the Jacobites' task: hold the line, survive and keep surviving.

On 20 August, Williamite assault troops crept into the furthest line of trenches, some 500 yards from the south-east corner of Irishtown, and waited. All throughout the day their cannons pummelled the walls and the outlying Jacobite forts, and at 2 a.m. the grenadiers were finally given the signal to attack. They sprung out of the trenches and sprinted maniacally towards one of the Jacobite mounds of earth, dubbed the 'yellow fort', which was 'within a pistol shot to the south wall'.[4] When they were at its base, they flung grenades up over the edges and lashed ladders to its sides. The few dozen Jacobites above them pointed their muskets down into the dark and began to spray the faceless figures with bullets. They beat back two waves of Williamite attacks before the enemy finally bludgeoned their way up and drove them out. Word flew back into the city, and within an hour some 1,800 Jacobite cavalry and dragoons rode out of Irishtown to counter attack. Seeing the swarm of horses closing in on them in the dark, the Williamites in the fort fired as fast as their muskets would let them. Cannon fire from batteries on both sides chewed up the ground around them. The Jacobite horsemen rode through the torrent of gunfire as they tried to fight their way up the fort. There were only shapes and explosions in the dark, as bullets whizzing in every direction cut through legs and chests and skulls. The Williamites then sent some of their own cavalry into the fray to even the numbers, and the Jacobite horsemen were forced to fall back.

The battle for the yellow fort had been the deadliest encounter of the war since Oldbridge. An estimated 300 Jacobites had been killed, while the Williamites lost 79 men dead and a further 192 wounded. 'The service was very desperate,' one Williamite soldier wrote in a letter,[5] while John Stevens wrote that 'our loss was considerable'.[6] At dawn on 21 August the Williamites held a vital mound of earth and brick less than a cannon shot from the city walls. Within two days they had dragged up some of the fresh heavy guns that had been sent for after Ballyneety and began to pound the rooftops of Irishtown without ceasing. The Jacobite guns mounted on the citadel, the black battery and at other points on the walls fired back when they could, but the sheer intensity of the Williamite artillery was unbearable. In the Williamite camp, Robert Southwell's pen started to crow: 'The enemy must be convinced there is no withstanding our men,' he wrote, though he admitted that, with their tenacity and refusal to surrender, the Jacobites 'have much outdone our expectation'.[7]

*

The life was being bled out of Limerick. When William and his army had first arrived, the city's defenders had jeered and lobbed defiant cannon shots right into their camp. Then word of Sarsfield's raid on the enemy supply train had electrified the place. But in the week that followed, morale started to sour. Life under an endless bombardment had become fraught and terrifying, and the prospect of survival dwindled every hour. When they were posted in the ditch outside the city, the Jacobite troops were at the mercy of splintering stones as the Williamites intensified their efforts to blow a breach in the east wall. In those few off-duty hours inside the city, they found 'as little rest as at other times'.[8] They bunked down on piles of straw or in filthy cots and waited for a bomb to crash through the roof and kill them. Irishtown began to stink of cinder and filth. There were a few hours of respite on 23 August, when both sides agreed a brief ceasefire to bury their dead, but afterwards the terror promptly resumed. The Williamites were digging around the clock to carve their trenches closer and closer to the walls. By 24 August their lines were just fifty paces from the Jacobites' outer ditch – no more than the length of a good garden. Governor Boisseleau feared that his men might buckle and warned that any soldier who abandoned his post would be shot. The Williamites threw up another battery of cannons outside the city, this time pointed towards Baal's Bridge, the only point of escape from Irishtown into Englishtown. Twelve heavy guns were likewise mounted on the yellow fort and began to fire almost without pause on one small section of the east wall. Every night the bombs and mortars kept landing, like hot stones falling from heaven. No one slept.

Then, on Monday 25 August, autumn arrived. Throughout the morning the rain fell 'at such a furious rate' that trenches were flooded with as much as two feet of water. The fuses of the Williamite cannons would not light. The sky cleared in the afternoon and the guns got back to work, but William's mood seemed to immediately sink. During a conversation in his tent that evening, William asked 'in his dark and reserved way' whether it would be quicker for a man to sail to England from Dublin or Waterford. Robert Southwell read between the lines and tried to jolt his king's confidence, replying that the best route would be via Cork and Kinsale after capturing Limerick. 'To this he would say nothing,' Southwell wrote. William had run his father-in-law out of the kingdom, captured Dublin and chased the enemy army into a crumbling old fortress. But now the one element he could not control, the one thing he feared the most – the weather – had charged in to have its say. 'Should such weather hold, it would make things impossible,' Southwell admitted.[9]

The first blast of rain was a reminder that time was running out. On 26 August the Williamite cannons stepped up their furious bombardment, and at some point during the afternoon the heavy effort finally paid off. A section of the east wall collapsed, creating a gap about fifteen yards across. Rubble and broken bricks tumbled down, creating an ominous ramp right up to the breach. For the rest of the day and well into the night, the cannons fired continuously to widen the breach and flatten the rubble below it, priming the ground for an imminent attack. The Jacobite infantry who had gone days without sleep remained welded to their posts out of fear and duty. Mortars, hot shots and incendiaries continued to pummel Irishtown throughout the night. Boisseleau ordered his troops to build a makeshift barricade in the streets behind the breach out of rubble, timber and up-turned carts and had cannons dragged up to the breach that was now 'above thirty paces in width'.[10] In a few hours' time, this entire war would shrink into a violent contest for that tiny patch of the kingdom. Everyone knew it.

*

The cannons were awake and snarling before first light on Wednesday 27 August. It was a hot and dry morning. William had decided that the assault on the breach would take place in the afternoon, and all throughout the morning barrels of ammunition, gunpowder and woolsacks for cover were carried down through the trenches. The most battle-hardened grenadiers in each regiment were plucked out and sent to the front with the perilous honour of leading the attack. By midday, 500 of them were crammed in the furthest trench like sardines, with an arc of English and continental troops behind them: Dutch blue guards on their right, Danes on the left, four English regiments in the centre and hundreds of Brandenburg mercenaries in the rear. William and his generals positioned themselves on Singland Hill to view the carnage.

By around 3 p.m., the Williamite cannon fire had died down and the Jacobites on duty along the ditch began to swap with the next shift. As the relief soldiers trudged down through Irishtown to take their posts, they found Governor Boisseleau anxiously zigzagging through the streets, as if searching for a burglar. He barked at every man to light the fuse on his musket and stay sharp. Then, at half past the hour, three successive shots from the Williamite battery gave the signal to attack. The 500 grenadiers clambered over the lip of the trench and began to charge towards the wall like demons. A blood-curdling cry went up, followed by the pop and flash of grenades. The Jacobite soldiers waiting to be relieved from the ditch panicked and began to scramble back through the breach in the wall behind them. Inside the city, the soldiers marching towards St John's Gate froze in the sudden crash of uncertainty. Boisseleau came sprinting past, his sword in hand, and roared at them to follow him to the wall.

The Williamite grenadiers leapt down into the abandoned outer ditch. They had been given orders to simply hold there and wait for support, but in the mad frenzy of the charge they climbed up the other side and began to pour over the rubble, through the breach and into the city. Time seemed to stop. Jacobite soldiers were lined up behind the barricades in the street, their eyes and muskets fixed on the gap in the wall. But no one fired. For a split second, no one knew if the dozen or so red coats now staggering down through the breach were the last of their retreating comrades or the first of the enemy. Then, after an eternity, someone spotted a sprig of Williamite green in one hat. In that same moment a Williamite officer climbed to the top of the breach, raised his sword over his head and roared out, 'The town is ours.' There was a crash of noise, as if two ships had collided in a storm. The Jacobite guns along the barricade opened fire, cutting down the first line of Williamite grenadiers and choking the narrow streets with smoke. With their orders to hold back no longer relevant, the next waves of Williamite troops began to pour through the wall and a gruesome fight for the breach began. Soldiers charged into a hailstorm of shot, climbing over the bodies of dead comrades and desperately trying to find cover. 'They pressed over, fresh men succeeding those that were killed or wounded,' one Jacobite wrote of the horrific scene. As each line of Williamite troops was ripped to pieces, more and more piled in behind them, the enemy army 'insensible of its losses'.[11] They pushed closer and closer to the barricades in the street, as grenades and bullets flew through the air like hail. 'The noise was so terrible that one would have thought the very skies ready to rent in sunder.'[12]

As the Williamite troops began to gain a foothold in the street beyond the breach, the Jacobite soldiers rushed out from cover and crashed into them. The most furious and cruel hand-to-hand fighting of the war began. For almost four hours men punched and clubbed and wrestled and stabbed each other, and a few square yards of Limerick city descended into a vision of hell. Eyes burned with dust and smoke, while men and women hurled rocks and broken bottles down on the Williamites from windows and rooftops. Humanity and mercy had no place. In the bloodlust of the moment, the only desire of all these humans was 'to ruin and undo one another'.[13]

Panic swept through Irishtown. Civilians and soldiers who were not sucked into the vicious struggle at the breach began to flee over Baal's Bridge into the northern half of the city. The new Williamite battery aimed at the bridge saw the commotion and opened fire. The Englishtown guards were forced to haul up the drawbridge under heavy fire to prevent a stampede. The desperate fighting at the wall continued, but the Williamites could not force their way through. The cannons and muskets at the barricades created a killing zone behind the breach. Corpses, rubble and muskets littered the ground. Then, as the waves of Williamite troops attacking the breach seemed to suddenly slacken, a French infantry officer, Lieutenant Colonel de Beaupré, leapt over the barricade and sprinted towards the breach. Deranged with adrenaline, dozens of Irish infantry raced after him and began to pour back through the wall into the enemy lines outside. Hundreds of Williamite troops climbed up out of the trenches to face them. A sea of limbs and fire washed out through the wall. Cannons on both sides roared into life, hurling shot down into this new tangled mass of human effort. The Jacobite guns on the citadel, the black battery and a small fort across the Abbey River on King's Island began to thrash the bulk of the Dutch, English and German infantry now pushing up towards the wall. Legs and skulls were blown apart, spraying screams and gore into the summer air. Five hundred Jacobite dragoons swept out of St John's Gate on the south wall, looped around at full speed and crashed into the Williamite flank. It was the most loud and brutal thing in the world. Men killed, killed and killed again. A company of Brandenburg soldiers climbed up and overran the black battery, like ants swarming over a tree stump. They were just about to seize its cannons when a massive, stunning explosion blew the tower to pieces. Masonry and shredded bits of flesh were thrown skywards 'with a most terrible noise'.[14] A magazine of gunpowder in the tower had accidentally ignited, but the Williamite soldiers caught in the fight below suddenly feared that the ground was mined with explosives. Some began to fall back. The Danish troopers on the left held their ground and 'fired upon the enemy with all imaginable fury'. The haze of gunpowder smoke became so thick that it formed 'one continued cloud' that drifted away into the distance, as if a volcano had erupted. The Williamite chaplain George Story looked out across the battlefield and saw only 'dust, smoke and all the terrors that the art of man could invent'.[15]

By seven o'clock that evening it was over. The Jacobites had driven their enemy back through the wall, and somehow Limerick had survived. Along the streets of Irishtown, up over the breach and down into the trenches beyond, there was a trail of slaughter and suffering. Dismembered bodies were strewn everywhere; wounded and dying men crawled and limped and moaned, many of them blinded by explosions and shrapnel. The Williamites staggered back towards their camp at Singland Hill filled with 'anger and sorrow' at the bloody cost of their failure.[16] Boisseleau, who had stood side-by-side with his men on the barricades all day, was milling through the streets inspecting the damage when a disoriented Williamite soldier staggered up and surrendered to him in person. 'God had not ordained the town should be lost at this time,' John Stevens wrote in his journal, relieved that he was still there.[17] The Williamites had suffered over 2,000 dead and wounded trying to storm the breach, while some 500 Jacobites had been killed trying to stop them. Somewhere among all the corpses was de Beaupré, the French officer who had inspired the Jacobite counter attack and paid for it with his life. The day after the battle, Robert Southwell wrote another letter to London. 'I have no good news,' he reported glumly.[18] Through sheer tenacity and sacrifice, Limerick had endured.

*

The day after the battle the rain began to pound once more. The Williamite cannons continued to fire on the breach, convincing everyone that another attack was imminent. But that night, William held a council of war to discuss what to do next. Reluctantly accepting that it was too late in the year to keep going, he decided to raise the siege. He ordered three frigates to sail down from Dublin to Waterford, from where he would later depart for Bristol, less than twelve weeks after he had arrived. The shattered Jacobites spent Friday 29 August crouched in cold and wet trenches, waiting for the enemy to try their hand again. But at first light the next morning, there was silence. Fearing some sort of trick, a few Jacobites crept out into the fields and ditches beyond the walls and discovered that the enemy had vanished. They 'stole away in the dead of the night', John Stevens wrote, leaving their shovels and pickaxes scattered about alongside hundreds of unburied bodies stripped of valuables.[19] A few Jacobites tiptoed up to Singland Hill, looked east and saw the Williamites trudging away towards Tipperary. It was over.

Men began to wander out of Irishtown gingerly, as if stumbling out of a dark room. They rummaged across the battlefield inspecting the wreckage and searching for loot. The Jacobites shadowed their retreating enemy for miles, finding tons of abandoned coal, hundreds of discarded bombs and cannonballs and the grizzly remains of a Williamite field hospital that had burned to the ground, killing every man in it. The Jacobite cause in Ireland, much like the city it had taken shelter in, was battered, breathless but alive. Victory was a pile of fetid and smouldering rubble, mounds of broken earth and charred rooftops. Outside the walls of Limerick, there were so many corpses on the battlefield that 'infinite numbers of crows and ravens' began to appear, picking at flesh and growing so fat that they waddled around like hens.[20]

27

Army of One

The ambassador was terrified. The Marquis of Albeville was an Irish veteran of James's diplomatic corps who knew trouble when he saw it. Back in the summer of 1688, as James's power was crumbling, Albeville had abandoned his post in The Hague and returned to London without permission to warn Whitehall of the Dutch threat. Two years later, in October 1690, less than eight weeks after the siege of Limerick had ended, Albeville was back in Ireland watching another government fall apart. By this stage the Duke of Tyrconnell had sailed for France to hold face-to-face discussions with James, and in the viceroy's absence order seemed to unravel. On 27 October Albeville decided that he had seen enough. He wrote two urgent dispatches to St Germain: one addressed to James and the other to Tyrconnell. Something, he begged both of them, had to be done.

Tyrconnell had been at Galway when he'd learned of the defence of Limerick, but rather than remain in Ireland for the winter he chose to sail to France with Lauzun and his French troops. It was a spicy decision. Tyrconnell claimed that he was leaving to personally lobby Louis and his ministers for further aid, but his rivals in the army suspected that Tyrconnell wanted to tell James his version of events before they could. The timing of Tyrconnell's departure on 12 September could not have been worse. Eleven days later John Churchill, now the Earl of Marlborough – the general who had infamously deserted James at Salisbury – landed with a small invasion force at Passage West, near the city of Cork. A few weeks earlier Marlborough had approached Queen Mary and her privy council with a bold plan to seize Cork and Kinsale and cut off the Jacobites' direct supply line to France. William had been informed of the plan by 14 August, when he was still camped at Limerick, and gave Marlborough his blessing. After landing at Passage West, Marlborough's force linked up with Wurtemburg and several thousand Danish, Dutch and Huguenot soldiers sent south after the withdrawal from Limerick. Cork was taken utterly by surprise and surrendered on 28 September after a brief siege. The entire garrison was taken prisoner.

The following day Marlborough and Wurtemburg turned south and arrived at Kinsale. The town was quickly overrun and the nearby garrison of Charles Fort, the most formidable modern fortress in Ireland, on paper, was surrounded. Despite having months' worth of food, gunpowder and ammunition, the fort was dangerously short of troops, having sent out much of its garrison to try and relieve Cork just before the city fell. Charles Fort had sharp angular walls and thick bastions but had also rather strangely been built at the bottom of a hill. Marlborough's artillery took brutal advantage. After a two-week siege and a ferocious bombardment from cannons aimed right down into the fort, the Jacobite garrison surrendered on 15 October. Marlborough's cannons blew a hole in the outer walls so big that Charles Fort's governor, Edward Scott, was able to ride out through it in his coach. In barely three weeks, the Williamites had snatched Cork and Kinsale, secured the entire Irish south coast and seized thousands of pounds of supplies and materiel. Marlborough returned to London with his reputation in slightly better nick than William's.

After failing to capture Limerick, the new king had sent a humiliating message to both houses of parliament expressing regret that 'my best endeavours' had not been enough to end the war.[1] Westminster was in little mood for sympathy. On 11 October parliament was presented with a bill of £48,247 for the cost of the Irish expedition so far, as well as for beefing up the defences at Hull, Portsmouth and the Isle of Wight. Securing William's kingdoms was becoming a costly business for the taxpayer, and there was still too little progress to show for it.

The survival of Limerick had been one of the most astonishing events of the war, but it was still not enough to unite the Jacobites. Before Tyrconnell left for France he appointed twelve commissioners to run the civil government in his absence and named the Duke of Berwick as commander-in-chief of the army. To ease concerns about the twenty-year-old duke's inexperience, Tyrconnell also appointed a council of senior officers to advise him. The Scottish Thomas Maxwell, the English Dominic Sheldon and the Irish John Hamilton – Richard Hamilton's brother – were chosen as conservatives to counter the mischief of the war party of Nicholas Purcell, Henry Luttrell, John Wauchope and the others who had been 'dissatisfied with the Duke of Tyrconnell's conduct since the business of the Boyne'.[2] Tyrconnell grudgingly handed the last seat on the military council to Patrick Sarsfield. The interim government proved to be a shambles. Before the siege of Limerick, the anti-Tyrconnell faction had tried to coax Berwick to be their leader. Now that they had him, the Marquis of Albeville wrote to Paris, it was not enough. Without fear of censure, several Irish officers began to grumble openly about having to 'commit the safety of the kingdom, their lives and fortunes, to the conduct of a young prince of nineteen or twenty years of age'.[3]

Berwick struggled to hold things together over the winter. With another campaign finished, the Jacobite troops once more cut loose and began to plunder from people that were nominally under their protection. Conditions were rough, and supplies were scant. In Limerick and Galway, the last two cities under Jacobite control, soldiers had to make do with sleeping in barns and abandoned houses 'where they had neither beds nor so much as straw to lie on'.[4] Many simply stormed into people's homes and 'thrust the citizens out of their beds'.[5] Fever and illness continued to linger. 'The whole country … is laid waste,' Albeville wrote to James. 'Nothing but devastation and desolation is seen in country and city.' Everywhere you looked, houses were being torn down and stripped of iron and timber, crops were rotting in the fields and soldiers were stealing 'the very shoes of one another's horses'. There was 'no obedience' in any rank of the army. 'Nothing but the utmost severity will ever bring this nation under discipline or order,' Albeville concluded. Unfortunately, his letters of desperation never made it to Paris. With the Williamites in control of the south coast, it had become almost impossible to smuggle information in or out of Ireland. As Albeville himself admitted in a letter that fell into enemy hands, 'we have the worst intelligence in the world'.[6]

*

It was a winter of whispers and doubt. After Tyrconnell's departure for France, his rivals in the army leadership were terrified of being outmanoeuvred. Patrick Sarsfield, Simon Luttrell and the new governor of Limerick, William Dorrington, strong-armed the Duke of Berwick into allowing them to send their own delegates to St Germain and challenge Tyrconnell's side of the story. Simon Luttrell, his brother Henry, Colonel Nicholas Purcell and the Catholic bishop of

Cork, Peter Creagh, set sail for France. Unknown to them, a concerned Berwick had earlier sent Thomas Maxwell, an ally of Tyrconnell's, to St Germain with a warning. Tyrconnell made the most of his head start. By the time he arrived at St Germain word had already arrived of the success at Limerick, and James was so pleased that he promoted his old friend from the post of lord deputy to lord lieutenant – a largely meaningless but nonetheless symbolic change in job title. The strain of the past two years had left Tyrconnell in tatters, and it showed. Courtiers in St Germain were shocked to see the 'old and infirm man' that Richard Talbot had become.[7] Tyrconnell admitted himself that his 'palpitation of the heart daily increases', as weight, age, gout and stress ate away at him.[8] Nevertheless, he 'showed himself a diligent and active courtier' in the few weeks he was in Paris and managed to secure a ninety-minute private audience with Louis.[9] The influential French war minister, Louvois, was still nipping in the French king's ear about how the Irish war was a waste of resources, particularly as Louis's cousin, the Duke of Savoy, had just broken with France and joined William's alliance. But the defence of Limerick was evidence that Ireland still had some fight in it. Tyrconnell was able to coax a clear – if unspecific – promise of continued support from Louis. With a new line of French credit, the freshly endorsed lord lieutenant of Ireland left Paris for Brest to oversee preparations for the spring campaign.

The rival delegates from the Jacobite army were almost thrown in gaol when they arrived at St Germain. Thomas Maxwell got to James before them and wasted no time painting an image of plots, arguments and attempted coups. Maxwell also briefed James on the precarious role that Patrick Sarsfield was playing in it all. Sarsfield had been promoted to major general, and his clout with the troops made him untouchable. It was suggested that Sarsfield's ego 'was quite out of its natural station', but that he could be coaxed back into line 'if his counsellors Henry Luttrell and Nicholas Purcell were kept from him'.[10] After everything he had suffered, James despised all talk of mutiny. He refused point blank to receive the Luttrells, Purcell and the bishop of Cork when they reached St Germain and even considered gaoling the officers out of principle. The army delegates held their ground, courted allies elsewhere in St Germain and eventually gained an audience with their king. In a makeshift presence chamber the delegates bowed, offered all the necessary missives about loyalty and service and proceeded to rip the Duke of Tyrconnell to shreds.

James was told that the viceroy of Ireland 'was not qualified' to run an army. His decision-making was erratic, his age and illnesses slowed him down and he was accused of corruption and nepotism. If Tyrconnell remained commander-in-chief, the army delegates warned, 'it would utterly dishearten the body of the nation'.[11] James was stunned. The army's blunt assault on Tyrconnell's competence was extraordinary. James's indecision flared up once more, and he began to wonder if Tyrconnell was the right man to direct a war. James's queen, who had long been a friendly correspondent of Tyrconnell's, insisted that if she and her husband were happy with the viceroy, then the rest of Ireland should be too. But James shuffled in his seat. The thought of an army abandoning him had driven him to the brink of a nervous breakdown in 1688, and now he was being told that it could happen again. As at almost every other moment of crisis since he became king, James froze. He considered recalling Tyrconnell altogether, but feared that Louvois would seize on it as proof that he could not manage his own shop. When the army delegates floated the idea of appointing a new French general as overall commander, James agreed. With the exception of Boisseleau at Limerick, French generals had been idle, unlucky, disinterested or useless since the war in Ireland began. It said a great deal about the army's lack of faith in Tyrconnell that they would rather take their chances with another Frenchman than trust their fate to a man they saw as 'better prepared to manage a treaty than to continue the war'.[12]

*

In early November 1690, William sent a letter to several English bishops giving them instructions to oversee the rebuilding of the Protestant Church in Ireland. As it stood, roughly a quarter of Ireland was still in Jacobite hands, and vast swathes of the countryside were little more than green deserts filled with bandits and murderers. But as it was in all things, William was in a hurry. In war-torn Ireland there were judges and officials to appoint, taxes to collect and a Protestant ascendancy to restore. A new government in Dublin was formed under three lord justices: Viscount Henry Sidney, one of the seven signatories of William's invitation to invade; Thomas Coningsby, a paymaster-general of the army; and Charles Porter, a former Irish lord chancellor who had been a victim of Tyrconnell's administrative purges of 1686. By the first week of December, the new lord justices had received their official instructions to administer Ireland's law, revenue and trade. Taking charge of a kingdom still in a state of war would be an unenviable task.

After the captures of Cork and Kinsale, the Williamite army withdrew into winter quarters. The Count of Solms had initially been left in charge after William's departure, but when Solms and the Dutch blue guards returned to England in October, command passed by default to the Dutch baron of Ginkel, the next most senior lieutenant general in Ireland. Ginkel set up his headquarters in Kilkenny and shuffled his lines about until the Williamites' frontier ran through Ireland like a crescent moon: starting in Ballyshannon and Enniskillen in the north, down through Mullingar and Birr in the midlands, into Tipperary, Cashel and Cork and then along the south coast. The Jacobites held the River Shannon and everything behind it. The country between the two armies became a desolate no-man's land where travelling unarmed was suicide. Throughout the winter of 1690–1, the diary of the Williamite chaplain George Story became a grim account of bandits in plain clothes raiding, stealing and murdering. The Williamites fought back in kind, and the mood was unmerciful. Dozens were reported dead at skirmishes between packs of bandits and Williamite troops across the Bog of Allen, Laois and Cork. Troops were 'encouraged by law' to kill as many bandits as they could, with fixed payment promised for every head.[13] Discipline was a rare luxury. On 1 November the Earl of Nottingham wrote to the lieutenant general James Douglas about 'complaints of great disorders committed by you and your officers', such as the indiscriminate theft of food and livestock. A commission of inquiry into army abuses was demanded in London. Major General Percy Kirke, who also received a rebuke about his troops' conduct, wrote to London insisting that while 'there have been great abuses committed of that nature', he had not stolen five shillings from anyone'.[14]

*

The winter was cold and stormy. Fuel ran short, and a black market trade in stolen goods flourished on both sides of the frontier. In February 1691 the Jacobites were forced to devalue their brass coins due to a shortage of currency. Mark Baggott, a former Jacobite sergeant-at-arms in Dublin, was caught sneaking into the capital dressed as a woman, tried as a spy and hanged. The Williamite lord justices issued an order prohibiting any Catholic from coming within ten miles of the frontier and ordered all those living in occupied territory to 'remove to some other parts of the kingdom'.[15] Before the turn of the year, Dublin was struck by rumours of a Catholic plot to smuggle supplies south to Limerick. City authorities raided several Catholic-owned homes and properties and made a number of dubious arrests. Suspicion was also festering on the other side of the Irish Sea. In London, William's personal physician was slipped an anonymous note warning that 'a person who is in the interest of the king' had been seen meeting with an Irish priest suspected of plotting to assassinate William. The note was passed on and found its way into the king's official papers. The threat was obviously taken seriously.[16]

In late November 1690 William notified Westminster of his intention to return to The Hague and finalise the treaty with Savoy. Before he left, he urged parliament to provide more money for the army, navy and civil government, which were all effectively broke. The Commons, as ever, murmured unhappily. A short time later it received another bill for over £23,000 in army expenses. The new Dublin administration was costing money too – an invoice for almost £3,000 was presented for a new great seal, a royal printing press, freight charges and 'entertainment' expenses for the Irish secretary Robert Southwell, who was recovering from illness in Waterford and clearly enjoying it. Irish taxes were difficult to collect in wartime. For the foreseeable future, Westminster would have to keep paying the bills. The Commons finally decided to take back something in return. Westminster began drawing up a bill of attainder that would speed up the confiscation of Jacobite estates in Ireland, which would then be sold 'to bear the charge of the war'. William was not impressed. Like Cromwell before him, William intended to grant confiscated estates to whomever he chose, rather than see them sold on the open market with the proceeds going to the exchequer. As the crown and parliament waded into a dispute over property rights that would last for years, an army of some 20,000 Jacobite troops remained dug in along the line of the river Shannon. As

William departed for The Hague, he decided once again to try and negotiate an end to the Irish war. Peace, however, would have to be on his terms.[17]

*

Back in the first days of August 1690, when William's army was bearing down on Limerick like a mammoth, a Catholic barrister from County Clare named John Grady entered the Williamite camp. According to various accounts, Grady had been sent by Tyrconnell in secret to discover if William might be inclined to offer better terms. Grady was waved away. Now, as the year drew to a close, Grady's name cropped up again. William had decided to authorise off-the-record talks with the Jacobites but needed an envoy with connections. Grady was given the task. During the autumn of 1690, Grady shuttled over and back between Limerick, Galway and London, clearing the path for a potential truce, one briar at a time. It was not the safest job. For one thing, he had to move in secret, knowing too well that if senior Jacobite officers learned what he was up to, his liberty and life could be at risk. Grady also had to deal with William's decision to squeeze the Jacobites into a truce with a four-pronged, mid-winter assault along the frontier from Sligo to Kerry, which failed miserably. Finally, Grady did not know exactly what he was allowed to offer. The one carrot that could coax most Jacobites into a deal – their property – was now being fought over like a carcass between William and Westminster. Nonetheless, Grady struggled on.

As early as September 1690, Grady was writing positive reports that leading figures in Galway, the temporary seat of the Jacobite civil government, were willing to listen to an offer. The Jacobite army leadership was too distracted to notice for now: the Luttrell brothers and Nicholas Purcell were in France, while Patrick Sarsfield had moved to Athlone and was currently tearing up and down the Shannon, fortifying crossing points and scaring off any Williamite scouts. Grady held private discussions with the chief justice Thomas Nugent and the secretary of state Denis Daly, who were both staunch Tyrconnell supporters. Nugent's brother-in-law, Alexander MacDonnell, the governor of Galway, was quietly brought in on the talks.

Rotten weather and bad roads scuttled William's plans to eat into the Jacobite frontier in counties Limerick, Sligo, Kerry and Longford. Mobilising in winter had been a predictable disaster. As spring drew closer, with the prospect of another violent campaign ahead, some of William's generals in Ireland began to wonder if their king was driving too hard a bargain. Ginkel, Wurtemburg and even William Bentinck, the king's great confidant, asked why realistic offers regarding property, religious freedom and amnesty were not on the table. Thinking like a foreign general bogged down in the badlands, Wurtemburg grumbled that 'a stroke of the pen could end the war in Ireland'.[18] Ginkel was eventually given permission to flesh out the offer a little and issued a public declaration promising that William and Mary had no intention to oppress Irish Catholics. But Grady's negotiations never found their feet on such murky ground. Besides, at some point in November Patrick Sarsfield finally discovered that back-door diplomacy had been taking place and moved swiftly to shut it down.

Leaning on the isolated Duke of Berwick, Sarsfield had Nugent and Governor MacDonnell removed from their posts. Denis Daly was arrested on suspicion of holding treasonous correspondence and thrown in gaol. A number of mid-ranking officers suspected of facilitating the talks were arrested. Almost overnight, it became impossible for Grady or any other peace envoy to move safely through Jacobite territory. Grady informed Ginkel on 1 January that it was now too dangerous for him to even give letters to couriers, while the Marquis of Albeville wrote that one man who arrived in Limerick suspected of having knowledge of the talks was 'clap'd prisoner in the castle'.[19] The peace tactics came to a screeching halt. Sarsfield was appointed the new governor of Galway but immediately handed the post off to a deputy and returned to Athlone to guard the frontier. As ever, the popular sentiment seemed to stick to Sarsfield like a limpet. In the days after the peace talks had been broken up, a French priest in Galway wrote of how Sarsfield's 'wisdom and penetration' had forced Berwick to remove 'those characters on whom there rested more than a little suspicion'.[20]

When Tyrconnell returned to Ireland in January 1691, Jacobite affairs were in a mess. Several of his allies and political appointees were in gaol, and the army was restless. The Ulster colonel Balldearg O'Donnell, who had arrived at Limerick with several thousand troops just as the siege was ending, had set himself up in Connaught over the winter as 'a sort of independent commander', whipping up his men with clannish rhetoric. O'Donnell had all the haughty pride of a Gaelic chieftain, spinning myths about his talents and styling himself as the true heir to the old earls of Tyrconnell. Volunteers flocked to his banner, forming what began to look suspiciously like a private army. His men were labelled 'a rabble that destroyed the country', pillaging supplies at whim.[21] Patrick Sarsfield, meanwhile, was now effectively in control of Galway, Athlone and most of the Shannon. Tyrconnell had left St Germain with honours, assurances and vindication. But he was not in St Germain anymore.

The viceroy travelled to Galway, where his return was celebrated throughout the city with a choreographed display of 'balls and banquets, bonfires and public rejoicings, as if the English were quite driven out of Ireland'.[22] He immediately had Denis Daly freed from prison and reappointed Thomas Nugent to the privy council. Richard Nagle, Tyrconnell's fixer who had returned with him from France, was named as James's new secretary of state for Ireland. Aware that the Luttrell brothers and Nicholas Purcell were still in Paris and probably slandering him to the heavens, Tyrconnell clamped down on correspondence in and out of Ireland, ordering that it be vetted first. He then issued a mischievous declaration on 27 January promising fixed payments of gold and silver to any Williamite soldier who wished to defect. Any enemy who presented himself at Galway, Limerick, Sligo or Athlone would receive free passage to France, from where they could either enlist in James's army or 'repair to their respective countries'.[23] Tyrconnell knew that his offer would be ignored, but the declaration was a useful tool. It allowed him to remind his enemies on both sides of the frontier that he was back in charge.

Preparing the army for war was a familiar and debilitating task. After returning from France, Tyrconnell conducted several troop inspections and was shocked at what he found. As well as the typical lack of muskets and powder, entire regiments were now without proper uniforms. Tyrconnell had been given the relatively modest sum of 14,000 livres when he departed France, but by the time that new coats, hats and shoes were purchased for the troops, the money was almost gone. Tyrconnell's shallow pockets did not go unnoticed. A few weeks prior to the viceroy's return from France, one ordinary Irishman's letters were almost giddy with the news that 'his majesty of France is resolved to stand by us' with men, money and resources.[24] But by the middle of spring 1691, all Tyrconnell had come up with was 8,000 new muskets, new uniforms and promises of French help that were looking emptier by the day. With the new campaign season drawing close, Tyrconnell's struggles to equip a disorganised army gave heart to his enemies, who were suffering their own troubles of indiscipline, lack of money and a shortage of supplies. Writing to London in February 1691, the Williamite lord justice Thomas Coningsby rattled off a list of complaints and stated that 'I see every day so many, many difficulties … that I cannot help wishing the war was ended upon any terms.' But despite all this, he took comfort in the knowledge that Tyrconnell had it worse. Word had already filtered through that the Jacobite viceroy had not brought as great a bonanza of money and supplies from France as was originally feared, and many within the Irish ranks were thought to be 'infinitely dissatisfied'. Coningsby suggested that if the Williamites took a step back and waited for hardship and scarcity to drive the Jacobites mad, 'a general pardon may, at some critical time, do the business'.[25]

*

Tucked away inside the stack of manifestos and letters that Tyrconnell had brought from France was one particularly valuable document. James had given Tyrconnell a royal patent naming Patrick Sarsfield as the first Earl of Lucan. Sarsfield was now a peer of the realm and a member of the Jacobite nobility. It was a tactical gift. James had told how strategically important Sarsfield was and tried to coax him away from the army faction with flattery. It would not be straightforward. During the winter of 1690–1, when Sarsfield was in *de facto* command of the Jacobite army, he kept contact with several of his allies in France, particularly Justin MacCarthy, who was now leading Louis's new Irish regiments in action against Savoy. Sarsfield's pen fizzed. On first learning that Henry Luttrell and the other delegates had been refused an audience at St Germain and labelled 'mutineers', Sarsfield angrily wondered if it was now a crime 'to oppose those who wished to treat with the Prince of Orange and put all Ireland into his hands'. He insisted that he and his allies were 'determined to die a thousand deaths rather than betray the king's interest, or to submit to a usurper'. He clearly believed that Tyrconnell and his close circle of barristers and judges lacked the stomach for a war. 'There is only one party here which perfectly unites all the Irish, [and] are resolved to sacrifice in the king's service themselves and all that they hold dear.'[26] These did not seem the words of a man who could be bought off cheaply. In January and February 1691 Jean Francois Fumeron, a French emissary who travelled to Ireland with Tyrconnell, wrote to Louvois that Sarsfield had failed to present himself at Limerick despite repeated requests from the viceroy. Sarsfield protested that he was sick in Athlone, but it was widely suspected that he was holding out to hear if Luttrell and the other delegates had managed to sway James's opinion. By late February, however, Sarsfield could not delay any longer. He travelled to Limerick and paid his respects to the viceroy and lord lieutenant of Ireland, gritting his teeth as he bowed.

Tyrconnell and Sarsfield could barely stand each other, but they put on a good show. After Sarsfield arrived in Limerick, Tyrconnell began to publicly court his friendship 'with all the earnestness imaginable'.[27] He formally granted Sarsfield his patent of nobility and handed him the task of reordering the army ahead of the new campaigning season. Sarsfield kept the viceroy at arm's length. He stayed in Limerick for little over a week before returning to Athlone and vented in a letter to Justin MacCarthy that Tyrconnell's sweetness made him sick. 'Tyrconnell incessantly compliments me and professes his friendship, but I have known him for too long not to know that I should place little trust in his false words.' Were it not for his loyalty to James, Sarsfield wrote, 'I would let [Tyrconnell] know that he does not deserve the slightest respect from anyone. He is very jealous and despairs of my reputation and of the influence I have over the army.' When Sarsfield had presented himself in Limerick, Fumeron hoped that his display of deference to Tyrconnell would 'do much to make the army follow suit'.[28] But now, just a few weeks before the army was due to take the field, the Jacobite leadership was as riddled with contempt as ever. Word of it all travelled as far as London, where a newsletter reported that 'Tyrconnell and Sarsfield cannot agree'.[29]

*

The thick and salty hulls of the French ships turned past Kerry Head and sailed up the Shannon estuary until they spotted the four turrets of St Mary's Cathedral in the distance. As the lead vessel crept towards the city docks, a huge crowd jostled and tiptoed for a better look. The cannons mounted on the highest walls of King John's Castle blasted a salute. At noon on 9 May 1691 the long-awaited French relief convoy finally arrived at Limerick, where it was 'received with real demonstrations of joy'.[30] As cheers rippled back through the crowds into the streets of Englishtown, Tyrconnell stood on the quayside and sized up the Frenchman walking down the gangplank towards him. He was broad, hard-featured and intimidating. His name was Charles Chalmont, the Marquis of St Ruth. He was the latest French general tasked by Versailles with shaping this useful mess of a war. St Ruth had arrived in Limerick with 146 officers, 24 surgeons, 180 stonemasons, 800 horses, 19 cannons, 16,000 muskets and crates of coats, stockings and shoes. Crucially, he had very little money and no soldiers. Louis had promised James and Tyrconnell after the siege of Limerick that he would continue to support the Irish war. He was obviously happy with the bare minimum.

St Ruth had a brutal reputation. He was a hardened soldier, the complete opposite of the snooty courtier Lauzun, and was infamous for his violent persecution of French Huguenots after Louis revoked their legal protection in 1685. He was described by the baron of Ginkel, the Williamite general he would soon face on the battlefield, as 'a great persecutor of the Protestants'.[31] At home, St Ruth's relish for war and the

Catholic faith was renowned. He was sent to Ireland because he had briefly commanded the Irish brigade in Savoy the previous August. He was bumped up to the rank of general and travelled to Ireland with two immediate deputies: the Marquis d'Usson and the Chevalier de Tessé. The arrival of St Ruth, coupled with the Duke of Berwick's recall to France earlier that year, had muddled the army hierarchy. Shortly after Patrick Sarsfield's meeting with Tyrconnell in Limerick, word reached Galway that a French general was coming to take command of the army. Sarsfield gleefully circulated the news, which 'did not a little rejoice the generality of the Irish' who believed that Tyrconnell was a stuffy old hack.[32] The fact that Henry Luttrell and Nicholas Purcell had returned to Ireland in St Ruth's company added colour to the idea that his appointment was a victory for the army. Simon Luttrell stayed behind in France as the army's eyes and ears in James's court. Accounts vary as to whether St Ruth officially outranked Tyrconnell on military matters or if the viceroy simply deferred to the Frenchman on James's request to avoid further dissent within the army. James's biographer specifically claims that Tyrconnell lost his power to appoint senior officers, 'which so lowered his credit in the army that little regard was had to his authority'.[33] Whether he was in charge on paper or not, Tyrconnell privately seethed. He was reduced at last to an army of one – distrusted, marginalised and out of the loop in the most defining days of the war.

*

The nagging had done the trick. After months of complaints by the lord justices about unpaid bills, irresponsible officers, bandits and every other calamity under the sky, the Williamite army slowly began to stir. By mid-March London had approved a battle plan for the coming season, which stated that Ginkel would attack Athlone, storm over the Shannon and pick off

Galway, Sligo and Limerick one at a time. Despite no one knowing how, when or even if Irish estates were to be confiscated and divided up, the carrot of forfeited lands was dangled in front of the troops to boost morale. Arms, materials and fresh recruits had been shuttled into Cork, Waterford, Dublin and Carrickfergus. Ginkel was confirmed as commander-in-chief, and final preparations were underway for what would be some of the most violent weeks in Irish history.

Ginkel was in no mood to repeat mistakes. By late April his men were already gathering at Mullingar, some twenty-eight miles east of Athlone. On 26 May his huge artillery train of thirty-six heavy cannons, eight mortars and hundreds of wagons of gunpowder and shot, 'such a one as never had been seen before in that kingdom', left Dublin in order to reach the front as early as possible.[34] Protestant militiamen were armed across Ulster, Cork and elsewhere to protect Williamite supply lines from bandits. Before Ginkel left Dublin on 30 May to bring the axe down on Jacobite Ireland, there were a few final pieces of housekeeping to attend to. Somewhere in the chancellor's office at Dublin Castle were binders filled with the documents connected to the Jacobite parliament of 1689. The papers had already lapsed into history, relics of a moment in time when Tyrconnell was the champion of Catholic Ireland and his kingdom was more than just an exercise in treason. On 9 May 1691, almost two years to the day since the Patriot Parliament had convened, Queen Mary issued an order for all its laws and attainders to be officially expunged. The Duke of Tyrconnell had lost control of the army, and now his laws were being torn up. Richard Talbot's Ireland had vanished.[35]

28

Hell upon Earth

Back when Ireland was a patchwork of Gaelic fiefdoms, before any man named Henry or James or William had claimed her lands and taxes, there was an old trade route that bisected the island from east to west. Carts loaded up with onions or kale or barley would be hauled for miles through Meath or Roscommon until they converged on a single ford across the Shannon, just where the river opens its jaws into Lough Ree. Luan's Ford, as it was known, was just a few dozen yards wide, and sometimes during summer the water would barely lick the knees. Straddling the border between Leinster and Connaught, and sitting almost dead centre in the middle of the island, Luan's Ford was a strategic jewel. Irish kings tried to bridge it with wood and wicker, and finally the Normans built a way over it with stone. The small town of Athlone rose up around it – part trading post, part frontier fort – one half on either side of the river. The hubbub of its daily markets became a magnet for merchants, farmers, tricksters and drunks. Eel fisheries, weirs and water mills harvested the river. Gatehouses and earthworks were built as a shield. A squat stone castle with high walls was constructed on the western riverbank. Yet for all its flesh and teeth, Athlone's greatest asset remained that single bridge over the Shannon, the tiny ligament connecting east and west.

As the Williamite army rumbled out of Mullingar in the first days of June 1691, Ginkel thought about everything that now hinged on the capture of that bridge. This was his first campaign as a commander-in-chief, and victory or failure would sleep at his feet alone. On the continent, France and the grand alliance were still clawing at each other everywhere from Flanders to Savoy, and as long as the Jacobite army survived in Ireland, William's efforts would be torn between two fronts. A line of invisible dominoes now stretched from the battlefields of the Spanish Netherlands, through the halls of Westminster and over the cobbled alleyways of Dublin, finally coming to a halt on that small bridge in Athlone. It was the gateway into Connaught, the last sanctuary of Jacobite Ireland. It was about to become the tiniest, most vicious frontier in an international war.

The forty-seven-year-old Ginkel was a cautious man. His various portraits all depict a flabby figure with a long, prominent nose; in some paintings his eyes are wide and generous – in others he squints and probes, as if the artist's brush was an enemy that needed to be studied. When William and Solms had departed Ireland the previous autumn, Ginkel had been left in charge by default. There were some who wondered if he had the grit for the job. Before Ginkel rode out of Dublin to join the army at the end of May, William had written to him from Flanders urging him to be fierce and decisive. 'You know what sort of people you have to deal with, such as cannot always be controlled by mildness.'[1] Ginkel also had to contend with a total overhaul of his general staff: Meinhardt Schomberg, the new Duke of Leinster, had been sent to take charge of the army in Scotland, while generals Percy Kirke and James Douglas had been dispatched to Flanders. The German Duke of Wurtemburg remained as Ginkel's deputy, while a Huguenot major general, the Marquis of Ruvigny, took over Schomberg's cavalry. The Dutch major general Adam van der Duyn, Lord Scravenmoer, was a stout and familiar old quartermaster who had been in Ireland since 1689. The English major general Thomas Talmash joined the senior staff, as did Hugh Mackay, the Scottish major general who had landed with William at Torbay in 1688. Ginkel and his new commanders were given firm instructions to shake the war out of its rut. As they were marching off into action in June, the lord justice Charles Porter was bubbling with confidence that 'the difficulty will be over' by the end of summer, as most Jacobites 'are in great discontent, wishing for nothing more than ... they might have opportunity to desert'.[2]

Porter was only half right. Squabbles continued to nag the Jacobite leadership like a toothache, while food, money and other supplies remained thin. St Ruth was all energy, travelling up and down the Shannon inspecting the frontier, giving particular attention to Athlone, where he now knew that Ginkel would strike. All horses in Jacobite-held territory were seized for army use – according to one Williamite account, hundreds of private horse owners were summoned to Limerick under the pretence of receiving a civil award only to have their animals confiscated when they got there.[3] But there was much to do and too little time to do it. Work had been underway to buttress Athlone's defences since March, but progress was sluggish. The Shannon was the quickest route to get materials upstream from Limerick, but St Ruth had only six boats fit for the task, and the flow of supplies reduced to a trickle. When the Jacobite army finally marched north from Limerick on 4 June – almost a week after Ginkel's troops had mobilised – many companies of infantry had as few as four tents between thirty or more men, often without poles or pins to hold them down. Then there was the humour of Irish summers to contend with. The first night of the Jacobites' march towards Athlone was 'extraordinarily wet and cold', and many troops were forced to sleep under bushes.[4]

*

There was only one barrier on the road between Athlone and Mullingar: the small Jacobite fort of Ballymore, which poked out from the edge of a tiny lake some thirteen miles east of Athlone. Ginkel captured it without breaking a sweat. On 7 June his army surrounded the fort, and after the Jacobites refused to surrender Ginkel's artillery and grenadiers got to work. Ballymore surrendered unconditionally the next day, and the Irish soldiers inside were carted off to Dublin as prisoners. As well as 51 officers and 780 soldiers, some 260 bandits were found among the garrison fighting like enlisted troops. Many of the soldiers' families had been cooped up inside with them, and after the fort was captured 400 women and children were turned out into the countryside, shell-shocked and bawling. They watched as their men were marched away like cattle to the improvised floating gaol of Lambay Island, a rocky outcrop a few miles off the coast of Dublin. The lord justice Charles Porter had no intention of holding a pack of soldiers and bandits in the capital. 'This city would not be safe whilst we had so many in the skirts of it,' he wrote.[5]

If Ginkel had known at that moment that St Ruth's army was still several days from Athlone, he might have sprinted west and overrun the town. Instead, he dug in at Ballymore for ten days. He had his reasons. Wurtemburg and the Danish troops were still marching north from Cashel, and the rest of his artillery train had not yet arrived from Mullingar. Likewise, Ginkel was waiting for several pontoons that he might need to cross the Shannon if the main bridge in Athlone was out of reach. The pontoons had to be shipped from Waterford to Dublin and then dragged painstakingly overland. In the meantime, Ballymore became a forest of canvas and muck as 18,000 soldiers whittled away the days waiting for orders. It left the lord justices in Dublin rather skittish: Thomas Coningsby moaned that 'we have lost ten days', a delay that might be 'almost irreparable'.[6] Even Ginkel grew restless, writing on 16 June that the delay of the pontoons and other supplies was 'an embarrassment' that had gifted the enemy precious time.[7]

*

St Ruth reached Athlone on Sunday 21 June. Ginkel had beaten them there. After finally departing Ballymore on 18 June, the Williamite army arrived at the eastern outskirts of Athlone the following day. The town was hardly a sight to inspire awe. A craggy old wall wrapped the eastern half in a semicircle, propped up by three old bastions and two gun batteries dating back to Cromwell's days. Inside, the Leinster half of the town – which had once been a thriving commercial centre – was now a pitiful ruin. The previous summer, when Lieutenant General Douglas had launched a brief and failed attack on Athlone, the Jacobites had simply set fire to Leinster town, retreated across the river and broken the last three arches on the bridge. The stubby tower of St Mary's Church was the only notch of any note on a dismal horizon. After a small force of Jacobite soldiers had been driven from the outlying ditches, Ginkel had nine of his heavy guns blast a hole in the outer wall on 20 June. About 300 Williamite grenadiers stormed through, flinging explosives like apples. The Jacobites rushed back over the bridge and pulled up the planks covering the broken arches. The enemy shock troops rushed after them, but when they reached the bridge a line of Jacobite muskets across the water opened up, killing several and forcing the rest to pull back out of range. Williamite engineers brought up wooden blinds to erect a barricade at their end of the bridge, and hundreds of Ginkel's troops poured into Leinster town as its new tenants. All through the night on 20 June, the Jacobites across the water on the Connaught side listened to a symphony of shovels and hammers and the creaking wheels of cannons being hauled into place. Both armies held one half of the old market town, with just 'a deep and rapid river between them and us'.[8]

St Ruth stared out across Athlone from a dense and boggy hillside some two miles to the west. He scanned the landscape methodically, picking out the tall lines of heaped earth that had been piled around the outskirts of Connaught town to make up for the lack of walls. He watched the Shannon cut through Athlone like an artery, widening as it passed under the bridge and then rolled south. Beyond, he could see featureless shapes scuttling about the ruins of Leinster town, dragging barrels and digging holes like ants. St Ruth was not concerned. He had arrived at Athlone with some 21,000 men, including 3,000 cavalry and 2,000 dragoons – a slightly larger force than his enemy. Ginkel's troops might have been more experienced and better equipped, but they would still have to fight their way across a single stone bridge barely a few paces wide. The odds seemed firmly on the Frenchman's side.

*

Out of pride, defiance or just plain stubbornness, the Duke of Tyrconnell had travelled to Athlone with the army. Patrick Sarsfield, Henry Luttrell and the other Irish officers could barely hide their disgust. The march had been miserable enough as it was: 'Long and tiresome' days in baking heat were broken up by sudden blasts of rain that churned up roads 'as if it had been the depth of winter'.[9] The lord lieutenant slogged along, despite his health being as poor as ever. Despite Tyrconnell's agreeing to defer to St Ruth on military matters, he had no intention of sitting things out. After making camp west of Athlone, Tyrconnell had recommended that St Ruth demolish the outer earthworks on the western edge of Connaught town, just so that the army could rush in unimpeded if the Williamites somehow made it across the river. St Ruth ignored him. Tyrconnell then heard whispers that a petition was being circulated among senior officers demanding his expulsion from the camp. Finally, a young Irish officer entered the viceroy's tent and threatened the viceroy that 'if his grace did not withdraw from the camp, he would cut the cords of his pavilion'. It was astonishing. Three years earlier, Tyrconnell would have had the officer hanged for treason. But now he was cornered, adrift and powerless. Since Richard Hamilton's capture at the Boyne, he had few friends left in the army. All Tyrconnell could do was protest. He appealed to Louvois in Versailles, complaining that the officers were caught up in schemes while the enemy was barely a cannon shot away. When he raised the matter with St Ruth, the Frenchman shrugged, feigned surprise and did nothing. With bitter reluctance Tyrconnell bent down, picked up the pieces of his dignity and rode away. Despite this brazen affront to his authority, the viceroy realised that 'the time and place were not proper for his vindication without endangering the common cause'.[10] He left the camp and rode back to Limerick, a sour and almost broken man.

*

At such close range there would have been only a fraction of a second between the flash of a muzzle, the blast of gunpowder and the sickening crunch of a cannonball tearing into brick or bone. There would be no time to scream or scramble for cover. Death was prompt and unfussy. At 5 a.m. on 22 June the first Williamite battery of five twenty-four-pound cannons and six mortars opened fire from inside the Leinster half of

Athlone. By 7 p.m. that evening a huge breach had been blown in the outer walls of the castle across the river, exposing its courtyard like a ribcage cracked open. Over the coming days, more and more heavy artillery was dragged into Leinster town and pointed across the water. One square yard at a time, the guns began to chew and demolish the western half of Athlone. The Williamite batteries were mounted on earth piled so high that hardly a nook of Connaught town was out of their sights. For the next nine days the western shore was pounded almost without pause, with cluster bombs and cannonballs and mortars 'never ceasing night and day'.[11] Any building taller than a few feet was smashed to rubble. Flaming shells stuffed with oil exploded on impact, set fire to thatched roofs and sent flames dancing from house to house. When Jacobite soldiers in the barricades by the bridge or along the river broke cover to douse the flames, snipers across the water would pick them off. Holes were blasted in the earthen ramparts along the riverbank, and the Jacobites' makeshift defences were pummelled with remorseless efficiency. Night and day, the skies rained fire and death. The western side of Athlone was not under siege – it was being slowly wiped off the face of the earth.

St Ruth had given his men two simple instructions: survive the bombardment and hold the bridge. His deputy, Lieutenant General d'Usson, had been given command of the town and was largely occupied directing engineers in clearing away rubble and repairing barricades that had been smashed by cannon shot. The Jacobite cavalry rode back and forth between their half of Athlone and their main camp to the west, bringing up supplies and bundles of wooden fascines to replace those shot away or blown up in the barrage. All tasks were carried out under a constant hail of mortar and cannon fire. Walking ten yards was a game of chance. The air choked with the smell of sulphur and charred timber. 'The place was so ruined, and the passages so filled up with lumber and stones, that there was not room for two men … to march any way,' one Jacobite officer wrote. The Williamites across the river 'raised their batteries and trenches very high, that a cat could scarce appear without being knocked in the head'.[12] The Jacobites fired back from their own small battery of six-pound guns whenever they could, and even picked off a few Williamite officers with lucky shots. But it was like throwing stones at a tidal wave. There was no sleep, no pause and no end to the horror.

After he had arrived on 21 June, St Ruth boldly declared that Ginkel 'deserved to be hanged for attempting to take Athlone … and that he himself deserved to be hanged if he should lose it'.[13] Confident that even the most ill-equipped troops could hold the bridge through sheer weight of numbers, St Ruth chose not to give d'Usson a permanent garrison of veteran troops. Instead, he decided that the entire Jacobite infantry would take turns manning the barricades. Many of the Irish soldiers were novice recruits levied the previous winter and had no experience of fighting. St Ruth decided that Athlone was as good a place as any to break them in. About three or four regiments at a time would be posted in the town, an average of about 1,500 men. All they would have to do, St Ruth reasoned, was hold their positions, keep their heads down and shoot anything that tried to cross the bridge. But war is never so simple.

By 26 June the Williamites had erected three huge gun batteries inside Leinster town, with a further line of mortars outside the walls to the north. Houses and earthworks on the opposite shore were being ripped to pieces with ease, and dozens of Jacobite soldiers were killed trying to repair them. Thirty wagonloads of fresh gunpowder were wheeled into Leinster town to continue the torment. A mill near the bridge on the Jacobite side caught fire after being struck by a bomb. According to one Jacobite prisoner, sixty-four men had been trapped inside and all but two were burned alive.[14]

Then, after four days of continuous shelling, Ginkel decided to test the bridge. Under the cover of darkness in the early hours of 27 June, a small party of Williamite soldiers rushed across under heavy fire, covered by thunderous shots from their own artillery behind. In just a few minutes they had managed to fasten planks over two of the broken arches, and then they fell back with bullets whizzing all around them. The following day, the Williamite guns worked in horrific unison to keep the Jacobites pinned down and prevent them from tearing up the planks. At around 1 a.m. on Sunday 28 June the Williamites decided to finish the job.

A small team of grenadiers lugging timber planks rushed towards the final arch, barely a few feet from the Jacobite barricades, and managed to cover the gap. Grenades and bullets were fired over and back at shockingly close range, and explosions, hot smoke and the screams of wounded men swallowed the bridge in a cloud. The Williamites pulled back, having at last repaired the bridge and snatched the momentum of the battle. But then, in a moment of incredible and senseless courage, a Scottish Jacobite sergeant named Custume leapt over the barricades followed by five or six men from his unit. They sprinted straight into a maelstrom of bullets from across the river and began throwing the planks down into the water. Men watching on both sides of the bridge were stunned. For a single moment all the noise and fury of the battle seemed to freeze, drift up into the air and then crash down again. Custume and his men were shot to pieces by gunfire. But just as de Beaupré had jumped over the barricade at Limerick and inspired the Jacobite counter attack, Custume's sacrifice stirred the troops behind him into furious action. Dozens of Jacobites swarmed out onto the bridge and threw down the last of the planks as shots cut through flesh like razors and limbs were blown off by cannon fire. The survivors sprinted back for the cover of the western bank. The planks covering the broken arches were pulled up, and the bridge had somehow been retaken. With so much blood and courage, the Jacobites had held the line.

The Williamite gunners across the river went looking for vicious retribution the next day. The wooden fascines covering the Jacobite barricades at the bridge were set on fire by exploding shells. John Stevens, who was on duty at the time, struggled to help quench the flames that swept higher and higher, leaping onto nearby buildings and throwing up an unbearable wall of heat. Mortars, cannon shots and bullets flew through the fire from across the river. The inferno spread. Houses yet to catch fire were pulled down in a panic to try and starve the blaze, while loose timber and blocks were thrown forward to prop up the battered barricades. Shrapnel and musket shot cut in every direction, ripping open throats and chests as men sprinted through the streets with buckets of water. It went on for four barbaric, exhausting hours. It seemed to Stevens that there was 'no likelihood of any man coming off alive'. He later wrote that 'This was the hottest place that I ever saw in my time of service.' Out of the forty men from Stevens's company who had scrambled to put out the fire, seven were killed and nineteen were wounded. Stevens was nearly killed twice. A cannonball struck the outer wall of the castle and sent a piece of shrapnel flying towards his head. Had he not been wearing his hat, it probably would have sliced his skull open. A short time later, Stevens and a few other officers were huddled together relaying orders when a bomb landed a few feet away, barely missing a barrel of gunpowder. Dozens of Jacobites were killed in the inferno of 28 June. The flames and artillery and smoke and noise were more horrific than anything seen at Derry or the Boyne or Limerick. Veteran French officers remarked that 'they had never seen such furious firing for so long a time'.[15] Others who had once scoffed at reports of Irish cowardice 'acknowledged they never saw more resolution and firmness in any men of any nation'. The Jacobite troops who lived through that day were described as 'brave fellows as intrepid as lions'.[16] Even their enemies across the river admired the bravery of Custume and the others, who 'all lost their lives as testimonies of their valour'.[17] Once the storm of fire had finally passed that afternoon, men with blackened faces staggered about the rubble clearing away pieces of dead comrades, their boots crusted over with a paste of blood and filth. They had held the bridge. But that terrible Sunday, John Stevens remarked, had been 'hell upon earth'.[18]

*

Ginkel held a council of war that afternoon. For a week his cannons had blasted Athlone to pieces, but their enemy refused to be dislodged. Ginkel's attempts to find a way around Athlone had been frustrated: three days earlier, a Williamite lieutenant scouted a small ford upstream towards Lanesborough but blew his cover and alerted the Jacobites into building earthworks to block the pass. Storming the bridge was beginning to look like an expensive exercise. However, there might yet be another way. Jacobite deserters had revealed the location of Luan's Ford, the old crossing that had given birth to Athlone, just a few dozen feet south of the main bridge. Three Danish soldiers tested the ford and reported that it was barely knee deep. Ginkel was convinced. At his council of war on 28 June, with the Jacobite half of the town still smouldering, he gave the order for a three-pronged assault over the river the next day. One wave of troops would cross the ford, another would attack the bridge and a third would use the pontoons to cross the river to the south.

Word of the planned offensive passed through the Williamite camp that night, and the 2,000 shock troops chosen to lead the attack stuffed their satchels with grenades, powder and bullets. With the Jacobite lines within earshot across the river, everyone was warned to tread as quietly as possible. The assault was due to begin at first light, but by 10 a.m. nothing had happened. There had been a delay in drawing up the boats to assemble the pontoon bridge, and by midday the game was up. The Jacobites, seeing so many soldiers massed and ready on the opposite bank, packed their barricades with extra men and waited for the attack. The tension was agonising. One Jacobite grenade flew across the bridge and exploded near the Williamite barricade, starting a blaze that 'suddenly flamed so violently, that our men could not endure the fire and smoke'.[19] With the element of surprise lost, Ginkel called off the attack. Williamite heads sank. The assault team of 2,000 men trudged back to their camp. Two days earlier one Williamite soldier admitted in a letter to England that the Jacobites had 'more courage than expected' and that taking Athlone might end with 'a great loss of men'.[20] Now, with their plans to storm the western shore on hold, many Williamites no longer knew what to think, 'seeing themselves defeated in so great a project'.[21] The Jacobites who had spent the morning gripping their muskets and waiting for an attack sighed with relief. The duty garrison was rotated and Thomas Maxwell, the Scottish major general who had aligned himself against Sarsfield's faction, temporarily relieved the exhausted d'Usson as commander. Another bleak day ticked by.

*

Tuesday 30 June was only the ninth day of the siege of Athlone, but Williamite spirits were already beginning to wither. Some of their artillery pieces were drawn away and some supplies were removed from the trenches, as if in preparation for a retreat. Ginkel held another council of war, and the dangers of remaining in Athlone were thrashed out: the cavalry were running out of forage, and morale was plummeting. However, the consequences of retreat were grim: if the Williamites withdrew, St Ruth would theoretically be able to pour into Leinster, seize huge tracts of open country and possibly force a battle somewhere near Dublin. If they retreated from Athlone, the Williamite army might suddenly be pedalling backwards, fighting a defensive war. Wurtemburg, Mackay, Ruvigny and Talmash all spoke up in favour of one last push. Then, at some point in the afternoon, a 'lucky omen' fell into Ginkel's lap. Two Jacobite officers had swum over the river to defect and revealed that at that very moment three of the greenest and 'most indifferent regiments in the Irish army' were currently on duty.[22] St Ruth was overconfident and had allowed the defences to slacken. The time to attack was now. The 2,000 grenadiers on standby since the previous day were quickly moved up into position. Ginkel ordered that each man be given a single gold guinea, embossed with the faces of William and Mary and worth about twenty shillings, to jolt their courage.

The bell of St Mary's Church chimed to signal the attack, and the Williamite cannons opened up with a synchronised crash. The first three lines of grenadiers, marching twenty-men abreast, waded into the river and began to cross the old ford. 'On a sudden we bounced over our works into the river, and were a good way on before the enemy perceived us,' one officer recalled. The guns behind them 'fired continually over our heads' to keep the surprised Jacobites across the water pinned down. The first line of Williamite grenadiers, drenched from the waist down, began to climb the embankment on the other side of the river and stumble up towards a breach in the outer earthworks. They flung their grenades ahead of them, whipping up a manic storm of explosions that terrified first lines of novice Jacobite troops. 'They were in such consternation that they made little or no resistance.'[23] Two of the Irish regiments on duty at the time 'were but raised the winter before' and 'were most unfit to be put upon the defence of a place'.[24] St Ruth's decision to rotate all of his infantry along the front lines, regardless of their mettle, was about to backfire spectacularly. Seeing the lines of grenadiers rush up the bank towards them, the Irish soldiers dropped their muskets and ran. The Williamites began to pour through the breach unchecked, like water through a crack in a dam. Panic swept through Connaught. Almost simultaneously, more Williamite shock troops surged over the bridge, covered the broken arches with planks and overran the Jacobite barricades. Downstream, the pontoon bridge was lashed into place and the third arm of the Williamite assault force started to rush across. After over a week of brutal, heroic defiance, the western half of Athlone was crumbling like a sandcastle.

Bolting Jacobites sprinted through tight avenues littered with rubble and debris, desperately trying to make it out of the town alive. Williamite soldiers swarmed over the bridge, seized the earthworks and began slashing and shooting any soldier in their path. D'Usson, who was in the rear of the town trying to wade through the crush, was trampled to the ground and knocked unconscious. His limp body had to be carried away to safety. Williamite soldiers poured through every street, slowed only by piles of wreckage. Within minutes they had seized the earthworks on the town's western edge, the same ones that Tyrconnell had urged St Ruth to tear down. The French general had finally decided that the earthworks be demolished just a few hours earlier, but the order came far too late. The main Jacobite camp two miles away up the hill was gripped by a sudden alarm, as Irish soldiers began streaming out of the town 'in great confusion'.[25] The Williamites had captured the western half of Athlone in less than half an hour. 'We were masters of the town before St Ruth knew anything of the matter,' one wrote.[26]

The news hit St Ruth like an avalanche. He had left a weak, nervous garrison in charge of the town, and the earthworks that he had tardily decided to remove were now in Williamite hands, blocking him from launching a counter attack. Athlone was lost. Thomas Maxwell was captured and taken prisoner, while St Ruth, Sarsfield, Purcell, Luttrell, Wauchope, de Tessé and every other man in the Jacobite camp watched helplessly as the last barrier into Connaught was kicked down. The Jacobites stared at each other with silent fear, 'as if utter ruin had been hanging over us'.[27] Within a few hours, their entire army was in full retreat towards Ballinasloe, fifteen miles away, its French commander dazed by how cheaply he had allowed Athlone to slip through his fingers.

*

The counting came next. The Jacobites had lost 1,200 men defending Athlone, with almost 500 killed in that gruesome, frenzied final attack. Dozens were butchered in the aftermath. 'The Danes found many of them under tubs and in dark corners, most of which they put to the sword,' one account claimed.[28] By comparison, Ginkel's army lost barely twelve soldiers and one officer during the final assault. Six cannons, two mortars, twenty barrels of gunpowder, twelve barrels of grain and vast amounts of other supplies were captured. The Williamite soldiers finally saw first-hand the awesome destruction their artillery had inflicted. A total of 12,000 cannonballs and 600 bombs had fallen on the western half of Athlone in those nine days. The Williamite batteries had swallowed fifty tonnes of gunpowder, while several more tonnes of loose stones had been fired across the river by mortars. The stink of gore and ash was sickening. Rubble, filth and the charred remains of homes, taverns and stables were all that remained. There was 'not one house left whole in all the town', the chaplain George Story grimly noted. The castle that had once towered over the water's edge 'was beat down to the ground'.[29]

The consequences were not lost on anyone. The fall of Athlone was a catastrophe for the Jacobites, as it now meant that 'a gate should be opened into Connaught … the last refuge of the nation'.[30] As the army staggered away to Ballinasloe, its morale evaporated. 'Such a panic fear … seized our men that the very noise of ten horsemen would have dispersed as many of our battalions'.[31] When the news reached London, it was celebrated like a feast day. 'The taking of Athlone in the view of a numerous army with the loss of so few men is not to be paralleled,' one correspondent remarked.[32] But the most relieved and satisfied man of all was Ginkel, who had exploited one of those extraordinary moments of luck that tend to decide the shape of history. 'The enemy retired during the night, I believe, towards Galway,' he wrote in a short dispatch to William. 'We shall pursue them as soon as possible and shall, I hope, soon be able to bring this war to a glorious termination.'[33]

29

God Will Make You All Saints

St Ruth took it personally. As the Jacobite commander-in-chief, he had forfeited one of the most impregnable places in Ireland. Reputations did not tend recover from such embarrassments. So, like a drunken brawler knocked off his feet in an alleyway, St Ruth's first instinct was to leap up swinging and pretend that it didn't hurt. In this sense, he was not alone. Several days after Ginkel's army had overrun Athlone, a Jacobite colonel named Felix O'Neill wrote a letter shrugging off the defeat. 'Everybody knows that Athlone could not be thought tenable,' he insisted, and though its loss after such a ferocious defence was sickening, the main Jacobite army was intact, hardy and ready to fight.[1] O'Neill was talking tough, but in the hours after the retreat from Athlone he would have found himself in small company. St Ruth's men staggered west to Ballinasloe in the same scattered manner as the Jacobites who had trekked from the Boyne to Limerick one year earlier. Less than half of John Stevens's regiment were accounted for, and some reports claimed that as few as 7,000 troops were present at the first Jacobite muster after Athlone. Stragglers began to trickle into the camp over the coming days, 'their fear somewhat abating', but morale had been gutted.[2] St Ruth had taken a thrashing, but he was keen to strike back immediately. Others were not so sure.

St Ruth held a council of war at Ballinasloe, but his design to draw the Williamite army into a major battle somewhere along the road from Athlone to Galway found little support. Opposition to the idea was one of the few things that Sarsfield and Tyrconnell found themselves agreeing on. Despite his popularity and status, Sarsfield had largely been kept out of St Ruth's inner circle and was in no mood to bandage the Frenchman's ego. Sarsfield pointed out that Ginkel's army was larger, more experienced and armed to the teeth. 'To hazard a battle against them with the Irish army, inferior in number and discipline, ill-clad, and not well fed, having no pay, and much discouraged for the loss of Athlone, was to endanger the whole kingdom.'[3] Tyrconnell, who was being kept up to date with things from Limerick by quick-footed messengers, echoed Sarsfield's point. They both believed that the only viable course would be to launch a guerrilla campaign to harass Ginkel's troops and drag out the war until more men and arms arrived from France. They proposed splitting the infantry in two, with one half each being sent to garrison Limerick and Galway. The cavalry would then sneak into Leinster and attack the Williamite supply lines, raiding and burning until Ginkel was forced to retreat from Connaught and cover his rear. The plan was remarkably similar to the Duke of Berwick's idea the previous summer, which Tyrconnell had scoffed at. But those were different days in a much-changed theatre. With the muck of Athlone still on their boots, the Jacobite general staff voted against a battle. Overruling them would have required political muscle that the humiliated St Ruth did not have.

Lieutenant General d'Usson, still battered from the stampede out of Athlone, was sent to Galway to begin preparations for its defence. The Scottish major general John Wauchope travelled to Limerick to do likewise. Sarsfield rode to Loughrea to oversee the withdrawal of Jacobite troops from a necklace of small river garrisons, which were now rendered useless with the loss of Athlone. Indulging his prerogative as commander-in-chief, St Ruth held tough at Ballinasloe and began to scout the unfamiliar terrain of County Galway, his temper still 'too sensible of the affront he received' from Ginkel and his pride 'longing for an opportunity to wash away that stain'.[4]

*

There were streets to clear, defences to fix and bodies to drag out from under the rubble. Before Ginkel could make his next move, the debris of what used to be Athlone had to be swept out from underfoot. His sick and wounded were sent back to Dublin, where the grand Royal Hospital at Kilmainham had been stocked with fresh tents, ample medical supplies and a new surgeon general. On the two-day march back to the capital, the Williamites limping away from the front passed hundreds of horse-drawn wagons heading the opposite way, wobbling under the weight of sacks of grain and barrels of gunpowder. The army paymasters had also sent a fresh consignment of coin to keep the soldiers focused. Before he was hauled off to Dublin Castle under armed guard, Ginkel chatted with Thomas Maxwell, the most notable Jacobite prisoner taken at Athlone. Maxwell whinged about St Ruth's incompetence, and Ginkel began to wonder if others in the Jacobite ranks were as miffed as he was. He decided to find out.[5]

On 9 July Ginkel published a declaration, co-signed by Thomas Coningsby and Charles Porter, which called for the Jacobites to surrender. The document, which had been signed and dated two days earlier, promised that any Jacobite soldier or officer who submitted would receive an equal or better-paid position in William's army and 'shall also be restored to, and put in possession of, all their estates forfeited for … treasons, crimes and offences'. It seemed generous on the surface, but beneath the dressing there was little meat. The guarantees of property only referred to the most recent round of attainders passed since William and Mary were crowned and did nothing to address the old sores of Charles's land settlement. Meanwhile, Jacobite officers seeking to avail of the terms would have to not only surrender themselves, but also 'yield up any such city, town, fort or garrison' under their command within three weeks. The terms were also extended to the ordinary citizens of Limerick and Galway, in the hope that they might be coaxed into throwing off St Ruth's protection and opening their gates to Ginkel. But the only prize that might have tempted them – the promise of Catholic liberty – was not on the table. On religious freedom, Porter and Coningsby's declaration stated only that William and Mary would convene a parliament in Dublin to discuss Catholic concerns 'as soon as their majesties' affairs will permit them'.[6] London and Dublin had been haggling over the wording of the declaration since that spring, but the final draft had been neutered of all substance – not least by the fact that William and Mary's signatures were absent from the bottom. Two days after it had been published and ignored, a grumpy Ginkel was unsurprised. The declaration 'promised nothing', he complained, before adding that the terms were so poor that they 'may be of more prejudice than advantage', as it would force the Jacobites to keep fighting for something better.[7]

*

The Jacobite camp near Ballinasloe had begun to swell, as soldiers who had been guarding crossing points along the Shannon joined up with the main army, and others who had simply scattered in the aftershock of Athlone returned to their regiments gingerly. By the end of the first week in July, around 15,000 or 20,000 men were crowded into the camp, which had since withdrawn a few miles west from Ballinasloe to the tiny village of Aughrim, a place 'without any other thing worth observing'.[8] St Ruth made it his business to trot around the hot maze of tents and carts and campfires, chatting with junior officers, followed at every turn by his retinue of aides-de-camp. If his men were going to fight, St Ruth knew he would have to salvage their morale. 'He used all the means possible to strengthen his army … now he begins to be very kind to and familiar with the Irish officers, whom he formerly treated with disrespect and contempt.'[9]

Just over the horizon, Ginkel was in the dark about his enemy's plans. His scouts were being chased off with only scraps of information: on 5 July a Jacobite patrol intercepted and killed twenty Williamite scouts near Aughrim, took five more prisoner and chased eleven others back to Athlone. The thin terms on offer for surrender had coaxed barely a handful of Jacobites into deserting, depriving Ginkel of a usually fruitful source of intelligence. On 10 July he believed that St Ruth was heading south to Portumna to make a stand somewhere near Lough Derg; the following day he had it that the Jacobites planned to split their army between Galway, Limerick and Sligo. For a man used to making meticulous decisions based on hard fact, fumbling around like this annoyed Ginkel immensely. Without any decent intelligence, he simply decided to press ahead with the original plan to take Galway, the Jacobites' last coastal port, before swinging south to finish the war in Limerick. On 7 July the last of the Williamite troops had crossed through Athlone, and two days later the army set out on the road west. The countryside before them bobbed and rolled like a gentle green tide, but the weather was wild and unpredictable. One moment they would bake under the 'violent scorching heat of the sun', and a few hours later the sky would crack with thunder which 'all men took for hot firing of cannon' in the distance.[10] One night a violent rainstorm washed away dozens of Jacobite tents, while two men and a boy travelling with the Williamite camp were struck by lightning and killed. It was not a good time to be superstitious.

Just after dawn on 8 July the Jacobite army gathered its baggage and supplies and shuffled one mile to a new camp on the slope of Kilcommodon Hill, just south of Aughrim village. It was 'plainer, pleasanter ground' than some of the barren and looted places where John Stevens had laid his head during the war.[11] St Ruth had chosen the location carefully. Kilcommodon Hill sloped gently down towards a thick bog that stretched along its feet for almost a mile, criss-crossed with briars and flooded with sticky water. The road from Athlone to Galway ran along the bog's edge, narrowing until it pinched into a small causeway some sixty yards long, 'where only two abreast could pass, and that too with great difficulty'.[12] Sitting at the end of the causeway was the shell of Aughrim Castle, an old ruin with some overgrown low walls and thick ditches. From there, the road hooked left in an arc up along the face of the hill and down the other side. Here, opposite the causeway on the other edge of the bog, was a clearing known as Urraghry Pass, which was narrow, uneven and barely passable. The entire field was a bottleneck pinched by the wild, sloppy work of nature. It was a great place to put an army.

St Ruth established his main camp on the hillside, summoned his senior officers and confidently told them that this was going to be their battlefield. St Ruth had deferred to his generals' opinions at the last council, but now he was enforcing his rank and issuing a direct order. In the days since Athlone he had worked tirelessly to galvanise morale, reorganise his forces and find a place where Ginkel's strength and firepower would be nullified by the terrain. Now, on this innocuous hillside near

Aughrim, a place he had never heard of before, St Ruth was sure he would have retribution. The battlefield would need to be manicured: the ditches between the bog and the hillside were clipped and shaped to create a mazy network of defences. Aughrim Castle and the narrow causeway were fortified with trenches. St Ruth's nine remaining field cannons were drawn up on the hillside, three guns each pointing left, right and straight ahead. The clink and squelch of shovels and pickaxes became a mid-summer chorus as piles of earth were cleared to shape the ground for the carnage to come. 'St Ruth showed good skill in choosing ground and in ranging his host for this fight, where his all and the all of the nation lay at stake,' one Jacobite wrote.[13]

St Ruth knew that many of his troops had never seen a battle before. Apart from the sprinkle of veterans who had served in the French army or had felt the mad heat of Oldbridge at the Boyne, most of the Irish soldiers were rookies and would shortly be expected to turn back an army of professionals from Germany, Denmark and Holland. They had never been asked to hold formation on a battlefield as men to their left and right were dismembered by cannon shot. They had never known the terror of a cavalry charge or heard the screams and whimpers of men dying from a bullet to the stomach or a bayonet through the eye. No one knows for certain what St Ruth said to his men – whether he was harsh and stout or warm and sympathetic. However, a piece of paper was later found in the pocket of a dead French aide, apparently containing a speech that some believe St Ruth gave on the eve of the battle. No one knows for sure if these were St Ruth's words, or the poetic thoughts of some junior officer, or simply a forgery. St Ruth's grasp of English was spotty at best, and the idea of him delivering passionate rhetoric to regiments of mostly Irish-speaking infantry seems remote. But if that moment was real, and St Ruth really did read this speech, then it is hard not to think that the hearts of the rank-and-file Jacobites were wrenched up to the heavens: 'You are not mercenary soldiers, you do not fight for your pay, but for your lives, your wives, your children, your liberties, your country, your estates; and to restore the most pious of kings to his throne; but above all for the propagation of the Holy Faith, and the subversion of heresy.' The speech soared and soared. 'King James will love and reward you; Louis the Great will protect you; all good Catholics will applaud you; I myself will command you; the Church will pray for you … God will make you all saints, and his holy mother will lay you in her bosom.'[14]

30

Aughrim

At sunrise on Sunday 12 July 1691 a thick fog lingered over the countryside, the kind that burns off on a summer morning to reveal a soft sky and a comforting sun. In another life it would have been a morning for an Irishman to trot out to the bog, a spade across his shoulder, ready for a day of slicing and stacking and turning the peat, because even the finest summers are just fleeting things, and turf for the winter needs saving. The fog might have smelled like one of those mornings when you were a boy, wandering idly along the docks of La Rochelle, listening as gangplanks crashed down and deck hands bickered and the great white towers of the harbour rose up like mountains; back before your family had to flee France because Louis decided that how men say their prayers was the state's business. In some other corner of the past, a misty summer morning would have meant work, family and home. But here, in the gentle lap of east Galway, the morning only brought fear and regret. Tens of thousands of anxious men who had barely slept the night before drew a deep breath in the mist and wondered.

Ginkel finally knew where he had to go. On Saturday 11 July his scouts were scouring the terrain near Aughrim village when they spotted the great, distant mass of the Jacobite army drawn up across Kilcommodon Hill. Ginkel hurried up to see for himself, scanning the enemy lines and making marks on a map of the area given to him by a French Protestant family who had settled in Galway. At a rough guess, he believed that the Jacobite lines were almost two miles long, running from the edge of the road, up across the face of the hill, through a large tangle of tents and carts and down the other side. He could see the narrow causeway, the ruined old castle and the thick expanse of bog that curled across the base of the hill, like a cat at its master's feet. It was a daunting image. The Williamite scouts could only guess how many tens of thousands of enemy soldiers were out there, 'very advantageously posted; with a large bog and entrenchments made before them'.[1] The fact that the main Jacobite camp was right up against the lines on the hillside was stark evidence that St Ruth had no plan to retreat. 'They were resolved to win the day or lose all,' one Williamite soldier wrote.[2]

The Williamite army had advanced two miles beyond Ballinasloe and was settling down for the night when orders arrived for every man to fix and clean his weapons, gather ammunition and prepare to march at first light. Quartermasters spent the night minutely dividing up supplies: each rifleman stuffed fifteen little packets of powder and shot into his satchel, or clipped them to his belt, while assault troops were given two grenades each – coarse, weighty things that rolled around in their packs as they walked, reminding them that when the time to attack came, they would be first in line to die. Ginkel sent for the rest of his field artillery to be brought up from Ballinasloe as quickly as possible and ordered that, when the army moved out, their tents and baggage would remain behind. They were marching to war, and they would be travelling light.[3]

St Ruth had overseen his final preparations. The Jacobite army was arranged like a man standing upright with his arms out wide and his back defiantly against a wall. The infantry were drawn up in two lines near the bottom of the hill to barricade the centre, while the cavalry and dragoons were posted in support at either end. The total Jacobite strength that day is disputed but is believed to have been somewhere between 18,000 and 20,000 men, all twisting stomachs and soggy boots as they stood there fingering their musket locks, praying silently, cursing this bloody wait. St Ruth had also dispersed his officers to their posts along the line: de Tessé was to be his second-in-command, while the infantry in the centre would be led by major generals William Dorrington and John Hamilton. Overall command of the crucial left flank by Aughrim Castle and the causeway was given to Major General Dominic Sheldon, while Henry Luttrell was to lead the first line of cavalry on the left. De Tessé and Patrick Sarsfield's places on the battlefield vary between accounts – some claim Sarsfield was on the left, others the right; others say he had been posted in reserve alongside the cavalry regiment of Lord Galmoy, who had led the first failed attempt to reduce Enniskillen in the summer of 1689. But the most critical post in the line – the pivot on which the entire battle would turn – was not handed to a veteran general or an elite troop of cavalry. The defence of Aughrim Castle, the crumbling makeshift fortress at the end of the causeway, was tasked to Colonel Walter Burke and a small regiment of 200 men. If Burke could hold the castle and its 'parcel of old garden ditches', and if his men could drive the Williamites off the main road, the enemy would be forced to find a way through a thick, sticky maze of bog instead.[4] That castle was everything.

*

Dawn. Ensigns and lieutenants barked at their men to form up and move. They marched through the chalky and cold morning fog. Each company was its own island, until slowly their borders shrank and they were swallowed by the great mass of the army: countless thousands of men shuffling and grunting with heavy human effort. The flags and banners that marked out the Danish, English, Dutch, German and Huguenot regiments were barely visible through the haze. The drums and fifes that normally set the rhythm were silent, as Ginkel had ordered his troops to march as discreetly as some 20,000 men and horses could. By eight o'clock in the morning the Williamite vanguard had followed the road to the edge of the battlefield, more than a mile from the foot of Kilcommodon Hill. The march stopped. Officers snapped and growled at their men once more, and the regiments were shuffled into position in roughly the same shape as St Ruth's lines: infantry in the centre, cavalry and dragoons at either end. It was noon before the mist began to roll back. Ginkel rode up a small slope to his right and scanned the battlefield once more, sizing up the terrain, the final alignment of the Jacobite forces and every other fraction a general must weigh as he calculates slaughter like mathematics. A small party of Jacobite scouts were spotted moving up towards Ginkel's left wing, and he promptly ordered about 200 of his own dragoons to drive them off. The Williamite dragoons raced up, eager for action, and a small skirmish broke out. The Jacobite lines along the hillside began to shuffle nervously, unsure as to whether or not this was the first move of the battle. Ginkel had his eighteen cannons towed up into the centre of his line, and the batteries on both sides of the battlefield began a deafening sequence of fire: probing, testing and finding their range. The sound of carbine rifles popping and whizzing from the skirmish grew louder as the Williamite dragoons climbed off their horses and took up firing positions in ditches. Both armies watched out of the corners of their eyes, and waited.

Ginkel called a council of war early in the afternoon. It was a typically frank exchange. The dragoons he had sent out to drive off the Jacobite outriders had held their ground and kept fighting, contrary to their original orders, and the sight of the skirmishing had drawn St Ruth's army closer down the hill 'in very considerable bodies', as if magnetically drawn to the bustle.[5] Ginkel had tweaked his own lines in response, but his gut instinct, as ever, was caution: tents were sent for from the main camp up the road, and it seemed as if the Dutch commander intended to hold off his attack until the following morning. However, 'perceiving the enemy to be in some disorder by what had already happened', the Williamite generals decided to fight while they had the chance, fearing that St Ruth might 'march off in the night'.[6] The Scottish major general Hugh Mackay leaned over Ginkel's map and proposed a simple plan: the Williamite left wing would drive forward and attack the Jacobite right up Urraghry Pass, hopefully baiting St Ruth into drawing away some troops from the causeway. Then, the Williamites' right wing of cavalry and dragoons would bludgeon their way up the causeway and overrun Aughrim Castle, the anchor of St Ruth's entire line. The Williamite infantry and grenadiers, meanwhile, would wade straight into the bog and attack the Jacobite infantry head-on in the centre. Everything depended on drawing St Ruth into the trap: as it stood, the narrow causeway was simply too tightly packed for the Williamites' heavier, stronger cavalry to flex their muscle.

The attack began at around five o'clock that evening – strangely late in the day, even in mid-summer. The Williamite left flank, comprised mostly of Danish and Huguenot regiments, began to inch forward up the spotty ground towards Urraghry Pass. Infantrymen and grenadiers went first, with packs of cavalry and dragoons swarming around the fringes, ready to pick off any stray Irishmen that might break cover. They were instantly taken back by the sheer ferocity of the Jacobite defence. Lined up in ranks behind hedges, the Irish soldiers 'behaved themselves like men of another nation, defending their ditches stoutly'.[7] With lethal precision, the Jacobites began to scramble from hedge to hedge, twisting and feinting, laying down thick fire on the disoriented Williamites from punishingly close range. The Jacobite cavalry posted on their right swooped down in waves, butchering the Danes and Huguenots with violent care. The Williamites pushed on 'with a great deal of bravery, but were beaten back'.[8] For an hour and a half Ginkel's men tried to find a way through, their eyes stinging from smoke. At the same time, four regiments of Williamite infantry in the centre marched down into the bog, raising their guns and packs over their heads as they struggled 'up to their middles in mud and water'.[9] Their boots sank in the marsh, and their coats sagged with wet muck. They had just managed to wade through the worst of it, and were within twenty yards of the ditches on the other side when St Ruth's troops finally opened fire. Men climbing out of the water were flung back by a hailstorm of bullets. Bodies began to crumple to the ground as men shot through the arm or leg cursed and crawled for cover. More Williamite infantry struggled out of the bog, but dozens were cut down before they could even catch their breath.

The Jacobites were fighting for every inch and contesting every clump of earth with anger. St Ruth had ordered that the ditches at the roots of Kilcommodon Hill be trimmed, knocked and realigned for this very moment. With lethal co-ordination the Irish infantry fired their muskets, scrambled back through clearings, waited for their enemies to follow and then fired again, killing and wounding dozens at a time. It was fierce and bloody work, and when the lines drew too close the soldiers flung themselves at each other, wrestling and punching and gouging and stabbing like feral beasts. The patch of ground where the fighting was worst became known as the bloody hollow, and it was apt. The Williamites suffered horrific casualties. 'They attacked ... with unbelievable bravery ... fought the enemy hand to hand, struck them with musket butts, and those without arms grabbed them by the necks and threw them to the ground.'[10] A hail of musket shot sliced through the air from every direction, and the men 'could scarce see one another for smoke'.[11] The slow, violent momentum of the battle was swelling behind the Jacobites, and they were determined to feel it. As the Williamite advance ground to a halt in the middle, huge numbers of Irish cavalry and infantry suddenly poured through the clearings in the ditches and crashed into their lines. The Williamite centre began to collapse as the infantry were driven back through the bog, tumbling, scrambling and panicking in the water. The Jacobites were gripped by some invisible frenzy – hacking and pummelling any man who tripped or got stuck. It was butchery. 'The English charged, and in their advancing the Irish slew numbers from their little old ditches; the English gained them and flew in boldly ... the Irish returned the charge, and broke and pursued them with great slaughter.'[12] The Jacobites drove their enemy so hard that they broke right through the bog and out the other side, briefly capturing some of the Williamite cannons before the English major general, Thomas Talmash, rallied the disintegrating lines and halted the rout. There was no other way to describe it – the Jacobites were winning, and winning violently. 'They had driven our foot in the centre so far,' wrote George Story, who was watching with concern from the hillside behind. 'The thing seemed so doubtful for some time.'[13]

Looking across the battlefield on horseback from Kilcommodon Hill, St Ruth saw vindication and glory stretch out before him, like some gruesome baroque painting. He was heard to exclaim, 'Le jour est á nous, mes enfants.' He watched as Ginkel's left flank was fought to a standstill up Urraghry Pass, while the Jacobite infantry and cavalry in the centre 'threw all down before them like thunderbolts'.[14] Ginkel was stunned. But at this seemingly despairing moment in the battle he spotted something across the field, through the smoke and the slaughter. Two regiments of Jacobite infantry and a cluster of cavalry were marching away from their positions in a cornfield near the edge of the causeway. As the Jacobite centre and left flank became tangled up in the manic fighting, St Ruth and William Dorrington feared that gaps might suddenly appear in their lines. As a precaution, the French commander decided to pull some troops away from his left to reinforce his right. Ginkel suddenly saw his chance. It had come at far bloodier a cost than he or Hugh Mackay could have imagined, but St Ruth had taken the bait.

The Williamite right wing of infantry and cavalry began to race up the road towards the causeway, bellowing from the pits of their lungs. It was every bit as vicious as the fighting in the centre, with men 'pressing and tumbling over a very dangerous place … amongst showers of bullets'.[15] St Ruth's decision to hoist two regiments of infantry away from the road gave Ginkel the tiniest of cracks to exploit. Grenadiers and infantrymen beat their way along the edge of the road, ducking, firing and scrambling forward, desperately trying to survive from one second to the next. The first swarm of cavalry from Colonel Francis Compton's regiment charged fearlessly up the narrow passage, straight into the jaws of Walter Burke's Jacobite garrison in the castle. The Jacobites fired, reloaded and fired again, their fingers aching from the clunky work of pouring the powder, packing the bullet and priming the fuse, which would occupy a good rifleman for thirty seconds and a bad one for longer. The Williamite cavalry pressed on into the tempest. Horses were shot in full gallop, sending their riders hurtling to the dirt with a sickening clatter of broken bone. The Williamites could not find a way through. Compton's men were driven back, charged a second time and were driven back again. The mouth of the causeway became littered with the mangled and twisted flesh of men and horses. The Williamite infantry along the crest of the road could only inch forward, the way ahead completely obscured by smoke blown into their faces by wind sweeping down the hill. 'There was nothing but a continued fire, and a very hot dispute all along the line.'[16]

The Jacobite left and the Williamite right were knotted in a horrific struggle for the causeway and Aughrim Castle. The furthest lines of infantry were barely thirty yards apart, and the nearby Jacobite cannons pounded the Williamites mercilessly. 'With the thrust of pikes and swords and the shots of muskets, carnage raged through the ranks,' one Danish eyewitness wrote. 'The very ridges of the hill seemed to be afire and to vomit flames like those of Etna.'[17] Walter Burke's men shot anything that staggered through the smoke and haze. They fired from behind shattered windows and mossy garden walls and every other scrap of cover they could use. They had shredded the first two waves of Williamite cavalry, but their ammunition was running low. As they turned to open fresh crates of bullets, disaster struck. The extra bullets they had been given were English-made rounds that were too big for the muzzles of their French guns. The storm of fire spitting out from the castle began to fade as horrified Jacobites tried to stuff oversized bullets into their muskets. Someone, somewhere had made a terrible mistake, one that was later decried as being 'as bad as treachery'.[18] A third wave of Williamite cavalry came hurtling up the road, and this time there was no fire to stop them. A great door seemed to swing open, and dozens of horsemen from Mackay and Ruvigny's regiments raced through the causeway and out the other side. The Williamite infantry by the roadside clambered up and joined the swarm, overrunning the hapless Jacobites in the castle, butchering almost three-quarters of Burke's regiment with bullets and sabres and bayonets.

St Ruth watched from near the base of the hill as his left flank started to crumble. Henry Luttrell's first line of cavalry, which was posted further down the road behind the castle, was supposed to charge and counter attack if the causeway fell. But fearing that Luttrell's horses would not be enough to hold back the flood, St Ruth snatched at his reigns, shouted for his aides to follow him and turned to charge over towards the castle. Across the battlefield, through a great wall of smoke and confusion, a Williamite artilleryman saw a cluster of horses galloping across the hillside in the distance. The cannon crew's work was swift and unthinking, like tying a shoelace: the inside of the barrel was swept; a charge of powder was stuffed in, followed by a cannonball; the contents were packed tightly and primed; and then the gun erupted with such force that it was flung backwards on its wheels. The shot cut through the air and took St Ruth's head clean off his shoulders. His decapitated body was flung from its horse. The colour drained from his aides' faces, and a crushing timeline of terror and consequence began. St Ruth was dead. Fearing what would happen if the men found out, the general's body was quickly wrapped in a cloak and whisked from the battlefield. But it would be impossible to keep such a thing secret.

This entire battle was St Ruth's vision, and without him no one knew to do next. The infantry were caught up in brutal fighting along the centre and were unaware of the disaster that had just occurred a few yards behind them. However, the news of St Ruth's death cut through the cavalry like a forest fire. Henry Luttrell, who was supposed to lead a charge and take back Aughrim Castle, turned with his brigade and fled. Dominic Sheldon, who was in command of the entire left wing, froze on the spot. Lieutenant General de Tessé, now in overall command, raced across from Urraghry Pass to try and turn back the Williamites, who had now broken through and were wheeling around to rip through the unguarded Jacobite infantry from behind. De Tessé was shot three times as he charged into Ruvigny's men. One bullet struck him in the face, while another pierced his metal chest plate. He slumped across his horse, barely alive, and was pulled from the field by his aide-de-camp. The Jacobite lines began to dissolve. Their cavalry turned and rode away from the field, and their stunned infantry were suddenly torn apart by a deluge of Williamite horses. 'Their army was soon in confusion for want of orders … their foot were miserably slaughtered by our horse and dragoons as they made towards the bog.'[19]

Fate and catastrophe had struck with incredible timing. The Jacobites began to break from the field in a panic, pursued with hatred by the Williamite cavalry. It was now about eight o'clock in the evening. What followed over the next few hours is considered to be one of the worst massacres in Irish history. Thousands of Jacobite infantrymen were stabbed and slashed to death as they tried to escape the field towards Loughrea. Had it not gotten dark, the butchery would have lasted for hours. It was 'a total rout', one Williamite officer recalled. 'Our horse made a great slaughter of their foot in the pursuit.'[20] The wives and children attached to the main Jacobite camp were forced to witness a living nightmare. It is almost impossible to imagine the scale of the cruelty. The account of one Danish eyewitness is devoid of any sense of triumph or pride:

> The Irish fled all over the fields … from all sides the inescapable violence meets them … many men and horses pierced by wounds could have neither flight nor rest, sometimes trying to rise they fell suddenly, weighed down by the mass of their own bodies; others with mutilated limbs and disabled by pain asked for the sword as a remedy… others spewed forth their breath mixed with blood and threats, grasping their bloodstained arms in an icy embrace, as if in readiness for some future battle … blood, as if drawn by the bite of a poisonous snake, flowed over the ground, and so

> inundated the fields that you could hardly take a step without slipping. Such and so horrible a sight, of the slaughtered bodies, remained all around untouched and unchanged for some days.[21]

*

The Jacobite army had been eviscerated. Those who managed to escape the field limped away to Galway, Limerick or some other corner of a shrinking nation where they could find refuge. Patrick Sarsfield and Lord Galmoy tried to cover the Jacobite retreat, harrying and driving off some Williamite cavalry. But there was only so much they could do. The Danish troopers, who were described as 'excellent pursuers', hunted down Jacobite stragglers for sport. The dead and the dying littered the land 'like a great flock of sheep, scattered up and down the country, for almost four miles round'. The corpses of those Jacobite infantrymen who had ferociously held the line and driven back the first Williamite assault were found piled along the crest of the bog, often as many as 150 at a time, 'most of them by the ditches where they were shot'.[22] The number of men who perished at Aughrim that day is disputed, of course, and will never be known for certain. Rival accounts vary, as always: some claim that just 673 Williamites died, others say over 5,000. Conservative estimates put the Jacobite losses at 2,000 dead, while a report from the front printed in the *London Gazette* crowed that 'of the enemy, about 5,000 were killed upon the place'.[23] Robert Parker, a Williamite officer who described the battle in his memoirs, offers the most credible tally: 4,000 Jacobites killed and 2,000 taken prisoner, with 3,000 Williamites dead and wounded. Either way, the Battle of Aughrim was an appalling exercise in savagery, roughly on a par with the Battle of Clontarf in 1014 as the most murderous day in Irish history.

The Jacobite leadership had been devastated. St Ruth was dead, and de Tessé was barely alive. Major generals William Dorrington and John Hamilton, who had commanded the centre of the Jacobite line, were both captured. Hamilton was gravely wounded and died a short time later. A number of Jacobite noblemen were taken prisoner on the field, including Lord Bophin, the Earl of Clanricarde's brother and Patrick Sarsfield's father-in-law. Sarsfield's uncle, Colonel Charles Moore, had also been killed. Walter Burke, who had commanded the fateful garrison at Aughrim Castle, was captured, as was Colonel Gordon O'Neill, who had led the Jacobite infantry as they charged through the bog and attacked the Williamite lines on the other side. Viscount Galway, Lord Bophin's brother, fell into the Williamites' hands but was executed 'by some of our foreign troopers … after he had surrendered himself a prisoner'.[24] A list of the surnames of the Jacobites who perished at Aughrim captures the breadth of their unlikely coalition: O'Neill, Moore, Bourke, MacGuire, Talbot, Mansfield-Barker, Morgan, Arthur. Some were noblemen who had refused to acknowledge a usurper; many were gentry fighting to reclaim their family's property and influence. Others simply saw themselves as holy warriors – men like the Catholic priest Alexius Stafford of Wexford, 'an undaunted zealot, and a most pious church man', who was killed while urging some Irish infantry to charge.[25] Norman, Gael, priest; they had all gathered under James Stuart's banner, and together they had suffered the same fate. One Jacobite writer lamented that Aughrim was 'a victory snatched out of the hands of the victorious'.[26] The Williamite officer Robert Parker could not help but praise his enemies' valour, writing that 'never did the Irish fight so well in their own country, as they did this day … and had it not been that St Ruth fell, it were [*sic*] hard to say how matters would have ended'.[27] The Duke of Wurtemburg wrote that the Jacobite infantry 'did wonders', and if their cavalry had done likewise instead of breaking from the field, 'we should have been totally defeated'.[28]

*

There were more trophies than Ginkel knew what to do with. Dozens of wagonloads of food, ammunition and other supplies were captured when the Jacobite camp on Kilcommodon Hill was overrun. The Jacobites' nine field cannons were seized, as were hundreds of muskets thrown away by soldiers attempting to flee. Eleven battle standards and thirty-two sets of regimental colours were sent to London as gifts for Queen Mary. 'This unexpected successful action at Aughrim', as one Williamite officer described it, had been an extraordinary feat and had annihilated the Jacobites' ability to wage war.[29] When word of the victory reached Brussels, the city's guns fired three blasts in salute to William's army. On 13 July Ginkel asked the lord justices in Dublin to declare a public day of thanksgiving. Two days later, the victory had still not sunk in. 'It was a great victory over the enemy; no time must be lost,' Ginkel wrote, before typically requesting fresh supplies of food, gunpowder and wages. Prisoners 'of all degrees' would shortly be arriving in the capital, he added.[30] Work began in an effort to clear the corpses away from the battlefield, but there were simply too many to bury. Four days later the Williamite army marched away, leaving behind a sea of carnage. 'The place where this battle was fought will make a noise in history,' George Story declared.[31] The Jacobite colonel Charles O'Kelly wrote that Aughrim had been a battle 'so glorious to Ginkel, and so fatal to St Ruth and the Irish, who lost there the flower of their army and nation'.[32]

31

A Mighty Edifice

The city of Galway had too much to lose. It was a trading post wrapped in old walls, shielded by water on two sides and a bog on another. Its houses were built like castles to withstand the endless siege of the weather, which swept in from the Atlantic like a battering ram. It was not a great city of fortune like Venice or Genoa, but it was still a tidy place to trade with France or the West Indies without drawing too much attention. Its wealth and commercial interests were largely in the hands of 'new interest' men – Catholics who had bought property from old Cromwellian investors and were distrusted by their peers for having 'purchased from usurpers the inheritance of their own countrymen'.[1] But Galway was a city of thick skins, where men argued that they lived in the world as it is, not as it used to be. It was a city of shipping agents and warehouses and customs inspectors, and like any place that made its living from the sea, it had learned to be sensible. 'Being always rather a place of trade than action of another nature', Galway would require only a gentle prod from Ginkel to realise that war was bad for business.[2]

It is not difficult to imagine a city strangled by hysteria on the morning of Monday 13 July as word of the rout at Aughrim began to spread: crowds gathering under porticos swapping hot rumours; mothers shaking and clutching their children tight, certain that their homes would be dust within days. The Williamite army was rampant and barely thirty-five miles away. Galway began to picture the terror of a siege, and few believed they would survive it. Lieutenant General d'Usson had been detailed to defend Galway, but he was not working with much. The city garrison had barely seven regiments of infantry, supplemented by those few hundred stragglers from Aughrim who did not head for Limerick with the rest. D'Usson had just over 2,000 men in all, many of them half-clothed and without working muskets. His appeals to Limerick for extra men in the days after Aughrim were rejected. The city's outer earthworks were slapdash and unfinished, and several cannons had not yet been fixed to batteries on the landward walls. The roving army of Balldearg O'Donnell, the unruly Ulster commander who styled himself as the true Earl of Tyrconnell, had been told to march south and relieve Galway, but he was cut off by Williamite troops and withdrew into Mayo without making a fuss. Talk within Galway quickly turned to surrender. The civilian governor Lord Dillon, the aldermen and various leading nobles, including the Earl of Clanricarde, argued the merits of fighting on, leaving d'Usson a frustrated bystander. Townsmen snuck messages out to Ginkel, assuring him that the city would fold. Judge Denis Daly, who had been briefly gaoled for his part in Grady's peace talks the previous winter, slipped out of Galway, met with Ginkel at Athenry and gave him 'an exact account' of 'all the Irish intrigues' within the walls.[3] D'Usson even had to arrest the mayor, Arthur Ffrench, after he sent the town clerk to negotiate with Ginkel without his consent. One Jacobite lamented that for all Galway's shortages of muskets and men, 'the greatest want of all was resolution and union'.[4]

It was a prompt and straightforward surrender. Ginkel arrived on 19 July and demanded that Galway open its gates. Dillon refused, and the following morning Williamite soldiers swarmed over the outer earthworks. Senior city officials held a meeting that same day without d'Usson's knowledge and agreed to seek terms. The French general was given no say in the matter. A ceasefire was proclaimed; hostages were exchanged as a customary token of good will, and on 21 July Ginkel granted Galway an unusually generous deal. The entire Jacobite garrison would be 'safely conducted' to Limerick with an armed escort, and Galway's officials, aldermen, sheriffs and other noted individuals 'shall enjoy and possess their estates … and all other liberties and immunities'. Named members of the local Catholic clergy would be free to preach 'without being prosecuted on any penal laws'.[5] A clause was also inserted allowing any Galway native not currently in the city three weeks to return, submit to Williamite authority and enjoy the same terms. Sensing Ginkel's desire to finish the war quickly, Galway had driven a hard bargain.

Ginkel seemed almost nervous as he forwarded a copy of the terms to William Bentinck for the king's approval, covering himself by stressing that Wurtemburg and the other generals thought it was a fair deal. In the meantime, he pressed ahead with the formalities: at midday on 26 July Ginkel entered Galway to a civic reception from the mayor and aldermen. Two hours earlier d'Usson, Dillon and some 2,300 Jacobite soldiers marched out of the city towards Limerick. Before the garrison traipsed off, a group of Irish soldiers attempted to siphon a gunpowder barrel in the street when it exploded, blowing out several men's eyes and maiming 'above twenty'.[6] It was a fittingly bungled end to the defence of Galway. An irritated d'Usson wrote that 'he who today is ready to die rather than submit to the Prince of Orange will tomorrow talk loudly about the need for a settlement'.[7] Hard-line Jacobites moaned that their last seaport had been handed over by men who 'considered nothing but their own security'.[8] Ginkel and his troops were not complaining. The very day that the surrender of Galway was agreed, Ginkel was already making preparations to march on Limerick. George Story walked along the top of Galway's thick old walls, inspected its magazines and thanked God that things had not gone the other way. 'This town with a good garrison in it might have given us more trouble,' he remarked.[9]

*

The news that woke the Duke of Tyrconnell from his bed in Limerick early on 13 July was stark. Aughrim had been lost and untold thousands were dead, St Ruth among them. The viceroy 'was struck with a deep wound of sorrow', one writer recalled. Tyrconnell had urged St Ruth to tear down Athlone's outer earthworks and then told him to avoid fighting Ginkel in the field. He had been proven right both times, but at great cost. Nonetheless, the new emergency in the aftermath of Aughrim seemed to reinvigorate Tyrconnell, and within days he had thrown off his pity and spite, like a man flinging a wet coat into a corner. He was old and sick, but he was still a political craftsman without equal. At this lowest point of the war Tyrconnell 'roused his courage' and prepared to step firmly back into the centre of affairs.[10] He began, naturally, with a letter to Paris.

Louis and James needed to be informed about Aughrim at once, and as he started writing Tyrconnell did not dilute his opinions. 'I am angry that the poor monsieur St Ruth has lost his life, he had certainly the best will in the world, but a temperament hardly suited to our affairs.' Tyrconnell stated that St Ruth 'did not consult me' on his decision to give battle and insisted that if he had been listened to neither St Ruth nor the army would be lost.[11]

Tyrconnell added the standard request for supplies and troops as a matter of urgency. He made three copies of his dispatch and gave one each to trusted members of his retinue: the Earl of Abercorn, one of James's lords of the bedchamber; Lord Thomas Howard, a kinsman of the famous dukes of Norfolk; and a Mr Doran, one of Tyrconnell's secretaries. Abercorn and Howard were both killed attempting to smuggle the message into France, and only Doran managed to deliver it to Paris intact. James, who was increasingly uninterested in Ireland, apparently greeted the news with a shrug. 'The best remedy he had was his usual resignation to the will of God,' one account claims.[12] Tyrconnell's request for arms and men was noted at Versailles, but the timing could not have been worse. The Marquis of Louvois, the ferocious war minister who had dominated French politics for over thirty years, had died on 16 July. His sudden death threw his ministry into a confused transition. Versailles was able to promise that 'provisions, ammunition, arms and other necessaries of war' would be shipped from Brest as soon as possible, but there could be no talk of fresh troops until at least the spring.[13]

While he awaited news from France, Tyrconnell did what he could. On 16 July he made a point of riding out to greet the first troops arriving at Limerick from Aughrim – a draining task as his poor health made all travel extremely taxing. He ordered that garrisons be reinforced in Clare and Kerry as a public show of strength. Patrick Sarsfield had already ridden into Tipperary with his cavalry, and rumours of a Jacobite plan to torch Cashel reached Ginkel as early as 25 July. Tyrconnell still hoped that his design to hold Galway and Limerick and fight a guerrilla war everywhere else could be salvaged. But when he received news of Galway's unexpected surrender, it hit him hard. 'Tyrconnell had great expectations that Galway would make a long resistance, which would be to his advantage; for thereby he hoped that the campaign would be so far spent, that the besieging of Limerick could not be undertaken in that season,' one officer wrote.[14]

Jacobite Ireland had been torn in half. All that remained was the city and county of Limerick, the counties of Kerry and Clare, some patches of Mayo and the stubborn garrison at Sligo, some 130 miles to the north, which was currently under siege by Colonel John Mitchelburne, the former governor of Derry. On 28 July Ginkel's army was marching out of Galway, ready for its next hurdle. The rumours of Tyrconnell's resurgence and Sarsfield's stalking of the supply lines in Tipperary rattled Ginkel into action. 'The enemy is endeavouring to get their stuttered forces together, in order to try their fortune once more,' he wrote from the front.[15]

Things were moving quickly. After the fall of Galway Balldearg O'Donnell, who saw himself as a Gaelic warlord but had barely lifted a finger during the past two campaigns, saw a chance to 'advance his own fortune' and sent a delegate to Ginkel's camp to discuss his swapping sides.[16] O'Donnell said that if he was given £2,000 to pay off his creditors, a commission in the Williamite army and a promise that William would consider naming him Earl of Tyrconnell, he would defect 'and bring a considerable body of the Irish along with him'.[17] Ginkel was naturally suspicious but believed it was worth a chance. He forwarded O'Donnell's terms to William Bentinck for approval and stated that 'the submission of this man would add much to the peace of the country'.[18] Ginkel had heard the gossip that the French and Irish could not stand each other. The chance to recruit O'Donnell and stir up more trouble in the enemy ranks would be worth the fuss. While his terms were being haggled over, O'Donnell decided to flex his muscle and marched north to Sligo, where a deadline had been negotiated between Mitchelburne and the Jacobite governor Teague O'Regan – the eccentric who had thumbed his nose at Schomberg in Carrickfergus in 1689. O'Regan had agreed that he would surrender Sligo if no relief came to his aid within fifteen days. With mischievous timing, O'Donnell's men marched over the horizon, Mitchelburne withdrew and Sligo exhaled with relief. His point made, O'Donnell then finalised his deal with Ginkel the following day and 'joined with the sworn enemies of his country'.[19] First Galway, then O'Donnell: Tyrconnell knew that if the Jacobites kept cutting their own deals, any prospect of prolonging the war or securing decent terms would vanish. The most testing scandal of all, however, was yet to come.

*

A few days after they had marched out of Galway, d'Usson and the city's former garrison arrived at the Clare village of Sixmilebridge, one of the last stops on the road to Limerick. Henry Luttrell was waiting there to escort them the rest of the way. Before they departed, Luttrell struck up a conversation with a Huguenot officer named Pierre de la Bastide Saint-Sebastian, who had accompanied d'Usson this far under the terms of the surrender. It was one of those cordial chats between gentlemen soldiers who attempt to murder each other one minute and then discuss brandy and affairs of state the next. Saint-Sebastian asked Luttrell 'why would not the Irish come to a treaty rather than to continue the war with so much misery?' Luttrell reportedly gave an off-hand reply that 'such a thing might well be, if general Ginkel had sufficient power' to offer a deal.[20] The Huguenot officer raised an eyebrow, bade his company farewell and disappeared up the road. Neither d'Usson nor Luttrell thought any more of it.

Some days later, a Williamite trumpeter approached the gates of Limerick to parley. Patrick Sarsfield, who had returned to the city after dropping his plan to raze Cashel, rode out to meet him. Sarsfield was almost as famous with his enemies as he was with his own men and he carried a daunting air. Swallowing hard, the trumpeter produced a list of Williamite officers who had been missing since Aughrim and asked if any of them had been taken prisoner. Sarsfield scanned the paper, shot a probing glance at the messenger and said no. The Williamite trumpeter stuttered, or looked away nervously, or gave some other betraying twitch. Sarsfield narrowed his eyes and demanded to know if the messenger was carrying anything else. The messenger said no. Sarsfield's voice hardened, like a father demanding to know where a child has hidden his pipe. He warned the messenger that if he was searched and found carrying another letter, he would have him hanged from the nearest tree. The Williamite buckled and handed Sarsfield a sealed express addressed to Henry Luttrell, his old friend and confidant. It was a message from Saint-Sebastian, the Huguenot Luttrell had wagged with at Sixmilebridge, confirming that Ginkel 'had full powers … to give ample conditions' for surrender.[21] Sarsfield felt as if he had been thrown overboard a ship. He did not know the context of the letter, but it did not matter – discussing surrender with the enemy like this was treason. Sarsfield set aside any thoughts of his friendship with Luttrell, returned to the city and brought the letter straight to Tyrconnell. Luttrell was arrested.

The scandal became the talk of Limerick. D'Usson and de Tessé were prepared to have Luttrell hanged immediately so as to avoid the showy spectacle of a trial. Word even reached Ginkel, who publicly threatened reprisals if Luttrell or any other Jacobite seeking to discuss surrender was harmed. Luttrell was brought before a court martial. Before a single word of evidence was heard, a letter had already been sent to France stating that 'we believe that the court martial will condemn him to be shot'.[22] Tyrconnell presided as chairman and stacked the tribunal with officers 'he thought he had an influence on', including several of his nephews and his illegitimate son, Colonel Mark Talbot, who had been wounded at Aughrim.[23] Tyrconnell held a boiling grudge against Luttrell, having always suspected him of being the architect of the army's attempted *putsch* the previous summer. Now was his chance for revenge.

The evidence against Luttrell was circumstantial but presented with damning flair – not just the letter, but also his decision to flee from Aughrim just as the left flank was collapsing. Luttrell spoke up desperately in his own defence, aware that if he were found guilty he would be taken out into the yard of King John's Castle and shot. The court martial was a war within a war, tense and unsettling. Luttrell's closest allies, Patrick Sarsfield and Nicholas Purcell, had been kept off the judging panel. His older brother Simon was still in France, out of reach and unable to help him. But it did not matter. Luttrell was acquitted. One observer who sat through the trial recalled that the evidence was so weak 'it was impossible he could be found guilty by men that had either honesty or honour'.[24] Tyrconnell, who had voted for Luttrell to be executed, was furious. Despite the verdict, he had Luttrell thrown into the castle gaol, where he remained until the war was over.

*

After Aughrim, Tyrconnell had fought harder than anyone to keep the Jacobite cause alive. Limerick's defences and stores were prepared for another siege. He issued a proclamation that all men between sixteen and sixty must enlist 'and be ready to fight immediately'. The Jacobite army was moved to Caherconlish, William's old staging post, for the first siege the previous summer. Regiments were arranged, and 'the whole city of Limerick and the army believed that there would be soon a second battle'.[25] In one of those remarkable feats of recruitment that had become his specialty, Tyrconnell pulled together a force of roughly 20,000 men by the first week of August – albeit only half of them with working muskets, too few cavalry and barely any artillery. Tyrconnell then made the unorthodox and slightly nervy demand that every soldier renew his oath of fealty to James and swear not to make terms with the enemy.

The pessimistic d'Usson and de Tessé wondered what the viceroy was up to, while Nicholas Purcell and Henry Luttrell – before his arrest – were among the Irish officers who urged the troops to ignore it. When word arrived that Ginkel's army had crossed back over the Shannon to attack Limerick from the east, Tyrconnell shuffled his troops back through the city into County Clare and prepared his infantry to man the barricades. It would have seemed odd to many that the viceroy was now so determined to continue the war, when twelve months earlier he had argued passionately to end it. It was simply a matter of spirit. After James had fled Ireland in the aftermath of the Boyne, Tyrconnell felt lost and adrift. Now, though his cause was weaker than it had ever been before, the frail old Richard Talbot was resolute. Perhaps he knew that he was dying and did not want a life of defiance to end in submission.

On the evening of Monday 10 August Tyrconnell was invited to dine with Lieutenant General d'Usson at the Frenchman's quarters in Englishtown. By all accounts it was a 'very merry' occasion and a few hours of welcome respite for Tyrconnell.[26] The weeks since Aughrim had shown that his instincts were as fierce as ever, but his body was struggling. 'He was now very infirm, and naturally slow in his motions as well as his resolutions,' one writer recalled.[27] The effects of poor health that had bothered him for years now had their own routine: the crippling pain of gout made it hard for him to stay on his feet for long, while his weight and the weakness of his heart left him tired and short of breath. His speech grew weary and slow. He would have seemed like a cranky old grandfather, scolding and admonishing all around him. But the fierce, sly and tactical courtier who had dominated men and affairs for decades was still there, hidden inside a failing vessel.

That evening, after he had finished dining with d'Usson, Tyrconnell complained of feeling very weak. He was put to bed but was unable to rise the next morning. Doctors were called for, but the viceroy's condition deteriorated rapidly. For two days he lay in bed panting and mumbling. He was heard to whisper 'ratafia' over and over, leading some to suspect that the brandy and crushed apricot stones he had drank at dinner had been poisoned. In truth, Tyrconnell had suffered a massive stroke. He waved his hand at a sealed packet from St Germain, which contained instructions from James about what to do in the event of his death. On Thursday 13 August the viceroy lost his ability to talk. He lingered for another day, alone with his suffering and his thoughts. At around 2 p.m. on 14 August, the Duke of Tyrconnell died. He had survived Cromwell and the malice of Westminster and the fall of his king. He had torn up laws, raised armies and demolished opponents, driven by an unshakeable belief that he was right. He would not live to see the end of his war. Richard Talbot's remains were interred in St Mary's Cathedral in a ceremony without the trumpets or heralds of state a dignitary of his stature could normally expect. 'Thus this great man fell, who in his fall pulled down a mighty edifice,' one Jacobite officer lamented.[28] Richard Nagle, who had been Tyrconnell's point man for so long, could now see only smoke and ruin without him. 'God in his infinite mercy preserve us,' he wrote.[29]

32

Before God and the World

Ginkel stood on Singland Hill and looked out once more over that damned city. It was almost twelve months to the day since he had last seen Limerick, and perhaps he thought he was stuck in some twisted loop. Once again there had been a great battle, and once again the Jacobites had limped back to their old Viking fortress, ready to make a bloody racket. William himself had failed to smoke them out the previous summer, and since then the defences of Irishtown, which had been the epicentre of the first siege, had been thickened with six bastions and a new ditch wider and deeper than the old one. The rain had been pounding down for over a week, and the city's marshy fringes were turning to soup. In Dublin and London the war in Ireland was already being discussed in the past tense. The lord justices congratulated Ginkel as if he had finished the job, praising the fact that in six weeks he had done more than most would have expected in three months. Five days after Aughrim Queen Mary's chief advisor, Lord Carmarthen, was already floating ideas for sending Ginkel's army into France – an invasion of Normandy, perhaps, or maybe Aquitaine. Ginkel felt like one of the few who remembered how ferociously stubborn Limerick could be. On 9 August he extended the deadline for surrender issued on 7 July, but despite his spies sneaking into Limerick to distribute copies of his latest offer, the Jacobites were unmoved. On 25 August, nine days after the Duke of Tyrconnell's death, Ginkel's army reached the outskirts of the city, overran the old forts on Singland Hill and began the slow, sloppy business of digging trenches up to the Irishtown walls. Over the next five days several Williamite troops were killed by potshots from the city's guns. If this war really was over, it certainly did not feel like it.[1]

*

Even in death Lord Tyrconnell cast a hard shadow, and no one man could replace him. Instead, James had ordered that control of the Jacobite government be split between three lord justices: Alexander Fitton, the Lord Chancellor; Francis Plowden, a revenue commissioner; and Richard Nagle, Tyrconnell's old fixer and the incumbent secretary of state. As the most senior lieutenant general in the army, d'Usson was given command of military affairs. There was still no official place in the hierarchy for Major General Patrick Sarsfield, but such things hardly mattered. The new Lord Lucan's influence was unmatched, despite the scandal of his friend Henry Luttrell's trial and acquittal. Deliberately or otherwise, Sarsfield was not given a specific command on the eve of the siege: the French major general Henri de La Tour Monfort was named governor of Limerick, while Dominic Sheldon – another man whose nerve had failed him at Aughrim – was given command of 3,500 cavalry and 1,000 infantry posted on the north bank of the Shannon to block the Williamites from crossing upstream. Sarsfield remained bottled up inside the walls with the garrison of some 15,000 men – almost a third of whom were unarmed. Sarsfield was loosely attached to d'Usson's general staff but also held his own independent councils and became a magnet for ripening anti-French sentiment within the army. On 2 September, for example, Sarsfield, Purcell, Lord Galmoy and several officials agreed that roughly £4,000 in wages should be given to the soldiers, who had not been properly paid in months. The fact that the money would have to come out of d'Usson's dry treasury – and that d'Usson himself had not been asked in advance – was of little concern. Sarsfield was throwing his weight around, and neither the Jacobite lord justices nor the French commanders had the sand to challenge him. With Henry Luttrell in gaol, Sarsfield allied himself more closely with John Wauchope, the Scottish major general who had a rare passion for Irish affairs and a useful dislike of the French. In this tiny world of scheming and manoeuvre, Wauchope became 'the only general officer Sarsfield had to rely upon'.[2]

Jacobite Ireland was now little more than a city-state, but it remained as dangerous as a cornered beast. Although deserters and spies from Limerick brought Ginkel accounts of flooded earthworks and soldiers 'mightily apprehensive' of being bombed into the dirt, Jacobite morale was firm. The Williamites heard accounts that Limerick was full of talk of imminent relief from France, 'by which they were encouraged to hold out'.[3] Ginkel was coming under pressure to attack Limerick immediately, rather than simply blockade the city and starve the Jacobites out. The lord justices in Dublin feared such a course would 'induce the factions to hold out; reconcile their animosities, and expect help from France'. Ginkel was crabby at having to continue the war when he believed that a full pardon, some religious guarantees and a few thousand acres of land would settle it. 'One month's war [will] cost the King more than all the forfeitures will amount to,' he grumbled.[4] He was forced to press on, cursing the stiffness of politicians. The little snags that filled Ginkel's days seemed to grate and multiply. An abundance of wages in the camp saw a spike in the cost of bread, brandy and ale, which forced Ginkel to fix prices and warn that any soldier dabbling in the black market would be locked up. His artillery train of eighteen heavy cannons, three mortars, eight hundred barrels of gunpowder and 'a great many carriages with bombs, ball, shovels and pickaxes' was delayed by mushy roads and only started to arrive at Limerick eleven days after it had departed Athlone. When he finally pushed his vanguard towards Irishtown on 25 August, Ginkel sent some 600 cavalry, 300 dragoons and over 1,000 infantry, all drawn out in a menacing arc 'so that the enemy might see we were resolved to spare no pains, rather than go without the town a second time'.[5] The only thing that annoyed Ginkel more than having to attack Limerick again, it seems, was the idea that it might once more get the better of them.

*

The bombardment of Limerick began on 30 August 1691, exactly a year to the day since William had abandoned the first siege. Ginkel did not send a messenger to summon the city to surrender. He knew there was no point. Three days earlier, a fleet of eighteen Williamite warships had sailed up the Shannon and begun to fire on Limerick from the water. The damage they inflicted was minimal, but their hulking, malevolent presence in the river was terrifying. 'This put several of the Irish much out of countenance, for till then they were made believe that either we had no ships in the river, or else those we had would quickly be swallowed up by the French fleet,' George Story wrote.[6] Unlike the previous summer, when William had angled his trenches and batteries towards the south-east tip of Irishtown, Ginkel shuffled his lines around to the south-west, where there were fewer bastions and more of the city to aim at. It also gave him a direct link to the river, which he was keen to exploit. On 28 August he had several of the ships' heavy cannons hoisted ashore to fatten up the main battery.

Two days later the barrage began. Instead of trying to blow a breach in the wall, which would suggest that he intended to storm Limerick by force, Ginkel instead ordered his gunners to pour all their fire on the rooftops. It was the usual cocktail of destruction, deployed with painful efficiency: heavy shells that would shatter entire houses; hollow bombs known as carcasses that were filled with oil and would explode on impact; and red-hot cannonballs attempting to burn the city to the ground. The gunners also began to fire on Thomond Bridge, some 500 yards upriver, to try and cut off communication between Limerick and Dominic Sheldon's cavalry on the north bank. This was not a strategic plan to capture a city; it was an assault on the last pieces of the rebel kingdom hiding inside.

Limerick had lived through heavy shelling before, but a familiar nightmare is never gentle. On 31 August the Williamite batteries pounded the city from dawn to dusk, dropping 101 bombs and 'setting it on fire in some places'. Limerick was jammed with soldiers, civilians and refugees, and the only rounds that did not cause carnage were the ones that flew clean over the city and landed harmlessly on the other side. The city was in a constant state of weary alarm, as fires broke out faster than they could be quenched. The Jacobites shot back as hard as they could from their own batteries in the castle and along the walls, but Ginkel's heavy firepower was in a different league. The squalid crush of the city became too much for the Jacobite lord justices and a flock of other gentlemen and ladies, who scrabbled together their belongings, squeezed out across Thomond Bridge and 'encamp'd under sheets and blankets' on the north bank, out of range of the Williamite guns and away from the horror of life under fire.[7]

Breaking Limerick's spirit before relief could arrive from France became Ginkel's obsession. It was already dangerously late in the year for his men to be squatting in filthy trenches. The ships blockading the river had only a few weeks' worth of supplies, and once these ran out their captains would have no choice but to sail back to port, leaving the Shannon wide open. On 6 September Jacobite deserters brought troubling news that 'the Irish resolve not to give us the town'. Limerick's storehouses and magazines were amply stocked, and there was no immediate prospect of the city being driven to starvation like Derry. Ginkel would have to squeeze harder. On 8 September work was completed on a new gun battery barely 300 yards east of King's Island, comprising a beastly twenty-five heavy cannons and eight mortars pointed directly at Englishtown, the ancient spine of the city. Eight more cannons were dragged up onto Singland Hill, and with synchronised precision all three of the Williamite batteries opened fire, creating a horrific roll of thunder. 'A great many of them wished themselves in another place, having never heard such a noise before,' George Story remarked. 'We threw bombs, fire-balls and carcasses all day long, and our guns were discharged almost without ceasing.'[8] In just a few hours the new battery near King's Island had blown a hole in the Englishtown wall. Englishtown was barely a few blocks wide with tall, ramshackle tenements and a narrow central street that ran from the castle down to Baal's Bridge. There was nowhere to hide. Day after day, the horrific haze of fire continued, 'reducing that famous city almost to ashes'.[9]

All the Jacobites could offer in response was mischief. One night, as Williamite soldiers were clearing the ground for a new battery, the city gunners used moonlight to drop mortars on their heads, 'killing five or six'. On 9 September a small party sallied out from Irishtown and set fire to piles of woolsacks that might have been used as cover during a ground assault. A ship was scuttled near the Merchant's Quay docks to prevent the Williamites from sneaking into the harbour at night. The rain continued to drown everything. Two weeks after the bombardment began, the Jacobites inside the city started to suspect that Ginkel had no appetite for storming the walls. 'They have already been fifteen days before the town without having come nearer than they were the first day,' the French commissary Fumeron wrote. 'I do not think they have resolved to take it by force … they will content themselves with bombarding us.'[10] The high silhouette of St Mary's Cathedral came under fire, after Jacobite deserters revealed that it was stocked with supplies. Dozens of barrels of brandy and oats caught fire after a bomb struck a different storehouse in Englishtown. Words were just as combustible: on 7 September a forged piece of propaganda claiming to be Tyrconnell's will was circulated throughout Limerick, designed to whip up a storm against d'Usson, de Tessé and the rest of the French. The paper warned that 'to wait for help from France is a mere chimera' and also contained an apparent insistence that Tyrconnell had only forced people to take new oaths to James 'because I knew that Lord Lucan and Luttrell were looking for an opportunity to ruin my reputation with the deluded masses'.[11] There was uproar at the thought that France had abandoned Limerick to its fate. The French commanders, who had no idea when the fresh supplies were coming, struggled to keep tempers in check. Very soon, however, a real disaster would overcome the hubbub of an imaginary one.

*

Ginkel's guns had ripped open the Englishtown wall on 8 September, but the Dutch general still refused to storm the city. A Jacobite deserter claimed that there was a deep ditch in front of the wall that was 'always full of water, and well palisaded'. The governor of the city had also apparently ordered that the streets behind the breach be barricaded with rubble and timber. It all stoked Ginkel's fears that sending grenadiers over the Abbey River and through the breach would be a violent and messy contract. Instead, he decided to stiffen his blockade and find a way to choke Limerick from both sides. He would need to act quickly: the weather was getting worse, and the mood within his own camp was limp. On 15 September Viscount Lisburne, a popular Williamite commander from Dublin and 'a remarkable zealot' for the cause, was killed when a Jacobite cannonball struck his tent. Meanwhile, Ginkel had already ordered that the County Limerick town of Kilmallock be prepared for winter quarters – hardly the most inspiring message for his troops. 'This was but melancholy news to both officers and soldiers, who were all willing to undergo hardships rather than go away without being masters of the place'.[12] Ginkel was keeping his options open. The River Shannon was scouted as far north as O'Brien's Bridge ten miles away to find a place where the pontoons from Athlone could be used. One promising site was found, but a Danish swimmer sent to test the crossing barely made it back alive, breathlessly reporting that the water was too fast, rocky and dangerous.[13]

Ginkel and the Duke of Wurtemburg were constantly pacing about in the trenches and batteries, discussing progress and gathering reports. They knew that the clock was ticking. On 15 September they received a promising piece of news: there was a small cluster of islands in the river just south of Parteen, barely a mile and a half from the Williamite camp. Willem Meesters, the engineer who had flung himself into a bush of nettles to escape Sarsfield's raid at Ballyneety the previous summer, inspected the location and sent back a solid report. The pontoons would be able to reach the nearest island, and from there the rest of the river looked shallow enough to ford on foot. Ginkel did not dither. At four o'clock that same afternoon he gave orders for cannons to be dragged up to cover the crossing, and once night fell his troops began the loud, conspicuous work of hammering the pontoons together. Dominic Sheldon's Jacobite cavalry were camped four miles away across the river, but a small detachment of dragoons under the command of brigadier Robert Clifford had been left to guard the riverbank. Clifford, an old acquaintance of Patrick Sarsfield's, was hardly the best choice for the post. He had a feckless reputation, and as an officer he was dismissed as 'vain and very airy, of shallow parts, and of no great action'.[14] In the early hours of 16 September, as the clank and thud of tools at work drifted through the dark across the river, worried Jacobite scouts told Clifford that something was up. He brushed off their concerns, insisting that the river was too deep to cross. His ignorance was about to be cruelly exposed.

By dawn the Williamite pontoon bridge had been completed, and just after six o'clock the first of 1,100 infantry began pouring over onto the Clare bank. The Jacobite dragoons were taken utterly by surprise and began to fall back almost immediately. Clifford and his men abandoned their camp in a white panic, leaving tents and saddles and satchels strewn about like confetti. 'They entirely broke,' one Williamite officer recalled.[15] Word whistled up to Sheldon's main camp a few miles away. Bizarrely, Sheldon ordered his cavalry to retreat. Thousands of Jacobite horsemen turned and fled from a few regiments of shivering Williamite infantry, their boots and coats still dripping with water. Sheldon raced north towards Ennis 'with such precipitation and disorder, that if 100 of the enemy's horse had charged him in the rear, they would, in all likelihood, defeat his whole party'.[16] The north bank of the river was swamped in baffling panic, as if a fox cub had been dropped into a coop of 10,000 hens. The alarm was raised in the civilian camp near Thomond Bridge, and hundreds of petrified civilians began to rush back into the city with all the belongings they could carry. The Williamite troops upstream had simply crossed the river and dug in, but it did not matter. Seeing Sheldon's cavalry in full flight threw the Jacobite camp into frenzy. The screams of lord justices and aides and wives rushing back over the narrow bridge into Englishtown could be heard in the Williamite trenches downstream. 'It's almost incredible what a noise and confusion there was,' George Story wrote.[17]

Clifford's negligence almost cost him his head. After sprinting back into Limerick he was hauled before a council of war to explain himself. 'Clifford protested himself innocent as to any treachery,' one Jacobite officer recalled, 'though he could not deny but he was guilty of an unpardonable neglect.'[18] Clifford was placed under arrest pending a full court martial, but the consequences of his failure threw an immediate gloom over the city. Limerick was now cut off, and though Ginkel had only sent a few regiments of men across the river, it was now in his power to completely surround the city on all sides. Sheldon's cavalry had disappeared, and most of his infantry had scattered into the hills. Hundreds of civilians squeezed back into the city in terror, and the hot temper within the walls increased. Ginkel issued a declaration that gave Limerick eight days to surrender. With the fiery gravitas of an Ottoman sultan, he stated that this was his final offer. If the Jacobites ignored it, he warned, 'they must be answerable for the blood and destruction they draw upon themselves; for I hereby acquit myself before God and the world, and wash my hands of it'.[19]

*

This great war of kings and disease and defiance had come down to a final test of nerve. On 17 September, the day after Ginkel's final demand for surrender, d'Usson and de Tessé co-signed a letter to Louis stating that almost everyone – including Sarsfield and Wauchope – were talking of surrender. Despite all the wreckage of the bombing, there was still enough biscuit left to feed the city garrison for about two months. But 'zeal was languishing', and the streets of Limerick began to clog with rubble and the sickly perfume of sulphur and filth.[20]

Scruffy and fretful soldiers were once more going days without sleep. When they were not on duty in the outer defences having cannonballs shot at them, the Irish soldiers bunked on damp floors and waited. They thought back to Athlone and Aughrim; those who had been in the service long enough remembered the hellhole at Derry and the songs and whistles of the march back from Dundalk, when they had spooked old Schomberg out of a battle. They remembered shapeless silhouettes charging through the breach in the Irishtown wall. They remembered those frenzied days after the Boyne, when James had vanished and Tyrconnell raced past them on the road to Limerick, his shoulders hunched under the weight of exhaustion and misery. They tried to think of life as it used to be, but war was the only thing left in their hearts.

D'Usson, Sarsfield and the other generals had almost completely detached themselves from the struggle, their faint hopes of French relief withering by the hour. According to one account, a Jacobite officer came up with a plan to sally out with 1,500 men and attack the main Williamite battery south-west of Irishtown, but 'dared not propose the project to the governor and general officers, because he believed that they would look upon it as impracticable'.[21] On the other side of the walls, Ginkel remained cranky and defensive. At a 'hotly disputed' council of war on 17 September, he once more decided against assaulting the city.[22] Over the next three days, he ordered that some heavy cannons be loaded back onto the warships in the river, as if preparing for a full withdrawal. In his letters to Dublin and Flanders, Ginkel was already shifting responsibility onto the navy, which had been making excuses for its failure to erect a full blockade of the Irish coast. 'The reduction of Ireland entirely depends on preventing the promised succour from France,' Ginkel wrote, insisting that it would not be his fault if a French fleet broke through the Shannon and relieved Limerick.[23] London was not happy with

Ginkel's efforts, and the political capital he had won at Athlone and Aughrim was already melting. Nerves were fraying. On 19 September three Irish bandits were arrested for murdering some Williamite troops who had wandered away from their camp. Ginkel's irritation spilled over. He ordered that the three be tortured to death on a breaking wheel – a crude medieval device that spun a victim around while his bones were smashed with a hammer. Ginkel was quietly informed 'that this way of torture was against the laws of England' and had to make do with having the bandits hanged, drawn and quartered.[24] Their limbs were nailed to hedges lining the main road to Limerick. Resolve on both sides of the walls was cracking. It was now just a question of who would blink first.

*

On Monday 21 September Ginkel received an urgent dispatch with news that Sligo had finally surrendered. The message galvanised him into making one final push against Limerick, knowing that it would end the war for certain. The following morning he personally led more than half of his army over the pontoon bridge onto the north bank. It was a daunting sight for the Jacobite sentries: ten regiments of infantry; almost all the Williamite cavalry and dragoons; fourteen field cannons and more than a week's worth of bread and ale, all creaking around the great hairpin in the Shannon and down towards Thomond Bridge. By midday they were all on the north bank, in full sight of the Jacobite cannons but tantalisingly out of range. Roughly 600 Jacobite infantry had been billeted in an old earthen fort and a twist of quarries and ditches near the top of Thomond Bridge. As Ginkel's force snaked around the river, Governor Monfort sent another 200 troops out to harass and slow their march. The Jacobites marched out over the bridge, swung right and began to tussle with the Williamite vanguard, briefly stuttering Ginkel's advance. The Dutch general had only intended to stretch his lines out in an arc and cut off the road to Sixmilebridge, but after the Jacobites started to pester his lines he decided to attack. Two regiments of Williamite grenadiers clawed their way towards the bridge, beating the Jacobites back with musket shot and grenades. Two hundred Williamite dragoons dismounted their horses and joined the assault.

For two hours the Jacobites dug in around the top of the bridge, covered by cracks of cannon fire and sharp shooters along the walls of King John's Castle behind them. 'The dispute was pretty hot at first,' George Story recalled. 'The attack seemed very hazardous.'[25] The ground at the Williamites' feet was churned by cannonballs, but the grenadiers fought their way forward with tremendous bravery, one inch at a time. The sheer weight of Ginkel's numbers began to tell. A handful of Jacobite soldiers threw down their muskets and began to sprint back across the bridge towards the city. Stooping down behind cover to reload, the rest of the Jacobites looked back and saw their comrades in flight. The panic was infectious. Within moments the Jacobite lines collapsed as hundreds clambered back towards the safety of the bridge, which was barely wide enough for three men to cross at a time. A crush formed. Seeing their enemies break with alarm, the Williamite troops broke cover and raced after them. They overran the earthworks, beating and hacking any Jacobite left behind, and began to fire into the crowd squeezing onto the bridge.

The French officer on duty in the gatehouse near the top of the bridge watched in horror as a tangled mass of bodies flooded towards him. Fearing that the enemy might fight their way through the crush and into the city, he ordered that a drawbridge covering one of the stone arches be pulled up. Barely more than a hundred Jacobite soldiers had so far made it across – the rest now watched in horror as the bridge was shut in front of their eyes, trapping them with their backs to the enemy. Curses and cries for mercy were drowned in an inferno of gunfire, as the Jacobites stuck on the bridge were butchered like cattle. Bodies began to tumble into the river. Corpses of Irish soldiers began to collapse on top of each other. Wounded men were trampled until their ribs shattered and their lungs burst. The Williamites fired into the crowd again and again, ignoring the waving handkerchiefs and pleas for quarter. It was hellish and sickening. 'Before the killing was over, they were laid in heaps upon the bridge higher than the ledges of it.'[26] The bodies of men who had drowned or were shot in the river trying to swim to safety bobbed downstream like apples. So much blood was spilled into the Shannon that the water looked like marble. Some 600 Jacobite soldiers had been slaughtered in just a few minutes. A stray bullet killed the French officer who had fatefully pulled up the drawbridge. Somewhere between 75 and 120 Jacobites who had survived the massacre were captured. The Williamites had lost about 26 men, with 200 or 300 more wounded. All that night, the horrific debris of the attack lay strewn across the bridge. The rain continued to fall, and a shocked silence fell over the city's cannons. Ginkel's soldiers pitched their tents and found shelter where they could. Most of them slept soundly. 'We did not at all fear a sally that night, for the bridge was so heaped with corpses,' one soldier remarked.[27]

*

The bloodbath of 22 September shredded what was left of the Jacobite officers' morale. The following day, d'Usson held a council of war where it was agreed to seek terms with Ginkel. It is difficult not to picture a meeting hot with anger and allegations: the Irish blaming the French for pulling up the drawbridge; the French accusing the Irish of incompetence for allowing the Williamites to cross the river in the first place.

Outside in the streets, the hatred of the French boiled over, with one deserter claiming that 'they were for flinging all the French over the walls'.[28] Had the officer who closed the drawbridge not already been killed, he probably would have been lynched. The official report of d'Usson's council of war is decidedly polite, referring to 'all these reasons maturely examined' that led to the agreement to surrender. However, one detail betrays a mutually self-serving disgust: the copy that d'Usson and de Tessé kept was entitled 'motives that led the Irish to capitulate', while another version was called 'the reasons the French generals gave major general Wauchope and Lord Lucan for the capitulation'.[29] The latter is particularly telling. Patrick Sarsfield, with the support of Wauchope, finally appeared to have seized control of the Jacobite army at this last, despairing moment of the war.

Throughout the day of 23 September the Williamite cannons continued to torment Limerick. From his new headquarters on the north bank, Ginkel sat at his desk as the cold afternoon rain danced on the canvas above. He began a letter to the lord justices in Dublin, but instead of being inspired by the brutal success of his men the day before, Ginkel was about to give up. His troops had fought 'with the utmost bravery', but it was now almost October, and the ferocity with which the outnumbered Jacobites had fought in those two hours before the massacre on the bridge unsettled Ginkel, who had seen up close 'how those people defend themselves'. The ships blockading the river had only four or five days' worth of supplies left. Despite all the pressure piling on him from Dublin, Westminster and Flanders, Ginkel flatly refused to storm the city. 'Taking the town by assault, as proposed, is impracticable.' With frank, gruff and almost sad honesty, Ginkel admitted that he 'can do no more'.[30] The letter was sealed, wrapped in a bundle and handed to a messenger to deliver to the capital. But at around five o'clock that evening, just as the rain stopped and the autumn sky began to darken and sink, an unusual drumbeat was heard coming from the city gates. A runner burst into Ginkel's tent with a short and momentous message. Sarsfield and Wauchope had called for a ceasefire.

33

Articles

It was fitting that the first words about ending the war in Ireland had to be translated twice. In the early evening of 23 September, after the patter of drums calling for parley had drifted out from Englishtown, John Wauchope, 'looking out of a tower', shouted for the Dutch lieutenant general Scravenmoer, an old acquaintance of his from the Dutch brigades before the revolution.[1] A small wooden dinghy was sent to fetch Wauchope, as Thomond Bridge was impassable with corpses. Speaking in Dutch, Wauchope and Scravenmoer had an awkwardly polite discussion about an initial twenty-four-hour ceasefire. When the deal was agreed, Wauchope asked if Patrick Sarsfield, who spoke French, could be fetched to explain the terms to the Huguenot Marquis of Ruvigny, as Hugh Mackay and Thomas Talmash – the only Williamite generals who spoke English as their first language – were camped on the other side of the city. Scravenmoer gave his blessing, Ruvigny and Sarsfield joined the conversation and the four generals began to translate for one another, back and forth, like foreign attachés at a dinner party. They took their leave; Sarsfield and Wauchope were rowed back across to the city and the news was delivered to Ginkel in a rush. The Williamite commander immediately wrote a letter to the lord justices in Dublin. 'Come at once,' he urged.[2]

The next morning Sarsfield and Wauchope met with Ginkel in person. Their conversation, by all accounts, was pleasant: Sarsfield broke the ice by presenting 'some bottles of good claret' as a gift, while Ginkel courteously recognised Sarsfield's title of Lord Lucan and insisted all his subordinates do likewise.[3] They were gentlemen, of course, and war required the same lick of manners as any other pursuit. Sarsfield sought an assurance that once this surrender was settled, he and the rest of the Jacobite army would be allowed to sail to France. Ginkel consented. A three-day extension to the ceasefire was agreed, and in exchange for releasing all Williamite prisoners in the city, Ginkel gave Sarsfield passports to send for Sheldon, Galmoy and several other Jacobite lords and dignitaries who had fled into County Clare. Later that afternoon the city gaol was opened and some 240 Williamite prisoners staggered out, most of them horrendously sick and injured, others too weak to walk. Like the rest of Limerick, they had endured the furnace of Ginkel's siege, and as many as thirty Williamite prisoners had been killed inside the walls by their own artillery. The chaplain George Story described the wretched state of the men as they limped into the Williamite camp: some collapsed and died on the spot, while one dragoon's hand had been 'shattered to pieces' by a cannon shot, but the wound had never been dressed. He died of infection a few hours after being set free.[4]

On the morning of 25 September the Jacobite delegates who had been summoned from Clare arrived at Ginkel's camp. As well as Sheldon and Galmoy, the party included Colonel Garrett Dillon, a barrister who had sat in Tyrconnell's parliament of 1689; the solicitor-general Toby Butler; Lords Westmeath and Trimlestown; and the archbishops of Armagh and Cashel, Dominick Maguire and John Brenan. They were all welcomed into the camp and dined with Ginkel that afternoon. When they were finished, the delegates went down to the river and climbed into boats waiting to ferry them into the city. Looking to their left as they crossed the Shannon, they saw the horrific human debris on Thomond Bridge. The stacks of pale and fetid corpses were only now being carried away for burial. The following day, after another round of talks between Sarsfield, Wauchope and Ginkel, both sides agreed to begin formal negotiations. Hostages were exchanged as collateral, and on 27 September the Jacobites made their opening gambit. They presented Ginkel with a list of proposals calling for – amongst other things – a full pardon and legal indemnity; the restoration of all estates owned by Catholics before the revolution; unrestricted freedom of worship, including a priest in every parish; and liberty for Catholics to hold civil, military and professional employment. Ginkel cut a deep frown and mumbled. While he had no personal qualms with most of this – he had, after all, spent the last year complaining that terms like these were not on the table – he knew that he could not break the law, nor write any new ones. The penal laws were still on the statute books, and Ginkel was not about to light a bonfire under his own career. He rejected the Jacobites' proposals and ordered that work begin immediately on a new battery on Singland Hill to remind the Jacobites that this was not a dance. They got the message.[5]

*

The articles of surrender were agreed on 28 September, and the Treaty of Limerick was formally signed five days later. For a war rooted in years of complicated legal strife and religious tension, the negotiations to end it were quite prompt. After Ginkel had dismissed the Jacobites' first offer, a formal conference took place in his camp involving Sarsfield, Wauchope, Nicholas Purcell, the two Catholic archbishops and three Jacobite lawyers – Toby Butler, Garrett Dillon and Colonel John Browne. To ensure that he did not feel outnumbered, Ginkel invited his entire general staff to sit in as delegates. George Clarke, William's secretary at war, kept note of the proceedings that went on for twelve hours. The final treaty was broken into two halves: one dealing with military affairs and the other to agree what would happen to Ireland after the war.

The army business was the easiest to settle. Once the basic principle had been agreed that every Jacobite soldier would be free to go to France, join up with William or simply turn in his musket and go home, the rest of the military articles just tidied up timetables and logistics. Ginkel agreed that the Williamites would provide fifty ships, fully stocked and supplied, to ferry the Jacobite army to France. All prisoners of war held throughout the kingdom were to be set free immediately, and the Jacobites would be allowed – rather astonishingly – to remain fully armed and in possession of Englishtown as a sort of ransom until arrangements for the voyage to France were made. The only role that d'Usson, de Tessé and Monfort played in the talks was to sign the treaty when it was all done. Since Sarsfield and Wauchope had seized command of the army, the French were lame ducks, forced to feign illness as the war was concluded without them.

The civil articles of the treaty were thornier, and like most contracts the sticky points were in the wording. After Ginkel had scoffed at the Jacobites' opening offer on 27 September, he sent back twelve counter-proposals that provided the cement for the final treaty. This first draft, however, stated that all the terms would only be offered to Jacobite soldiers in Limerick, Clare, Kerry, Cork and Mayo. Toby Butler pointed out that this would ignore the thousands of ordinary Irish people in those counties who were under the Jacobites' protection. George Clarke snipped that this was not a deal for the entire kingdom of Ireland, merely those bits of it that the Williamites did not yet control. Sarsfield slammed his fist on the table and warned that 'he would lay his bones in those old walls rather than not take care of those who stuck by them all along'.[6] His point made, the second draft of the treaty was amended to extend the terms to the common folk. It would not be the last time that the syntax of the deal would be ripped apart.

After an exhausting debate in which every syllable was scrutinised, the delegates finally reached an agreement late on 28 September. Ginkel quickly sent a letter to the navy vice-admiral, Ralph Delaval, warning him not to open fire on the French fleet if it suddenly appeared in Irish waters. 'I have entered into a treaty with the city of Limerick, and the Irish army … we have a cessation of arms at land, and have agreed there shall be one too at sea.'[7] The Williamite lord justices arrived from Dublin late on 1 October, and after a run through of the terms, Coningsby and Porter gave their blessings for a final copy to be drafted. On 3 October the entire Jacobite delegation dined with the Duke of Wurtemburg, before crowding into Ginkel's tent to put their names to history. After the three French generals had signed the military articles, the next man to scrawl his name was Patrick Sarsfield. He wrote the word 'Lucan' with a tight and curving script, leaning on the last flick of the 'n' as if lingering in the moment or caught in some daydream of things passed and things to come. Wauchope was next, then Colonel Mark Talbot, the illegitimate son of the old viceroy who was now just a shadow in the corner. Galmoy and Nicholas Purcell were the last to sign, ending almost three brutal years of rebellion and war. The civil articles, meanwhile, were presented as a contract between Ginkel, the lord justices and the seven principal men of Jacobite Ireland, a kingdom now moments away from being dissolved: Sarsfield, Galmoy and Mark Talbot; colonels Nicholas Purcell and Nicholas Cusack; and the lawyers Butler, Dillon and Browne. Tellingly, the names of three Jacobite lord justices appointed after Tyrconnell's death are nowhere to be found.[8]

There were thirteen civil articles in the Treaty of Limerick, but only six of them had any real meat. The first and most fateful clause stated that Irish Catholics would receive 'such privileges in the exercise of their religion as are consistent with the laws of Ireland, or as they did enjoy in the reign of King Charles the Second'. Once the war was finished, it went on, William and Mary would convene a parliament in Dublin to explore giving Catholics greater freedom. The second article confirmed that all Jacobites still in arms would be entitled to whatever property they held at the end of Charles's reign. The fifth article promised a general pardon, and the sixth ensured immunity from any lawsuits for theft, destruction of property or other crimes committed during the war. The ninth article promised that Jacobites who submitted would only have to take oaths of allegiance to William and Mary, rather than disavow the Holy Communion or deny James's claim to the throne. The twelfth article promised that William and Mary would ratify the treaty within three months 'and use their utmost endeavours' to ensure an Irish parliament would do likewise in the future. The other clauses were simply provisos and clarifications; the final article, meanwhile, was a late addition specifically for John Browne, whose ironworks in Mayo had been commandeered for the Jacobite war effort. A once-off property tax was to be levied on every estate secured by a Catholic under the treaty in order to compensate Browne for the loss of goods he needed as collateral for his loans. It was a peculiar detail at the end of a peculiar war.[9]

The next morning the Williamite army marched into Irishtown, more than a year after they had tried and failed to batter their way in. They found the southern half of Limerick city to be little more than a charred and crumbling ruin. Its streets were 'disordered' and clogged with rubble, beneath much of which were the crushed remains of men, women and children. There was hardly a single house or tenement left intact, and every gutter was clogged with human filth. Even by the foul standards of an army camp, the stench was nauseating. Cleaning it up was so demoralising that Major General Thomas Talmash personally mucked in to try and encourage the men.[10]

*

Over the coming weeks, the Treaty of Limerick resembled a sort of marriage contract forcing two divorced spouses to live under the same roof. The Jacobites remained holed up in Englishtown as preparations to transport their army to France were made. A nervous cloud hung over the city, as George Clarke and other senior Williamites worried what could happen if 'a squadron of eighteen or twenty frigates from France' suddenly appeared in the river.[11] For a short while both sets of soldiers had mingled and chatted with each other, until Sarsfield complained that some Williamites had begun to 'plunder and strip' the Irish, forcing Ginkel to confine his men to their posts. The Jacobites started locking the Englishtown gates to try and keep their soldiers from defecting or wandering off. One Jacobite lieutenant colonel snuck out a letter protesting to Ginkel that he had been gaoled for refusing to go to France. Ginkel was irate, believing that the spirit of the treaty was being trampled on, and had four cannons dragged up to Baal's Bridge and pointed ominously into Englishtown. Sarsfield stormed into Ginkel's quarters and 'several strong words passed'. He protested that the Jacobite officer had been gaoled for insubordination, not for refusing to go to France, and snapped that how he chose to discipline his soldiers was his own damn business. Ginkel had already heard rumours that Jacobites were being told they would be sent to Hungary as cannon fodder for the Turks if they joined William. To try and cut through the muddle, Ginkel issued a declaration insisting that no man would be sent anywhere 'contrary to their inclinations and desires'. Sarsfield and Wauchope hit back, telling a crowd of troops in Englishtown that any man who came with them would not be stuck in France for long, as 'next spring, or soon after, they would either be landed in England, or else in Ireland, with a powerful army'.[12]

As part of the deal to end the war, Ginkel and the Williamites were to be allowed to make their pitch to the Irish soldiers directly. On 6 October all 14,000 or so Jacobite troops in Limerick filed out across Thomond Bridge where Ginkel, his senior officers and the Williamite lord justices were waiting. An aide delivered a speech urging them to stay and fight for William, pointing out 'how unnatural it was for them to choose to go serve in a foreign country against the real interest of their own'. It was a waste of breath. Earlier that day a huge Mass had taken place inside Englishtown, in which the soldiers were assured that travelling to France was the will of God and that fighting for the heretic William would lead to 'certain damnation'. Casks of brandy were then cracked open to buff any nervous edges. When the speeches were finished, drums began to ripple and the Jacobite soldiers were given the choice to either march back into the city and head for France or stay outside and remain in Ireland. Sarsfield had choreographed the moment well. As the most ardently loyal regiments shuffled back into the city first, the pressure for the rest to do likewise became stifling. Little more than 1,000 Jacobites chose to stay behind, but there were some surprising faces among them. Nicholas Purcell, one of the signatories of the treaty, decided to return to his estate in Tipperary, while brigadier Robert Clifford, who had allowed the Williamites to cross the Shannon and probably feared that he would be court martialled the moment he set foot in France, also chose to stay put. And then, sitting astride his mount, was Henry Luttrell, who had spent the siege in the castle gaol. Not only did Luttrell decide privately that he would stay in Ireland, but he is also reported to have made a spirited speech to his regiment urging them to do the same. It was a sharp and final turn for Sarsfield's old friend, who had always been a divisive figure. The consequences of his decision would linger with Luttrell and his family for years.[13]

*

Piece by piece, the armies drifted away. On 8 October Ginkel ordered his men to disperse to winter quarters, and on 3 November he arrived back in Dublin to an elated reception from the lord mayor, a guard of honour from the city militia and the ecstatic acclaim of the city's Protestants. The following day was William's birthday, and in the Irish capital it was marked with banquets, bonfires, a great service in Christchurch Cathedral 'and all the demonstrations of joy that could be made upon such an extraordinary occasion'.[14] William and Mary had already proclaimed a day of public thanksgiving to mark 'a wonderful success of their arms to reduce the kingdom of Ireland'.[15]

It is the natural way of things that the joy of victory in one place is met by the gloom of defeat in another. As 1691 crept into winter, the orphans of Jacobite Ireland struggled to make sense of it all. On 20 October, almost a month after the ceasefire, a French fleet of eighteen frigates, four fire ships and twenty transports stuffed full of food and ammunition finally arrived in the Shannon. There was a brief panic in the Williamite command that the French could restart the war. However, Admiral Chateaurenault, who had led the French fleet at Bantry Bay in 1689, chose to honour the new peace, much to Ginkel's relief. For the Irish preparing to embark for France, the belated arrival of the fleet was a hard glimpse of what might have been. Sarsfield rode to Cork to oversee the departure of an army of which he was commander-in-chief in all but name. His vigorous pursuit of peace in the last days of the war had left everyone bemused. The Jacobite colonel Charles O'Kelly wondered how Sarsfield, 'in whom the Irish nation reposed their greatest confidence and who … would be the last man to harken to a treaty, was now the most earnest to press it on'.[16] George Clarke suspected Sarsfield was vain and 'reckoned on making himself considerable in France by bringing over such a body of troops'.[17] Another Jacobite account scoffed that 'it is comical to hear the great commanders of Limerick blame Clifford for not defending the pass … and yet they themselves with as much ease do yield their fortress'.[18] Others grumbled that Tyrconnell would not have struck a deal if he were alive. Sarsfield's motives were raked over, again and again. Ginkel had been authorised to coax Sarsfield over with the promise of a large estate. His Jacobite peerage might also have been formally recognised in London. But the truth is that Sarsfield was a soldier. His first and highest loyalty had always been to the commission held from James, and if it were no longer tenable to fight for his king in Ireland, he would gladly leave and fight for him somewhere else. In a war cooked with so many layers of faith and property and influence, basic loyalty was the most tragic ingredient of all.

Hauling the Jacobite army across the sea to France was a drawn out, arduous and heart-breaking affair. Sarsfield and Ginkel haggled with each other about whether space should be kept on the ships for soldiers' wives and children. A constant leak of Irish deserters streamed out of Limerick, with many more slipping away along the road as they marched to Cork. The first wave of Irishmen arriving in Brest received a cold introduction to their new life: the governor of the town refused to give them quarters or provide clothes and supplies; reports came back to Ireland of men being forced to sleep in 'lanes and hedges', exposed to the punishing weather sweeping in from the coast.[19] The French took a dim view of the Irish officers, believing that most were unfit for their commissions. With cold efficiency, almost every Irish officer was demoted by one rank. There were reports of some Irishmen immediately changing heart and trying to barter passage back home, only to be refused. Others wrote letters from Brest urging their countrymen not to bother coming over, which apparently caused at least three Jacobite regiments to turn in their muskets and walk away before departure. The French fleet that had arrived at Limerick carried away the last of the Englishtown garrison on 1 November, with the help of several Williamite supply ships. One such vessel, the *Rose of Chester*, struck rocks before it even left the Shannon and sank, dragging 120 Irishmen with it to the bottom of the river.

On 8 December, after the first wave of Jacobite troops had been shipped to France, Sarsfield wrote to Ginkel from Cork, telling him that one more trip would be enough, and after that he would be released from his end of the bargain. The news that the final ships were about to leave seemed to stir people into a panic, as men and women scrambled for the last spaces out of Ireland. There were heartrending accounts of bawling wives being turned away from ships after their husbands had boarded, and of people snatching at ropes and rigging as the last vessels sailed away, only to be kicked into the water to drown. Charles O'Kelly wrote of brothers embracing each other for the final time in tears and of women and children crying out for their husbands and fathers, lingering in grief on the cold dockside for hours. 'The saddest day is come that ever appeared above the horizon of Ireland. The sun was darkened, and covered over with a black cloud, as if unwilling to behold such a woeful spectacle.'[20]

*

The generals, lords and men of state all began to depart, seeking out their next frontier. Ginkel, Coningsby, Porter, Clarke and much of the Protestant gentry of Dublin sailed away on 5 December for an audience in London with William, who had returned from Flanders in late October. Mackay, Talmash, Wurtemburg and most of their troops had already left. Sarsfield departed Cork on 22 December with the three Jacobite lord justices he had swept aside after Tyrconnell's death. Many Jacobites with estates to keep remained in Ireland, but others – most notably Lord Galmoy and Colonel Garrett Dillon, who had both signed the Treaty of Limerick, chose to forfeit their lands and follow their oaths across the sea. John Wauchope, Dominic Sheldon, Gordon O'Neill and most of the other senior officers journeyed to France. In all, some 12,000 Irish Catholics left their homeland behind, unwilling or unable to live in an utterly conquered kingdom. The man whom they had given up their lives for did not even bother to receive them at Brest in person. Instead, James simply sent a messenger with a few short words of thanks and a promise that 'we shall never forget this act of loyalty'.[21]

In Dublin, there was a new era to build. At the end of January 1692 the new legal year began. Every judge, privy counsellor, lawyer and 'several other persons of different qualities and employments' swore public oaths to William and Mary. With a sharp glimpse of what was to come, the lord justices issued a declaration ordering all colonels and senior officers in Ireland to dismiss any Catholics in their regiments. The mood in the capital was sharp. The Protestant gentry, clergy and businessmen who had been criminalised under Tyrconnell read the Treaty of Limerick with scorn. After suffering three wars in 100 years, they had wanted nothing less than the complete purge of all Catholic wealth and influence in Ireland, so that men like Richard Talbot would never have the means to challenge them again. They feared that leaving the natives with even the tiniest scraps of clemency was dangerous. One month after the Treaty of Limerick was signed, a Protestant in Dublin wrote to an acquaintance that Westminster and Whitehall would have to take hard steps to keep Ireland in check. 'They cannot sink it into the sea,' he warned.[22]

In London, William paced about his privy chambers at Kensington Palace, where the air was easy on his lungs and hard questions about Ireland had at last been shaken away. His shoulder still creaked from that clip of a cannonball at the Boyne, and every time he rolled it loose he wondered what might have happened if it had struck three inches closer. No matter. Too many uncertainties lay ahead to dwell on those in the past. For the first time since he had landed at Torbay in 1688, William was content with the present. When he had arrived back in London from Flanders two weeks after the Treaty of Limerick had been signed, it seemed that all of England had come to greet him. His carriage crept through a sea of waving arms, 'the continual shouts of the people, and the streets full of bonfires and illuminations'. The stern and uncomfortable mask he had always worn in public began to slip. 'The king seemed to take more notice of the people's acclamations than ever before,' one eyewitness remarked.[23]

On 3 March 1692, just as he had signed off on the final arrangements for his new government and privy council in Ireland, William told his secretary to draft one more letter. It was a proclamation 'hereby declaring that the said kingdom of Ireland is reduced to our obedience, and the war and rebellion there ended'. Before it was dated, sealed and sent to every corner of the realm, one last line was inserted at the bottom, with greater relief and certainty than ever before:

'God save the King and Queen.'

Epilogue

Time and Violence

In the end it was a fall from a horse that sent William of Orange – *stadtholder*, king, husband, general, conqueror, usurper – from this life to the next. In late February 1702, William was riding through Richmond Park in London when his horse stumbled over a molehill and sent him crashing to the ground. He escaped with just a broken collarbone – once more displaying, it seems, his uncanny knack for survival. But on returning to Kensington Palace that evening, William seemed strangely wistful. His thoughts began to linger on his beloved Mary, who had died of smallpox in those very halls in 1694. Her death had seemed to tear away a piece of William, leaving a silent wound. On the evening of his accident, William sat down by an open window overlooking the prim, geometric gardens that he and his wife had planned together. He fell asleep beneath a cold draught and contracted pneumonia. His weak, asthmatic lungs could not endure the attack. As he lingered in bed, William sent for his old companion William Bentinck, the Earl of Portland. Their relationship had grown distant in recent years, but in his final hours Bentinck was once more at William's side, just as he had been in 1675, when they were younger men with other cares. Then, on the morning of 8 March 1702, the fifty-one-year-old William of Orange lost his final battle.

His father-in-law was waiting for him. James Stuart, the king in exile, had lived out his days as a devout and listless pensioner at St Germain. In May 1692 a French fleet that had been primed to invade England was scattered at the battle of La Hogue off the Normandy coast. In the aftermath, France began to lose interest in England's domestic affairs. When the war between Louis and William's grand alliance ground to a halt with the Treaty of Ryswick in 1697, Louis was required to publicly recognise William as king and abandon any future design to stir trouble on James's behalf. When Louis and the rest of Europe next went to war in 1701, the new prize was the crown of Spain. James was left to pray and contemplate on the outskirts of Paris as the cruel course of history left him behind. In the autumn of 1701, the sixty-one-year-old's health had begun to fade. Attendants were fussing around the bedridden old king when Louis le Grand, the man who had once used James's tragedy like a chess piece, paid his cousin a visit. 'I am going to pay that debt which must be paid by all kings, as well as their meanest subjects,' James whispered.[1] Louis gave his kinsman parting comfort by stating that he would, after all, support his son's claim to the throne. On 6 September, after embracing his now thirteen-year-old son, James Francis Edward, for the last time, James II died of a brain haemorrhage. His son and his grandson would agitate for their birthright for years, leading two great uprisings in Scotland in 1715 and 1745. Both would fail with brutal consequences, and Jacobitism would drift away, the stuff of haunting ballads echoing through the Scottish highlands.

Back in 1692, when the defeat at La Hogue and Limerick seemed to have finally strangled James's ambition, he sat down to write a letter to his son. It was the moment he realised that he would never see London again and decided to pass his quest on to the next generation. The letter was a long ramble of advice, touching on everything from the value of piety to selecting counsellors. 'A king ought to be the father of his people,' James wrote. Towards the end of the letter, he finally turned his pen to Ireland, that harshest of places, now on the cusp of deep and binding change. James had little sympathy for the Catholics of the kingdom that had risen to defend him and paid for it with their blood and dignity. 'There must be great care taken not to trust them too far, they being generally ill principled,' he warned. The sons of great Irish families should be raised in England, even at the expense of the crown, in order to wean them 'from their natural hatred against the English'. The men of Munster and Ulster could not stand each other, James added, and both tended to spit on the machinery of power in Dublin, which was now firmly back in Protestant hands. No Gaelic man should ever be lord lieutenant or the governor of a garrison, James warned; and no matter how time or circumstance might change, the Irish 'will always be ready to rise in arms'. It was a sneering dismissal of a kingdom that had once more suffered in the name of the Stuarts. Catholic Ireland would never rise up for a king again. From now on, it would fight for itself.[2]

*

The Treaty of Limerick was a contract between war-weary officers written in a tent. It was supposed to be some vision of Ireland where Catholics would be ruled but not suppressed. History and circumstance would tear the treaty to pieces.

William upheld the terms as long as he needed his Catholic allies, most notably Emperor Leopold in Vienna, to fight with him against France. But when the war against Louis ended, William no longer felt the need to hold his subjects in check. In 1697 a Protestant-controlled Irish parliament was finally summoned in Dublin to ratify a heavily edited version of the treaty. The first clause, promising a debate on freedoms for Catholics, was erased. Back in 1691, Sarsfield, Butler and the other Jacobites had agreed that Catholics should receive all privileges and protection they had enjoyed under Charles II. It was a naive mistake – the only leniency Catholics ever received in those times came from Charles's whims. The penal laws had never been scrubbed from statute, and when the time came for the Irish parliament to interpret the treaty, there was a very low ceiling on how much Catholics could expect. It was a shock, but hardly a surprise, when William approved the Dublin parliament's Banishment Act in 1697, which expelled every Catholic bishop from Ireland. It was the opening strike in a century of methodical legal suppression of the Catholic people. It was the hardest sort of victors' justice.

Demolishing the second article of the treaty, which guaranteed the estates of all Catholics who submitted to the new reign, required greater finesse. The Irish gentry's thirst for their old mansions and prestige had been a crusade passed from one generation to the next. It would not be passed on anymore. After William's death in 1702 the crown passed to Anne, James's youngest daughter, the shy, lazy, elusive princess who had snuck out of Whitehall in the dead of night in 1688 and broken her father's heart. Anne had neither the will nor the inclination to hold back the temper of parliament. In 1703 the Dublin assembly drew up the Popery Act, which sought to pluck the last of Irish land from Catholic hands. When a Catholic owner died, his property would be divided into smaller pieces between all his Catholics sons, dwindling further and further through the generations, until there was barely anything left. However, if one son converted and became a Protestant, he would inherit everything and his brothers would be turned out. Toby Butler railed against the law, believing it a betrayal of the treaty he had helped to write. He and other protestors were waved away, like beggars demanding a penny. When Charles O'Kelly, the Jacobite colonel, sat down to write his coded memoir of the war, Ireland was being squeezed in a new era of penalty and 'all the miseries that a conquered nation could rationally expect'.[3] One day, change would come. But the Catholics of Ireland would suffer unspeakable ruin before it did.

*

One by one the men whose bullets, wounds and words had made Ireland the epicentre of Europe fell to time and violence. Ginkel and Ruvigny were both elevated to the English nobility: the former as Earl of Athlone, the latter as Earl of Galway. Both died in their early seventies. The Duke of Berwick became one of the most celebrated generals in Europe, rising to Marshal of France and securing his most legendary victory at Almanza in Spain in 1707. He wrote a memoir of that first campaign in Ireland and was killed aged sixty-three when a cannonball blew his head off at Philippsburg. Others did not have the chance to live long and reflect. The Count of Solms, who had marched into Whitehall and effectively placed James under arrest in December 1688, had his leg shot off at the battle of Landen in 1693 and died a few days later. John Wauchope, who became

Sarsfield's right arm in those final hours of the war, was killed in the French victory at Marsaglia in 1693, as was Thomas Maxwell, the Scot who had watched Athlone melt around him like a house of wax. Justin MacCarthy died fighting in the Pyrenees. In April 1693, the long-mooted prisoner swap between the Jacobite general Richard Hamilton and the ill-fated Ulster commander Lord Mountjoy finally took place. Mountjoy went straight into William's service in Flanders and was dead within six months. Hamilton entered the Jacobite court-in-exile in St Germain but fell from favour and died in poverty in 1717. D'Usson and de Tessé, the last gatekeepers of France's lacklustre Irish mission, were both dead by 1705. Richard Nagle, Tyrconnell's enforcer and briefly a lord justice of Ireland, lived out his days in France. The Earl of Melfort, who had once been the most powerful counsellor in James's circle, suffered a fall from grace that ultimately saw him banished from court. He died of illness in 1714. The Earl of Clarendon, the Irish viceroy whom Tyrconnell had elbowed out of Dublin Castle, died in 1709, having long been suspected of hidden sympathy for James's cause. John Keating, the Irish Protestant judge who had made the back-door overtures to London for peace in 1689, was driven from favour by the new Williamite administration. He put a gun in his mouth in October 1691.[4]

John Mitchelburne, who had defiantly hoisted his red flag in the last chapter of the siege of Derry, died in 1721 and is buried in the old Glendermott cemetery outside the city. Resting nearby – his date of death unknown – is Adam Murray, the firebrand colonel who had helped turn the tide when the city was on the edge of the abyss. Robert Lundy, the callow governor who had abandoned Derry to its fate, was arrested in Scotland, imprisoned in the Tower of London and questioned by the House of Commons. Though he never stood trial and his fate is unknown, his legacy endured. Lundy's name became a byword for cowardice, treason and conspiracy in Protestant Ulster.[5]

Henry Luttrell became an enigma. The man who held Patrick Sarsfield's ear as he prodded the Duke of Tyrconnell was awarded an annual pension from the Williamite government for his surprise volte-face after the Treaty of Limerick. He attempted to lead an Irish brigade into Venice's war with the Turks in the Mediterranean but was unsuccessful. He likewise tried and failed to make a mark with the Dutch army in the years before William's death. He leapfrogged his brother Simon, who died in 1698, to inherit the grand family estate of Luttrellstown Castle in County Dublin. He became embroiled in a bitter legal dispute with his brother's widow, which saw petitions travel all the way to the House of Lords in Westminster. Luttrell was a sixty-two-year-old gentleman, plump and content in his retirement, when an assassin shot him dead as he was being carried on a chair through Dublin in 1717. The murderer was never caught and his motive never discovered. Luttrell's name became dirt: he was Luttrell the Traitor, and the path along which he had fled from Aughrim became known as Luttrell's Pass. More than eighty years later, when Ireland was once more swept by rebellion, Luttrell's grave was opened and his skull was smashed with a pickaxe.

Then there is Patrick Sarsfield, the man revered by one Gaelic poet as 'a champion of chieftains'. His raid at Ballyneety in 1690 is cherished in Irish folklore as one of the few moments worth remembering in a war of misery. The troops he brought to France with him would be remembered as the Wild Geese – a weary flock far from home but one that established a tradition of Irishmen fighting in Spain, France, Poland, Hungary and Flanders right up until the Napoleonic wars. Sarsfield's own thirst for the frontlines quickly caught up with him. He was shot in the chest holding the line at Landen in August 1693, and died a few days later. Lord Lucan's last words, it is said, were of home and sorrow. 'Oh, that this were for Ireland.'[6]

For a moment that would sink down the well of time, Ireland had been a kingdom of Catholic law and privilege, rallying to the banner of a Catholic king. The mason who had built it brick by brick – the destruction of the land acts, the internment of Protestants, the raising of an army and the waging of a war – was Richard Talbot, the Duke of Tyrconnell. The boy who cowered among the corpses of Drogheda became an irresistible titan. It was Talbot who held the door open for James and Louis, scoffed at William's first overtures for peace and made Ireland the wild west of a European war. Talbot was the final fury of the Norman barons. He tailored a kingdom with finesse and brute force. And, in the end, he did as much as anyone to provoke the brutal and lasting malice of England. When Talbot was gone, Oliver Cromwell's tactic of caging all Irish Catholics in the same cell was mastered. After Theobald Wolfe Tone's romantic insurrection of 1798 was crushed, Ireland was fused into a United Kingdom with England and Scotland, with one crown and one parliament. One day, after so many others full of tears and tragedy, Ireland would break free, and break in two, its points of division marked with the same ink as 1688 and 1641. That, of course, is a story of other men: O'Connell, Parnell, Redmond, Carson, Craig, Pearse, Collins and de Valera.

The relics of Tyrconnell's war are everywhere – the great lump of stone on which the Treaty of Limerick was apparently signed is now mounted on a plinth a few paces from where 600 men were massacred on Thomond Bridge. The walls of Derry are the thick, defiant vertebrae of a modern city. The frame of Charles Fort still looms menacingly over the harbour in Kinsale where James had arrived in splendour and fled in disgrace. Aughrim Castle is an overgrown tower of stones near a motorway. The walls of Limerick have been torn down, with only tiny fragments left peeking out invisibly behind terraced flats and car parks. The kingdom they had once all belonged to became an awkward and cruel memory. Today, it is barely a memory at all.

Bibliography

Manuscript collections

Correspondence of Henry Hyde, Earl of Clarendon, and his Brother Laurence Hyde, Earl of Rochester, vols I & II, 1828.

Correspondence of John Ellis, vol. II, 1829.

Eighth Report of the Royal Commission of Historical Manuscripts, 1881.

Fourth Report of the Royal Commission of Historical Manuscripts, part I, 1874.

Franco-Irish Correspondence 1688–1692, vols I–III, ed. Sheila Mulloy, 1983–4.

Manuscripts of the Duke of Portland, vols I & III, 1891–94.

Manuscripts of the Earl of Dartmouth, 1887 (Historical Manuscripts Commission, eleventh report, appendix part V).

Manuscripts of the Earl of Fingall, 1885 (Historical Manuscripts Commission, tenth report, appendix part V).

Manuscripts of the Marquis of Ormonde, vols I & II, 1895–99

Papers of F. W. Leyborne-Popham of Littlecote, Co. Wilts, 1899.

Report on the Manuscripts of George Allan Finch, vols I–III, 1922.

The Rawdon Papers, 1819.

Diaries and pamphlets

A Diary of the Siege and Surrender of Limerick, with the Articles at Large, Both Civil and Military, 1691.

Anonymous, *The Song of Dermot and the Earl*, c. 13th century (available online).

Cavelli, Marquise Campana de, *Les Derniers Stuarts á Saint-Germain en Laye*, 2 vols, 1871.

Coke, Roger, *A Detection of the Court and State of England during the Last Four Reigns and the Inter-regnum*, 1703.

Ferrar, John, *A History of Limerick, Ecclesiastical, Civil and Military from the Earliest Records to the Year 1787*, 1787.

Hamilton, Andrew, *A True Relation of the Actions of the Inniskilling Men*, 1690.

King, William, *The State of the Protestants of Ireland under the Late King James's Government*, 1730.

Lansdowne, Marquis of (ed.), *Petty–Southwell Correspondence 1676–1687*, from the Bowood Papers, 1928.

MacKenzie, John, *Mackenzie's Memorials of the Siege of Derry, Including His Narrative and Its Vindication*, 1690.

Mullenaux, S., *Journal of the Three Months Royal Campaign of His Majesty in Ireland, Together with a True and Perfect Diary of the Siege of Limerick*, 1690.

Ó Cianáin, Tadhg, *The Flight of the Earls, 1607–1609*, Dublin, 1916.

Pepys, Samuel, *Diary*, entries from 1660–1 (available online).

Richards, Col. Michael, *Diary of the Siege of Limerick*, 1691.

Stevens, John, *The Journal of John Stevens, Containing a Brief Account of the War in Ireland 1689–1691*, ed. Robert H. Murray, 1912.

Story, George, *An Impartial History of the Wars of Ireland*, 1693

Story, George, *A Continuation of the Impartial History of the Wars of Ireland*, London, 1693.

Temple, Sir W., *Letters to the King, the Prince of Orange, the Chief Ministers of State and Other Persons*, 1703.

The Negotiations of the Count d'Avaux, vols I–III, 1754.
Walker, Rev. George, *A True Account of the Siege of London-Derry*, 1689.
Wolseley, William, *Letters from Colonel William Wolseley, 1690: Pursuit of Irish Tories*, 1892.

Articles and calendars

'A Diary of the Siege of Athlone', *The Irish Sword*, 4.15, 1959.
Archives of the *London Gazette*, 1688–1692 (available online).
Calendar of State Papers, domestic, Charles II, 1660–85, 25 vols.
Calendar of State Papers, domestic, James II, 1685–89, 3 vols.
Calendar of State Papers, domestic, William and Mary, 11 vols.
'Franco-Irish correspondence' (review), *Journal of the Armagh Diocesan Historical Society*, 4.1, 1960–1.
'French naval affairs and the surrender of Limerick', *The Irish Sword*, 2.6, 1954–5.
Gleeson, Willie, 'King John's Castle', *Old Limerick Journal*, 12, 1982.
Grey's Debates of the House of Commons, vol. IX.
Hayes-McCoy, G. A., 'The Battle of Aughrim', *Journal of the Galway Archaeological and Historical Society*, 20.1–2, 1942.
History and Proceedings of the House of Commons, Vol. I, 1660–1680, 1744.
Jordan, John, 'The Battle of Aughrim: Two Danish sources', *Journal of the Galway Archaeological and Historical Society*, 26.1–2, 1954–5.
Journal of the House of Commons, vols VIII–X.
Journal of the House of Lords, vols XIII–XV.
'Letters of Richard Cromwell, 1659', *The American Historical Review*, 3, 1902.
Mulloy, Sheila, 'Limerick and France during the Jacobite War, 1689–1691', *Old Limerick Journal*, 25, 1989.
'Note concerning an account, written by Adrian Adornes, a Dutchman, of his dangers in Ireland, 1689–91', *Journal of*

the Historical and Archaeological Association of Ireland, series 4, vol. 5, part 1, 1879.
Ó Danachair, C., 'The Danish Corps in Ireland', *The Irish Sword*, 5, 1961–2.
Old Limerick Journal, 28, 1990 (1690 Siege edition – 54 articles)
'Sarsfield's defence of the Shannon, 1690–91, including correspondence with Lord Mountcashel', *The Irish Sword*, 1.1, 1949–50.
Simms, J. G., 'The Battle of Aughrim, history and poetry', *Irish University Review*, 7.1, 1977.
Simms, J. G., 'The making of a penal law, 1703–04', *Irish Historical Studies*, 12.46, 1960.
Simms, J. G., 'Williamite peace tactics, 1690–91', *Irish Historical Studies*, 8.32, 1953.
Swords, Liam, 'The Jacobite War: a dispatch from Limerick, 1691', *Journal of the Armagh Diocesan Historical Society*, 16.1, 1994.
Tate, Lilian (ed.), 'Franco-Irish correspondence: December 1688–August 1691', *Analecta Hibernica*, 21, 1959.
The 1641 Depositions, Trinity College Dublin (available online).
Wheatley, C. J., 'Heroic Palimpsest: Robert Ashton's "The Battle of Aughrim"', *Eighteenth Century Ireland*, 11, 1996.
'Wurtemburg at Limerick, 1690', *Studies: An Irish Quarterly Review*, 43.170, 1954.

Memoirs, secondary texts and further reading

Annals of the Kingdom of Ireland by the Four Masters, vols I–VII, Dublin, 1856.
Bagwell, Richard, *Ireland under the Stuarts and during the Interregnum*, vols I–III, London, 1908–9.
Bardon, Jonathan, *A History of Ireland in 250 episodes*, Dublin, 2008.
Barratt, John, *Battles for the Three Kingdoms: The campaigns for England, Scotland and Ireland 1689–92*, Stroud, 2007.

Browning, Andrew, *English Historical Documents, vol. VIII, 1660–1714*, London, 1995.

Burghclère, Baroness W., *The Life of James, First Duke of Ormonde, 1610–1688*, vol. II, London, 1912.

Burnet, Gilbert, *Bishop Burnet's History of His Own Time (with Notes)*, vol. IV, Oxford, 1833.

Carte, Thomas, *The Life of James, Duke of Ormonde*, vols IV & V, Oxford, 1851.

Childs, John, *The Williamite Wars in Ireland 1688–1691*, London, 2007.

Cibber, Colley, *An Apology for the Life of Mr Colley Cibber, Written by Himself*, vol. I, London, 1740.

Clarke, J. S., *The Life of James the Second, King of England*, vols I & II, London, 1816.

Connolly, S. J., *Divided Kingdom, Ireland 1630–1800*, Oxford, 2008.

Corp, Edward T., *A Court in Exile: The Stuarts in France 1689–1718*, Cambridge, 2004.

Crouch, Nathaniel (aka Richard Burton), *The History of the Kingdom of Ireland*, Westminster, 1693.

Crowley, Roger, *Empires of the Sea: The Final Battle for the Mediterranean, 1521–1580*, London, 2008.

Dalrymple, John, *Memoirs of Great Britain and Ireland*, vols I–II, London, 1771–8.

D'Alton, John, *Illustrations, Historical and Genealogical of King James's Irish Army List 1689*, Dublin, 1855.

Davies, Norman, *Europe: A History*, London, 1997.

Davies, Norman, *Vanished Kingdoms: The History of Half-Forgotten Europe*, London, 2011.

Deane, Seamus, *A Short History of Irish Literature*, London, 1986.

Dennehy, Coleman (ed.), *Restoration Ireland: Always Settling and Never Settled*, Farnham, 2008.

Doherty, Richard, *The Williamite War in Ireland, 1688–91*, Dublin, 1998.

Edwards, David, Lenihan, Padraig and Tait, Clodagh (eds), *Age of Atrocity: Violence and Political Conflict in Early Modern Ireland*, Dublin, 2007.

FitzJames, James, *Memoirs of the Marshal Duke of Berwick*, vol. I, London, 1779.

Gilbert, J. T. (ed), *A Jacobite Narrative of the War in Ireland*, Dublin, 1892.

Hardinge, W. H., *On the Townland Surveys of Ireland, 1640–1864*, Dublin, 1865.

Harris, Tim, *Revolution: The Great Crisis of the British Monarchy, 1685–1720*, London, 2006.

Hogan, James (ed.), *Letters and Papers Relating to the Irish Rebellion between 1642–46*, Dublin, 1936.

Hull, Eleanor, *A History of Ireland and Her People*, London, 1931.

Hume, David, *The History of England in Three Volumes*, vols I & II, London, 1754–56.

Jones, Dan, *The Hollow Crown: The Wars of the Roses and the Rise of the Tudors*, London, 2014.

Jones, Dan, *The Plantagenets*, London, 2012.

Jouvin, Albert, *Le Voyageur d'Europe*, vol. III, Paris, 1672.

Kelly, James and Lyons, Mary Ann (eds), *The Proclamations of Ireland, 1660–1820*, vols I & II, Dublin, 2014.

Kinsella, Eoin, *The Articles of Surrender and the Williamite Settlement of Ireland: A Case Study of Colonel John Browne 1640–1711* (PhD paper), Dublin, 2011.

Lenihan, Maurice, *Limerick: Its History and Antiquities*, reprint, Cork, 1991.

Lenihan, Padraig, *The Last Cavalier: Richard Talbot 1631–91*, Dublin, 2014.

Macaulay, Thomas Babington, *The History of England from the Accession of James II*, vols I–V, Philadelphia, 1848.

MacErlean, John, *The Poems of David Ó Bruadair, Part 3*, Dublin, 1917.

Mackay, Hugh, *Memoirs of the War Carried on in Scotland and Ireland, 1689–1691*, London, 1833.
Mackay, John, *Life of Lieutenant General Hugh Mackay of Scoury*, London, 1836.
Milligan, C. D., *History of the Siege of Londonderry*, Belfast, 1951.
Moody, T. W., Martin, F. X. and Byrne, F. J. (eds), *A New History of Ireland, Volume III: Early Modern Ireland, 1534–1691*, Oxford, 1976.
Ó Ciardha, Eamonn, *Ireland and the Jacobite Cause, 1685–1766: A Fatal Attachment*, Dublin, 2004.
Onnekink, David, *The Anglo-Dutch Favourite: The Career of Hans Willem Bentinck, First Earl of Portland, 1649–1709*, Farnham, 2007.
O'Kelly, Charles, *Macariae Excidium, or The Destruction of Cyprus*, Dublin, 1850.
Parker, Robert, *Memoirs of the Most Remarkable Military Transactions from the Year 1683 to 1718*, London, 1747.
Penn, Thomas, *Winter King: The Dawn of Tudor England*, London, 2011.
Plantavit de la Pause, Guillaume, *The Life of James Fitz-James, Duke of Berwick*, London, 1738.
Potter, Matthew, *First Citizens of the Treaty City: The Mayors and Mayoralty of Limerick, 1197–2007*, Limerick, 2007.
Pringle Thomson, James, *The Jacobite Rebellions 1689–1746* (Bell's Scottish History Source Books), London, 1914.
Prunty, Jacinta and Clarke, H. B., *Reading the Maps: A Guide to the Irish Historic Towns Atlas*, Dublin, 2011.
Salmon, Thomas, *Modern History, or, The Present State of All Nations*, vol. XXIII, London, 1734.
Sergeant, Philip, *Little Jennings and Fighting Dick Talbot: A Life of the Duke and Duchess of Tyrconnell*, vols I–II, London, 1913.
Simms, J. G., *Jacobite Ireland*, Dublin, 1969.

Sharpe-Grew, E. & M., *The Court of William III*, London, 1910.
Sharpe-Grew, E. & M., *The English Court in Exile: James II at Saint-Germain*, London, 1911.
Stuart-Wortley, J., *Memoirs of General George Monck, Duke of Albemarle*, London, 1838.
Troost, Wouter, *William III: The Stadtholder King*, Farnham, 2005.
Volatire, *The Age of Louis XIV*, vol. I, Paris, 1751.
Wauchope, Piers, *Patrick Sarsfield and the Williamite War*, Dublin, 1992.
Whitelocke, Bulstrode, *Memoirs, Biographical and Historical of Bulstrode Whitelocke, Lord Commissioner of the Great Seal*, London, 1860.
Witherow, Thomas, *Derry and Enniskillen in 1688–1689*, Belfast, 1873.

Endnotes

1. Pieces of Paper

1 Pepys, *Diary*, 25 May 1660.
2 Calendar of State Papers, domestic, Charles II, May–September 1660.
3 Pepys, 23 April 1661.

2. Predatory Incursion

1 Crouch, *The History of the Kingdom of Ireland*, pp. 58–100.
2 *Annals of the Kingdom of Ireland*, vol. II, p. 1138.
3 Texts of the papal bull *Laudabiliter* 1155 and the confirmation of Pope Alexander III taken from Hull, *A History of Ireland and Her People*. The poem 'The Song of Dermot and the Earl', written by an unknown author and translated from Latin, is one of the best accounts of the first Norman incursion into Ireland.
4 *Annals*, vol. V, p. 1449.
5 *Ibid.*, pp. 1445–49.
6 *Ibid.*

3. Avalanche

1 Edwards, Lenihan and Tait (eds), *Age of Atrocity: Violence and Political Conflict in Early Modern Ireland*, p. 163, pp. 176–92.
2 Crouch, p. 51.
3 Manuscripts of the Duke of Portland, vol. I, pp. 36–7.
4 Letter from Mayor of Londonderry to the Lord Justices, 8 January 1642, taken from Hogan (ed.), *Letters and Papers Relating to the Irish Rebellion between 1642–1646*, pp. 1–5.
5 *Ibid.*, W. St Leger to Mr Speaker, 23 March 1642.

6 Corish, 'The Cromwellian Conquest, 1649–53', taken from Moody, Martin and Byrne (eds), *A New History of Ireland, Volume III: Early Modern Ireland, 1534–1691*, p. 340.

4. Oliver's Shoemakers

1 Connolly, *Divided Kingdom: Ireland 1630–1800*, p. 128.
2 'His Majestie's Gracious Declaration for the Settlement of his Kingdom of Ireland', taken from Connolly, p. 132.
3 FitzJames, *Memoirs of the Marshal Duke of Berwick*, vol. I, p. 95.
4 Gilbert (ed.), *A Jacobite Narrative of the War in Ireland*, p. 156.
5 O'Kelly, *Macariae Excidium, or The Destruction of Cyprus*, p. 146.
6 Dennehy (ed.), *Restoration Ireland: Always Settling and Never Settled*, p. 60.
7 Crouch, pp. 52–4.
8 Burghclere, *The Life of James, First Duke of Ormonde, 1610–1688*, vol. II, pp. 66–7.
9 Report on the Manuscripts of George Allan Finch, vol. I, p. 256.
10 Connolly, p. 135.
11 Burghclere, pp. 105–6.
12 Gilbert, p. 178.
13 O'Kelly, p. 14.
14 *Ibid.*
15 Gilbert, p. 35.
16 Jouvin, *Le Voyageur d'Europe*, vol. III, p. 414.
17 *Ibid.*, p. 401.
18 Gilbert, p. 17.
19 Burghclere, p. 108.

5. Forever Incapable

1 Lenihan, *The Last Cavalier: Richard Talbot 1631–91*, pp. 78–9.
2 *Journal of the House of Commons*, vol. IX, 25 March 1673.
3 Text of 'An Act for Securing the Protestant Religion by Disabling James Duke of York to Inherit the Imperial Crown of England and Ireland', 4 November 1680.
4 *History and Proceedings of the House of Commons, Vol. I, 1660–1680*, p. 435.

5 Correspondence of Henry Hyde, Earl of Clarendon, and His Brother Laurence Hyde, Earl of Rochester, vol. I, pp. 105–6 (hereafter referred to as Clarendon Correspondence).
6 Burghclere, p. 325.

6. Jacobus Rex

1 J. S. Clarke, *The Life of James the Second, King of England*, vol. II, p. 32.
2 *Ibid.*, p. 2.
3 Clarendon Correspondence, vol. I, p. 110.
4 Clarke, vol. II, p. 3
5 Harris, *Revolution: The Great Crisis of the British Monarchy, 1685–1720*, pp. 49–54.
6 Clarendon Correspondence, vol. I, p. 115.
7 O'Kelly, p. 15.
8 Harris, p. 54.
9 Clarendon Correspondence, vol. I, pp. 184–7.
10 Sergeant, *Little Jennings and Fighting Dick Talbot: A Life of the Duke and Duchess of Tyrconnell*, vol. I, p. 298.
11 Clarendon Correspondence, vol. I, p. 346.
12 Lansdowne (ed.), *The Petty–Southwell Correspondence 1676–1687*, p. 234.

7. All Prudent Courses

1 Calendar of State Papers, domestic, James II, September–November 1685.
2 Clarke, vol. II, p. 49.
3 Clarendon Correspondence, vol. I, p. 189.
4 Declaration of Indulgence of King James II, 4 April 1687, in Browning, *English Historical Documents, vol. VIII, 1660–1714*, pp. 399–400.
5 Clarendon Correspondence, vol. I, pp. 533–42.
6 J. G. Simms, *Jacobite Ireland*, p. 31.
7 Sergeant, vol. II, p. 353.

8. Nineteen Parts of Twenty

1 Voltaire, *The Age of Louis XIV*, vol. I, pp. 169–72.
2 Manuscripts of the Marquis of Ormonde, vol. II, pp. 373–4.

3 *Ibid.*, p. 303.
4 Lansdowne (ed.), p. 214.
5 Manuscripts of the Marquis of Ormonde, vol. II, p. 371.
6 William King, *The State of the Protestants of Ireland under the Late King James's Government*, p. 92.
7 Sergeant, vol. II, pp. 356
8 Clarendon Correspondence, vol. II, p. 156.
9 Clarke, vol. II, p. 155.
10 Harris, p. 271.
11 *London Gazette*, 12 July 1688.
12 Clarendon Correspondence, vol. II, p. 179.
13 Clarke, vol. II, p. 165.
14 Letter of Invitation to William of Orange, 30 June 1688, taken from Dalrymple, *Memoirs of Great Britain and Ireland*, vol. I, appendix (book V), pp. 109–10.

9. Invasion

1 Calendar of State Papers, domestic, James II, 8 September 1688.
2 Clarendon Correspondence, vol. II, p. 189.
3 Sergeant, vol. II, p. 386. See Manuscripts of the Marquis of Ormonde, vol. II, pp. 378–87 for Tyrconnell's declarations on army affairs in the summer of 1688.
4 Clarke, vol. II, p. 169.
5 Troost, *William III: The Stadtholder King*, p. 198.
6 Clarendon Correspondence, vol. II, p. 194.
7 Clarke, vol. II, p. 198.

10. Villainy upon Villainy

1 Calendar of State Papers, domestic, James II, 8–10 November 1688.
2 Stevens, *The Journal of John Stevens*, pp. 4–8.
3 Clarendon Correspondence, vol. II, p. 204.
4 Harris, p. 292.
5 Clarke, vol. II, p. 217.
6 Clarendon Correspondence, vol. II, p. 205.
7 Correspondence of John Ellis, vol. II, pp. 314–19.
8 Stevens, p. 4.
9 Wauchope, *Patrick Sarsfield and the Williamite War*, pp. 37–9.

10 Correspondence of John Ellis, vol. II, p. 320
11 Sergeant, vol. II, p. 393.
12 Clarke, vol. II, p. 225 (appendix).
13 Clarendon Correspondence, vol. II, p. 206.
14 Clarke, vol. II, p. 226.
15 Clarendon Correspondence, vol. II, p. 211.

11. Nothing Less Than Despair

1 Sharpe-Grew, *The Court of William III*, pp. 208–12.
2 Clarendon Correspondence, vol. II, p. 215.
3 Manuscripts of the Earl of Dartmouth, p. 220.
4 Clarke, vol. II, p. 220 (appendix).
5 Manuscripts of the Earl of Dartmouth, p. 224.
6 Clarendon Correspondence, vol. II, pp. 215–17.
7 Manuscripts of the Earl of Dartmouth, p. 226.
8 Clarke, vol. II, pp. 249–50.
9 Correspondence of John Ellis, vol. II, pp. 350–60, and Manuscripts of the Duke of Portland, vol. III, pp. 420–1.
10 Clarendon Correspondence, vol. II, p. 224.
11 Clarke, vol. II, p. 262.
12 Clarke, vol. II, pp. 261–5.
13 Clarendon Correspondence, vol. II, p. 231 (appendix).
14 Clarke, vol. II, p. 274.

12. House of Fear

1 King, appendix, pp. 71–3.
2 Gilbert (ed.), p. 36.
3 Calendar of State Papers, domestic, James II, 11 December 1688.
4 Cavelli, *Les Derniers Stuarts á Saint-Germain en Laye*, vol. II, p. 591.
5 Manuscripts of the Marquis of Ormonde, vol. II, pp. 388–9.
6 Witherow, *Derry and Enniskillen in 1688–1689*, pp. 18–21.
7 MacKenzie, *MacKenzie's Memorials of the Siege of Londonderry, Including His Narrative and Its Vindication*, p. 15 and appendix pp. 61–2.

13. We Shall Never See Each Other Again

1 Gilbert (ed.), p. 43.
2 King, p. 113.

3 Correspondence of John Ellis, vol. II, pp. 362–73.
4 Manuscripts of the Duke of Portland, vol. III, p. 423.
5 *Ibid.*, pp. 422–3.
6 Clarendon Correspondence, vol. II, pp. 237–49.
7 FitzJames, vol. I, pp. 37–8.
8 Stevens, pp. 12–17.
9 Clarke, vol. II, pp. 288–319.
10 Descriptions of Lord Melfort taken from Corp, *A Court in Exile: The Stuarts in France 1689–1718*, p. 21, and E. and M. Sharpe-Grew, *The English Court in Exile: James II at Saint-Germain*, pp. 277–9.
11 Manuscripts of the Duke of Portland, vol. III, p. 422.
12 Sergeant, vol. II, pp. 403–08.
13 Clarendon Correspondence, vol. II, p. 274.
14 King (appendix), p. 71.
15 Cavelli, vol. II, p. 530.
16 *Ibid.*, pp. 531–5.
17 *Ibid.*, pp. 537–43.
18 *Ibid.*, pp. 540–1.
19 Corp, p. 22.
20 Stevens, pp. 28–32.
21 Grey's Debates of the House of Commons, vol. IX, pp. 2–39, and Manuscripts of the Duke of Portland, vol. III, p. 423.
22 Manuscripts of the Marquis of Ormonde, vol. III, p. 392.
23 *Ibid.* and King, pp. 126–7.
24 Simms, *Jacobite Ireland*, p. 62.

14. Now or Never, Now and Forever

1 Clarke, vol. II, p. 327.
2 FitzJames, vol. I, pp. 41–3.
3 Sergeant, vol. II, p. 426.
4 MacKenzie, appendix, pp. 62–3.
5 *Ibid.*, pp. 16–18.
6 *Ibid.*, p. 19.
7 Manuscripts of the Marquis of Ormonde, vol. II, pp. 395–6.
8 MacKenzie, p. 21.
9 Childs, *The Williamite Wars in Ireland 1688–1691*, pp. 56–7, and Simms, *Jacobite Ireland*, p. 57.
10 Sergeant, vol. II, pp. 426–7.

11 Gilbert (ed.), p. 46.
12 Clarke, vol. II, p. 330.
13 Simms, *Jacobite Ireland*, p. 64.
14 Manuscripts of the Marquis of Ormonde, vol. II, pp. 398–9.
15 Cavelli, vol. II, p. 586.
16 *Ibid.*, p. 582–3.
17 Clarke, vol. II, p. 331.
18 Gilbert, p. 52, and Cavelli, pp. 587–93.

15. To Derry

1 Gilbert (ed.), p. 41.
2 MacKenzie, p. 28.
3 Cavelli, pp. 587–93.
4 *Ibid.*
5 Gilbert (ed.), p. 52.
6 Sergeant, vol. II, p. 440.
7 Clarke, vol. II, p. 334.
8 MacKenzie, p. 26.
9 Calendar of State Papers, domestic, William and Mary, 8 March 1689.
10 MacKenzie, p. 31.
11 Citations from the fighting at Clady taken from FitzJames, p. 44, and MacKenzie, p. 31.

16. No Surrender

1 MacKenzie, p. 32.
2 *Ibid.*, pp. 31–2.
3 *Ibid.*, p. 33.
4 *Ibid.*, pp. 33–6, and Witherow, pp. 100–2.
5 Cavelli, pp. 587–93.
6 Gilbert (ed.), p. 62.
7 Clarke, vol. II, p. 330.
8 Walker, *A True Account of the Siege of London-Derry*, p. 25.
9 MacKenzie, pp. 29–34, and Report on the Manuscripts of George Allan Finch, vol. II, p. 203.
10 Walker, pp. 26–7.
11 Gilbert (ed.), p. 63
12 Walker, p. 27.

13 MacKenzie, pp. 36–7.
14 Stevens, p. 61.
15 FitzJames, pp. 44–8, and Clarke, vol. II, p. 334.
16 Calendar of State Papers, domestic, William and Mary, February–April 1689.
17 Report on the Manuscripts of George Allan Finch, vol. II, p. 204.

17. Cruel Consistency

1 MacKenzie, p. 39.
2 FitzJames, p. 49.
3 Quote taken from Gilbert, p. 68. For accounts of the skirmish at Pennyburn see also MacKenzie, p. 39, Walker, p. 30 and Childs, pp. 87–8.
4 Quote from Gilbert (ed.), p. 68. Account of Berwick's injuries taken from FitzJames, p. 51.
5 MacKenzie, p. 41.
6 *Ibid.*, p. 42.
7 FitzJames, p. 51.
8 Walker, p. 37.
9 FitzJames, p. 52.
10 Walker, p. 40.
11 MacKenzie, p. 45.
12 Clarke, vol. II, p. 365.
13 Walker, p. 42.
14 A daily tally of shells that fell on Derry from April to July can be found in MacKenzie, appendix, p. 72.
15 *Ibid.*, p. 43.
16 Gilbert (ed.), p. 76.
17 Walker, p. 41.
18 MacKenzie, p. 43.
19 Quote from Gilbert (ed.), pp. 77–8. Account of Williamite injuries taken from MacKenzie, pp. 43–4.
20 Eighth Report of the Royal Commission of Historical Manuscripts, p. 494.
21 Sergeant, vol. II, p. 451.
22 Walker, p. 43.
23 MacKenzie, p. 47.
24 *Ibid.*, p. 46.

18. Dividing the Skin

1 Clarke, vol. II, p. 355.
2 Gilbert (ed.), pp. 70–1 and Simms, *Jacobite Ireland*, pp. 68–9.
3 King, p. 167.
4 O'Kelly, p. 34.
5 Clarke, vol. II, pp. 356–7.
6 King, p. 151.
7 Stevens, p. 68.
8 Clarke, vol. II, p. 360.
9 Manuscripts of the Marquis of Ormonde, vol. II, p. 402.
10 Stevens, p. 70.
11 Gilbert (ed.), p. 70.
12 Stevens, p. 71.
13 Manuscripts of the Marquis of Ormonde, vol. II, p. 407.
14 Gilbert (ed.), p. 75.
15 King, p. 167.

19. This, I Hope, Will Be Your Destiny

1 MacKenzie, p. 48.
2 *Ibid.*, p. 49.
3 Walker, p. 51.
4 Text of Rosen's message taken from MacKenzie, pp. 49–50.
5 MacKenzie, pp. 48–50.
6 Walker, p. 54.
7 *Ibid.*, pp. 55–6.
8 *Ibid.*, p. 56.
9 Clarke, vol. II, p. 367.
10 Calendar of State Papers, domestic, William and Mary, 11 July 1689.
11 Calendar of State Papers, domestic, William and Mary, 13 June 1689.
12 Quotations and figures taken from Walker, pp. 56–61.
13 Gilbert (ed.), p. 81.
14 MacKenzie, pp. 52–3 and appendix, pp. 71–2.
15 *Ibid.*, p. 53.
16 Calendar of State Papers, domestic, William and Mary, 26 June–10 July 1689.
17 Eighth Report of the Royal Commission of Historical Manuscripts, p. 495.

18 Schomberg to William, Calendar of State Papers, domestic, 21/22 July and 26 July 1689.
19 Walker, pp. 59–63.
20 MacKenzie, p. 55.
21 Gilbert (ed.), p. 84.
22 Walker, p. 63.
23 Gilbert (ed.), p. 84.
24 *Ibid.*, p. 85.
25 Walker, p. 64.
26 Gilbert (ed.), p. 85.
27 Eighth Report of the Royal Commission of Historical Manuscripts, p. 495.

20. Outlive the Day

1 Clarke, vol. II, p. 368.
2 Hamilton, *A True Relation of the Actions of the Inniskilling Men*, pp. 1–9.
3 *Ibid.*, pp. 17–20.
4 Eighth Report of the Royal Commission of Historical Manuscripts, p. 494.
5 Hamilton, p. 27.
6 FitzJames, pp. 53–4.
7 Hamilton, pp. 25–34.
8 Gilbert (ed.), p. 81.
9 Hamilton, pp. 37–8.
10 *Ibid.*, p. 42.
11 *Ibid.*, pp. 42–4.
12 Accounts of MacCarthy's capture taken from Gilbert (ed.), pp. 81–2, and Clarke, vol. II, p. 368.
13 FitzJames, p. 56.
14 *Ibid.*, pp. 55–6.
15 Hamilton, p. 47.
16 Quote from Hamilton, p. 44. See also Simms, *Jacobite Ireland*, pp. 118–19.

21. A Noisy World

1 Sharpe-Grew, *The Court of William III*, pp. 55–7.
2 *Ibid.*

3 Clarendon Correspondence, vol. II, p. 295.
4 Sharpe-Grew, *The Court of William III*, p. 61.
5 Calendar of State Papers, domestic, William and Mary, 4–12 November 1689.
6 Story, *An Impartial History of the Wars of Ireland*, p. 6.
7 FitzJames, p. 56.
8 Corp, p. 24.
9 Clarke, vol. II, p. 389.
10 Sergeant, vol. II, p. 460.
11 Story, *Impartial History*, pp. 11–15.
12 Clarke, vol. II, p. 376.
13 Stevens, pp. 78–9.
14 *Ibid.*, p. 80.
15 Story, *Impartial History*, p. 22.
16 *Ibid.*, p. 23.
17 Gilbert (ed.), p. 88.
18 Stevens, p. 82.
19 Story, *Impartial History*, pp. 22–39.
20 Calendar of State Papers, domestic, William and Mary, 4 & 14 November 1689.
21 Stevens, pp. 82–6.
22 Quote from Story, *Impartial History*, p. 35. Further information from Calendar of State Papers, domestic, William and Mary, December 1689.
23 Gilbert (ed.), p. 90.
24 Stevens, pp. 89–92.
25 Manuscripts of the Marquis of Ormonde, vol. III, p. 419.
26 Gilbert (ed.), p. 90.
27 Sergeant, vol. II, pp. 469–74.
28 Journal of the House of Commons, vol. X, November–December 1689.
29 Quote from Simms, *Jacobite Ireland*, p. 135. For further reading see Onnekink, *The Anglo-Dutch Favourite: The Career of Hans Willem Bentinck, First Earl of Portland, 1649–1709*, pp. 78–80.

22. Fishing with a Golden Hook

1 Report on the Manuscripts of George Allan Finch, vol. II, p. 285.
2 O'Kelly, appendix p. 338.

3 Story, *Impartial History*, pp. 64–5, and Stevens, p. 101.
4 *Ibid.*, pp. 54–61.
5 *Ibid.*, pp. 58–61.
6 Sergeant, vol. II, p. 485.
7 Stevens, pp. 103–10.
8 Sharpe-Grew, *The Court of William III*, p. 220.
9 Story, *Impartial History*, pp. 66–8.
10 Clarke, vol. II, p. 391.
11 Report on the Manuscripts of George Allan Finch, vol. II, p. 279.
12 Clarke, vol. II, pp. 393–4.
13 Stevens, p. 119, and Story, p. 71.

23. The Boyne

1 Papers of F. W. Leyborne-Popham of Littlecote, Co. Wilts, p. 272.
2 Story, *Impartial History*, p. 75.
3 *Ibid.*, p. 78.
4 *Ibid.*
5 Papers of F. W. Leyborne-Popham, p. 273.
6 Stevens, p. 121.
7 Story, *Impartial History*, p. 81.
8 *Ibid.*, p. 82.
9 Gilbert (ed.), p. 102.
10 Report on the Manuscripts of George Allan Finch , vol. II, p. 330.
11 Stevens, p. 122.
12 *Ibid.*, p. 123.
13 Story, *Impartial History*, p. 84.
14 *Ibid.*, p. 85
15 FitzJames, pp. 64–5.
16 O'Kelly, pp. 51–2.
17 Papers of F. W. Leyborne-Popham, p. 272.

24. They Gave the Kingdom for Lost

1 Simms, *Jacobite Ireland*, p. 153.
2 Gilbert (ed.), p. 105.
3 Stevens, p. 130.
4 O'Kelly, p. 52.
5 Stevens, pp. 130–2.
6 Report on the Manuscripts of George Allan Finch, vol. II, pp. 332–60.

7 *Ibid.*
8 *Ibid.*
9 Manuscripts of the Marquis of Ormonde, vol. II, pp. 309–16.
10 Stevens, p. 149.
11 O'Kelly, p. 56.
12 Stevens, pp. 132–56.
13 Manuscripts of the Marquis of Ormonde, vol. II, pp. 440–1.
14 Franco-Irish Correspondence, vol. III, pp. 146–7.
15 Gilbert (ed.), p. 111.
16 O'Kelly, p. 58.
17 Stevens, pp. 158–9 (appendix).
18 FitzJames, p. 96.
19 Gilbert (ed.), p. 111.
20 FitzJames, pp. 79–80 and p. 96.
21 Report on the Manuscripts of George Allan Finch, vol. II, pp. 362–83.
22 *Ibid.*
23 Papers of F. W. Leyborne-Popham, p. 275.
24 Report on the Manuscripts of George Allan Finch, pp. 362–97.
25 Stevens, pp. 148–50.
26 *Ibid.*, p. 142 and p. 149.
27 *Ibid.*, p. 156.
28 Quotes taken from FitzJames, pp. 79–80. Account of the failed plot in Stevens, pp. 145–6.
29 O'Kelly, p. 54.
30 Simms, p. 159.
31 Gilbert (ed.), p. 113.

25. Sarsfield's Pyre

1 Manuscripts of the Marquis of Ormonde, vol. II, p. 444.
2 Story, *Impartial History*, p. 111.
3 Report on the Manuscripts of George Allan Finch, vol. II, p. 408.
4 *Ibid.*, p. 427.
5 Stevens, p. 163.
6 FitzJames, p. 72.
7 The Journal of Rowland Davies, 9 August 1690, taken from *Old Limerick Journal*, 28, 1990, p. 163.
8 Stevens, p. 166.

9 Report on the Manuscripts of George Allan Finch, vol. II, p. 406.
10 Stevens, p. 166.
11 Report on the Manuscripts of George Allan Finch, vol. II, pp. 408–9.
12 Story, *Impartial History*, p. 116.
13 Sarsfield to Mountcashel, 24 February 1691, taken from *The Irish Sword*, 1.1.
14 The Rawdon Papers, p. 330.
15 Story, *Impartial History*, p. 119.
16 Report on the Manuscripts of George Allan Finch, vol. II, p. 413.
17 *Old Limerick Journal*, 28, 1990, p. 165.
18 Story, *Impartial History*, p. 119.
19 *Old Limerick Journal*, 28, 1990, p. 165.
20 Report on the Manuscripts of George Allan Finch, vol. II, p. 412.
21 O'Kelly, p. 64.
22 The Rawdon Papers, p. 332.
23 Report on the Manuscripts of George Allan Finch, vol. II, p. 412.
24 The Rawdon Papers, p. 332.
25 MacErlean (ed.), The Poems of David Ó Bruadair, vol. III, p. 143.

26. Thirty Paces Wide

1 Report on the Manuscripts of George Allan Finch, vol. II, p. 416.
2 Stevens, p. 169.
3 Story, *Impartial History*, p. 127.
4 Gilbert (ed.), p. 114.
5 The Rawdon Papers, p. 334.
6 Stevens, p. 173.
7 Report on the Manuscripts of George Allan Finch, vol. II, pp. 422–6.
8 Stevens, p. 174.
9 Report on the Manuscripts of George Allan Finch, vol. II, pp. 428–9.
10 Stevens, p. 177.
11 *Ibid.*, p. 178.
12 Story, *Impartial History*, p. 129.
13 *Ibid.*
14 *Ibid.*
15 *Ibid.*, pp. 129–30.

16 *Ibid.*, p. 130.
17 Stevens, p. 180–1.
18 Report on the Manuscripts of George Allan Finch, vol. II, p. 434.
19 Stevens, pp. 183–6.
20 *Ibid.*

27. Army of One

1 Journal of the House of Commons, vol. X, 1688–93, October 1690.
2 Report on the Manuscripts of George Allan Finch, vol. II, p. 472.
3 *Ibid.*, pp. 475–8.
4 Stevens, p. 193.
5 Report on the Manuscripts of George Allan Finch, vol. II, p. 478.
6 *Ibid.*, pp. 475–8.
7 Clarke, vol. II, p. 422.
8 Sharpe-Grew, *The English Court in Exile*, p. 227.
9 Clarke, vol. II, p. 422.
10 *Ibid.*, p. 424.
11 *Ibid.*, p. 423
12 O'Kelly, p. 127.
13 Story, *Impartial History*, pp. 138–52, and *Continuation*, pp. 53–63.
14 Calendar of State Papers, domestic, William and Mary, November 1690–February 1691.
15 Manuscripts of the Marquis of Ormonde, vol. II, p. 447.
16 Calendar of State Papers, domestic, William and Mary, November 1690–February 1691.
17 Calendar of State Papers, domestic, William and Mary, October 1690–February 1691; Journal of the House of Commons, October 1690; and Manuscripts of the Duke of Portland, vol. III, p. 454.
18 Simms, *Jacobite Ireland*, p. 190.
19 Report on the Manuscripts of George Allan Finch, vol. II, p. 478.
20 For more on Williamite peace tactics of 1690–1, see Simms, Irish Historical Studies, 8.32.
21 Clarke, vol. II, p. 434.
22 O'Kelly, p. 113.
23 Calendar of State Papers, domestic, William and Mary, January 1691.
24 *Ibid.*, November 1690.
25 *Ibid.*, January–February 1691.

26 Wauchope, pp. 191–4.
27 O'Kelly, p. 112.
28 Wauchope, pp. 191–4.
29 Calendar of State Papers, domestic, William and Mary, March 1691.
30 Stevens, p. 197.
31 De Ros Manuscripts, p. 321, taken from Fourth Report of the Royal Commission of Historical Manuscripts, appendix.
32 O'Kelly, pp. 111–12.
33 Clarke, vol. II, p. 451.
34 Story, *Continuation*, p. 90.
35 Calendar of State Papers, domestic, William and Mary, March–May 1691, and Story, *Continuation*, p. 80.

28. Hell upon Earth

1 Simms, *Jacobite Ireland*, p. 202.
2 Calendar of State Papers, domestic, William and Mary, March–June 1691.
3 Story, *Continuation*, p. 86.
4 Stevens, p. 199.
5 Calendar of State Papers, domestic, William and Mary, June 1691.
6 *Ibid.*
7 De Ros Manuscripts, p. 320, taken from Fourth Report of the Royal Commission of Historical Manuscripts, appendix.
8 Parker, *Memoirs of the Most Remarkable Military Transactions from the Year 1683 to 1718,* p. 29. See also *London Gazette*, 29 June 1691.
9 Stevens, pp. 202–3.
10 Gilbert (ed.), p. 132.
11 O'Kelly, p. 121.
12 The Rawdon Papers, p. 347.
13 Gilbert (ed.), p. 131.
14 Story, *Continuation*, p. 99.
15 Stevens, pp. 208–9.
16 The Rawdon Papers, p. 347.
17 Story, *Continuation*, pp. 102–3.
18 Stevens p. 208.
19 Story, *Continuation*, p. 104.

20 The Rawdon Papers, p. 345.
21 Story, *Continuation*, p. 104.
22 *Ibid.*, p. 106.
23 Parker, p. 32.
24 Gilbert (ed.), pp. 134–5.
25 Stevens, pp. 210–11.
26 Parker, p. 33.
27 Stevens, p. 211.
28 Simms, *Jacobite Ireland*, p. 211.
29 Story, *Continuation*, p. 116.
30 O'Kelly, p.124.
31 Stevens, p. 211.
32 Manuscripts of the Duke of Portland, vol. III, p. 471.
33 Calendar of State Papers, domestic, William and Mary, July 1691.

29. God Will Make You All Saints

1 The Rawdon Papers, p. 347.
2 Stevens, pp. 210–11.
3 O'Kelly, pp. 129–30.
4 Gilbert (ed.), p. 137.
5 Story, *Continuation*, p. 116; Calendar of State Papers, domestic, William and Mary, July 1691; and De Ros Manuscripts, taken from Fourth Report of the Royal Commission of Historical Manuscripts, appendix, p. 310.
6 Text of the declaration taken from Story, *Continuation*, pp. 118–19.
7 De Ros Manuscripts, p. 310.
8 Stevens, p. 212.
9 Story, *Continuation*, p. 114.
10 Stevens, p. 213.
11 *Ibid.*
12 Story, *Continuation*, p. 131.
13 Gilbert (ed.), p. 138.
14 Story, *Continuation*, pp. 123–5.

30. Aughrim

1 The Rawdon Papers, p. 352.
2 Parker, p. 34.

3 Story, p. 122.
4 Parker, p. 34.
5 The Rawdon Papers, pp. 353–4.
6 Story, *Continuation*, p. 128.
7 *Ibid.*, p. 129.
8 The Rawdon Papers, p. 349.
9 Story, *Continuation*, p. 129.
10 Swords, 'The Jacobite War: a dispatch from Limerick', Journal of the Armagh Diocesan Historical Society, 16.1, p. 72.
11 Story, *Continuation*, p. 130.
12 Gilbert (ed.), p. 140.
13 Story, *Continuation*, p. 131.
14 Gilbert (ed.), pp. 141–2.
15 Story, *Continuation*, p. 131
16 *Ibid.*, p. 133.
17 Jordan, 'The Battle of Aughrim: two Danish sources', Journal of the Galway Archaeological and Historical Society, 26.1, p. 5.
18 Gilbert (ed.), p. 147.
19 Story, *Continuation*, pp. 134–5.
20 Parker, pp. 35–6.
21 Jordan, pp. 6–7.
22 Story, *Continuation*, pp. 135–7.
23 London Gazette, 16 July 1691.
24 Story, *Continuation*, p. 136.
25 Gilbert (ed.), p. 148.
26 *Ibid.*, p. 147.
27 Parker, p. 36.
28 Jordan, p. 12.
29 The Rawdon Papers, p. 352.
30 De Ros Manuscripts, p. 322.
31 Story, *Continuation*, p. 136.
32 O'Kelly, pp. 133–4.

31. A Mighty Edifice

1 O'Kelly, p. 71.
2 Story, *Continuation*, p. 160 and O'Kelly, p. 71.
3 De Ros Manuscripts, p. 322.
4 O'Kelly, pp. 137–8.

5 Story, *Continuation*, pp. 166–8.
6 *Ibid.*, p. 172.
7 Simms, *Jacobite Ireland*, p. 235.
8 Clarke, vol. II, p. 459.
9 Story, *Continuation*, p. 172.
10 Gilbert (ed.), p. 148.
11 Tate (ed.), 'Franco-Irish correspondence: December 1688–August 1691', Analecta Hibernica, 21, p. 219.
12 Gilbert (ed.), pp. 149–50.
13 Clarke, vol. II, p. 459.
14 Gilbert (ed.), p. 152.
15 De Ros Manuscripts, p. 323.
16 O'Kelly, p. 141.
17 Story, *Continuation*, p. 182.
18 Calendar of State Papers, domestic, William and Mary, August 1691.
19 O'Kelly, p. 143.
20 Gilbert (ed.), p. 149.
21 *Ibid.*
22 Swords, p. 73.
23 Ferrar, *The History of Limerick, Ecclesiastical, Civil and Military, from the Earliest Records to the Year 1787*, p. 354.
24 *Ibid.*
25 Gilbert (ed.), p. 152.
26 *Ibid.*, p. 155.
27 Clarke, vol. II, p. 461.
28 *Ibid.*, p. 155.
29 Sergeant, vol. II, pp. 560–1.

32. Before God and the World

1 Calendar of State Papers, domestic, William and Mary, July 1691, and De Ros Manuscripts, p. 323.
2 O'Kelly p. 147.
3 Story, *Continuation*, p. 190.
4 De Ros Manuscripts, p. 323.
5 Story, *Continuation*, p. 188.
6 *Ibid.*, p. 191.
7 Quotes taken from Story, *Continuation*, pp. 191–204. See also Gilbert (ed.), p. 159.

8 Story, *Continuation*, pp. 207–10.
9 O'Kelly, p. 149.
10 Simms, *Jacobite Ireland*, p. 246.
11 Wauchope, p. 250.
12 Story, *Continuation*, pp. 212–13.
13 Richards, *Diary of the Siege of Limerick*, p. 291.
14 O'Kelly, p. 152.
15 Richards, p. 293.
16 O'Kelly, p. 149.
17 Story, *Continuation*, pp. 216–17.
18 O'Kelly, pp. 151–2.
19 Story, *Continuation*, p. 220.
20 Gilbert (ed.), p. 167.
21 *Ibid.*, p. 167.
22 Story, *Continuation*, p. 220.
23 De Ros Manuscripts, p. 323.
24 Story, *Continuation*, pp. 221–2.
25 *Ibid.*, p. 224.
26 *Ibid.*, p. 224.
27 The Rawdon Papers, pp. 361–3.
28 Richards, p. 296.
29 Simms, *Jacobite Ireland*, p. 249.
30 De Ros Manuscripts, p. 323.

33. Articles

1 *London Gazette*, 5 October 1691.
2 De Ros Manuscripts, p. 323.
3 The Rawdon Papers, pp. 361–2.
4 Story, *Continuation*, pp. 228–9.
5 *Ibid.*, pp. 229–30.
6 Papers of F. W. Leyborne-Popham, p. 280.
7 Story, *Continuation*, p. 232.
8 Papers of F. W. Leyborne-Popham, pp. 281–2, and Story, pp. 231–2.
9 Story, *Continuation*, pp. 246–66.
10 *Ibid.*, pp. 256–60.
11 Papers of F. W. Leyborne-Popham, p. 281.
12 Story, *Continuation*, pp. 258–9.
13 *Ibid.*, p. 260.

14 *Ibid.*, pp. 280–2.
15 *London Gazette*, 22 October 1691.
16 O'Kelly, p. 155.
17 Papers of F. W. Leyborne-Popham, p. 281.
18 Gilbert (ed.), p. 173.
19 Story, *Continuation*, p. 290.
20 O'Kelly, pp. 156–7.
21 Story, Continuation, pp. 289–90.
22 Manuscripts of the Duke of Portland, vol. III, pp. 477–9.
23 *Ibid.*, pp. 477–9.

Epilogue: Time and Violence

1 Clarke, vol. II, p. 598.
2 *Ibid.*, pp. 621–37.
3 O'Kelly, p. 157.
4 Manuscripts of the Duke of Portland, p. 477.
5 Witherow, appendix, p. 351.
6 'The Triumph of Patrick Sarsfield' in MacErlean (ed.).

Index